THE GREAT WAR AT SEA

THE
GREAT WAR
AT SEA

1914–1918

RICHARD HOUGH

Oxford   New York

OXFORD UNIVERSITY PRESS

Oxford University Press, Walton Street, Oxford OX2 6DP

Oxford New York Toronto
Delhi Bombay Calcutta Madras Karachi
Petaling Jaya Singapore Hong Kong Tokyo
Nairobi Dar es Salaam Cape Town
Melbourne Auckland
and associated companies in
Berlin Ibadan

Oxford is a trade mark of Oxford University Press

First published 1983
Reprinted 1984, 1985
First issued as an Oxford University Press paperback 1986
Reprinted 1988, 1989

British Library Cataloguing in Publication Data
Hough, Richard, 1922–
The Great War at sea, 1914–1918
1. World War, 1914–1918—Naval operations
British
I. Title
940.4'5941   D581
ISBN 0–19–285181–0

Printed in Great Britain
Richard Clay Ltd.
Bungay, Suffolk

*To the memory of
Arthur Marder*

CONTENTS

PLATES

We are grateful to the following for their kind permission to reproduce the illustrations in this book: Associated Newspapers Ltd: 21; BBC Hulton Picture Library: 6, 8; Imperial War Museum: 1, 2, 7, 9, 11, 12, 15, 16, 17, 18, 19, 20, 22, 23, 24, 25, 26, 27, 28, 29, 30, 31, 33, 35, 39; Illustrated London News Picture Library: 5; Mansell Collection: 4, 10; National Archives, Washington: 38; Ullstein Bilderdienst: 32; WZ-Bilddienst, Wilhelmshaven, W-Germany: 3, 34. We have been unable to trace the copyright holders of 13, 14, 36, and 40, and we hope that any possible owners of these pictures will accept our apologies.

MAPS

PREFACE

Following the publication of his third volume of 'Jacky' Fisher's letters in 1959, Professor Arthur Marder suggested that I should write a biography of his hero, and gave me much assistance and advice when I agreed to do so. Then, some time before his untimely death on Christmas Day 1980, he and the Oxford University Press approached me with the suggestion that I should embark on a one-volume history of the Royal Navy 1914–18. In this proposed new work I was to have additionally the bonus of access to all Marder's papers and, of special value, the papers he had accumulated since the publication of the five volumes of *From the Dreadnought to Scapa Flow*. On his death this material was all in characteristic Marder order in preparation for further revised and expanded editions of his own work.

Arthur Marder and I had been friends and mutual critical admirers since the late 1950s. I was never so professionally stimulated as when with him, either in England or southern California. In Marder's company, 'shop' ruled everything, and I can recall with some embarrassment a private dinner at the Garrick Club during which, at opposite ends of the table, we found ourselves overwhelming all other conversation and rearranging the cutlery in a prolonged Jutland debate. We did not agree on all matters, nor all judgements, but that only added a spice to our relationship.

In the last months of his life he asked me to read and comment upon the manuscript of his last great work, *Old Friends, New Enemies*; and in his last letter to me written a few days before he died he wrote warmly about my biography of our mutual friend, Lord Mountbatten.

I was able to talk to Marder, all too briefly, about my preparatory work for this book. I most earnestly hope that he would have approved of it in this final form. I know that he would have been gratified that I had the continuous and invaluable advice of Lieutenant-Commander Peter Kemp, who proved himself Marder's own 'ready and constant counsellor' for so many years, and to whom I, too, owe a great deal over twenty-five years of writing naval history.

RICHARD HOUGH

ABBREVIATIONS

ADC	Aide-de-camp
AP	Armour-piercing (shell)
BC	Battle-cruiser
BCF	Battle Cruiser Fleet
BCS	Battle Cruiser Squadron
BEF	British Expeditionary Force
C and M	Care and Maintenance
CID	Committee of Imperial Defence
C.-in-C.	Commander-in-Chief
DF	Direction finding
DNI	Director of Naval Intelligence
DNO	Director of Naval Operations
DOD	Director of Operations Division
DSC	Distinguished Service Cross
DSM	Distinguished Service Medal
DSO	(Companion of the) Distinguished Service Order
GFBO	Grand Fleet Battle Order
HSF	High Seas Fleet
LCS	Light Cruiser Squadron
NID	Naval Intelligence Division
OD	Operations Division
RN	Royal Navy
RNAS	Royal Navy Air Service
RNVR	Royal Navy Volunteer Reserve
USN	United States Navy
VC	Victoria Cross
W/T	Wireless telegraphy

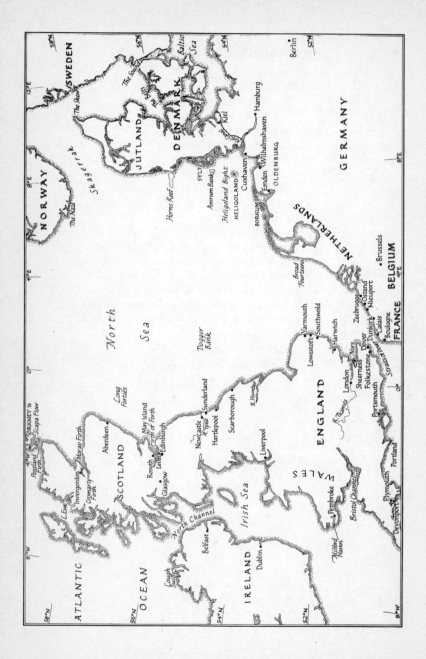

1

'AN ENORMOUS SHIP'

The influence of the German Emperor – Britain's new alliances – Admiral Fisher appointed First Sea Lord – The need for naval reforms – The conception of the Dreadnought, *and her critics*

AN onlooker described the launch of HMS *Dreadnought* as 'the greatest sight I have ever seen – it made me proud of my country and of the Navy'. 'She went in without a hitch,' a naval cadet wrote home, 'She is an enormous ship.'[1]

The battleship was launched by Edward VII at Portsmouth on a chill, dour day in February 1906. The King sang 'For those in peril on the sea' as ardently as anyone present. He was afterwards presented with an oak casket, carved from Nelson's flagship, HMS *Victory*. It contained the mallet and chisel used in simulation to sever *Dreadnought*'s last cable securing her to the slip.

The first *Dreadnought* had been built in 1573 and fought against the Spanish Armada, the sixth distinguished herself at Trafalgar. This was the ninth ship in the Royal Navy to carry the name, and her historical associations were as numerous as her innovations. Almost every feature of this battleship was notable and novel. As those who had been chiefly responsible for her proudly proclaimed, the *Dreadnought* was to be the biggest, fastest, and most heavily gunned battleship in the world. She was also to be heavily armoured and protected from fatal damage by elaborate compartmentation. For the first time in a battleship, the *Dreadnought* was to be driven by efficient and clean turbines in place of reciprocating engines.

This battleship, floating high out of the waters of Portsmouth harbour, flags taut in the breeze, and, to the sound of music and cheers, being nursed towards her fitting-out basin by paddle tugs, was to lend her name to every subsequent capital ship built for the world's navies. Even the Germans, the future enemy who built almost as many as the British, called them *Dreadnoughtschiffe*. It was a breed of fighting ship that in its size and grace and provocative appearance celebrated appropriately the last generation of the big-gun man o'war.

The *Dreadnought*, built at unprecedented speed and at once making every other battleship of the world outdated, became a political and material factor in the naval arms race already under way between

Britain and Germany. 'Germany has been paralysed by the *Dread-nought*', Admiral Sir John Fisher, First Sea Lord, wrote gloatingly and with every word underlined, to King Edward VII. Germany was dismayed, even outraged, but not paralysed for long. Ten years later Germany could put to sea a fleet of twenty-one dreadnought battleships and battle-cruisers in the greatest naval battle in the war: a war which the dreadnought and the competition she intensified, had in large measure brought about.

Fifteen years earlier Germany had possessed a negligible navy of small coast-defence vessels, and though the Germans were powerful on land, the sea was not an element that had previously inspired their interest or ambition. For Britain the Pax Britannica had been sustained since Trafalgar and the Napoleonic wars by a Navy which incontestably 'ruled the waves', boasting a numerical strength greater than that of any likely combination of navies afloat. The strength and quality of the Royal Navy were as unquestioned by the mass of the people as those of God and Queen Victoria. Everyone gave

> . . . three cheers and one cheer more,
> for the hardy Captain of the *Pinafore*,

and 'the ruler of the Queen's Navee' would still have been an object of veneration even if Gilbert and Sullivan had not kept the nation humming. The Diamond Jubilee review of the fleet in 1897 was described by the *The Times* as 'this unexampled scene . . . Nothing could be more impressive than the long lines of ships anchored in perfect order, spreading over miles of water in apparently endless array.'

The Navy's influence and presence were world-wide. From the rivers of China to the Navy's coaling station in the Falkland Islands, from Newfoundland to Simon's Town in South Africa, and from Malta to Wellington, New Zealand, the white ensign flew and gunboats or second-class protected cruisers, battleships, or torpedo boats, were available for any occasion, ceremonial or unruly.

Sir Walter Raleigh at the time of an earlier great queen had written that 'There are two ways in which England may be afflicted. The one by invasion . . . the other by impeachment of our Trades.' Few English people read Raleigh in the 1890s, and even fewer bothered to define or comprehend the meaning of the maritime supremacy the nation enjoyed. This task became the responsibility of an obscure American naval captain, Alfred Thayer Mahan, who wrote several works of history on the influence of sea power.[2] These were read with wonder and admiration in Britain, and alerted many people to the importance of retaining the superiority they had taken for granted for almost a century. If her Trades were impeached, Britain's industry would be silenced, her people starved.

Mahan's work was timely. In those final decades of the nineteenth century the colonial appetite of other nations was growing apace, and with it an interest in trade and the sea upon which it depended. Mahan was read in Washington and Berlin, Tokyo and Paris, and a consciousness of the value of naval strength spread through the defence councils of nations which would benefit from it, as well as many others concerned with prestige and power over their neighbours.

Soon after the completion of the *Dreadnought*, others of her kind even larger, more expensive, and more powerful were ordered by three South American republics, by Spain, Italy, Greece, and Turkey, as well as by the major powers. In Japan, newly built shipyards constructed some of the finest men o'war of their time. The United States Navy, so insignificant that it had been openly challenged by Chile in 1891, expanded rapidly and began ordering battleships.

Before the end of the nineteenth century the growth of navies all over the world was already shaping the direction of twentieth-century history. Nowhere was the course more sharply and uncompromisingly delineated than in Germany; nowhere were the lessons of Captain Mahan studied more zealously.

The rise of the German Navy from the early 1890s to 1914 was a remarkable achievement. A navy demands a multitude of special skills both in the construction of ships and the training of the men to serve in them. The Germans lacked experience equally in the manufacture of armour-plate and heavy naval ordnance as in gunnery, signalling, and manoeuvring a large number of ships at sea. Nor did they possess any naval traditions or history. They were starting from the first riveter working on the first strake and the first gunlayer behind the sights of an 8.2-inch naval gun in a choppy sea. But the Germans learned fast and – like the new United States and Japanese navies – largely from the British Navy.

The inspiration for the German *Kriegsmarine* came from the Emperor himself, Kaiser Wilhelm II. He was a ruler whose withered left arm was matched by a flawed mind, who laboured under grievances all his life, the most dominant in the early years of his reign being envy for the navy of his grandmother, Queen Victoria. It caused the Kaiser real suffering not to be supreme. He boasted the greatest army in the world as well as the grandest personal uniforms and decorations. When he saw his nephew enjoying Cowes Week, and winning races there, the Kaiser set about building the finest ocean cutter in the world and applying himself with earnest seriousness to the art of racing. After expressing his complaints about the handicapping, his will to win prevailed until the future Edward VII could bear it no longer: 'The regatta at Cowes was once a pleasant holiday for me,' he remarked sadly, 'but now that the Kaiser has taken command there it is nothing but a nuisance.' And he never went again.

Kaiser Wilhelm did not care to be seen in an inferior Royal Yacht to his grandmother's so he ordered a bigger and grander one. Wherever the Kaiser sailed in his glittering *Hohenzollern* he saw evidence of the dominant power of Britain at sea. He resented deeply the Royal Navy's size, strength, and apparent efficiency. He resented the respect for and acquiescence to the Royal Navy by the rest of the world, and Britain's pride in the service which he saw as no more than arrogance.

The Kaiser's partner who shared and encouraged his ambition was Alfred von Tirpitz, who was ten years older (born 19 March 1849) and had originally served in the old and unesteemed Prussian Navy. Tirpitz showed no special distinction as a sailor in this minor service, but revealed himself as a brilliant and ambitious administrator and political manipulator. He strongly attracted the attention of the Emperor, and became Secretary of State for the Imperial Navy in June 1897, a date which marks the birth of the mighty High Seas Fleet.

Tirpitz needed all his Machiavellian qualities, and all the Kaiser's powerful support, to persuade the Reichstag to pass the first of his German Navy Laws in 1898 against the liberal-pacifist element on one side and the Prussian Army element which was equally hostile. This law provided for the considerable expansion of the service, and was followed by a second in 1900 of a much more ambitious nature. It called for a fleet including 38 battleships, 20 armoured cruisers and 38 light cruisers – a fleet which he justified in these momentous and threatening words:

In order to protect German trade and commerce under existing conditions only one thing will suffice, namely, Germany must possess a battle fleet of such a strength that even for the most powerful naval adversary a war would involve such risks as to make that Power's own supremacy doubtful. For this purpose it is not absolutely necessary that the German fleet should be as strong as that of the greatest naval Power, for, as a rule, a great naval Power will not be in a position to concentrate all its forces against us.

These words were heard with dismay in Britain. Germany's colonial expansion in Africa and the East – the *Weltpolitik* – and hostile events such as the despatch of the provocative anti-British 'Kruger Telegram' of 1896, and the Anglophobiac chorus conducted by German statesmen and the Press during the Boer War, all combined to cause alarm and a massive reappraisal of the naval position of Britain and her Empire at the end of the old century.

The death of Queen Victoria on 22 January 1901 caused conflicting shocks of grief and disbelief that the old lady was not after all immortal. Her eldest, once recalcitrant and much abused son succeeded at a moment in the nation's history of anxiety and the need for far-reaching decisions. France, Russia, and Germany were all hostile. No one approved of Britain's war against the Boer farmers, and suspicion and disapproval of her imperial power and stance were widespread. Now her Navy was being directly threatened by the most powerful military nation in the world.

As one writer was to put it, 'Without the supremacy of the British Navy the best security for the world's peace and advancement would be gone. Nothing would be so likely as the passing of sea-power from our hands to bring about another of those long ages of conflict and returning barbarism which have thrown back civilization before and wasted nations.'[3] Between them, Kaiser Wilhelm II and the head of his navy had brought about an end to the Pax Britannica even before the first keel of the first of the new German battleships was laid down.

For Britain, the end of the old century and the death of the old Queen marked also the end of isolation. The accession of that most gregarious of monarchs, Edward VII, could not have occurred at a more appropriate time for the nation. Britain was in need of friends.

Within a few years, the Anglo-Japanese Treaty of Friendship (30 January 1902) and the *Entente Cordiale* (8 April 1904) with France, lovingly prepared by Edward VII, permitted Britain eventually to withdraw the greater part of her naval strength from the Far East and the Mediterranean, and concentrate her battle fleets in home waters. This was just what Tirpitz had declared Britain would not be able to do.

Would these steps be sufficient to meet the growing threat from across the North Sea, which had already been renamed in German atlases 'German Ocean'? Were the *matériel* and the fighting efficiency of the Royal Navy equal to the task?

The Royal Navy at the outset of the twentieth century was like a rich, vain old man, swollen with self-confidence and living on the memory of past glories. He cannot move quickly nor see very well. He is a gregarious clubman but has as little regard for modern times and trends as he has for those outside his circle.

The best that can be said of the Royal Navy in 1904 is that it had known worse days quite recently. In the early 1880s the service could look back forty years without pride on a record of ultra-conservatism. As far as the sailors were concerned they were fed, treated, and paid as if Nelson were still their commander-in-chief. Hardships were made tolerable by companionship and the ever-liberal rum ration. The officers were indifferently educated, unimaginative, their style and conduct ruled by elaborate protocol, custom, and tradition. For them the Navy was as exclusive as a Guards regiment. In war they would doubtless have performed with all the valour of their ancestors. In peace, for decade after decade, the old brotherhood which had linked them in battle with the lower deck had withered.

The Lords Commissioners of the Admiralty had long since established a principle that experiment and innovation must be avoided. Others could be inventive if they wished. Britain might follow in due course if she thought fit. This principle applied to all manner of advances, most conspicuously to the acceptance of steam propulsion and the end of masts and yards. When the battleship *Inflexible* was commissioned in 1881 she was the wonder ship of her day, with the biggest (16-inch) guns in the service and armour-plate of 24 inches, a thickness never exceeded. She could steam at almost 15 knots. But she was a sort of nineteenth-century hybrid, linking the eighteenth and twentieth centuries. While she enjoyed the unique advantage of electric light she was also fully rigged, and as much time and skill were devoted to hoisting sail and taking in a reef as if she had been Sir John Jervis's flagship at St Vincent. Traditionalism in the Royal Navy had been strengthened after the introduction of pioneering breech-loading guns in 1860 and their hasty abandonment after several accidents. Twenty years were to pass, when the breech-loader was long since established in foreign navies, before the Admiralty would countenance their return.

The emphasis was on smartness, speed in hoisting sail, precise conformity to signal-book diagrams in fleet drills, pride in pulling races and inter-ship boxing and tug o'wars. Admiral 'Pompo' Heneage, who was born three years earlier than Queen Victoria and retired three years before she died, was the complete Victorian naval officer, but by no means the most eccentric nor exceptional in his concern for a ship's cleanliness or smartness. 'When inspecting ships he always wore white kid gloves,' according to one naval writer, 'and his coxswain followed him with a dozen spare pairs . . . He liked to put his hands on the tops of pipes running over his head, or into the most inaccessible nooks and crannies. If one speck of dust appeared on the immaculate gloves, he would turn to the Commander waving two fingers. "Dis is not de dirt of days," he would observe, "nor de dirt of veeks, nor de dirt of months. It is de dirt of ages. Coxswain, gif me a clean pair of gloves." [4]

Practice 'shoots' were not considered of first priority by the commanders-in-chief nor by their captains. The shine on the decorated tampion, which closed off like a cork the guns' barrels, was more important; and it was not unknown for the meagre ration of practice ammunition to be tossed overboard for fear that gun-firing might spoil the brasswork.

During this long period of decay, a handful of exceptionally talented officers somehow achieved positions of influence ashore and afloat. Among them were Philip Colomb, a questioning intellectual who wrote provocatively for service journals, and Admiral Sir Frederick Richards, a great reformer and administrator.

Far above them all as an administrator, reformer, inspirer, persuader, manipulator, charmer, and politician was John Arbuthnot Fisher. Fisher, the counterpart and chief adversary of Alfred von Tirpitz, did more than any single officer to drag the Royal Navy out of its nineteenth-century sloth, inefficiency, and drowsiness, and make it fit to stand up to the superb force Tirpitz created.

In his years of greatness a friend of kings and princes, politicians and newspaper proprietors, 'Jacky' Fisher entered the Navy in the 1850s, 'penniless, friendless and forlorn' as he later wrote. His family was certainly without power or influence, his father being an ex-army officer turned tea-planter of mixed fortunes in Ceylon. Fisher never saw him after the age of six, when he was sent to England to live with an uncle. It seems likely that Fisher's exceptional qualities of intellect and moral and physical courage were inherited from his mother, who is described as having a 'powerful mind, organizing capacity and taste for power'.[5]

Within twenty years Fisher had made his mark as an 'apostle of progress' with a special interest in torpedoes, mines, gunnery, and advanced machinery like the water-tube boiler and the turbine.

From captain of the Navy's gunnery school, Fisher became Director of Naval Ordnance and Torpedoes in 1886, a department he found in a state of chaos and confusion. Within less than five years he had totally reorganized it, and successfully withdrawn from the Army its remarkably anomalous responsibility for naval guns. This performance was a preview in miniature of his future period as First Sea Lord. Fisher gathered about him a group of ambitious and patriotic officers attracted by his dynamism, self-assurance and extreme style: they were the cream of the Navy's intellect, soon to be known as members of the 'Fishpond'. And heaven help any non-member (he called them 'the syndicate of discontent') who opposed Fisher's policies! Fisher inevitably made enemies with every reform but it was not necessary for him to have made as many as he did, or to be so unforgiving. Nonetheless it can fairly be said that when Fisher was appointed First Sea Lord in October 1904, six months after the signature of the *Entente Cordiale*, the Royal Navy's course towards decay was reversed.

Fisher recognized, ahead of many politicians, the deadly danger emerging from across the North Sea. He also knew that the men who would one day have to face it must be of the highest quality. With this in mind he transformed recruitment, manning, and status in the Navy. He introduced schemes to encourage promotion from the lower deck and at the same time abolished fees at naval colleges through which only the well-off had once passed. He introduced a nucleus crews system of reserves, based on French practice, and greatly improved the standing of the once-despised engineer officers.

All this was recognized by his followers in the service to be of inestimable value. Fisher's *matériel* reforms were more conspicuous. Ignoring the cries of fury from deprived commanders and far-flung diplomats, Fisher brought home numerous ships, most of which 'could neither fight nor run away' (as Fisher expressed it) and were scrapped. Even the Mediterranean Fleet was reduced to a shadow of the great fleet he had commanded from 1899 to 1902. Through influential friends and through his press contacts, Fisher concentrated the nation's eye on Germany, and Germany alone, as the threat to Britain's dominance at sea. The people loved it, and the Navy League flourished. By economies as ruthless as his reforms, Fisher reduced the Navy Estimates three years running. The Liberals loved him for that.

Above all else, Fisher gave the nation the dreadnought. This statement requires qualifying for it can also be argued that the all-big-gun ship was inevitably the final stage in the design of the old ship-of-the-line. In the nineteenth century the battleship had passed through numerous developments, from the three-decker wooden walls, little improved from the mid-eighteenth century, to mixed sail and steam propulsion, to the 'mastless' ironclad. Guns had developed from smooth-bore 68-pounders firing solid shot, to the 16-inch, rifled, breech-loading guns of the *Inflexible*.

As defence against the explosive charge of these massive shells, armour-plate had grown in thickness and resistance until (again in the *Inflexible*) it was responsible for 27.5 per cent of the ship's total displacement. By the end of the century, a typical modern first-class battleship was armed with four guns of 12-inch calibre in two turrets fore and aft, and a mixed battery of medium-calibre guns, from 6-inch to 9.2-inch.

By this time there was a growing consciousness of the threat of the torpedo and the mine. Cheap, nippy little torpedo boats, capable of speeds twice that of a battleship, could race in and send to the bottom a man o'war costing a million pounds and taking four years to build. This very real threat led to radical alterations in the design and defences of the battleship and to radical new thinking on tactics. Massive and cumbersome nets were carried and hoisted out like a steel crinoline by battleships at anchor. Battleships bristled with anti-torpedo boat light guns. It was deemed prudent to extend greatly the range at which lines of battleships fought one another.

All these new fears for the security of the battleship appeared to be confirmed in the Russo-Japanese War of 1904–5. Japanese torpedo boats opened hostilities by attacking the Russian Fleet. The Japanese suffered critical battleship losses from mines. Both sides became increasingly preoccupied with the new underwater weapons.

Other lessons were learned in this naval war which crystallized all the problems argued over by theoreticians for years. 'Spotting' the fall of shot accurately from ships firing mixed armament was seen to be almost impossible, the varying size splashes only confusing the spotter. According to the official British observer with the Japanese Fleet at the first-ever battle of ironclads, 'when 12-inch guns are firing, shots from 10-inch pass unnoticed, while for all the respect they instil, 8-inch or 6-inch guns might just as well be peashooters'. To the astonishment of this same observer (and to the whole naval world when it was informed) the Russian battleships opened accurate fire at 18,000 yards: 3,000 yards was still the standard range of British battle practice at this time. It was clear that heavy guns could prove decisive long before medium-calibre guns could come into effective range.

Here was proof for far-sighted naval designers that only the heaviest guns would count in naval warfare, and that future battles would be fought at ranges of between five and ten miles (as visibility permitted) with flotillas of torpedo boats attempting to get within range of the enemy in order to launch their 'tin fish'. Clearly, then, only the heaviest and anti-torpedo boat guns must in future be mounted in battleships.

The Japanese and Russians were, naturally, the first to recognize the lessons of the battles they fought. The United States Navy Board drew up plans for two battleships mounting ten 12-inch guns before the end of 1904, and succeeded in getting authority through Congress to lay down only marginally smaller all-big-gun battleships early in 1905. In Italy the naval architect Vittorio Cuniberti had made public his design for a battleship mounting twelve 12-inch guns, and none smaller except anti-torpedo boat guns.

The American ships were built at a leisurely pace, the Italians had not got the money to follow Cuniberti, the Japanese had not sufficiently developed their ordnance facilities and eventually produced a hybrid with mixed 12-inch and 10-inch guns. Only Britain had the facilities and need to produce an all-big-gun battleship without delay and set a pace which no other nation could match. Within a few days of his appointment as First Sea Lord, Fisher set up a Committee on Designs. It included a number of the best 'brains' in the Navy, all imbued with Fisher's sense of urgency. Less than a year later, the *Dreadnought* was laid down at Portsmouth, and eight months after her launch was steaming on her trials.

The effect at home and abroad was all that Fisher had hoped for. The *Dreadnought*, with ten 12-inch guns, had a broadside of twice as many heavy guns as any ship afloat. When few battleships could make 18 knots, the *Dreadnought*'s turbines speeded her along at 21 knots, and of even greater significance, she crossed the Atlantic at over 17 knots average without a breakdown. The German naval authorities were stunned by the superiority and speed of construction of this ship, and temporarily halted construction on battleships that would now be obsolete on completion. In the competition – the 'battleship race' – which was rapidly increasing in scale and intensity, the first round between Britain and Germany, between Fisher and von Tirpitz, had been won by the Royal Navy.

At home there was great satisfaction and rejoicing. Models of the *Dreadnought* appeared in the shops, boys could recite every detail of her statistics, and wherever she could be seen crowds collected. But among navalists, and Fisher's detractors, there was vocal criticism of the battleship. Her cost of construction was high and the cost of her loss in battle would be commensurately high. There were those who favoured smaller battleships with 10-inch guns, which could be built in greater numbers. Above all, if she made every battleship in the world obsolete, as Fisher loudly claimed, then Britain's great superiority in numbers over Germany was wiped out at a stroke. Fisher fought back at what he regarded as counsels of doom and timidity, claiming that Britain could outbuild Germany and would have a dreadnought battle squadron before Germany could complete her first *Dreadnoughtschiff*. In all the arguments that raged to and fro on the platforms, in the Press and West End clubs, the one undeniable and supremely important fact appears never to have been mentioned: the all-big-gun ship was as certain to come as day follows night, was already on the design boards of many foreign admiralties, was already under construction in the United States.

What Britain had done under the 'ruthless, relentless and remorseless' (as he liked to claim for himself) methods of Fisher was to produce a world-beater overnight. The *Dreadnought* reasserted once again British paramountcy at sea, and in a style of theatricality which only Jacky Fisher could sponsor.

2

THE ANGLO-GERMAN BATTLESHIP RACE

Admiral Fisher's attributes – The dreadnought race begins – Admiral Beresford's vendetta against Fisher – The German Emperor's intransigence – The dreadnought battle-cruiser – The 'We want eight and we won't wait' campaign and Winston Churchill's opposition – The Prime Minister's committee to enquire into the conduct of naval affairs – Fisher's resignation

ADMIRAL FISHER led the Royal Navy as First Sea Lord for five of the most critical peacetime years in the service's history, working with a white hot intensity that sharpened his beliefs and prejudices, made him more bellicose than ever, and illuminated more brightly year by year the colourful characteristics that had made him the greatest naval administrator since Lord Barham.[1] He became towards the end of his term of office a self-drawn caricature of the Admiral who had stormed into the Admiralty on Trafalgar Day 1904, the double underlinings in his cryptic letters and quotations from the Bible more numerous, his exclamations and imprecations more extreme, his response to opposition ever more violent. Power, rather than Acton's tendency to corruption, had always brought out the actor in Fisher. Sustained and supreme power turned the public figure of the man into a sort of naval Henry Irving bestriding the stage with exaggerated postures. But his effectiveness remained as sharp as ever, and it was not until his years in office were over that the toll they had exacted from himself and from others became fully apparent.

Fisher was not a man of war. He hated war. He had seen it at first hand out in China as a young man and had barely escaped with his life. 'War is hell!' he repeatedly declared. But if it came his beloved Navy would be ready. Then half measures would be dangerous and futile. As an inappropriate choice of delegate to the first Hague Peace Convention (1899) which was intended to bring about a reduction in armaments and laws for reducing the awfulness of war, Fisher had shocked the assembly by exclaiming, 'You might as well talk of humanizing Hell!' 'War is the essence of violence', was one of Fisher's oft-repeated aphorisms. 'Moderation in war is imbecility. HIT FIRST. HIT HARD. KEEP ON HITTING!'

Whatever this Hague Peace Conference may have accomplished, and Fisher regarded it as a waste of time, the second in June 1907 was accepted by everyone as a failure. For political and economic reasons alone, Britain was anxious to bring about a reduction in naval armaments and put a brake on the battleship race which had been accelerated by the construction of the *Dreadnought*. A proposal to bring this about was answered by Tirpitz: ' . . . look at the facts. Here is England, already more than four times as strong as Germany, in alliance with Japan, and probably so with France, and you, the collosus, come and ask Germany, the pigmy, to disarm. From the point of view of the public it is laughable and Machiavellian, and we shall never agree to anything of the sort.'[2]

It was this atmosphere of mutual distrust that this second conference was intended to reduce, but so choleric were Press comment and exchanges between the two nations' statesmen before the delegates met, that expenditure on armaments was not even raised at the Hague. The only benefit to Britain stemming from the Hague Conference was a settlement of Anglo-Russian differences in Asia, which Germany regarded as the first stage leading to an alliance. This would leave Germany flanked on three sides by potential foes, increasing further her paranoia. Germany responded with an amendment to the 1900 Navy Law, which would effectively give the *Kriegsmarine* no fewer than fifty-eight dreadnoughts ten years hence.

The high summer of 1907 marked the sombre starting-point of the headlong gallop to war seven years later. There were efforts to draw in the reins and audible laments, not all of them hypocritical. But as far as naval armaments were concerned, and they were the dominating factor, both powers were now hell-bent on a race to conflict.

A counter-campaign in Britain against the new German increase called for 'two keels to one', a difficult target to achieve with a Liberal government dedicated to public welfare and the easing of the inequalities in the land. But as an indication of how deeply even the Liberal and Labour factions were involved in the nation's naval preoccupation, the *Manchester Guardian* expounding the radical view accepted that naval rivalry with Germany was 'rapidly becoming the principal outstanding question of European politics'[3] and that Britain should certainly construct four new dreadnoughts a year to Germany's three.

The Conservatives and the Conservative Press continued to be alarmed for the future. 'Is Britain going to surrender her maritime supremacy to provide old-age pensions?' was typical of the bellicose questions sounded out by the *Daily Mail*. Fisher's enemies in and out of the Navy were now aroused to create a further contest within the Anglo-German contest by organizing a campaign for his removal. The faction's idol and leader was Lord Charles Beresford, once a national hero, now elderly and bloated by extravagant living. An Irishman of aristocratic lineage and immense wealth, Beresford had once been Fisher's ally in the reform movement in the Navy. But the two men, of equally volatile temperament and very different background, had fallen out, and the split had widened when Fisher was appointed First Sea Lord and was then promoted Admiral of the Fleet, ensuring the extension of his term of office to deprive Beresford of any prospect of succeeding him.

With its most important aim of ousting Fisher and replacing him with Beresford, an Imperial Maritime League was founded at the end of 1907. Lord Esher, whose support of Fisher was steady and whose influence was great in the land, gave to *The Times* a copy of the letter he wrote to the League defending Fisher. 'There is not a man in Germany, from the Emperor downwards, who would not welcome the fall of Sir John Fisher,' it concluded.

This letter led to the most bizarre incident in this Anglo-German naval rivalry. When it was shown to the Kaiser, he sat down and wrote in his own hand a letter nine pages long addressed to Lord Tweedmouth, political head of the Navy as First Lord of the Admiralty. In extravagant language, the Emperor of Germany stated that he was unable to understand British fears about the rise of the German Navy, which was not being created to challenge British naval supremacy. He also described Esher's opinion that Germany would be glad to see Fisher out of office as 'a piece of unmitigated balderdash'.

This new exercise in conducting Germany's foreign policy caused amazement in Britain, and King Edward felt impelled to write his nephew a reprimand. *The Times* expressed outrage: 'If there was any doubt before about the meaning of German naval expansion,' it thundered, 'none can remain after an attempt of this kind to influence the Minister responsible for our Navy in a direction favourable to German interests.'[4]

In Germany, where the heavy warship building facilities were being expanded at high speed and at great cost, Anglophobia grew apace, too. Ever sensitive to being patronized, watchful for evidence of interference in national affairs, envious of the size and wealth of the British Empire, resentful of Britain's apparent failure to regard Germany as a great power, anti-British feeling was easily whipped up by the Press, politicians, and the Emperor himself. 'You English are mad, mad as March hares,' he declared to an English newspaper correspondent, and made it clear that the great majority of his subjects were hostile to England. The well-informed and percipient

British naval attaché in Berlin declared that he doubted now whether the Emperor, 'much as he might desire it, could restrain his own people from attempting to wrest the command of the seas from Great Britain, if they saw a fairly good chance of doing so'.[5]

Fisher, always a target for sniping in the Royal Navy's own internecine war, was also involved in the complex and anxious task of improving the efficiency of the service, protecting it from politicians of radical-Liberal persuasion, and observing from his own Whitehall-based fighting top the threatening expansion of the German Navy.

Fisher had scored a second surprise moral victory over Germany by building and putting into service at great speed a new class of dreadnought-type armoured cruiser, bigger and faster than anything Tirpitz had contemplated, and with an all-big-gun armament twice that of any pre-dreadnought battleship. These formidable men o'war were what Fisher proclaimed to be his 'New Testament ships', 'hares to catch tortoises', scouting vessels of unprecedented speed (25+ knots) and power that could hunt down any warship anywhere in the world and sink it at leisure with its 12-inch guns. The battle-cruiser was to add a new element in the Anglo-German race, and by 1912 Germany had six built or building against Britain's ten.

However exuberant and confident Fisher remained in the strength, numbers, and quality of the British fleets, information from his intelligence department revealed the rapid improvement in the seamanship and gunnery of the *Kriegsmarine*'s personnel and the excellent design of the first German dreadnoughts.

In 1909 there occurred the biggest peacetime naval crisis in British history, a 'navy scare' which made those of the late nineteenth century (when the French and Russians were the source of anxiety) seem trivial. Towards the end of 1908, when the mood of Germany was clearly more hostile than ever towards France as well as Britain, informed sources in London told of further German acceleration in dreadnought building. The speed of construction of heavy men o'war was conditioned by the months occupied in building the guns and gun mountings. Previously, German shipbuilders had shown that they could build a heavy ship in three years. Now, thanks to increased facilities at Krupp's for building armour and guns and their mountings, this time had been reduced, it was believed, to little more than two years. Moreover, so rapid had been the increase in building slipways and training new men in the skills of shipbuilding, it was believed possible that Germany now had the capacity to build no fewer than eight dreadnoughts a year, equal to British capacity.

Statistics quoted to predict the size of the German battle fleets in 1912 or 1914, the speed of construction, and building capacity, all depended on inspired guesswork, and could be juggled to suit the needs of politicians, journalists, and naval officers. As Churchill wrote a few years later, 'in the technical discussion of naval details there is such a wealth of facts that the point of the argument turns rather upon their selection than upon their substance.'[6] But early in 1909 it was believed by Fisher and the Board that Germany would be able to put to sea a fleet of seventeen dreadnoughts by April 1912 against Britain's eighteen: scarcely the two-keels-to-one standard previously regarded as minimal for the nation's security.

The public and private argument that shook the nation early in 1909, leading up to the presentation to Parliament of the naval estimates, was whether four or as many as six new dreadnoughts should be provided for. The radical-Liberal element led by Lloyd George and Winston Churchill (then at the Board of Trade) stated emphatically that the nation could afford only four new ships if the Liberal welfare commitments were to be met, and that the Admiralty was being alarmist in asking for more.

The Conservatives, the conservative Press, and big-navy members of the Liberal Cabinet, however, kept up a sustained campaign for a minimum of six. There were threats of resignations inside the Cabinet and the Admiralty, and the whole country rapidly became involved with passions running high among extreme 'patriots' or 'panic-mongers' and the 'pacifists' or 'little Englanders'. Lloyd George came in for much abuse. The feeling at Buckingham Palace can be judged by referring to a letter the King's private secretary wrote to Lord Esher about Churchill: 'What are Winston's reasons for acting as he does in this matter?' he asked. 'Of course it cannot be from conviction or principle. The very idea of his having either is enough to make anyone laugh.'[7]

In the end the violent storm abated and the arguments were settled by the wily and ingenious Prime Minister, Herbert Asquith. He proposed to his split and outraged Cabinet that there should be provision for the construction of four dreadnoughts in the 1909–10 financial year, and a further four later if they were deemed essential. In the event, they were wanted, of course; for within months anxiety about German intentions had become even more widespread.

It was left to Churchill to make the comment: 'In the end a curious and characteristic solution was reached. The Admiralty had demanded six ships: the economists offered four: and we finally compromised on eight.'[8]

This 'compromise' had been reached as much because of news from the Mediterranean as from Germany. On the night of Easter Sunday 1909 a special messenger arrived at the Admiralty from the Prime Minister. Asquith had just learned that Austria, no doubt under pressure from her ally, Germany, was to build three or four dreadnoughts and he wished to know what information Fisher had on this dramatic news. Fisher rapidly learned that this was indeed true, and moreover that Italy, as alarmed as Britain, was about to put in hand her own dreadnought building programme. The anti-navalist view was that the two programmes cancelled each other out as far as Britain's security in the Mediterranean was concerned. The Prime Minister, the Board of Admiralty, and a majority in the Cabinet remained anxious and unconvinced, and the 'contingent' dreadnoughts were authorized. The ships provided for, including the 'contingent' ships, were the battleships *Colossus* and *Hercules*, four ships of the *Orion* class, and the battle-cruisers *Lion* and *Princess Royal*. All but the first two mounted 13.5-inch guns at Fisher's insistence. The Germans had nothing larger than 12-inch guns until 1916.

Fisher's supporters regarded this unprecedented programme as his culminating triumph. His enemies at home did not see it in this light, and conveniently forgot the fact, five years later when war broke out, that only the four extra 'contingent' dreadnoughts gave the Royal Navy its dangerously slim margin of strength over the High Seas Fleet. Instead, these enemies concentrated their considerable forces, which included the Prince of Wales, on ousting Fisher before he could (as they believed) damage the Navy fatally.

The Beresford pack of hounds, those excluded from the 'Fishpond' as they saw themselves, motivated by spite and jealousy, scarred from being passed over or slighted, were relentless in the pursuit of their quarry, and used the most unscrupulous methods, and their wealth and influence with the Press and Society.

The burden of their argument was that Fisher, by his neglect and starvation of the Navy and refusal to stand up to the politicians, had brought the service to the brink of disaster and all but destroyed its superiority and magnificence, and the esteem in which the world held it no more than five years ago.

The closed world of the Navy which occupies so much of its time on shipboard has always suffered from gossip and backbiting. Resentments and divisiveness build up all too readily in wardrooms, where unusual behaviour and 'braininess' were discouraged and class divisions were accentuated. The same could be said of London Society.

Given that Beresford was nearly mad by 1909, his proposed toast to celebrate the day he succeeded in driving Fisher from office is not an exaggeration of the language he used in his struggle against the First Sea Lord: 'To the death of Fraud, Espionage, Intimidation, Corruption, Tyranny, Self-Interest . . . '

A leader of 20 March 1909 is no less typical of the passions expressed in Fleet Street by the ultra-conservative, anti-Fisher Press: 'The sole responsibility for the fact that in a few months Great Britain will be in a more vulnerable position than she has been since the Battle of Trafalgar belongs to the First Sea Lord . . . We arraign Sir John Fisher at the bar of public opinion, and with the imminent possibility of national disaster before the country we say again to him, "Thou art the man!" '9

Beresford, seen by the vast mass of the uninformed as the ultimate patriot, was cheered at Portsmouth as a national hero when he was obliged to haul down his flag prematurely in March 1909. He at once went into battle in a final attempt to topple his enemy. The nation was in a highly emotional state over the Navy and the threat from Germany. 'We want eight and we won't wait!' sounded up and down the land at public meetings as the people cried out for more dreadnoughts.

It was difficult for a politician to ignore a sailor like Beresford with such influential as well as wide popular support. Asquith listened to his complaints, and to the outrage of the Board and Fisher's supporters, agreed to set up a committee to investigate the charges made by Beresford about the conduct of naval affairs.

This occurred during the behind-the-scenes fight by Fisher and the Board to increase above four the proposed dreadnought programme. Fisher was in despair and threatened to resign. First Esher, and then the King (who contrary to his eldest son admired and supported Fisher) begged him to remain in office. The King's letter put new steel into the First Sea Lord. 'I'm not going till I'm kicked out!' he wrote, and characteristically underlined every word.

The committee of four cabinet ministers with the Prime Minister in the chair held fifteen meetings and filled nearly 600 pages with their proceedings and appendices. The main charges against the Board concerned the organization and distribution of the fleets in home waters, the deficiency in small craft due to the concentration on dreadnoughts, and the inadequacy of war plans.

Fisher and the Board were cleared of all charges, but with one or two provisos which suggested that Asquith, while avoiding a bland conclusion, did not want to be too hard on either admiral. The main criticism was of the lack of trust and cordial relations between Beresford and Fisher, which hardly caused surprise. But there was also a hint that a Naval War Staff with a brief to prepare war plans should by this time have been established.

Beresford and his supporters persuaded themselves that they had won, and were publicly jubilant, the newspapers and magazines hostile to Fisher renewing their attacks with a lack of restraint unusual even for that time. There was, the *National Review* claimed, 'no end to the catalogue of his high crimes and misdemeanours'. And 'Should it come to hanging, [Fisher] will be entitled to the nearest lamp-post.' Fisher's supporters were equally certain they had won. But Fisher himself, still outraged that the committee had even been formed, also resented in a typically over-sensitive manner the shadow of censure in the report. Weary and disgusted, disregarding even the King's congratulations, he determined to resign.

The date agreed with the First Lord, Reginald McKenna, and others in the Cabinet was 25 January 1910, his sixty-ninth birthday. On the King's birthday a few weeks earlier Fisher had been raised to the peerage as Baron Fisher, an almost unprecedented honour for a naval officer in peacetime. Beresford was livid.

There can be no question that Fisher laid the foundations upon which the Royal Navy of 1914 was built and that he did much of the subsequent structural work, too. In his earlier years Fisher had entered upon the Royal Navy scene like some gift from Neptune, performing prodigies on behalf of gunnery, torpedoes, mines, manning and many other departments. Those in the 'Fishpond' found themselves thinking more radically and working with a new pace and energy. He was a great inspirer and attracted stalwart loyalty, and his charm could be irresistible. Of medium height and unspectacular appearance, he remained one of those rare people whose presence could be felt in any gathering.

Fisher's mind was crisp and deep, his memory prodigious. Such was his dedication to the Navy that his marriage to a worthy but colourless woman faded. But he loved the company of women and they loved him in return, from Queen Alexandra to Pamela McKenna and the Duchess of Hamilton, with whom he shared a deep relationship for the last fifteen years of his life.

Fisher's work in Whitehall from 1904 to the end of 1909 stands unique in British naval history. While Tirpitz, starting from scratch, worked wonders in creating a superb fighting force in some fifteen years, Fisher's task was infinitely more difficult. He had to break outworn traditions, and like Hamlet 'reform it altogether'. A servant given an hour to clean a house has no time for tenderness with spiders. Fisher's broom was wielded without restraint. His enemies within the service multiplied with the passing of years and his own certainty in the urgency of his task. There was a touch of waspishness in the man and his enemies' accounts of his vendettas were mostly true.

The state of the Navy when he came to supreme power, although improved on what it had been ten years earlier, remained largely inefficient. His reforms in every department, from the fundamentals of warship design, i.e. HMS *Dreadnought*, and the virtual creation of a submarine service, to the eradication of time-serving sinecurists like the department responsible for the distribution of cutlasses to HM ships in 1905, were swift and complete. (This last reform was shortlived. Cutlasses were retained on board RN ships throughout the 1914–18 war.) Fisher prepared the Navy for modern war in 1914 on the greatest scale. It was not by a wide margin a perfect service. It lacked, for example, the support of an experienced Naval War Staff, which was introduced after his resignation. But, as an unprejudiced admiral remarked as he surveyed the Fleet assembled for review a few days before the outbreak of war, 'All that is best and most modern here is the creation of Lord Fisher.'[10]

Winston Churchill was one of his warmest admirers and became one of his closest friends. While opposing Fisher's demands for increases in expenditure by the Navy, he had been watching him closely and concluded that 'There is no doubt that Fisher was right in nine-tenths of what he fought for. His great reforms sustained the power of the Royal Navy at the most critical period in its history . . . After a long period of serene and unchallenged complacency, the mutter of distant thunder could be heard. It was Fisher who hoisted the storm-signal and beat all hands to quarters.'

Without Fisher's work Britain could not have survived against Tirpitz's magnificent High Seas Fleet from 1914. If Britain had lost the war at sea she would have been forced to surrender, succumb to the tide, and become a subservient satellite.

But Fisher's departure from the Admiralty was by 1910 essential. The overdose of the purgative was already having damaging effects. 'He shook them and beat them and cajoled them out of slumber into intense activity,' concluded Churchill, qualifying his summary: 'But the navy was not a pleasant place while this was going on. The "Band of Brothers" tradition which Nelson handed down was for the time, but only for the time, discarded.'[11]

After accepting the necessity for his resignation, Fisher began to understand how tired he was after his arduous campaigns. He told Esher of his 'relief to be free of having to run the British Navy all over the world. It makes one think of St. Paul! "And besides all this, there came upon me the daily care of the churches." '[12]

He had often spoken facetiously of retiring to the country to grow cabbages. He did settle at his son's home, Kilverstone Hall in Norfolk. But there was no gardening there for him. His interest and active participation in things naval and political was in for a brief hibernation, no more.

3

CHURCHILL AT THE ADMIRALTY

Churchill becomes First Lord following the Agadir Crisis – Admiral Wilson superseded – Churchill's over-extended travels, lack of tact, and disagreement with the King – The 15-inch gun and Queen Elizabeth *class of super-dreadnought – Churchill switches the Navy to oil – His enthusiasm for submarines and aviation – Fisher's support and guidance – Percy Scott's director and the opposition to it – Dreyer's fire control system – The creation of a Naval War Staff – Lower deck reform*

WINSTON CHURCHILL'S interest in the Royal Navy and his romantic affection for it had been known to his friends for some time. He also entertained a deep sense of admiration and affection for Fisher, which incidentally was not shared by Churchill's wife, who felt only suspicion and distrust for him.

On Fisher's resignation Churchill wrote to him, congratulating him on his elevation to the peerage as well as on the 'great services you have rendered to British Naval Supremacy'. He also ruefully recounted how, since he had been at the Home Office, he had 'stretched out several feeble paws of amity – but in vain – & I am only sorry that the drift of events did not enable us to work together . . . I have deeply regretted since that I did not press for the Admiralty in 1908. I think it would have been easily possible for me to obtain it. I believe it would have been better for us all.'[1]

Asquith had been aware for some time of Churchill's wish for the Admiralty, and less than two years after Fisher's resignation he offered it to him. Fisher had been superseded by a sturdy, steady, dour old salt, Admiral of the Fleet Sir Arthur ('old 'ard 'eart') Wilson, upon whom Fisher relied to sustain his policies and methods. Lacking the fiery stimulus of Fisher as his partner, McKenna did not thrive. On 25 October 1911 McKenna was transferred to the Home Office much against his will, and Churchill crossed Whitehall and exchanged jobs with him. 'As soon as he [McKenna] had gone,' wrote Churchill of this crowning moment, 'I convened a formal meeting of the Board, at which the Secretary read the new Letters Patent constituting me its head, and I thereupon . . . became "responsible to Crown and Parliament for all business of the Admiralty". I was to endeavour to discharge this responsibility for the four most memorable years of my life.'[2]

Asquith's concern about the readiness of the Navy had been intensified during the diplomatic conflict in Morocco between France and Germany, which also affected Britain. In the spring of 1911 the French despatched a small military force to Morocco, ostensibly because French lives in that country were threatened by a revolt against the Sultan of Morocco. The Germans rightly suspected that this was only a first move towards part-annexation, which would thwart the long-term German intention of establishing a naval base on the Atlantic coast.

The Germans emulated Britain's long-established corrective for trouble abroad by sending a gunboat to Agadir. Britain's own response was for a time confused, although everyone agreed that the situation could become dangerous. The Press response was varied, from the *Manchester Guardian* preaching peace and deploring panic, to the *Standard* on the far right: 'The plain truth of the matter,' ran an editorial, 'is that no Government . . . could consent to allow a great foreign navy to station itself on the flank of our Atlantic trade and on the line of our route to the Cape.'[3] Sir Arthur Nicolson, Permanent Under-Secretary at the Foreign Office agreed. The Admiralty, however, made light of the affair to the Foreign Office claiming that the Germans would require a powerful detachment to support this distant base, which would mean weakening the Fleet in the North Sea. Informed opinion also believed that Germany was much more interested in interfering with France's suspected annexation of Morocco, humiliating her and driving a wedge into the newly formed *Entente Cordiale*.

It was an indication of the gravity of the crisis that, with bellicose words thick in the air in Germany, France, and Britain, Lloyd George, arch-pacifist radical-Liberal, made a speech at the Mansion House. Peace with Germany at the price of loss of vital interests 'won by centuries of heroism and achievement', was unacceptable he stated in his best patriotic manner. 'National honour is no party question.'

During August and the early part of September 1911, while France and Germany tried to patch up their differences, war between Britain and Germany appeared for a time imminent. Grey sent for McKenna to warn him that the Fleet might be attacked at any moment.

The crisis and likelihood of war slowly receded, but it was noted by Asquith that the Fleet, though ready, had no war plans. Further enquiry revealed the absence of any progress on the formation of a Naval War Staff. Admiral Wilson was even more intractable over this question than Fisher. Both men believed that any plans should be locked up securely in the mind of the First Sea Lord, although it was rumoured (no doubt apocryphally) that Wilson had once scribbled his plans on one side of a piece of paper which was somewhere in his desk. When questioned at a meeting of the Committee of Imperial Defence at the height of the Agadir Crisis about the Admiralty's strategy, Wilson could only mutter – he was no orator – that, briefly, the plans were for a close blockade of German ports, the capture of advanced bases, and possible landings on the enemy's coast. He was against the Army sending an expeditionary force to help France until the enemy's Fleet had been destroyed.

Churchill found that Fisher's successor was quite out of his depth in terms of modern strategy, weapons, and conditions, with no intention of consulting with anyone, certainly not the Army, or even his civil master, the First Lord. Churchill's admiration for Wilson as a man was boundless.

He was, without any exception, the most selfless man I have ever met or even read of. He wanted nothing and he feared nothing – absolutely nothing. [He had earned the VC fighting the Dervishes] . . . He impressed me from the first as a man of the highest quality and stature, but, as I thought, dwelling too much in the past of naval science, not sufficiently receptive of new ideas when conditions were changing so rapidly, and, of course, tenacious and unyielding in the last degree.[4]

Churchill selected as Wilson's successor the C.-in-C. of the Home Fleet, an unexceptional man, Sir Francis Bridgeman, who seemed intelligent and alert and malleable, whom Churchill understood looked forward rather than back and was in favour of a Staff. Bridgeman's first duty was to hand to Wilson Churchill's letter demanding his resignation and offering him a peerage if he wanted one. When Wilson had hauled down his flag for the last time, in contrast with Beresford he had expressly forbidden even the smallest demonstration. Now he accepted the demand for his resignation in silence, and 'without any grace whatever,' according to Bridgeman, 'promptly declined the honour'.[5]

This incident was only an early clue to the nature of the new regime. Suspicion of Churchill before he came to the Admiralty was widespread. Established Conservatives of all classes saw him as the man who had fought against increasing the strength of the Navy and now was its civil head with the responsibility for keeping it strong. 'A self-advertising mountebank', was the *National Review's* opinion. Even the service and semi-service magazines were muted in their enthusiasm. *The Navy League Annual* stated that his arrival was not regarded with much favour. Nor could *The Navy* 'feel much satisfaction at the change which has taken place'.

Traditionally, the First Lord of the Admiralty is not expected to know, or wish to know, much of the detail of the Navy of which he is political chief. The First Lord, who was responsible for the Navy to Parliament, presided at Board meetings and acted as spokesman for the Cabinet among his functions. Churchill was not content with these limited activities. To the concern of his Board and senior officers with whom he was immediately in touch, he revealed himself as a civilian Fisher, investigating, questioning, reforming where reforms were not thought to be needed, formulating plans – and not just Naval War Plans – where plans already existed or were not seemingly essential.

Churchill did not sit at his desk in Whitehall like McKenna or Lords Tweedmouth and Selborne before him. He dashed out to inspect dockyards and new ships, barracks and torpedo training establishments. He even went to sea. His position entitled him to the use of the Admiralty Yacht *Enchantress*, a 3,500-ton steam vessel, as graceful and comfortable as the Royal Yachts. During his first eighteen months in office Churchill spent a total of six of them at sea in the *Enchantress*, sailing with his senior admirals, fellow politicians, and friends on board. He took Asquith to sea to observe gunnery practice, and, according to the Prime Minister, was soon 'dancing about behind the guns, elevating, depressing and sighting'.[6]

None of this rushing about helped to improve the traditional naval establishment's opinion of Churchill. Almost everywhere he went he left behind him hostility and suspicion for his methods and manner. He even succeeded in raising the wrath of his sovereign who already distrusted him. George V, the new King, was not only an Admiral of the Fleet of great experience: he loved his Navy and its traditions and high reputation. In Churchill he saw only the clever, opportunistic politician, and had agreed to his appointment with many reservations.

A month after Churchill became First Lord names had to be submitted to the King for new battleships under construction. This duty was the prerogative of the civil head of the Navy and Churchill took much satisfaction in it. The names he sent to Buckingham Palace were *Africa*, *Oliver Cromwell*, *Liberty* and *Assiduous*. These were scarcely traditional or ringing names and the King rejected them all except *Africa*. With extraordinary lack of tact and discretion, Churchill put forward *Oliver Cromwell* a second time and had it turned down again.

In reply Churchill sent the King's secretary a long and strongly argued case for using the name of this militaristic, anti-monarchist and anti-Irish figure, adding that he was 'satisfied that the name would be extremely well received'. He received a sharply-worded reply from Lord Stamfordham reminding him of the animosity aroused recently by the proposal that a mere statue to Cromwell should be erected, with the government of the day being overwhelmingly defeated in a vote on the issue. Why not *Valiant?* was the King's counter-suggestion. Churchill yielded, and in fact the super-dreadnought lived up to its name through two reigns and two world wars.

There is no doubt that Churchill was arrogant, overbearing, opinionated, and generally insufferable in the eyes of the traditional naval officer of the time. He also had a consistently hostile Press from the more traditionally-minded newspapers. 'The methods of Mr. Churchill,' the *Globe* contended, 'are wholly unfitted for the great Service of which for the time being he is the responsible head.'[7]

No one judged Churchill better than Asquith, who regarded his First Lord's more extreme activities with a mixture of wry amusement and mild vexation. Asquith once described a letter he had received from Churchill as 'very characteristic: begotten by froth out of foam'. But Asquith had every confidence that Churchill would eventually settle down. He was too clever, and had too clever a wife, to continue to exasperate his friends and create hostility among his colleagues for very long. And, as usual, Asquith was proved right. Two months before war broke out, Tirpitz received a letter from the German naval attaché in London which stated that 'on the whole the Navy is satisfied with Mr Churchill, because it recognizes that he has done and accomplished more for them than the majority of his predecessors . . . The intensive co-operation of all forces for an increase in the power and tactical readiness of the English Navy has under Mr. Churchill's guidance . . . experienced rather energetic impulses and inspiration. The English Navy is very much aware of it.'[8]

Churchill's prodigious work and fundamental reforms for the Royal Navy in 1912–14 were in line with and in scarcely broken continuity with those of Fisher, from whom he encouraged letters (as if that were necessary) containing a torrent of facts and advice. 'As the man wrote about white leather hunting breeches to his tailor,' quipped Churchill once to Fisher about his letters, '"Keep continually sending".'[9] Thirty years ahead of his time, and in characteristically violent style, Fisher wrote to Churchill on 16 January 1912.

Sea fighting is pure common sense. The first of all its necessities is SPEED, so as to be able to fight –

> *When* you like
> *Where* you like
> and *How* you like.

Therefore the super-*Lion*, the super-*Swift* and the super-Submarine are the only three types for fighting (*speed* being THE characteristic of each of these types). AVIATION has wiped out the intermediate types . . .[10]

There was a brief cooling-off when Fisher disapproved of some naval appointments but Churchill soon charmed him back with an irresistible invitation to cruise in the Mediterranean in the *Enchantress* with his wife, the Prime Minister, the First Sea Lord, and numerous other bigwigs on board.

Churchill took Fisher's advice to heart on the construction of super-fast big ships, submarines, and 'AVIATION' as on much else, and Fisher, out of office but by no means out of power, took a material as well as an inspirational part in all three developments. A division of powerful battleships had been called for. They had to be fast enough to storm ahead of the two parallel lines of contesting battleships in order to 'turn' the enemy vanguard and 'cross the T' – the classic naval manoeuvre that allowed your full broadside to bear on the bows of the enemy – just as the Japanese Admiral Heihachiro Togo had done in his defeat of the Russians at the Battle of Tsu-Shima (May 1905). They would in theory, fulfil Fisher's requirement and be able to fight *when* they liked, *where* they liked, and *how* they liked.

Churchill was now determined to go one better in gunpower as well as speed. The 12-inch gun of the *Dreadnought* firing an 850-pound shell had been followed, at Fisher's direction, by the 13.5, whose shell weighed 1,400 pounds. In the United States, 14-inch guns were already being developed, and there could be no doubt that Krupps in Germany would eventually go to at least this calibre. Churchill consulted Fisher. A 15-inch gun would fire a shell of almost 2,000 pounds and would be devastatingly effective up to a range of 35,000 yards. Fisher was enthusiastic. 'No one who has not experienced it', wrote Churchill in the chapter headed *The Romance of Design* in his war memoirs, 'has any idea of the passion and eloquence of this old lion when thoroughly roused on a technical question . . . So I hardened my heart and took the plunge. The whole outfit of [15-inch] guns was ordered forthwith.'[11]

Like everything else, the cost of these new battleships was about double that of the original *Dreadnought*, itself approaching obsolescence. A speed of 25 knots and 15-inch guns demanded a displacement of 27,500 tons, and to achieve these statistics, Churchill learned from his technical experts, required oil rather than coal fuel. The consumption of oil in Britain in 1912 was extremely modest. The nation's and the Navy's energy needs were met almost entirely by God-given coal, the nation's foundation in both meanings. 'To commit the Navy irrevocably to oil was indeed "to take arms against a sea of troubles" ', Churchill wrote later.

Fisher was an enthusiast not only for the 15-inch gun but also for oil-fired ships. Oil was efficient and clean. It gave a battleship 40 per cent greater radius of action for the same weight of coal. A coal-burning fleet at sea lacked 25 per cent of its ships which were perforce away refuelling, an exhausting and filthy process anyway. An oil-fired fleet could refuel by turning a tap, and, in all but rough weather, refuel at sea. Oil required less than half the number of stokers. The arguments in favour of oil were incontrovertible, with one exception. It was a foreign not a home mineral.

Churchill passed the problem to Fisher. In June 1912 he wrote: 'The liquid fuel problem has got to be solved, and the natural, inherent, unavoidable difficulties are such that they require the drive and enthusiasm of a big man. I want you for this viz to crack the nut. No one else can do it so well. Perhaps no one else can do it at all . . .'[12]

Fisher agreed to chair a Royal Commission on oil. Its report favoured the momentous switch by the Navy from coal to oil. Churchill entered into negotiations with the Anglo-Persian Oil Company and carried through the House of Commons the Anglo-Persian Oil convention which led to the Navy having what was believed to be a guaranteed supply of oil without any risks of foreign control or interruption.

There thus came into being the magnificent class of five 15-inch-gunned *Queen Elizabeth* battleships whose service in two world wars was pricelessly valuable. And from this time virtually all new British men o'war were fuelled by oil.

Fisher's demand for 'super-Submarines' was even more difficult to meet. Disregarding early experimental craft, the submarine was scarcely a decade old, the first practical vessels being designed by an Irish-born American, J. P. Holland, and introduced into the United States Navy in the 1890s. Fear of underwater weapons went back earlier than this, but it was the fixed mine and the automobile torpedo carried by small craft that were most influential in modifying the tactics and strategy of the battle fleet and the defences of the battleship.

The submarine was at first regarded as a defensive weapon for the protection of harbours, bases and coastlines. The German Navy saw them in this role until after the outbreak of war, and Tirpitz was astonished at the damage the U-boat was able to inflict far from its own base. In Britain, the submarine service grew slowly and in face of the hostility of the great majority of senior officers and members of the

Board. When submarines took part in manoeuvres and war games, their successes tended to be discounted. Wilson judged the submarine as 'Underhand, unfair and damned un-English'. Most officers regarded them as playthings for the eccentric young men who dressed up in oilskins (very necessary) and looked like scruffy North Sea fishermen. The submarine in all major navies was patronizingly regarded as 'the weapon of the weaker power'.

Churchill, under the influence of Fisher, the submarine's most ardent advocate, a small number of intelligent and far-sighted senior officers, and politicians, supported the submarine branch and the construction of more submarines and new long-range torpedoes. As early as January 1912 he was in earnest correspondence with a number of politicians about the influence of the modern submarine and torpedo on the nation's defensive as well as offensive plans. Arthur Balfour, recently Prime Minister (1902–5) and destined to succeed Churchill as First Lord, was especially encouraging. 'I have been thinking over what you wrote about submarines,' Churchill wrote to him. 'They seem to me a great advantage to us. They make invasion look more difficult than before. They are the most formidable defence for their own coasts . . . On balance we are the gainers of this new type [of submarine] . . . Another thing which properly employed will be helpful to us is the long range torpedo. 10,000 yards! And it is a mere calculation of odds to see how many must be fired from one line of ships at another to hit every vessel – bar accidents.'

Balfour replied that he entirely agreed. 'I have long been strongly of the opinion that submarines will modify the whole question of Home Defence', he answered.[13]

By 1912 the size, range, and power of the submarine had much increased and its influence on manoeuvres could only be denied by blinkered officers, which unfortunately included a majority of the Board. In the 1913 manoeuvres submarine officers claimed to have accounted for 40 per cent of the men o'war present, in spite of the rule that after making a claim the submarine was obliged to surface for half an hour and not attack any vessel within three miles, in simulation of what were judged to be real-war conditions.

Nonetheless, under Churchill's regime the submarine was rapidly developed. The E-class which was to play such an important part in the war, was a vessel 178 feet long with a radius of action of 4,000 miles, a surface speed of over 15 knots and submerged speed of almost 10 knots. No one could totally disregard the threat of a swarm of such vessels on a battle fleet in misty typical North Sea weather. Recognition of the threat from German U-boats was reflected in the

fundamental and highly secret strategical decision taken in 1912 to
cancel a close blockade of the German coast in the naval war plans
and substitute distant blockade. In debates inside and outside the
Admiralty in the months leading to war the submarine threat was
argued exhaustively. Even the possibility of having to keep the
dreadnought fleet out of the North Sea altogether because of what was
euphemistically termed 'the small-craft menace' was aired.

Admiral Sir Percy Scott, a figure almost as dynamic, controversial,
and far-seeing as Fisher (but lacking his charm and wiliness), and a
revolutionary figure in the field of naval gunnery, contributed an
article to *The Times* a few weeks before war was declared arguing that
the Fleet of the future would require only aircraft and submarines.
'Submarines and aeroplanes have entirely revolutionized naval
warfare; no fleet can hide itself from the aeroplane's eye, and the
submarine can deliver a deadly attack even in broad daylight.'[14]

The outraged chorus of protests at this suggestion included the
voices of all those of conservative inclination and with vested interest
in the continued paramountcy of the dreadnought, from shipbuilders
and steel-plate manufacturers to most officers serving in the Fleet.
Scott's modest weight of supporters included the Liberal Press which
saw in his argument a means of reducing the crippling cost of
armaments.

Nevertheless the threat of the submarine was taken seriously
enough for an Admiralty Submarine Committee to be set up to
consider proposals for weapons to counter the menace. It remained
barren of ideas. 'It is high time', declared one admiral at a War
College lecture in April 1914, 'we put the fear of God into these young
gentlemen who lie about the North Sea attacking all and sundry
without let or hindrance.' How this was to be accomplished remained
for the present unanswered.

The hard prejudice which hindered the development of the
submarine did not apply to naval aviation. It is true that when offered
the Wright brothers' patent in 1907 Lord Tweedmouth on behalf of
the Board had turned it down. But two years later when the Hon.
C. S. Rolls of the infant Rolls-Royce motor car company offered the
Government the use of his Wright aeroplane he used for recreation, it
was gladly accepted. Before he resigned Fisher was showing interest
on behalf of the Admiralty and had ordered the construction of an
airship. As soon as Churchill was appointed, Fisher determined that
the subject should not be allowed to drop. '*Aviation* supersedes small
cruisers & Intelligence vessels. You told me you would push
aviation . . . '[15]

Churchill himself needed no pushing. From the first he was an enthusiastic supporter of early experiments and, in the teeth of Treasury opposition, put an Air Department to work. Soon he was able to write to Fisher. 'Aviation is going ahead. In a few months the Navy List will contain regular flights of aeroplanes attached to the battle squadrons.'[16] There was little or no opposition within the service. The aeroplane and airship were proving useful for scouting, for observing the fall of shot in action as well as locating submerged submarines and minefields. They were seen as an aid to and not a threat to the battleship.

In Germany, under the inspiration of Count Ferdinand von Zeppelin and with the support of Tirpitz, the lighter-than-air machine was favoured, and before war broke out the German Navy could call on a powerful force of some twenty highly reliable and effective Zeppelins based on Cuxhaven. Churchill respected this force but determined that the Royal Navy should concentrate on the aeroplane which was less vulnerable, cheaper, more adaptable and could be flown off the water on floats or carried in seaplane-carriers.

At Eastchurch on the Thames estuary a small but efficient naval air arm came into being. In 1913 the *Hermes*, the world's first aircraft (seaplane) carrier, was commissioned. The enthusiastic pilots and some admirals (Wilson, surprisingly, was among them) saw an important and wider future for aircraft. By 1914 plans were already being made for seaplanes to carry a charge of gun cotton fused to explode close to submerged submarines. An article in a service magazine in the same year drew the attention of its readers to aircraft as future torpedo carriers.[17]

Amidst the mass of work for which Churchill had made himself responsible outside as well as inside the Admiralty, he made a study of the new machines in the greatest detail. He took lessons in flying and was thus able to correct with authority what he regarded as detail flaws, such as inferior seating and flimsy controls. Charles Rolls had already become the first flying fatality and others had been killed or injured. Churchill's wife and his fellow politicians and friends begged him to desist. He was about to solo when his own instructor was killed and this led him at last to give it up, though with many regrets.

It was typical of Churchill that he regarded the detail of his work as important as the broad sweep of policy. After two years of his insistence, for example, on examining the working of a submarine's periscope or a Barr and Stroud range-finder, the cooking equipment at Dartmouth naval college, or the functioning of the feed equipment in a new fleet tanker, the Navy gave up taking offence and (as the German naval attaché had learned) Churchill was generally treated with respect and admiration.

Gunnery and fire control was one of the largest and most important subjects to come under his critical eye. Percy Scott had for long been concerned at the shortcomings, which could prove fatal under certain conditions, of the practice of individual gunlayers and trainers being responsible for the accuracy of their own gun or guns. With the increase in range of modern gunnery, Scott contended that the gunlayer in action at his relatively low station might well be so blinded by smoke, haze, spume, shell splash, and mist that he might not fire on the correct target, let alone hit it.

From about 1904 Scott began his fight for single, centralized gunnery control, or 'director firing', from a station high up in the foremast, using a master sight electrically connected to the sights of each gun, fire being controlled by pressing a single key. He soon gathered disciples about him. Among them was Captain Frederick Ogilvy, whose cruiser *Natal* was top of the Navy at the gunlayers' test anyway. This enthusiasm had originally been inspired by Scott when Ogilvy had served under him in HMS *Terrible*. Ogilvy's gunnery lieutenant was William James, one of the best in the service (known to his friends as 'Bubbles': as a child he was the model for Millais's famous painting).

Ogilvy decided to make his own centralized gunnery control with what he could find. 'I used to visit old ships lying in the dockyard', James recounted. 'I was caught one day by a dockyard policeman and there was a devil of a row. The Admiral Superintendent took a poor view of an officer stealing bits and pieces of sights etc from the old ships but Ogilvy fortunately was able to pacify him and I was not court-martialled.'[18] Ogilvy's 'master sight' was rigged on the top of the cruiser's conning tower, mounted on a Maxim Gun stand, and it came up to all Scott's expectations. Scott himself, as Inspector of Target Practice from 1905, continued his own experiments and spread wider the gospel of centralized firing. There was deeply entrenched opposition from individual captains of guns and crews who saw the responsibilities of their skills being diminished.

At a higher level it was also legitimately argued that an error by the Principal Control Officer and his two assistants, the Rate Keeper and Deflection Keeper, (all of them vulnerable to enemy fire) affected every gun in the ship.

A battleship's gunnery officer recalled another objection, and the simple counter-argument to the directors' supporters.

I remember that what they [the detractors] feared was that the long line of communications from the top to the guns was vulnerable and might be severed by an enemy shell in the first few minutes of battle. What they forgot was that if the Director was put out of action by a shell, there was no difficulty in changing over to the older system – the gunlayers and trainers at once leaving their instruments and going to their sights.[19]

The official acceptance of director firing was delayed by more than prejudice and reasonable argument. Pioneers' misfortunes inevitably occurred. 'The instruments gave us a lot of trouble. They were not reliable', recalled James, now gunnery lieutenant in HMS *Neptune*, the first dreadnought to be fitted with the full director equipment devised by Scott in conjunction with the shipbuilding and armaments company, Vickers. 'As the time approached for our battle practice I realized that if the training pointers went out of step we might fire a salvo at the towing ship. I explained this to the Captain and he decided we should carry out the battle practice in the usual way, the layers and trainers laying and training their guns by their sights.'

This episode became widely known in the Fleet. By chance, James took his Christmas leave that year in Switzerland. 'The first day I was on the ice, one of the skaters came up to me and said, "Why the devil didn't you use the director for your battle practice?" It was Percy Scott, a very skilled performer on skates. I told him the reason but he was not satisfied and did not speak to me again.'[20]

It was not until November 1912 that the die was finally cast in favour of the director. On the 13th two dreadnoughts steaming at 12 knots in rough weather at 9,000 yards range were in turn given three and a half minutes' firing on the target with their heavy guns. HMS *Thunderer* fitted with a director fired 39 rounds making 23 hits if the target had been the second ship, *Orion*. The *Orion* which employed independent gunlayer firing, then fired 27 rounds and made 4 theoretical hits.

A second contentious gunnery issue, related to director firing, was the development of fire control. A fire control instrument would provide an automatic plot of one moving ship against another in order that guns could be laid for future positions of the moving enemy target. As the range of guns increased, range-finders found their way into the British fleet in 1892 and into the Japanese Navy the following year. But this did not anticipate and plot the relative course and bearing of the target.

A man of exceptional ingenuity and originality of mind, Arthur Pollen, began to interest himself in the subject of fire control as the result of witnessing a warship's target practice at a mere 1,400 yards, and not accurate at that. Yet these same guns, manned by naval gun crews, were at the time engaging Boer targets at Ladysmith accurately at 10,000 yards. Pollen had been a barrister, parliamentary candidate, inventor, and businessman, one of whose hobbies was big game hunting. He now gave much of his time to devising what was in effect a mechanically operated computer decades ahead of its time, an apparatus which produced a true plot which gave an accurate prediction of the deflection and range required to allow for the time of flight of the ship's shells.

Pollen was not alone in the field. The son of an astronomer naval gunnery officer, F. C. Dreyer, was working independently along the same lines as Pollen. But it was not until 1913 that, after exhaustive trials, the Dreyer system using a fire control table was accepted by the Admiralty and began to be installed in big ships.

The competition between the two similar systems aroused a great deal of acrimony among their proponents. In some respects the Pollen system was ahead of the Dreyer, and there can be no doubt that the Admiralty chose the Dreyer system in the end because it originated more or less from within the service and Pollen himself lacked tact and discretion in promoting his case. He had also made himself an enemy of Fisher.

The Dreyer system was far ahead of any navy's, and in 1914 too elaborate and complex for the Royal Navy to get the best out of it. Like Pollen's system, Dreyer's finally depended for its accuracy on the quality of the range finder.

In his first days of office Churchill drew up an exhaustive memorandum on the need for setting up a Naval War Staff. It was a brilliant piece of writing, broad in its vision, profound in its historical understanding, masterly in its display of knowledge of sea power and the functions of a modern navy. 'In the past history of this country the Navy has carried out many maritime campaigns without the help of such a body of trained experts', ran one paragraph. 'But this is no proof either that such a body is not required under modern conditions, or that satisfactory results would not have often been obtained with less loss of life and waste of time if it had previously existed . . .'[21] Pointing to the development of new *matériel* of all kinds in 1911, he related this breathtaking twentieth-century speed with the time when 'progress in naval architecture was so gradual that the science of naval strategy, as based upon the capabilities of ships and the science of administrative preparation as regards foreseeing their wants, were simple and unchanging'. For centuries only the wind

could move the fleets, and for generation after generation the stores
and even the ammunition required to fight were identical.

The case for a Staff was incontrovertible as expressed by the young
new First Lord. But his old First Sea Lord remained quite unconvinced. Wilson's own memorandum opened:

The agitation for a Naval War Staff is an attempt to adapt to the Navy a
system which was primarily designed for an army . . . The requirements of
the Navy are quite different. In the aggregate probably more thinking has to
be done to produce an efficient Navy than an efficient Army, but it is on
entirely different lines . . . The staff that does this thinking is not called by
that name. It is comprised of the principal members of every department of
the Admiralty . . .

The core of the argument of this old, traditionalist but highly
intelligent sailor was contained in the paragraph: 'The Navy has
learned, by long experience, thoroughly to distrust all paper schemes
and theories that have not been submitted to the supreme test of trial
under practical conditions by the Fleet at sea, and the whole
Admiralty has been gradually developed to make the most of the
experience so gained.'[22]

The first reason why Asquith had sent Churchill to the Admiralty
was to do what everyone before him had failed to do, and Churchill
rode roughshod over Wilson and the great majority of senior officers
in Whitehall. The admirals who were lined up against him went as
unceremoniously as Wilson. By 8 January 1912 Churchill had an
Admiralty War Staff, with a Chief responsible to the First Sea Lord in
charge of the three divisions it comprised: Operations, Intelligence,
and Mobilization.

Lord Esher sent his congratulations among a chorus of others. 'It is
the most pregnant reform which has been carried out at the Admiralty
since the days of Lord St Vincent', he declared. The Press was solidly
in favour of the step taken by Churchill, which was a new experience
for him.

Churchill suspected, with all the evidence supporting him, that war
could start at any time, and the fact remained that after an upheaval
as profound as this the Admiralty would take time to settle and the
Staff would take time to play themselves in. There was not an officer
in the service trained in staff work.

Another department in urgent need of Churchill's attention and
general reform was the lower deck. Not only had the social
restlessness of 1911–12 spread to the lower deck due to poor
conditions and pay, but there was a great need to recruit many

thousands more sailors to man the growing fleet. Just one penny had been added to the pay of 1*s* 7*d* a day granted in 1852, the food was at the best basic, and the system of maintaining discipline was petty and undignified. Churchill's reforms in 1912 did away with many injustices, and led to higher pay and more generous leave and restrictions on the powers of the ships' police. Promotion to commissioned rank for petty officers and warrant officers began a process of democratization in the Navy. The fact that it slowed to a snail's pace after the first rush of reform, that insurmountable class barriers remained in the Navy for decades, and that until very recently a rating or petty officer who rose through hard work and merit to the ward room was treated as a social inferior, was no fault of Churchill. What he accomplished in 1912–14 was enough to lift the spirit and self-respect of the lower deck and lead to an improvement in efficiency and fighting spirit when war came.

THE ACCELERATION TOWARDS WAR

*Relative dreadnought construction figures, and the worsening relations with Germany –
The Hankey mission and Churchill's proposed 'naval holiday' – Austrian and Italian
dreadnought construction and the Mediterranean scene – Opposition to the withdrawal of
British strength from the Mediterranean – Ever-increasing naval expenditure – The
qualities of British and German dreadnoughts compared – Inferior British mines and
torpedoes – British and German personnel, their training and contrasting characters –
The shortage of exceptional talent among British and German admirals*

THE naval 'scare' of 1909, which had been the undoing of Fisher,
stemmed from predictions of German near-equality in naval strength
by 1912. These figures were calculated on German official figures of
shipbuilding enlarged by unofficial reports, rumours, and claims from
those many in Britain with a vested interest in laying down
more dreadnoughts. Typical of the doubtful sources on which 'scare'
figures were based was the account given to Fisher by members of an
Argentine naval mission to Germany in 1909. They had been
impressed by the vast resources of Krupps where they had seen
stockpiled armour-plate, no fewer than one hundred 11-inch and
12-inch guns nearing completion, and had heard that twelve
dreadnoughts were under construction and a thirteenth about to be
laid down. Perhaps the German hosts had been deliberately
exaggerating in order to impress their visitors: if so, it did them no
good as the Argentinians ordered their two dreadnoughts from
American yards.

In fact there was no acceleration of German dreadnought building
and no secret ships laid down. The substantiated figures available to
Churchill in April 1912 showed Germany with nine completed against
the seventeen predicted as possible or thirteen stated to be 'certain'.
To set against this, predictions of Britain's own dreadnought strength
had also been excessive and only fifteen had been commissioned. 'The
gloomy Admiralty anticipations [of 1909] were in no respect fulfilled
in the year 1912', Churchill wrote later. Lloyd George and he, then,
had been 'right in the narrow sense' in demanding a reduction in
British building. But he continued, 'We were absolutely wrong in
relation to the deep tides of destiny.'[1]

More firmly than in 1909, every sign, every portent, pointed to war
with Germany. The first communication from Buckingham Palace

received by Churchill after assuming office confirmed all that he feared.

Secret   Buckingham Palace.
                                                            Oct. 25th, 1911

My dear Churchill,
   The King wishes me to let you know that yesterday he heard from a relation in Germany who had recently been in Berlin to the following effect:—

> 'Admiral Tirpitz said, at the time when the Morocco [Agadir] crisis had reached its acute stage, that Germany would have gone to war with England but her Fleet was not ready yet and would *not* be until 1915 when the Canal would be finished so that all the largest ships could pass through, and by that time they would have enough Dreadnoughts launched to deal with any Power. The mines from Heligoland to the mainland would not be ready until 1914. If war broke out now', the Admiral said, 'the German Fleet would be smashed for no reason at all': (i.e. with no advantage to Germany).

The writer then went on to say:

> 'That is the reason why Germany gave in: so far as I can see we shall be fighting in 1915.'

If he did not hear these views expressed by Admiral Tirpitz himself, he heard them second hand.

                          Yours very truly,
                  (Sgd:)   Stamfordham[2]

   The strength of the German Fleet in 1912 may have fallen short of British predictions, but there could be no doubt that the tempo of the 'race' was increasing. The settlement of the Agadir Crisis had left Germany publicly humiliated and her people exasperated and angry. Tirpitz, always the masterly opportunist, now pressed for a supplementary navy bill to achieve a 2:3 ratio in dreadnoughts with the British Navy. 'The purpose and aim of our naval policy is political independence from England – the greatest possible security against an English attack – and a promising chance of defence if war should come', Tirpitz stated.[3]
   The figures 2:3 sounded to the uninitiated comparatively modest. But there were other factors to take into account. As had been witnessed in past years, battleship figures in particular could be manipulated. For example, pre-dreadnought battleships could count as half a battleship or none. The last British pre-dreadnoughts completed after HMS *Dreadnought* were formidable enough to be

counted as full dreadnoughts by some calculations. Moreover, British maritime responsibilities were world-wide, and in spite of Fisher's concentration of power at home, there remained substantial forces in the Mediterranean and the Far East. Then, Britain as an island, with her much longer and more vulnerable coastline, was more open to surprise attack – the 'bolt from the blue'. The Director of Naval Intelligence (DNI) predicted that 'a sudden and dramatic outbreak would be distinctive of future wars, especially of warfare at sea. The advantages . . . are so enormous as to quite outweigh any lingering scruples of international comity.'[4]

Churchill's grasp of the naval situation he had inherited was confirmed to all those who heard him at a meeting of the Committee of Imperial Defence. 'The ultimate scale of the German fleet is of the most formidable character', he told members.

The whole character of the German fleet shows that it is designed for aggressive and offensive action of the largest possible character in the North Sea or the North Atlantic . . .

We are sometimes told that the Germans only think of fighting a battle which will leave that greater Power seriously weakened after the battle is over; they will have destroyed themselves and the greater naval Power will be weakened . . . Anything more foolish than to spend all these millions year after year to make all these efforts and sacrifices and exertions for .no other purpose than certainly to come off second best on the day of trial cannot well be imagined.

The German Navy, Churchill emphasized, 'is intended for a great trial of strength with the navy of the greatest naval power'.[5]

In spite of these firm and determined words spoken publicly as well as within the confines of a Whitehall meeting, Churchill remained strong for peace and for reducing naval expenditure so long as Germany showed, however slightly, similar sentiments. In his first public speech as First Lord, in the Guildhall on 9 November 1911, he asserted that a large reduction in the British naval estimates was certain if no increases in the German Navy Law were introduced. Three months later, he declared himself in favour of what came to be known as 'the Haldane peace mission' to Germany.

Alarmed by the increase in tension following the resolution of the Agadir Crisis, Sir Ernest Cassel, the multi-millionaire British banker, and his friend Albert Ballin, the German shipping magnate, had conversations on how relations between the two powers might be eased. These promised well and resulted in an agreement, warmly approved by the Emperor of Germany and conditionally agreed to by the British Cabinet, on a basis for opening official negotiations. Lord

Haldane who, as Secretary of State for War, had entirely reformed
and remodelled the Army, was selected to lead the British mission.
Haldane was not only a statesman. He was a philosopher and lawyer
who had been educated partly in Germany. The talks were long and
exhaustive and led nowhere. Tirpitz was adamant that Germany
must go ahead with her supplementary bill for the Navy, offering only
to decrease the rate of dreadnought construction. The Germans
demanded a more neutral policy by Britain as the price for any real
reduction in naval expenditure. This Britain could not entertain. The
ties with Russia and France were essential for defence and for
practical considerations.

With the acceptance of failure, Britain's ties with her allies were
strengthened, and increased naval rivalry once again made certain. In
spite of this breakdown, attempts that were not all political or
half-hearted were made over the next two years to bring about some
sort of decrease in naval building. Churchill placed his faith in a 'naval
holiday', a break from dreadnought construction, but suspicion of his
motives was too strong in Germany for any hope of success. This can
be seen in a letter on the subject from the British naval attaché in
Germany to the Foreign Secretary Grey.

Tonight, after the Yacht Club dinner, the Emperor sent for me. His Majesty
was somewhat serious and remarked that he had heard that Mr Churchill, in
his expected speech on naval shipbuilding intended again to refer to the
'naval holiday' . . . His Majesty continued to the effect that if Mr Churchill
did make a further suggestion of a naval holiday he could not answer for the
state of opinion in Germany . . . His Majesty went on to say: 'It is absurd
England always looking at Germany. I have information from Russia and
France that they are spending so many millions on fleet expansion and I
must make my fleet expenditure sufficient to meet that. I am no longer able
to enter into a fleet agreement with England.' (This is practically verbatim).[6]

After reading a copy of this letter, Churchill noted in a memorandum addressed to Grey and the Prime Minister:

It is very natural that the German Emperor . . . should not relish the
prospect of proposals being made by this country, the good sense of which
will be increasingly appreciated the longer they are studied. We are,
however, face to face with the declaration of the German Chancellor in the
Reichstag on the 7th of April 1913 that they 'awaited' the formulation of
'definite proposals' from us. The German Government cannot expect to
enjoy the advantages of saying in public that they 'await proposals' and of
saying confidentially that they will resent it if they are made. If therefore it is
decided that no further reference to a 'naval holiday' should be made at the
present time, I ought to be at liberty to state that we have received

representations from the German Government to the effect that they do not desire to discuss any such proposals.[7]

This fencing in the dark while, outside, real sabres were being rattled, continued through the last fateful months of 1913 and 1914. On 13 March 1913 Churchill presented the new naval estimates to Parliament, which provided for a further five dreadnoughts and twenty-four cruisers and destroyers. The Liberal Press had now reduced its alarm and opposition to a muted and resigned groan. The Conservative newspapers thought that the proposals were inadequate and that there should be six dreadnoughts. Churchill raised again his idea for a 'naval holiday': if you promise not to lay down dreadnoughts for twelve months, we'll do the same. Millions will be saved with no loss to either side – this, in effect, was what he was offering.

The response in Germany was as outraged as the British naval attaché and British ambassador had warned it would be. There were accusations that arrogant Britain was again attempting to interfere with German internal policy and her right to be strong at sea, cause unemployment in German shipyards and industry generally, to hurl insults at the Emperor. The German naval attaché in London said the proposal was bogus and made only as a sop to the radical-Liberals.

When Churchill repeated the 'naval holiday' proposal yet again in October 1913 he was made a target for the vituperation of British Conservatives and German diplomats and defence chiefs alike. It was remarked in Germany that it was time for Churchill 'to take a holiday for a year'.

Like Neptune's trident with which cartoonists frequently linked Churchill as First Lord of the Admiralty, his motives were three-pronged. As a Liberal he genuinely wished for a reduction in defence expenditure and an increase in social benefits. As a politician he recognized the kudos he gained in his party by his efforts, even if they were by now futile. And as a naval administrator he recognized the difficulties already being experienced in finding the yards to build these ever more gargantuan men o'war and the sailors to man them.

In 1913 the Mediterranean had again become a grave anxiety to the Admiralty. The fact was that dreams of battleships among the Mediterranean nations, which had been known for some time, were rapidly becoming reality. Dreadnought fever was infectious. France, Italy, Spain, and Austria-Hungary were building their own, and Greece and Turkey had already ordered dreadnoughts from foreign yards. By 1915, more than twenty dreadnoughts would be completed and commissioned; and in the ever-changing fortunes of diplomacy, who could say which nation might be an ally or an enemy in some future war? Only France could be relied upon as a friend to help the much-reduced British naval force in the Mediterranean.

On 10 July 1912, Grey assured the House of Commons that there was no intention of withdrawing further strength from the Mediterranean, and that Britain would maintain a fleet there capable of dealing with either Austria or Italy, but not both. If there was a general conflagration in Europe, Austria and Italy were unlikely to be on the same side, and in any case France would then become involved. At this time, Churchill announced that a force of eight dreadnoughts would be provided for the Mediterranean by 1915, in time for the completion of the Austrian programme. For the present, there would be a battle-cruiser force based on Malta.

The Mediterranean position worsened soon after these announcements with the inevitable outcome of the Italo-Turkish war, a particularly cruel conflict. When peace was concluded in October 1912, Italy was in occupation of Tripoli, with its first-class naval base at Tobruk, the Dodecanese Islands, and a number of Aegean islands. Italy, in possession of a powerful navy and a string of strategic bases in the eastern Mediterranean, had swiftly become a serious threat to British interests and communications at a time 'when our whole fleet is insufficient to provide for a sure preponderance in the North Sea coincidentally with an effective protection of our Mediterranean interests'. This memorandum from the C.-in-C. of the Mediterranean Fleet, concluded: 'The situation would plainly be aggravated by the establishment of a hostile Naval Station in the Aegean.'[8]

On 15 November Grey warned the Italians that if they set up a base in the Aegean 'we would certainly want something of the kind ourselves'. The Germans, quick to seize the opportunity, formed for the first time a Mediterranean squadron consisting of their newest dreadnought battle-cruiser supported by fast light cruisers. At almost the same time, Turkey approached Britain about an 'arrangement'.

With his mind now deeply concerned about the growing British difficulties in the Mediterranean, Churchill addressed Grey on the subject of a recent friendly approach by Turkey:

I could not help feeling that our [Cabinet] colleagues were rather inclined to treat a little too lightly the crude overture wh the Turkish Govt have made . . . Italy has behaved atrociously; and I cannot myself measure what the feelings of our countrymen will be as the news of these abominable massacres, resulting as they do from an act of wanton & cynical aggression is amplified and confirmed. I am sure, judging by what I hear from every quarter, that all the strongest elements in Liberal opinion must be stirred against the Italians . . . Turkey has much to offer us. In fixing our eyes upon the Belgian frontier & the North Sea we must not forget that we are the greatest Mahomitan power in the world . . . Turkey is the great land weapon wh the Germans cd use against *us*.[9]

Both Germany and Britain had been exerting influence on Turkey and taking practical steps to support her armed forces for several years. Turkey turned naturally to the German Army for military guidance, and Britain had set up a naval mission to reorganize the deplorable Turkish fleet and, incidentally, to balance German diplomatic influence. The British mission also carried the responsibility – like similar naval missions elsewhere – of obtaining orders for British shipyards. Two dreadnoughts were already under construction by Vickers at Barrow and Armstrongs on the Tyne. Churchill sought to increase this British naval influence to the extent of selling at a knock-down price two pre-dreadnought battleships immediately. This met with the hostility of some politicians and the indifference of most. It was also against the advice of his First Sea Lord, Vice-Admiral Prince Louis of Battenberg, whose eldest daughter, (Prince Philip's mother) had married into the Greek royal family. He was in favour of closer ties with Greece instead. It was, in fact, already too late. German influence was implacably growing in Constantinople and British influence waning.

The naval position in the eastern Mediterranean remained anxious and unsatisfactory. The only consolation – and it was a double one – was that an assessment of the quality of the Italian and Austrian Fleets was low, no matter how numerous their future dreadnoughts. It might not be as low as the Turkish Navy, but the Austrians were observed to be pantomime sailors, with high jinks and parades, glittering epaulettes and bursts of song like some Viennese operetta. And the Italians had long since lost the skills and feel for the sea of the old-time Genoese and Venetians.

For Britain the position in the western Mediterranean should have been a great deal more satisfactory. The French Navy could never be a match for the German High Seas Fleet, although its quality had enormously improved in recent years. Therefore, sensibly judging that their British allies could be safely left to deal with Germany in the north, the French in September 1912 moved their Brest squadron to Toulon to face any threat from Austria or Italy, leaving their northern and western coasts unguarded. At the same time, the French naval authorities approached Britain on the subject of exchange of plans and mutual co-operation in time of war.

The British response was not entirely negative but it was very cautious. In spite of the *Entente Cordiale*, a suspicion of France engendered by old conflicts and rivalries and a national reluctance to surrender her independence of policy and action still remained. In London the French naval attaché was informed by Churchill that nothing arising from any conversations between the two naval authorities 'could influence political decisions'. 'The point I am anxious to safeguard', wrote Churchill to Asquith and Grey, 'is our freedom of choice if the occasion arises, and consequent power to influence French policy beforehand. That freedom will be sensibly impaired if the French can say that they have denuded their Atlantic seaboard, and concentrated in the Mediterranean on the faith of naval arrangements made with us.'[10] And this is exactly what the French did say.

The hard core of the Conservative Press trumpeted that reliance on the French in the Mediterranean was 'absolutely repugnant to the mass of Englishmen' (*Daily Express*) and 'marked the limits of what a self-respecting people should endure' (*The Globe*). In the end, so pressing was the need and so intense was the threat of war, that limited naval conversations led to limited agreement on naval co-operation from the Straits of Dover to the Mediterranean. The preparation was authorized of a joint book of signals to be used in time of war with Germany in which both parties were engaged as allies. That was all. The British Admiralty, and the whole nation, were to pay a high price for their blinkered and selfish attitude towards the French under the guise of patriotic pride in independence. It is a heavy mark against Churchill and his naval administration that they were responsible for bringing this about.

As for similar conversations and co-operation with Britain's likely ally in the east, Russian approaches were rebuffed with thinly veiled contempt for the Tsar's navy in the Baltic and the Black Sea. When the Russians pressed again for some sort of mutually beneficial arrangement in the event of war, Prince Louis indicated that perhaps he might talk to the Tsar about it when he went to Moscow in August 1914. His sister-in-law was the Tsarina and the children of the two families liked to play together on holiday.

In the two years before war broke out in Europe, Churchill's endeavours to increase the strength of the Navy and maintain superiority over Germany while pacifying the little-navy radical-Liberals and Labour critics at home, ran in parallel with his attempts to bring about a pause in the dreadnought race which was so severely stretching the resources of both nations.

'Bloated and profligate expenditure on armaments' was an expression frequently used by radical and anti-navalist elements in Britain, and was quoted again by Lloyd George in an important statement he made in the columns of the Liberal *Daily Chronicle* on New Year's Day 1914 in which he made a strong appeal to the European nations to reduce their expenditure on arms. He opened with a back-hander against his old ally and colleague, Churchill, by reminding his readers that Churchill's father had resigned rather than support further expenditure on arms. There was a hint that now Churchill himself might face enforced resignation for his opposite policy.

This was an openly hostile attitude for a Chancellor of the Exchequer to assume in referring to his Cabinet colleague. When asked to comment publicly, Churchill retained his dignity and put the Chancellor in his place, declaring that he had made a rule 'not to give interviews to newspapers on important subjects' while they were still under discussion by the Cabinet as a whole.

In the weeks that lay ahead, Churchill had a last fight on his hands with his fellow Liberals and opposition Conservatives before the strife assumed a mightier dimension in August. The dreadnought figures being bandied about in public and in the Cabinet had indeed become bloated since Fisher had laid down the original nine years earlier. One official calculation was that the Navy must have in commission in less than six years fifty-six dreadnoughts in order to keep a minimum 60 per cent superiority over the Germans. The cost as well as the size of battleships had risen from one million to over two and a half million already, and was certain to go higher. The cost of maintenance had similarly multiplied, together with pay for the crew. The trained men required to man this gigantic fleet – it took eight years to train a lieutenant, two and a half years to train a rating – would be around 75,000 for the dreadnoughts alone, plus thousands more for the supporting cruisers and destroyers, and many more thousands supporting and servicing them in dockyards and barracks.

The expenditure of £49,970,000 made the head reel, but in the nation's defence councils the need to keep a clear margin ahead of the rival was as vital as it had been when the starting pistol had cracked out at the turn of the century. Now the Dominions were persuaded to offer material help. New Zealand chipped in with a dreadnought battle-cruiser, and so did Australia, although the Admiralty had not control over this vessel. The people of Malaya went one better and found the cost of an additional *Queen Elizabeth*-type super-dreadnought. The Canadian prime minister determined to assist, too, and for many months Churchill's hopes were high that three dreadnoughts would come from this Dominion; but in the end the Canadian parliament turned down the idea.

On 17 March 1914 Churchill produced his last peacetime estimates. They were the highest on record (£51,580,000) and his speech was the longest on record (two and a half hours). They provided for four more dreadnoughts and acceleration in the pace of construction of three more already under construction to offset partially the loss of the expected Canadian contribution.

The usual cries were heard. The Conservative Press was predictably pleased, the Liberal Press loud in lamentation, broken by a crisp practical note: 'The dreadnought can no longer live with the submarine; in nine years we have therefore wasted 360 millions which could have been used to alleviate some of our social diseases.'

Behind the scenes five members of Asquith's Cabinet had earlier sent a letter to him:

The effect of so enormous an increase in our Naval expenditure upon the German programme and policy is a matter of surmise: but such excuses as may be suggested cannot obscure the main fact – that the total is unprecedented; the increase is unexampled at a time of international calm; and the impression powerfully created that we are leading the way in yet more rapid outlay . . . [11]

The 'international calm' was shortly to be broken by the sound of an exploding bomb in an obscure Serbian town. A few weeks later British and German dreadnoughts went to their war stations.

Ship for ship the Germans had built dreadnoughts better equipped for battle than the British, who had originated the dreadnought's all-big-gun specification. By conforming to the now-superseded British policy of following the successful innovations of their rivals, the Germans benefited by avoiding British mistakes. Tirpitz also had the advantage of starting from scratch. He was unburdened by countless aged men o'war and numerous distant and often neglected bases and coaling stations, as well as the odium suffered by Fisher in scrapping and closing them down.

Tirpitz and his naval architects, and their successors, built the most difficult-to-sink warships in naval history. The German dreadnoughts were wider in the beam than their British counterparts, permitting more comprehensive underwater protection, including watertight subdivision. Although Fisher scrapped old ships, sometimes excessively, he could not bring himself to scrap undersized old docks, preferring to spend the money on new ship construction. As the

Kaiser boasted to a British admiral visiting Kiel, 'We build docks to fit our ships not ships to fit our docks.' This was another important advantage in starting from scratch.

Also, the *Kriegsmarine* never envisaged operating its main fleet outside home waters and therefore the crews could endure the discomforts of cramped accommodation as they were never at sea for long. British men o'war had to be global, German men o'war were not intended for distant seas although some were to operate in them. The beam of the *Dreadnought* was 82 feet, that of the first German dreadnoughts, which could not have been accommodated in British docks, was 89 feet.

British dreadnoughts were less heavily armoured and overall less protected than German contemporaries. SMS *Kaiserin* of 1912 had a wide main belt of armour of 13¾ inches, tapering to 7¾ inches at the bows and stern. The contemporary HMS *Thunderer*'s main belt of armour-plate was narrower and only 12 inches thick, her bows and stern totally unprotected. The German gun turrets and decks (important against plunging fire) were also better protected.

British dreadnoughts, on the other hand, were more heavily armed than their German counterparts. The *Kaiserin* was equipped with 12-inch guns, the *Thunderer* had gone one better with 13.5-inch guns, giving her an almost 50 per cent advantage in weight of broadside. Moreover, the 13.5-inch shell could be fired to a greater range with a greater accuracy and did more damage on impact. The German naval authorities answered their critics at home with the claim that the projectiles from their 11-inch guns against the British 12-inch, and their own 12-inch against the British 13.5-inch had a higher muzzle velocity and greater penetrating power. The greater reliability as well as the greater penetrating power of German shell was to be proven in battle.

The greater offensive power and inferior defensive strength of the British battle fleet was a product of the British character and naval tradition. The offensive spirit had been deep-rooted in the British Navy since Elizabethan times and had guided Drake and Hawke, Anson and Nelson. It was not so much that British officers and men were trained to be offensive; it was rather that the defensive spirit was unthinkable. This was one of the reasons why there was such strong suspicion of a Naval War Staff whose 'brains' might counsel caution or delay. The Nelsonian principle, modified to meet modern conditions, that all a commander had to do was to lay close alongside an enemy and sink or capture him remained as deep-rooted as an old oak tree.

British dreadnoughts were swifter and more heavily gunned in order that an enemy could not escape and would be sunk. The risk element of being sunk by the enemy because you were not sufficiently protected took a low place in the priorities. Fisher himself despised armour as much as he loved the big gun.

The Germans, lacking naval history or tradition but rich in military experience and accomplishment, followed a more logical and dialectic policy, always keeping in mind that their ships would have to survive in the face of a more numerous enemy. This was one of the reasons why German torpedoes and mines were superior. Tirpitz envisaged from the earliest days of the High Seas Fleet that in time of war the Germans must attempt to whittle down British numerical superiority piecemeal. This could be done only by bringing to bear a superior German force against an inferior British force – a difficult tactical achievement – or by picking off individual ships by laying mines or torpedoing them, most likely by destroyers or submarines. The Germans applied their scientific minds to the thorough development and testing of mines and torpedoes for a decade before the war. Their torpedoes ran straight and steadily, their mines soon proved lethal. The few British mines were scandalously inefficient.

The short German coastline in the Baltic and North Sea with its deep indentations, shoals, sandbanks, and river estuaries, was ideal for minefields and the Germans had no trouble in sealing it off for the duration of the war.

The first weapons priority in the British Navy was guns and gunnery, with torpedoes a long way behind, and mines out of sight. Gunnery had always been the elite branch of the service, and even before the all-big-gun *Dreadnought*, battleships carried as many guns of as large a calibre as practicable. The most important reason why the British Navy was confident that their dreadnoughts were superior to German dreadnoughts was because the weight of their broadside was almost always superior, often by a wide margin. Churchill frequently referred to 'undoubted superiority of our ships unit for unit'. Very few senior officers doubted this. One of them was Admiral Sir John Jellicoe, himself a gunnery officer and a protégé of Fisher. Fisher had for long determined that this 'new Nelson' should become C.-in-C. of the British Fleet at the outbreak of war. Jellicoe thought it 'highly dangerous to consider that our ships as a whole are superior or even equal fighting machines'.

The offensive character of British ships was matched by a similar quality in the personnel. Throughout the lower decks the Nelsonian spirit of optimism, aggression, and contempt for the enemy was widespread. The warrant and petty officers were a sturdy, immensely able, and highly conservative breed. Like housekeepers and butlers in big houses, they were conscious of their responsibilities, firm with those of inferior rank, and loyal to those above them.

The officers themselves were variable in quality, in part because of the immense expansion of the Fleet. Cadets were accepted after a moderately stiff examination at the age when they would normally be going to public school and spent two initial years at Osborne Naval College in the Isle of Wight under strict discipline and an austere regimen. This was followed by two more years at the new college (replacing the ancient and unhealthy *Britannia* training ship) at Dartmouth. With the successful passing of their examinations, the cadet put up his midshipman's patches at the age of around eighteen.

Efforts had been made to modernize the curriculum and there was emphasis on mechanics and engineering as well as gunnery, navigation, etc. But no efforts were made to impart any historical knowledge or an intellectual view of the meaning of sea power. Debate and 'braininess' were not encouraged, unlike the traditional virtues of competition, sportsmanship, and leadership. Bullying was rife, class distinction reflected the times. The fraternity between officers and the lower deck which was the strength of Nelson's Navy, through storm-wracked blockade and action, had diminished, just as the 'band of brothers' spirit among officers at the time of the Napoleonic wars had been diluted by years of internecine strife exemplified by the Fisher–Beresford vendetta.

One hundred years of peace had not improved the overall spirit of the Royal Navy. The Navy had not experienced the shock of the Boer War which had led to widespread reforms in the Army. In 1914 the Army was relatively more efficient and better prepared for war than the Navy. The Navy continued to be regarded as a career for the less intellectually endowed and young men who liked the 'clubbable' closed world and looked forward to steady rather than swift advancement.

At the same time, the improvements already made in the reform movements of the late nineteenth and early twentieth centuries were evidenced in the quality of some of the young officers coming up the promotion ladder, men like Reginald Tyrwhitt, Roger Keyes, Stephen King-Hall, Bruce Fraser, Ernle Chatfield, Andrew Cunningham, William Goodenough, and that brilliant theorist and critic, Herbert Richmond.

Unfortunately many in this group had little opportunity to exercise senior command during the war, and it was in this department that the Navy was weakest. The generation who had been brought up with sail in the dark years when novelty was heresy had found it hard perforce to accept turbines, torpedoes, director systems, and gunnery practice at 14,000 yards. They were now, in accordance with the promotion system, in command of big ships and in their late forties and fifties, steady, experienced, good seamen, full of sound common sense but lacking in initiative and originality of thought: a dull lot on the whole. The exceptions among them shone like searchlights on night exercises, but it remained a dark night.

Among this precious band were Jellicoe, David Beatty, Henry Jackson (Chief of Admiralty War Staff), John De Robeck, Charles Madden, Reginald Bacon, Horace Hood, William Pakenham, and Prince Louis of Battenberg. Many people (including Churchill, who had him as First Sea Lord from December 1912, and Fisher) regarded Prince Louis as the outstanding flag-officer. He had, it was thought, lived down his German ancestry and English naturalization, was a brilliant tactician and seaman as well as an efficient and original administrator who, more than anyone in the service, was responsible for setting up the Naval War Staff. He can be credited with the most highly developed intellect in the Navy. After fleet manoeuvres in 1909, Beatty wrote, 'We have eight Admirals, and there is not one among them, unless it be Prince Louis, who impresses me that he is capable of great effort.'[12] Without condition, Lord Selborne, whose experience and judgement were unsurpassed, wrote of Prince Louis, 'He is the ablest officer the Navy possesses.'[13]

Prince Louis and Churchill made an inspired and stalwart pair at the top. But it was a thin crust, and below them there was not much substance. The pie had one great credit mark, however. From the highest among flag-officers to the lowliest ordinary seaman, the Royal Navy was imbued with self-confidence. And this was something lacking in the *Kriegsmarine*.

Like the architects of their dreadnoughts, which were welcomed with unanimity and pride in the fleet, the German officer class did not have to struggle with the octopus of reaction. Tradition and a glorious naval past were not wholly advantageous. The German Navy possessed all the merits and some of the demerits of youth. The officers were superbly trained, especially in technology. They were immensely proud of their young service which, thanks to the Emperor and Tirpitz, shrugged off the early social inferiority of the Navy compared with the traditional standing of the Army. The German Navy revelled in its own modernity, its up-to-date weapons and equipment.

Equally characteristic of the German character was a reluctant acceptance of the British Navy's superiority in numbers, in size of guns, in speed, and – more intangibly but very powerfully – of the British Navy's long record of dominance and almost unbroken victory at sea. There was an unease in the German Navy quite lacking in the British Navy.

The *Kriegsmarine* possessed two more tangible disadvantages. The first was that in spite of its proud name High Seas Fleet, the German Fleet had been created to challenge Britain in home waters, with the certain expectation that from the outset the British Navy would close blockade the German coast and ports. Much of its training was carried out in sheltered waters, there were few long cruises, and there were long periods in harbour. As could be seen in the lines of identical buildings at Kiel or Emden, it was as much a 'barracks' navy as a seagoing navy. The British sailor lived in his ship and was at sea for much of the time. The German sailor went on board as a soldier goes on parade.

The second serious drawback was that, by contrast with the British Navy's voluntary system of recruitment for a minimum of twelve years, the German Navy was manned by conscripted three-year servicemen, with the instructors and officers 'every year called upon to make trained men out of a fresh lot of conscripts totally strange to sea life'.[13] In spite of this serious lack of continuity, their training was first class, and their morale at the outbreak of war high.

As to the higher commands, Germany was as handicapped as Britain in her search for top-quality admirals, but for a different reason. In spite of the radical up-to-dateness of the *Kriegsmarine*, the higher echelons were riddled with admirals who had risen on their social connections as much as on their merits. It was the good fortune of the service that on 31 May 1916, its day of supreme need, an exceptionally talented flag-officer was in command of its scouting force, Admiral Franz von Hipper.

Facing one another across the North Sea in August 1914 were two contrasting navies, the Royal Navy stronger statistically but by an uncomfortably narrow margin, stronger in offensive qualities, and carrying much greater and wider responsibilities. The *Kriegsmarine* was like a new army corps equipped with new weapons, conscious of the need to make its mark and show the nation it was worthy of the trust and pride invested in it.

Both navies possessed one common characteristic: such heavy emphasis had been laid on the quality and high cost of the ships that the practice of preservation had overtaken the practice of risk-taking

which had governed war at sea since the galley battles in the
Mediterranean a thousand years before Christ. British and German
tactical doctrines pointed to self-protection and evasion rather than a
reckless eagerness to get at the enemy. An objective examination of
these doctrines even led to a conclusion that the Fleets might never
meet in full-scale battle. Not that anyone would allow themselves to
express such blasphemy. At the same time there was not a
commander on either side likely to repeat, 'Damn the torpedoes – full
speed ahead.' There was just too much at stake and the torpedoes –
and mines – were too threatening.

WAR AND EARLY MIXED FORTUNES

The July 1914 Test Mobilization – Battenberg's order to 'stand the Fleet fast' – The close blockade of Germany, and its consequences – The lack of east-coast bases: a weakness revealed – Jellicoe as C.-in-C. – The submarine and mine perils – The loss of three armoured cruisers and the super-dreadnought Audacious *– Frustration and pessimism among Grand Fleet commanders – The Battle of Heligoland Bight a tonic, but Staff weaknesses exposed*

THE Royal Navy was blessed with an unexpected advantage when war became inevitable in the early days of August 1914. As long before as October 1913 Churchill and Battenberg had discussed substituting a test mobilization of the Third Fleet for the usual summer manoeuvres. The Third Fleet, or Royal Fleet Reserve, was made up of ships normally manned by skeleton crews, which could be brought to war readiness only if some 20,000 reservists were mobilized, an elaborate logistical exercise which had not recently been practised. This was also a costly business but nothing like as costly as the usual summer manoeuvres, which entailed not only the consumption of great quantities of fuel but also heavy wear and tear on the ships. It is not known whether Churchill and the Board of Admiralty were guided in their decision to call up the reserves in the summer of 1914 in preference to manoeuvres by prophetic powers or sound judgement, or for the political advantage of economy. It is most likely that Churchill thought that war was coming and Battenberg agreed.

The calling up of the reserves went off without a hitch on 10 July 1914 as planned. A week later George V reviewed at Spithead what Churchill called 'incomparably the greatest assemblage of naval power ever witnessed in the history of the world'.[1] Another week passed, the reserve ships dispersed to their home ports, the 20,000 men prepared to return to their homes. Following the assassination in Sarajevo of Archduke Ferdinand of Austria and his wife, the Austrians were mobilizing and had sent a threatening ultimatum to Serbia. On Saturday 25 July Churchill and Battenberg met briefly at the Admiralty before Churchill left for the seaside where his wife (who had been unwell) and his family were staying, leaving Battenberg in sole command, although Churchill made arrangements to be available on the telephone.

Churchill was not the only member of the Cabinet to leave London at this time of crisis and imminent war. 'Ministers with their week-end holidays are incorrigible', complained the First Sea Lord to his young sailor son, Dickie, the future Earl Mountbatten.[2]

On the Sunday, Battenberg learned that the Austrian-Serbian situation had worsened which, in the complex web of alliances and agreements involving also Russia, Germany, France, and Britain, brought war even nearer. He spoke to Churchill at Cromer in Norfolk. Within hours the reservists would have scattered, to remobilize them would be immensely complicated and take days or even weeks because many would then be joining their families on holiday. But to halt their dispersal ('Stand the Fleet fast') would be politically provocative. Battenberg was told that, as the man on the spot, the decision must be his. 'Churchill wanted to pass the political buck', observed Battenberg's son many years later.[3]

That evening as mobilization of armies began all over Europe and diplomatic relations were severed, Battenberg took the necessary steps to retain the reservists and ensure that the fleets remained concentrated. Then he told his cousin, the King, and Grey at the Foreign Office what he had done. Churchill returned to London where, over the next hours and days, the final preparations were made for war.

By Wednesday 29 July all that remained to put the Navy on a war footing was to despatch the First Fleet (or Grand Fleet as it was renamed) to its war station at Scapa Flow in the Orkneys.

We may now picture this great Fleet, [wrote Churchill in his richest vein] with its flotillas and cruisers, steaming slowly out of Portland Harbour, squadron by squadron, scores of gigantic castles of steel wending their way across the misty, shining sea, like giants bowed in anxious thought. We may picture them again as darkness fell, eighteen miles of warships running at high speed and in absolute blackness through the narrow Straits, bearing with them into the broad waters of the North the safeguard of considerable affairs.[4]

When at 11 p.m. on 4 August 1914 the Admiralty flashed the signal, 'Commence hostilities against Germany', every vessel of the Navy's vast armada was stationed according to the contingency plans long since prepared. The dispositions were faultless, the advantage of the advance planning and warning incalculable, and an unpleasant surprise to the enemy. The German Navy was to receive another shock when it was forced to recognize over the coming weeks that the British close blockade of their coast, upon which all their war plans were based, was not to materialize after all. Instead of being in a position to make harassing attacks on the blockading British battle fleet, the North Sea had been made a marine no man's land, with the British Fleet bottling up the exits and patrolling only especially sensitive areas with light forces.

As in the days of the Dutch wars of the seventeenth century, Britain held a priceless natural advantage in her geographic position. By closing the 20-mile-wide Channel in the south and the 200-mile-wide channel separating the Orkneys and Shetlands from Norway, Britain could block German trade with the outside world. Germany would have to smash the steel doors which had been slammed shut and chained the instant the British Fleet reached its war stations, before the High Seas Fleet could interfere with a single vessel of Britain's 19 million tons of merchant shipping (almost half the world's total).

As one historian expressed it, 'So long as Admiral Jellicoe and the Dover Patrol held firm, the German Fleet in all its tremendous strength was literally locked out of the world. The Hohenzollern dreadnoughts could not place themselves upon a single trade route, could not touch the outer hem of a single overseas Dominion, could not interfere with the imports on which the British Isles depended, could not stem the swelling stream of warriors who came from every land and clime to save the cause of civilization.'[5]

This geographic advantage had been supplemented by recent weapons which could virtually close off narrow waters to enemy heavy ships. A Committee of Imperial Defence (CID) report of 29 November 1912 defined this advantage: 'Owing to recent improvements in submarine mines, submarine boats, torpedo-craft, and torpedoes, the passage of the Straits of Dover and the English Channel by the ships of a Power at war with the United Kingdom would be attended with such risks that for practical purposes the North Sea may be regarded as having only one entrance, the northern one.'[6]

It was upon this Grand Fleet at Scapa Flow that the survival of the nation now depended. It comprised 21 dreadnought battleships, 8 pre-dreadnoughts, and 4 battle-cruisers, against the High Seas Fleet's 13 dreadnoughts, 16 pre-dreadnoughts, and 5 battle-cruisers. Both Fleets were supported by cruisers and destroyers. It was in this last category that the High Seas Fleet held the greatest numerical advantage, some 80 to 40.

In the event of a mass surprise attack by the German Fleet on the Channel defences, the Channel Fleet's three battle squadrons of nineteen pre-dreadnoughts would rapidly be reinforced from Scapa Flow, and from the Patrol Flotillas based on the east coast and the strong force of light cruisers and destroyers based at Harwich.

British naval planners were confident that the locks and chains that secured these steel doors would hold under the severest test. But the Naval War Staff in all its deliberations and Winston Churchill and his Board in all their planning for every contingency, had wrought some weak links which were to become alarmingly evident in the first days and weeks.

The first of these weaknesses, which could well have proved fatal, was the lack of suitably situated, fully prepared, and fortified bases on the east coast. That immense armada which Churchill proudly described silently and speedily slipping through the Straits of Dover into the North Sea was like an army stranded in the open country, without a fortification in which to restore and defend itself. The dreadnoughts' compasses would lead the Grand Fleet to Scapa Flow. But that great anchorage with its inclement weather, bleak hills, and fast-flowing tides and currents was unprotected by a single fixed naval gun or even searchlight against surface attack, and lacked booms or nets to guard the entrances against surprise surface or submarine torpedo attack, or fast minelayers.

It is difficult to account for the fact that there had been little outcry within or outside the service about this astonishing lapse in the nation's defences, no shrieks of 'Scandal!' from the sensationalist Press, no secret enquiry from the CID or the new Naval War Staff. The eyes of the steady, conscientious Battenberg and the all-enquiring Churchill never discerned the anomaly of a fleet upon which the security of the country rested having no secure place to anchor, coal, replenish its stores, repair, or refit. The tide ran so high at Scapa that a floating dock, even if present, could not reliably operate.

For two centuries before the challenge of the new German Navy, any threat to Britain's maritime supremacy had come from the south and the west, from France and Spain. Plymouth, from which Drake had sailed, and Portsmouth, where Nelson had embarked for Trafalgar, were the traditional homes of British sea power, well defended and comprehensively equipped. They were supplemented by Milford Haven in Wales, Portland and Dover in the south. The only long-established and first-class naval base facing east was Chatham in the Thames estuary, an excellent base from which to operate a close blockade of the German coast but useless for the Grand Fleet in 1914.

Paradoxically, the need for east-coast bases had been accepted in the highest quarters for eleven years. In 1903 the Cabinet approved an Admiralty request to build a first-class base at Rosyth, upriver from Edinburgh on the Forth. The advantage of this location was that it could be readily defended against sea attack and was equidistant from Heligoland and the Skagerrak in the heart of German seaspace. There was ample accommodation and rail communication was first class. One drawback was the giant railway bridge on the Edinburgh side which spanned the river and, if demolished by sabotage or shellfire, might trap the entire fleet.

The creation of this Rosyth base was a fumbled exercise from the start. The defence of ports was a joint Army–Navy responsibility: the Navy fixed a notional 'scale of attack' for the guidance of the Army, which then took over, built the forts, supplied the guns and garrisoned the place. The friction between the Admiralty and War Office was ceaseless, the delays prodigious. Procrastination bred on *matériel* advances. The development of mines, torpedoes, and submarines, it was said, made the narrow estuary of the Forth dangerous for large ships. The dreadnought, by making earlier ships unfit for the line of battle, released them for shore bombardment with their heavy guns, requiring a new calculation of the 'scale of attack'. Rosyth required the building of a small town to accommodate the dockyard workers, and money was short.

The catalogue of delay and ineptitude swelled year by year. There were protests, but they were not vehement or sustained. Churchill blithely told the House on 18 March 1912 that the two docks at Rosyth would not be ready for another four years. At the same time, the secret decision to apply a distant instead of a close blockade made it essential to base the main body of the Fleet farther north. Already by 1910 Cromarty, outside Inverness, was being studied for suitability as an advanced temporary fleet base, and Scapa Flow as a base for minor forces.

As the size of the Fleet increased, Rosyth's accommodation was judged inadequate anyway, and even Cromarty with its generous firth would be a cramped anchorage. By early 1913 the Admiralty and the CID between them had reached the conclusion that Scapa Flow should be the war anchorage for light forces and Cromarty the main fleet base. At first the Admiralty asked for permanent defences for Scapa Flow and then withdrew the request when it was learned they would cost nearly £400,000 – the fifth of the cost of a dreadnought.

In August 1914, therefore, of the east-coast bases considered for the Fleet in war, Scapa Flow was undefended, Cromarty incomplete and only lightly defended, Rosyth judged too limited in capacity and also incomplete, and the other bases too far south.

The first reason for this grave deficiency, however, had nothing to do with changing conditions, policies, and weapons, tidal currents and the threat of toppling bridges. It was, as always, a matter of priorities. The Navy was restricted to a fixed annual sum of expenditure. It thought first of its guns and the ships in which to mount them, it thought of offence rather than defence, and – at least until 1912 – it did not think hard enough anyway. Fisher and his disciples, for all that they did to strengthen and modernize the Navy, were too preoccupied with the one offensive weapon. The power and awesome magnificence of the dreadnought hindered their sight of other considerations, and blinded them to the associated and equally important need for protective defences and bases when they were not at sea. A preoccupation with the big gun excluded thorough preparation of bases for the Fleet just as it excluded thorough research into alternative weapons such as the mine and the torpedo.

The first shock experienced by the Grand Fleet was not warlike. No U-boat, no night attack by German torpedo boats or powerful battle-cruisers disturbed its passage north. But even before this armada dropped anchor in the wide, undefended spaces of Scapa Flow, it had lost its experienced and admired C.-in-C. George Callaghan, a man renowned for his cheerful toughness. His only offence was his age – he would be sixty-two in December – and this was used by Churchill as the reason for his sudden supersession by fifty-four-year-old Admiral Sir John Jellicoe. Jellicoe was about to leave overland to take up his post at Scapa as second-in-command when he was given this news. He reacted sharply. 'The step contemplated is most dangerous', he telegraphed Churchill, who stood firmly by the decision he had reached with Battenberg that Fisher's nominee would make the best commander in war. David Beatty, the brilliant and dashing commander of the Grand Fleet's Battle Cruiser Squadron since he had left Churchill's side as his Naval Secretary, also believed that this was a disastrous step at the very outset of war. 'The moral effect upon the Fleet at such a moment would be worse than a defeat at sea',[7] he wrote in defence of Callaghan.

Jellicoe despatched no fewer than six telegrams of protest. He believed that the timing and manner of Callaghan's dismissal would arouse renewed suspicions of Churchill's methods and resentment and jealousy among numerous flag-officers senior to himself. He was right on both counts. Churchill's wife added her own note of warning. 'Don't underrate the power of women to do mischief', she wrote to her husband. 'I don't want Lady Callaghan and Lady Bridgeman [wife of the previous First Sea Lord] to form a league of retired Officers' Cats, to abuse you.'[8] The King thought Callaghan had been 'very badly treated', and made him his Chief Naval ADC. Jellicoe wrote, 'My position was horrible . . . the tragedy of the news to the C.-in-C. was past belief, and it was almost worse for me.'[9]

The two admirals were good friends and Jellicoe was no doubt right when he said that he had suffered even more than Callaghan. He also added that it was 'a grave error', and this was not true. Churchill's error was in failing to make the appointment earlier and at a much less critical time than at the outbreak of a war for which the whole Navy had been poised expectantly for so long. Callaghan's appointment had already been extended by one year, and it was due to expire on 1 October anyway. By terminating it earlier the offence given would have been much diminished and Jellicoe would have had time to work himself into his appointment instead of being cast unexpectedly into the highest seagoing command. 'Quite impossible to be ready at such short notice', he complained in one of his telegrams of appeal.

John Rushworth Jellicoe was a modest man who sincerely placed the unity of flag-officers and the well-being of the Fleet far above his own ambitions. There must be few occasions in history when an officer, appointed to the command of a great force at the outbreak of a great war, has acted so self-effacingly that his behaviour has bordered upon a disciplinary offence. Jellicoe's appearance seemed to justify his modesty. He was short in stature (5 feet 6 inches), with a straight tight mouth and a prominent nose. Battenberg's young son, a worshipper of the flamboyant David Beatty, described him as having the appearance of 'a frightened tapir'. But at fourteen one tends to underestimate the importance of eyes. Jellicoe's were clever and all-seeing as well as kind. Like the few officers of his generation who faced the challenge of battle, Jellicoe showed his physical courage during the Egyptian rebellion of 1882 and later in China. To be a gunnery officer of unusual distinction ensured promotion, and his intellectual powers were spotted by Fisher when Jellicoe was still only twenty-nine, ensuring his appointment as Assistant Director of Naval Ordnance. From that time, Jellicoe could do no wrong in Fisher's eyes, although he never became known as an inmate of the 'Fishpond'.

Jellicoe reached flag rank at forty-seven, and followed the sure way up the path to the summit by accepting sea and Admiralty appointments of ever increasing responsibility.

The Grand Fleet rapidly transferred their loyalty and affection from

Callaghan to Jellicoe. All ranks came to love and admire him, just as he had been universally loved and admired throughout his career. No detail of a rating's domestic or professional woe was too small for his consideration and sympathy. And in this quality, alas, lay his greatest professional weakness.

John Jellicoe was so conscientious that he wished the corrections of all troubles to be in his hands. Delegation was agony to him, and far too rarely practised. His staff were frequently at a loss to know how to release him from some of the weight of his burden so that they could carry out their own appointed tasks. He embraced the whole Grand Fleet and its more than 100 men o'war and 60,000 officers and men into his care, cherishing them all with proprietorial affection, as if they were his own family. Beneath his cool and agreeable exterior, Jellicoe was a worrier and also a hypochondriac. And like most hypochondriacs, he had reason to be one. He had always suffered from intermittent ill-health, and this had not improved with a bullet wound in his lung during the Boxer rebellion in China when he was forty.

Jellicoe was an enlightened admiral and also a superb seaman and handler of ships. He was reckoned to have the swiftest brain of any serving flag-officer, and in a tight corner his orders were instant and crisp. By the standards of his time and his service, he was an intellectual who thoroughly understood the meaning of maritime power and its history. Except for his reluctance to delegate, he was a first-class administrator.

Contrary to the spirit of the great majority of his subordinates, Jellicoe's policy from the beginning was conditioned by caution and the contradictory needs to preserve his ships and attract the approbation he had enjoyed all his service life. It was a difficult role for him to play for among his commanders there were many fire-eaters lusting for battle.

Everything that happened at sea in the first weeks of war tended to confirm Jellicoe's fears and support his policy of caution. A new Battle of Trafalgar which would destroy German sea power as decisively as Nelson had destroyed French and Spanish sea power had been expected throughout the land and by all classes. The power of the Navy had been extolled so loudly and for so long, the sacrifices to pay for it had been so burdensome, that anything less than a quick victory was unthinkable. Disillusion soon set in.

Almost at once the threat from submarines, which had been greatly underrated, as much by the Germans as the British, and which were to become the dominant class of fighting ship, materialized in a most unpleasant form. Within a week U-boats were operating as far as

Scapa Flow and beyond. This was as much of a shock to the British as it was a pleasant surprise to the U-boat commanders who had underestimated their own prowess and capability. It should not have been a shock. It was only necessary to glance at the freely available latest *Jane's Fighting Ships* to read that the radius of the new U-boats was 2,000 miles, and any atlas would show the distance from Scapa Flow to the Elbe estuary is a mere 600 miles.

Genuine sightings of periscopes were few, imaginary sightings frequent and disturbing, to the extent that some cynical wag thought up the name of a new epidemic sweeping through the Fleet: periscopeitis. On 1 September, with the main body of the Grand Fleet's dreadnoughts at anchor in Scapa Flow, a light cruiser near the north-eastern entrance suddenly opened fire. It was dusk, the evening was misty, the eyes of lookouts strained by long observation. Jellicoe immediately ordered steam to be raised and the Fleet put to sea. Before it could do so, there was another 'sighting' and several ships fired at the supposed periscope. There was a great deal of frantic signalling and racing about by escort craft before the twelve dreadnoughts put safely to sea in the last light of the day. There they remained until dawn, with all the effort, use of machinery, and consumption of fuel this entailed. That seal had a lot to answer for!

It was generally agreed that the 'First Battle of Scapa Flow' had been drawn. Five days later the flotilla leader *Pathfinder* fell victim to the first real U-boat, *U-21*, with heavy loss of life. Farce had become tragedy. Worse was to follow. On 22 September, three old armoured cruisers manned largely by the reservists who had missed their family summer holidays, were patrolling off the Dutch coast. Ships of this class had been 'peddling up and down', as Battenberg described their activity, since the beginning of the war, ostensibly to keep an eye on German light craft which might make tip-and-run raids on Channel shipping. Officers of the Grand Fleet, who were having their own troubles, dubbed them 'the live bait squadron'. Five days earlier, Churchill's attention had been drawn to the vulnerability of the cruiser patrol and in a memorandum he recommended that it should cease. The always outspoken Commodore Roger Keyes, senior naval officer at Harwich, had written an appeal a month earlier to the Director of Operations of the Admiralty War Staff, 'For Heaven's sake take those "Bacchantes" [armoured cruisers] away!'

But even Keyes, who had been Inspecting Captain of Submarines and should have known better, feared only attack by a superior surface force. No one seems to have thought of U-boats; and when the usual destroyer screen had to withdraw owing to the equinoctial weather, the three 10,000-ton sister cruisers, *Aboukir*, *Hogue*, and *Cressy*, continued their patrol nonetheless, at an economical speed of 10 knots and without zig-zagging, their captains comforted in the knowledge that seas a destroyer could not endure were equally impossible for submarines.

However, the weather moderated on the night of 21–22 September, and at 6.30 a.m. the *Aboukir* was struck by a torpedo and sank twenty-five minutes later. The *Hogue* was beginning to do what she could for the survivors, and intermittently firing at a number of real or imaginary periscopes, when she, too, was struck by two torpedoes and went down in ten minutes. The *Cressy* remained hove to, making a wireless signal to the Admiralty, when her lookout reported the track of a torpedo and a periscope. The time was 7.17, and when she too capsized and sank after two hits, all her boats were away picking up survivors from her sister ships. Her loss of life, especially, was appalling.

It was a salutory and expensive lesson on how not to conduct a patrol in this new age of the torpedo. The loss of the ships was of little consequence, but some 1,400 men in all went down with them. The attack had been carried out not by several submarines as thought at the time but by a single small and obsolescent U-boat.

'Nothing that had yet occurred had so emphatically proclaimed the change that had come over naval warfare,' wrote Sir Julian Corbett in his official history, 'and never perhaps had so great a result been obtained by means so relatively small.'[10]

Jellicoe's fear of the U-boat was intensified by this disaster. Already his preoccupation with undersea weapons had extended to mines. In the second week of the war, he wrote to Battenberg:

There is, of course, an element of considerable risk in traversing the North Sea with the Battle Fleet. It does not appear that mines are laid yet, but at any moment they may be, and even with mine-sweepers ahead, which can only be done at 10 knots speed, there is no certainty they will be discovered before a ship hits one. An objection to having the mine-sweepers ahead is that the slow speed this entails on the Battle Fleet makes it an easier prey to submarines.[11]

Some modest precautions had been taken before the war, against the threat of enemy minelaying. As for British mines and minelaying, one reason why it was the Cinderella branch was that the Hague Convention of 1907 had outlawed the laying of minefields outside an enemy's territorial waters and the mine as a weapon was regarded as even more 'damn un-English' than the torpedo. As well, the German delegation in particular had expressed the strongest repugnance to the idea of indiscriminate mining on humanitarian grounds. Nevertheless on the first day of the war, a German minelayer planted a field thirty miles off the English east coast which claimed a brand-new British cruiser two days later. The Germans stepped up their minelaying in total disregard of outraged British and neutral protests, drawing on the considerable store of highly efficient mines accumulated before the war.

British losses mounted, culminating in the catastrophe Jellicoe had most feared and the Germans had so ardently wished and worked for. The strain and risk of anchoring, especially overnight, in the unprotected base of Scapa Flow, had driven Jellicoe first into the North Sea where his fleet could be screened by its flotillas, and eventually into the Atlantic. As a makeshift while the defences of Scapa were completed, Lough Swilly on the north coast of Ireland became the Grand Fleet's base. It was a considerable victory, unknown to the Germans, for the submarine branch to have forced the British Fleet out of the North Sea. But that was not the end of it. In mid-October the fast German liner *Berlin*, now armed and equipped with minelaying gear and a large complement of mines, succeeded in breaking out of the North Sea. 'By fairy tale chances she achieved the impossible', according to the official account, and succeeded in laying a large number of mines off the northern Irish coast. It was a lethal location near the entrance to the North Channel which carried most of the shipping into and out of Liverpool.

Merchantmen and liners steamed out of this area in great numbers, but the *Berlin*'s first catch was a prize indeed. Early on the morning of 27 October the 2nd Battle Squadron of eight super-dreadnoughts put out from their anchorage for firing practice and was twenty miles off Tory Island, steaming in line ahead, when the *Audacious* suffered an explosion on the port side which brought her to a standstill. In spite of a prolonged attempt to tow her to safety, witnessed by a number of amazed American tourists on their way from New York in the White Star *Olympic*, she blew up that evening and went down. On this occasion the loss of life was negligible, the loss of this new battleship potentially catastrophic. Due to calls on its strength from other oceans, and mechanical trouble suffered by several of its ships, the Grand Fleet now had an advantage of only three dreadnought battleships over the High Seas Fleet (nineteen to sixteen) and was actually inferior in numbers in battle-cruisers as well as destroyers. In the vital area of home waters, the 60 per cent advantage which had been regarded as a minimum before the war had been whittled down to under 20 per cent, a totally inadequate figure when the enemy had the choice of time and place. Although these figures were not known to the man in the street, and for a while the Admiralty attempted to hush up the loss of the *Audacious* (in spite of the clicking of box Brownies at the *Olympic*'s rails) there was a deep sense of unease at the performance of the Navy so far, within the service, in Whitehall, and in the country at large.

Certainly audacity appeared to be lacking. Beatty blamed the Admiralty. 'Our principal and almost overwhelming handicap in the struggle . . . has been our Administrators . . . We are only playing at war', he wrote to his wife despairingly. 'We are all nervous as cats, afraid of losing lives, losing ships, and running risks. We are ruled by Panic Law, and until we risk something shall never gain anything.'[12]

Ten days before the *Audacious* disaster Beatty wrote to Churchill:

At present we feel that we are working up for a catastrophe of a very large character. The feeling is gradually possessing the Fleet that all is not right somewhere. The menace of mines and submarines is proving larger every day, and adequate means to meet or combat them are not forthcoming, and we are gradually being pushed out of the North Sea and off our own particular perch. How does this arise? By the very apparent fact that we have no base where we can with *any* degree of safety lie for coaling, replenishing, and refitting and repairing, after two and a half months of war. This spells trouble . . . [13]

Beatty then told the First Lord how, as he wrote this letter, his flagship, *Lion*, and the rest of his squadron were in a loch on the Isle of Mull, guarded by picket boats and nets from submarines, low in coal. 'We have been running hard now since 28th July; small defects are creeping up which we haven't time to take in hand.' Still lacking a secure base, 'the question arises, how long can we go on, for I fear very much, not for long, as the need for small repairs is becoming insistent'.

Jellicoe was even gloomier and more pessimistic than his subordinate. Churchill did all he could to bolster up the C.-in-C. 'I am sure you will not be discouraged by *Audacious* episode', he wrote. 'We have been very fortunate to come through three months of war without the loss of a capital ship. I expected three or four by this time . . . Quite soon the harbours will be made comfortable for you. Mind you ask for all you want.'[14]

Jellicoe had been doing that from the 4th of August, despatching telegrams and memoranda, sometimes daily, with complaints and requests, especially for more ships of all kinds, and – not unreasonably – a harbour that was secure enough to contain the Grand Fleet. This nagging was not the positive spirit on which Churchill always flourished, and he, too, became frustrated and gloomy. Captain Herbert Richmond, one of the Navy's 'brains' and a founder member of the Naval War Staff, observed Churchill's decline into pessimism by late October. 'He was in low spirits,' Richmond confided to his diary after dining with him, ' . . . oppressed with the impossibility of *doing* anything. The attitude of waiting, threatened all the time by submarines, unable to strike back at their Fleet . . . and the inability of the Staff to make any suggestions seem to bother him.'[15]

But it was a lack of the offensive spirit that worried everybody most. 'If we harried the Germans more, they would be less free to harry us', wrote Richmond four days later. The future Admiral Sir Bertram Ramsay, who certainly was never short of the offensive spirit when he was head of the naval forces at the D-Day landings thirty years later, wrote in his diary, 'I don't like the feeling of waiting to see what the enemy will do first . . . we should have a plan ready which will force the Germans to fight under the conditions we desire . . . '[16] Even the Prime Minister confided to Mrs Edwin Montagu on 4 November 1914 that he believed the Germans 'are so much better than we are at sea'.[17] And on the same day he reported to the King that the Cabinet, after reciting a list of disasters, declared that they were not 'creditable to the officers of the Navy'.[18]

Fortunately, and to their undying credit, this state of depression and hopelessness did not extend to the lower decks. Morale remained high among the men, who were both more philosophical and more resilient than their officers. They were also sustained by the outcome of the one action in home waters when they had been allowed to get to grips with the enemy.

Weeks earlier, when the war was young and 'the boys would be home for Christmas', there had been a fleeting but bloody brush with German light forces. Commodore Reginald Tyrwhitt, commander of the Harwich force, and Roger 'When-are-we-going-to-make-war?' Keyes were close friends and shared a bullish belligerence which endeared them to their subordinates. With no Battle of Trafalgar in immediate sight, and lacking the means to do more, these two officers concocted a plan to nip the enemy off Heligoland Island. The Germans laid on daily defensive destroyer patrols against British submarines and minelayers. Tyrwhitt with his two light cruisers and two destroyer flotillas, and three of Keyes's submarines, was to lure these destroyers and any other ships that might come out to support them onto a strong force of more submarines. Two battle-cruisers based at that time on the Humber were to come up in support.

Churchill and Battenberg were in favour of this show of strength and offensiveness and approved the plan on 24 August. When Jellicoe heard of it he thought it too risky without the support of the whole Grand Fleet. The Admiralty told him, in effect, that it was nothing to do with him but that he could send Beatty as additional support if he wished. When Beatty belatedly heard what Keyes and Tyrwhitt were up to, he successfully pressed Jellicoe to allow him to go and took with him for good measure the First Light Cruiser Squadron. The Admiralty was not told until later. Even when they were told that Beatty was storming south to support the operation, the news never reached Keyes and Tyrwhitt. The signal was sent to Harwich where it lay in someone's 'In' file until the force had returned.

Before action was joined, the operation had taken on the guise of farce and near-tragedy. No one told anyone anything and confusion of identity led to several hair-raising avoidances. 'Our battle cruisers were scattered by, & made violent attempts to sink, a squadron of our own submarines', observed the future Admiral the Hon. Sir Reginald Aylmer Ranfurly Plunkett-Ernle-Erle-Drax. 'Our light cruisers, sent in to support, were in 2 cases supposed to be enemy by our destroyers sighting them. In 1 case 2 of our light cruisers chased 2 of our torpedo boat destroyers at full speed to the west, each supposing the other to be the enemy. They blocked the air with wireless at the very time when *Arethusa* & her destroyers were being overwhelmed by superior forces.'[19]

No one present at this engagement was prepared to give a clear account of just what occurred on that typical North Sea late summer day of uncertain visibility, mist, and funnel-smoke clouds of ever increasing density. Both sides were shocked at how reality differed from peace-time evolutions and gun practice, and how readily you could be confused when you were uncertain where the fire was coming from and from whom – friend or foe?

All that could be recounted with some sort of certainty was that Tyrwhitt with his new armoured light cruiser *Arethusa* and the Third Flotilla of thirteen destroyers, closely followed by the First Flotilla and the cruiser *Fearless*, raced into Heligoland Bight, spotted and pursued their prey and engaged in a running battle until the cliffs of Heligoland Island itself suddenly loomed up out of the mist. The Germans had got wind of the operation, had laid their own trap, luring Tyrwhitt onto a strong force of cruisers which engaged him with rapid and very accurate fire.

Tyrwhitt was soon in serious trouble and called urgently for assistance. When it arrived, in the nick of time, he was amazed at its strength, having no idea that Beatty's battle-cruisers were participating.

Beatty himself had hesitated for only a moment at the prospect of entering waters that were certainly mined and probably thick with U-boats. 'If I lose one of these valuable ships the country will not forgive me',[20] he remarked to his flag-captain, who encouraged him to take the risk at once. It was what Beatty wanted to hear, and with the *Queen Mary* and *Princess Royal*, sped south into the Bight. Soon after midday, the 13.5-inch guns of the battle-cruisers together with the smaller guns of the light cruisers, had accounted for three modern German light cruisers and a destroyer sunk, and another three light cruisers badly damaged. Germans killed, wounded, and taken prisoner numbered 1,200, including the Flotilla Admiral and the Destroyer Commodore. Although the *Arethusa* had take a severe battering and had to be towed home, British casualties numbered a total of only seventy-five.

This operation greatly cheered the Navy, especially the lower deck. But weak, uncoordinated planning, poor communications, and ineptitude ashore and afloat were all revealed and unfortunately were a portent of the future. For all the confusion and misunderstanding that prevailed from first to last, a Naval War Staff might never have been set up by Churchill. The real trouble was that it had been set up too late. Two years was not long enough to correct the bad habits of individualism masking regardlessness, and heroism covering up for blind rashness; to teach the Navy to think things out and organize itself in mutual co-operation; to note and respond rationally to information provided.

An officer who served in the Operations Division (OD) in the Admiralty at this time made these comments on the War Staff in 1914:

Neither the Chief of the War Staff nor the Director of Operations Division seemed to have any particular idea of what the War Staff was supposed to be doing, or how they should make use of it; they had been brought up in the tradition that the conduct of the operations of the fleet was a matter for the admiral alone, and that he needed no assistance in assimilating the whole situation in all its ramifications, and in reaching a decision, probably instantaneously, upon what should be done and what orders should be issued in order to get it done.[21]

The irony was that in the Battle of Heligoland Bight all these Staff failings were manifested, but a minor victory had been achieved and a disaster avoided by old-time individualism and blind courage, assisted by more than a fair share of good luck. It was, as Churchill declared proudly, 'a fine feat of arms'. With a little more thought it could have been a major success. With the loss of a dozen or two German destroyers and the greater part of her scouting cruisers, the High Seas Fleet would have been severely crippled. Even so, the arrival of heavy British units in the German porch, with some savage knocks on the door, hurt German pride and infuriated the Kaiser. He gave instructions that the policy of caution must be intensified and the main body of the fleet be risked in a major action only with overwhelming odds on its side.

6

MEDITERRANEAN MISFORTUNES

Admiral Milne's responsibilities – The Goeben *threat – She shows a clean pair of heels – Unclear Admiralty instructions – Admiral Souchon's shadower – Admiral Troubridge's opportunity and failure to exploit it – A false report from London – Milne's dilemma – The* Goeben *successfully finds her way to Constantinople – Dire consequences for the Allies*

THE Battle of Heligoland Bight was no more than a wild skirmish, but it remained a victory at sea nonetheless, and it cast a brief cheerful light when everywhere, on sea or land, was shrouded in the darkness of defeats and retreats. For it was not only in home waters that the tide had generally flowed against the Royal Navy; nor was public uneasiness caused only by default or disappointment at the failure to achieve a new Trafalgar. There had been a major blunder in the Mediterranean, a lesser one in the Caribbean, and a severe defeat in the Pacific. Behind these sombre events were the same faults that characterized the Heligoland Bight operation: weak Admiralty planning, ill-advised and confusing interference by the Admiralty, and poor judgement on the spot. Additionally, sad to relate, there was weakness bordering on cowardice in one episode.

In the Mediterranean at the end of July 1914 the British had a relatively small force of fast cruisers as deployed by Churchill two years earlier. None of the eight dreadnought battleships promised for 1915 had yet arrived, but there were three dreadnought battle-cruisers, the *Indomitable*, *Inflexible*, and *Indefatigable*, inferior in speed and gunpower to Beatty's 'big cats' (as the fleet called them) like the *Lion*, *Tiger*, and others with 13.5-inch guns and a speed of around 28 knots. In addition to this powerful battle-cruiser squadron there were four good armoured cruisers, predecessors of the I-class battle-cruisers, *Defence*, *Warrior*, *Black Prince*, and *Duke of Edinburgh*. There were also four modern light cruisers and a flotilla of sixteen destroyers.

The C.-in-C. was Admiral Sir Archibald ('Arky-Barky') Milne, a 'social' officer who had been Flag-Officer Royal Yachts and was a friend of Queen Alexandra. Although a harmless enough man, he represented the worst kind of flag-officer for responsible war duties, being dull, slack, and ultra-snobbish even for his day. He would never have been appointed to the Mediterranean had it not been for his connections. 'Winston has sacrificed the Country to the Court',[1] Fisher wrote in outrage to Esher, and it was a disgrace that Churchill and Battenberg, fearful of royal disapproval, had not since replaced him, especially as they had no compunction in replacing George Callaghan, who was able and steady.

Milne's second in command, flying his flag in the *Defence*, was Rear-Admiral Ernest Troubridge, a descendant of Thomas Troubridge, one of Nelson's 'Band of Brothers'. He was a big, fine-looking man, the epitome of a sailor, much liked but with not too much 'up top'. His flag-captain was Fawcet Wray, a gunnery officer who was good-looking, immensely arrogant and pleased with himself, one of Beresford's disciples, and loathed by Fisher.

The German battle-cruiser sent out to the Mediterranean in 1912 was the *Goeben*, a fine, strong, fast ship, armed with 11-inch guns against the British battle-cruisers' 12-inch, but superior to those ships in all departments. Her despatch from Germany had been precipitate and political. She had not completed her delivery trials and her engines had given a good deal of trouble, but at her best could make at least 27 knots. She had in her company the modern, fast light cruiser *Breslau*. This tight, efficient little force was commanded by the very able Rear-Admiral Wilhelm Souchon.

Of the other Mediterranean fleets, the French had a powerful force of battleships at Toulon but only one of them a dreadnought. Their first concern was the safe transit of the Algerian Corps to Marseilles in support of the French Army. Both the Austrians and Italians had completed their first dreadnoughts. The Austrians were restricted strategically by their coastline which bordered only on the Adriatic. The Italians were rated high up among the second-class naval powers. Their ships were excellent, their personnel and leadership an unknown quantity. They were also presently and historically hostile to Austria and anxious about her growing naval strength. Italy was more sympathetically inclined towards the western allies, France and Britain, than the Central Powers, Germany and Austro-Hungary.

Greece, with whom Britain had good relations, did not figure in Mediterranean calculations. But Turkey did. Turkey held the key to the Black Sea and communications with Russia, Britain and France's ally. Relations with Turkey had continued to deteriorate and the British naval mission had lost all influence. Turkey's two powerful battleships which had been constructed in Britain were completed and ready for delivery. In the case of one of them, which mounted more heavy guns than any battleship ever built, the Turkish crew was about to take over. Shortly before war was declared, Churchill ordered the compulsory transfer of both dreadnoughts to the British Fleet, an act which the Turks considered outrageous.

On the last occasion when Britain had fought a major war in the Mediterranean, the 'men on the spot' – Horatio Nelson, and later Cuthbert Collingwood – operated entirely on their own initiative, making far-reaching decisions of a political as well as a naval nature. Now, by means of the cable and wireless telegraphy (W/T), orders could be despatched night and day from the OD in the Admiralty in London.

On 30 July Admiral Milne at Malta received a telegram warning him of the possibility of war and instructing him that his 'first task should be to aid the French in the transportation of their African army by covering, and, if possible, bringing to action individual fast German ships, particularly *Goeben*, who may interfere with that transportation . . . Do not at this stage be brought to action against superior forces, except in combination with the French as part of a general battle.'

This message could well be cited in a staff college lecture as containing every fault that orders to a distant commander at the outset of war could include. To start with it made no mention of any other contingency than the transportation of the French army to the west, no suggestion of action by Turkey with whom relations were abysmal and whose new dreadnoughts Britain was at the moment acquiring. Milne was to 'bring to action' the *Goeben* but only with 'superior forces' although (by any reading of this woolly prose) it was all right to engage the battle-cruiser in combination with the French (strength undefined) in 'a general battle', whatever that was. But it was 2 August before Milne was given authority even to communicate with the French, a direct consequence of the British Government's refusal to co-ordinate with this ally until war was declared or imminent. Even so Milne could not raise the French C.-in-C. by wireless all next day, and eventually was obliged to send a cruiser to Bizerta 'in quest of his colleague', Admiral de Lapeyrère.

Milne then learned of the British ultimatum to Germany and that France and Germany were already at war, although he had still received no word from the French Admiral. Intelligence had now reached London (3 August) of the arrival and coaling of the *Goeben* and *Breslau* at Messina on the north-east coast of Sicily. The War Staff at the Admiralty suddenly concluded, for no apparent reason, that the two fast German ships would sail west, not to interfere with the

French troop convoys which would be well protected, but to escape
out of the Mediterranean altogether through the Straits of Gibraltar
and prey on unprotected British Atlantic trade. A patrol was
accordingly set up at Gibraltar, and two of Milne's battle-cruisers
which were now watching the entrance to the Adriatic in case
Admiral Souchon should return and link up with the Austrian Fleet,
were ordered (8.30 p.m. 3 August) to proceed to Gibraltar at high
speed to intercept the *Goeben*.

Admiral Souchon had indeed sailed west, but he was heading for
north Africa not the Atlantic, and on the morning of 4 August he
bombarded two French ports, Bône and Philippeville. The shellfire
gave the French a nasty shock but did little damage, and the *Goeben*,
still with the *Breslau* in company, headed back east again, straight into
the arms of the two British battle-cruisers sent to intercept them.

The *Indomitable* and *Inflexible*, under the command of Captain
Francis Kennedy, sighted the big battle-cruiser at 10.30 a.m. dead
ahead and some fifty miles west of Galita Island. Neither side was
technically at war, and neither Captain Kennedy nor Admiral
Souchon could anticipate the consequences of their mutual adherence
to international law. After a suspicious shying away by both sides,
like the sudden meeting of two men surprising one another in the
dark, the British and German ships found themselves passing one
another, both at high speed and on opposite courses, guns trained fore
and aft but ready at an instant's notice to open fire. None of the
customary courtesy signals was exchanged.

The British ships then turned in a wide circle to begin shadowing
the *Goeben*, and were later joined by the light cruiser *Dublin*. For five
hours through that long day, Captain Kennedy kept station astern of
the *Goeben*, with some speed in reserve in case permission came
through to attack. It seemed unlikely that this would happen before
nightfall. Soon after 2 p.m. he was told of the ultimatum to Germany,
which was due to expire at midnight. Perhaps Admiral Souchon
intercepted the signal, for soon afterwards he ordered full speed, and
the shadowing exercise suddenly became a stern chase.

It was an intensely hot Mediterranean afternoon, and the stokers in
the *Goeben*'s boiler room were already under severe pressure. While
the battle-cruiser's speed built up to 23 knots, then to 24 and 25, the
men began to fall unconscious over their shovels. A number had to be
dragged up and laid out in the open air on the upper deck. At the
height of the chase, with the *Goeben*'s engineer petty officers urging the
men to do their utmost, there was a mechanical failure causing fatal
scalding to four men.

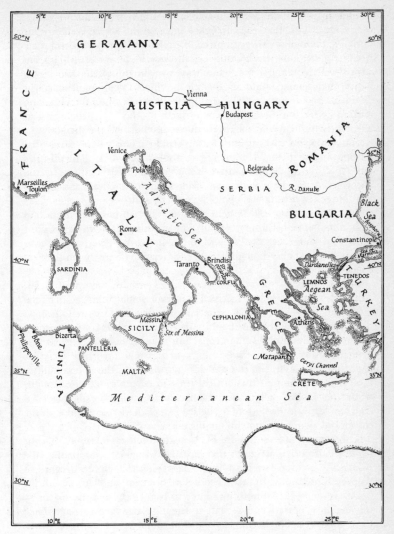

Map 2. The chase of the *Goeben*, August 1914

The *Indomitable* had achieved 26.1 knots on her trials, the *Inflexible* a shade more. But that was six years ago, the dreadnoughts had foul bottoms, their engines were in need of a refit, and the numbers of their stokers inadequate. Both ships logged close to 24 knots through the smooth Mediterranean sea, white waves washing high up their bows, black coal smoke staining the clear blue sky for miles astern. Conditions were not much better in the engine-rooms of the pursuers, and at least the *Goeben*'s men worked in the knowledge passed frequently to them that they were out-stripping their pursuers.

Souchon knew that the hunt was to be a long one, wherever his final destination might be. He knew, too, that if he could plant into the minds of his antagonists that his were the fastest ships in the Mediterranean, it would give him a great tactical and moral advantage. In this he was completely successful.

The light cruiser *Dublin* held on after the two battle-cruisers had been out-stripped. But at 7.37 p.m. she signalled, '*Goeben* out of sight now, can only see smoke; still daylight.' Soon even the smoke disappeared, and as daylight faded, the Germans were lost in the vast spaces of the ocean.

Six hours before a state of war with Germany became official, Admiral Milne at Malta received a further signal from his masters. 'The Italian Government have declared neutrality. You are to respect this neutrality rigidly and should not allow any of HM ships to come within six miles of the Italian coast.' In the first hours of a great war the authorities may be excused for making some incorrect decisions based on false premises. But it is difficult to forgive the Foreign Office (Grey) from failing at this critical time to perceive that the Italians would have been delighted and relieved to see the small, powerful German force at the bottom of the sea rather than linking up with the closer and even more potentially hostile navy of Austria.

This order, and the failure of the Admiralty to relax, modify, or broaden the original instructions to Milne suggest that neither the Admiralty nor the Foreign Office was paying the slightest regard to Turkey's intentions. In fact, even before Souchon had carried out his bombardment, it had been intimated to him (somewhat prematurely but he was not to know) that a friendly arrangement had been concluded between Berlin and Constantinople, and that the *Goeben* and *Breslau* should proceed – the order was marked of 'extreme urgency' – to the Bosphorus where he would be allowed free entry.

A ship with ample coal had been ordered for Souchon at Messina, and it was to this port again that the German Admiral now proceeded with his ships through the night after throwing off his pursuers. The

Italian authorities told him sharply that he would be given the legal twenty-four hours and no more.

With the news that his enemy had reached Messina, Milne adjusted his dispositions accordingly. To him everything seemed to point to Admiral Souchon either heading west again – this time continuing into the Atlantic – or slipping back into the Adriatic. Milne's primary instructions to protect the French troop convoys had never been cancelled. But on the afternoon of 5 August, he was additionally ordered to watch the Adriatic for the 'double purpose of preventing Austrians emerging unobserved and preventing Germans entering'. The first was straightforward enough, but it was quite impossible for him to prevent Souchon slipping through the Messina Straits from north to south and, ignoring international law, following the Italian coastline within the six-mile limit until he had outpaced his pursuers again.

Milne therefore concentrated his heavy ships, the only ships which could be reasonably certain of out-gunning the *Goeben*, midway between Sicily and Tunisia in the expectation of cutting off Souchon before he could attack the French troop convoys or race for Gibraltar. At the entrance to the Adriatic he stationed Admiral Troubridge with his four armoured cruisers, a sufficiently powerful force to deal with any Austrian men o'war except her new dreadnoughts. The French Toulon squadrons had now put to sea in overwhelming strength to deal with the two German ships. Their convoys required no British protection. But Milne knew nothing of this, and if the French had informed the Admiralty in London no one had thought it necessary to telegraph the news to Malta.

On 6 August, just before nightfall, the *Goeben*, closely followed by her satellite, left Messina, slipped south through the Straits, and in the open seas headed first due east before making sure that the only British ship in sight, the light cruiser *Gloucester*, observed him feinting north-east as if for the Adriatic.

Just before midnight, the *Goeben* and *Breslau* altered course again, this time to the south-east. Admiral Souchon, in accordance with his orders and supported in his self-confidence by his earlier demonstration of speed, pointed his bows towards Constantinople.

The British dispositions at midnight were: Troubridge with his four armoured cruisers was patrolling off the island of Cephalonia, south of Corfu, where he could keep an eye on the entrance to the Adriatic as instructed. He was shortly to be reinforced by the light cruiser *Dublin* and two destroyers, his own flotilla having departed to Malta for coal. Milne with two of his battle-cruisers was patrolling north of Sicily when he heard that Souchon had left Messina. In the belief that his quarry might proceed south of the island and then west, he headed west and then south to cut the Germans off. Milne's third battle-cruiser, the *Indomitable*, was coaling at Bizerta.

None of these dispositions was known to the German Admiral, and he would have been greatly relieved if he had learned that his most dangerous enemy was far to the west and had not even considered that he might be shaping course for Turkey. Souchon's anxieties remained burdensome. He had to pass through the islands of the Aegean with all their opportunities for waylaying and trapping his force or at best observing his movements. The state of the *Goeben*'s engines was another worry. Under extreme pressure they had worked wonders three days earlier but the Admiral knew he would never be able to put his boilers under such pressure again. He could not reach the Bosphorus without coaling. The enemy numbered not fewer than seven big armoured ships, without French support, and there were British submarines and destroyers to take into account, too. Most dangerous of all, he was being followed through the night. His feint north had been observed, but so had his turn onto an easterly course again.

The light cruiser *Gloucester*, 4,800 tons and completed in 1911, was armed with 6-inch and 4-inch guns, and on her trials had shown a speed of over 26 knots. She was a fine ship, built for scouting and warding off destroyer attacks. She was commanded by forty-year-old Captain Howard Kelly. His brother John, two years older, commanded the slightly more modern and powerful *Dublin*, which was racing north-east to join Troubridge. From calculations based on his younger brother's signals, his track should cross those of the two German ships. And in fact at 1.30 a.m. John Kelly signalled Troubridge that the *Breslau* was right ahead and that he was following her. One hour later the *Dublin* reported the position of the *Goeben* and her speed as 27 knots. John Kelly had misidentified the ship, which was understandable. It was the *Breslau*, steaming flat out to come up wth her big consort, and the *Dublin* soon lost her anyway.

Howard Kelly was having better luck and was playing the part of shadowing with skill and tenacity. Earlier in the night, in this pursuit within a pursuit, and when close to the Italian coast, the *Gloucester* had been forced to steer straight for the mighty *Goeben* in order to get between her and the shore and keep her in sight in the failing light. The *Breslau*, fearful of the *Gloucester*'s torpedoes, made threatening passes, and at any moment the German battle-cruiser might have opened fire and blown the relatively small cruiser out of the water.

The bright moonlight was an assistance and a danger in about equal parts. Kelly could keep his watch at a greater range but the visibility would speed his destruction if the *Goeben* opened fire. All through the night, in spite of the *Goeben*'s efforts to jam his transmissions, Kelly continued to report the speed, course, and position of the battle-cruiser.

The next day, off the Gulf of Kalamata, the *Breslau* took positive steps to deal with the shadower, dropping astern of the *Goeben* and crossing the *Gloucester*'s course repeatedly as if dropping mines. Kelly answered by opening fire at 11,500 yards with his forward 6-inch gun. The *Breslau* instantly answered with salvoes of rapid and extremely accurate fire. Kelly replied again by increasing speed, turning, and closing the range so that he could employ his full broadside. This movement finally provoked Souchon into action.

From the British cruiser's bridge the *Goeben*, no more than a distant smudge in the heat haze, could be seen to turn. Pin-point glows marked the instant of firing. Almost half a minute later, tall white fountains appeared in the sea. Kelly turned away, having accomplished his purpose of provoking the *Goeben* and forcing her to turn. At 2.45 p.m. Kelly signalled to Milne: 'Have engaged at long range with *Breslau* and retreated when *Goeben* turned. I am now following again.' Kelly's retreat was wise. A single hit from the *Goeben* might, at best, slow the *Gloucester* so that she could no longer continue her prime role of shadowing and reporting.

Two hours later, short of coal and with orders from Milne not to go farther than Cape Matapan, Captain Howard Kelly broke off after observing Souchon's course into the Aegean. At 4 p.m. he signalled, 'Enemy's ships in Cervi Channel steering east 15 knots. I am off Cape Matapan and returning N55W, 15 knots.'

Kelly could do no more, and what he had done was brilliant. 'The *Goeben* could have caught and sunk the *Gloucester* at any time,' ran the Admiralty minute on his report, ' . . . She was apparently deterred by the latter's boldness, which gave the impression of support close at hand. The combination of audacity with restraint, unswerving attention to the principal military object . . . constitute a naval episode which may justly be regarded as a model.'

The other side of the picture is dark by contrast. Rear-Admiral Troubridge had under his command the only ships that could have, at worst, damaged and delayed the *Goeben*'s flight, and with skill and luck might have sent her to the bottom, with a well-co-ordinated gun and torpedo attack. Although they pre-dated the dreadnought battle-cruiser, Troubridge's armoured cruisers packed a heavy punch with their biggest guns. The oldest had been commissioned nine years earlier, the *Defence* and *Warrior* were only six years old.

Defence   Warrior   Black Prince   Duke of Edinburgh
Average displacement: 14,000 tons
Total weight of broadside: 8,480 pounds
Maximum speed: 22–23 knots
Armoured belt: 6 inches

Goeben
Displacement: 23,000 tons
Total weight of broadside: 8,272 pounds
Maximum speed: 28 knots
Armoured belt: 11 inches

Both Souchon and Troubridge had a light cruiser under their command, and Troubridge would soon enjoy the advantage of having destroyers with him. On the night of 6–7 August, thanks to the *Gloucester*'s shadowing and reporting, Troubridge knew the *Goeben*'s position, course, and speed throughout the hours of darkness. His first mistake was to interpret the *Gloucester*'s urgent signal, received at 11.08 p.m. that the *Goeben* was altering course southward, as a feint, when in fact Souchon's earlier turn to the north-east had been an attempt to mislead his pursuers. As a consequence Troubridge lost an hour before continued signals from the *Gloucester* appeared to confirm that the *Goeben* was not making for the Adriatic. At a few minutes after midnight, Troubridge ordered his 1st Cruiser Squadron to alter course south.

For the ensuing four hours, the big armoured cruisers steamed south at close to their maximum speed, with the prospect of action by daybreak in the men's mind: the manoeuvring, the gunfire, the impact of enemy shells, the smoke and deafening noise – all the sound and fury towards which their professional lives had gravitated during the years leading to this war. Of the 3,000 or so men under Troubridge's command, there was probably not a stoker or a commander who had not rehearsed in his mind the moment of contact.

At 2.54 a.m. Troubridge signalled the Kelly brothers in their respective light cruisers: '1st Cruiser Squadron position 2.30 a.m. 38° 25′N, 20° 0′E, course south 20 knots. Am endeavouring to cross *Goeben*'s bows at 6 a.m.' Brave words. In the message there was no suggestion of failing to challenge Souchon, any more than there had been earlier when Troubridge had prepared to cut off the *Goeben* in the Adriatic. Under the critical circumstances of the past hours and days, calculations had surely been made of the relative strength of the four

1. Admiral of the Fleet Lord Fisher of Kilverstone, architect of Britain's naval renaissance [*bust by Jacob Epstein, 1916*]

2. HMS *Dreadnought*, precursor of the last generation of battleships

3. SMS *Nassau*, Germany's first dreadnought

4. Admiral Alfred von Tirpitz, naval pioneer and co-founder with the
Kaiser of the twentieth-century *Kriegsmarine*.

5. Winston S. Churchill, First Lord of the Admiralty October 1911–May 1915

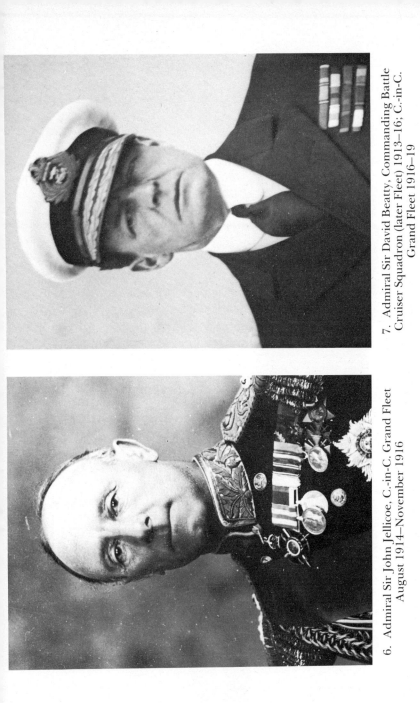

6. Admiral Sir John Jellicoe, C.-in-C. Grand Fleet August 1914–November 1916

7. Admiral Sir David Beatty, Commanding Battle Cruiser Squadron (later Fleet) 1913–16; C.-in-C. Grand Fleet 1916–19

8. HMS *Good Hope*, Cradock's flagship

9. Vice-Admiral Sir Doveton Sturdee, C.-in-C. South Atlantic and Pacific November 1914–February 1918

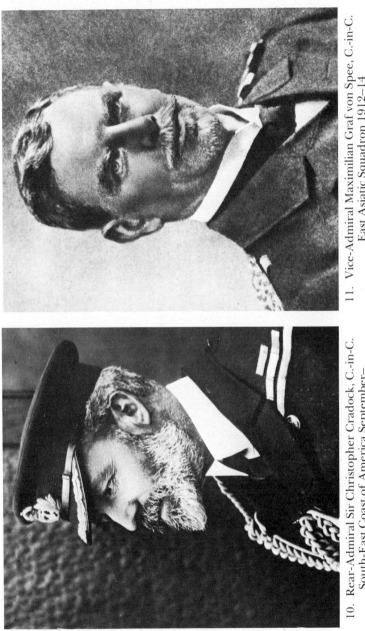

10. Rear-Admiral Sir Christopher Cradock, C.-in-C. South-East Coast of America September–November 1914

11. Vice-Admiral Maximilian Graf von Spee, C.-in-C. East Asiatic Squadron 1912–14

12. HMS *Invincible* working up to full speed at the Battle of the Falkland Islands, December 1914

armoured cruisers and the single battle-cruiser; contingency plans drawn up; methods of attack discussed in consultation with his captains.

Later, Troubridge was to claim that his decision to attack was 'a desperate one' made in the face of clear orders, by his immediate superior and by the Admiralty, not to engage 'a superior force'.

What was 'a superior force'? Was it a battle-cruiser in company with a light cruiser with 4.1-inch guns? There was no doubt of the answer in the mind of Troubridge's flag-captain, who always gave the impression that he knew everything. At 2.45 a.m. Troubridge was in the *Defence*'s chart room when Wray came in. He was clearly disturbed as he asked at once, 'Are you going to fight, sir? because if so the squadron ought to know.'

The Admiral replied, 'Yes, I know it is wrong but I cannot have the name of the whole Mediterranean Squadron stink.'

Fawcet Wray had done his sums and did not like this answer. Three-quarters of an hour later he again approached Troubridge and told him he did not fancy the prospect of taking on the *Goeben*. 'Neither do I; but why?' asked the Admiral, who, according to later testimony, was clearly worried.

Captain Wray had given much thought to the problem, and now (seemingly for the first time and within two and a half hours of the interception time) he explained to the Admiral how the *Goeben* would circle round the squadron at her superior speed 'at some range outside 16,000 yards which her guns would carry and which your guns will not. It seems to me', he continued, 'it is likely to be the suicide of your squadron.'

Troubridge, already half won over, said lamely, 'I cannot turn away now, think of my pride.' Wray was ready with the noble answer: 'Has your pride got anything to do with this, sir? It is your country's welfare which is at stake.'

Troubridge called for his navigator and asked him if there was any chance of the squadron closing in to the range of its 9.2-inch guns. He was told that there was no chance whatsoever. A few minutes after 4 a.m. Troubridge called off the interception. He was in tears as Wray remarked with gravity, 'Admiral, that is the bravest thing you have ever done in your life.'

At 4.49 a.m. Troubridge told Milne that he had called off the chase and requested instructions. He received a dusty answer. 'Why did you not continue to cut off *Goeben*?' Milne asked, well aware that 'chase' was an inappropriate word. 'She only going 17 knots, and so important to bring her to action.'

For the first of numerous exhausting times, Troubridge gave his reasons at about 8.30 a.m. on 7 August:

With visibility at the time [he signalled] I could have been sighted from twenty to twenty-five miles away and could never have got nearer unless *Goeben* wished to bring me to action which she could have done under circumstances most advantageous to her. I could never have brought her to action. I had hoped to have engaged her at three-thirty in the morning in dim light but had gone north first with the object of engaging her in the entrance to the Adriatic.

I was too late to intercept her when she altered course to the southward. In view of the immense importance of victory or defeat at such early stage of a war I would consider it a great imprudence to place squadron in such a position as to be picked off at leisure and sunk while unable to effectively reply. The decision is not the easiest of the two to make I am well aware.

Meanwhile, far to the south-east the *Gloucester* continued her hazardous shadowing and reporting. But nobody seemed any longer to care.

At Malta, 460 miles to the west, Admiral Milne continued his coaling. The *Indomitable* could have sailed on her own and many hours before the other two battle-cruisers, in spite of some boiler defects which Milne used as an alibi later.He finally cleared Valetta harbour with his three 12-inch-gunned ships in the early hours of the morning of 8 August, shaping course for Cape Matapan where the German force had last been sighted some eight hours earlier by the *Gloucester*. Still under the impression that the *Goeben* would eventually reverse course for the western Mediterranean and the Atlantic, he did not hurry, and merely cruised along awaiting intelligence from the Admiralty. When it came it was of a critical nature and demanded an instant response. 'Commence hostilities against Austria', it ran.

Milne at once altered course northwards in order to concentrate his force with Troubridge's and 'watch the Adriatic'. The *Goeben* was momentarily forgotten in this new critical turn of events and Milne anticipated having to face the full might of the Austrian Fleet, of untried quality but material strength greater than his own. From possession of overwhelming strength against a single German ship, he was reduced to conducting arithmetic to a reverse formula.

Four hours later he was told from London that the earlier message was a false alarm, although the situation with Austria remained critical. What had happened was typical of the mixture of accidents and follies, dashed with both courage and caution, that marked the *Goeben* business from beginning to end. The 'Commence hostilities . . .' signal had been merely a contingency message prepared in case the worst happened. An Admiralty clerk had found it lying in a tray, and recognizing its urgency, he had despatched it forthwith on his own initiative. At 1.45 p.m. on 8 August, Milne's flagship took in: 'Negative my telegram hostilities against Austria. Acknowledge. Urgent.'

Leaving Troubridge to 'guard' the Adriatic (what he would have done against three new Austrian dreadnoughts when a single German one was too much for him no one explained), Milne proceeded east at no more than 10 knots, still concerned more with the *Goeben* when she turned west again, and with guarding the approaches to the Suez Canal than in her rapid pursuit.

Souchon had, in fact, coaled at record speed from a collier at the island of Denusa in the Aegean, and on 10 August, with British wireless signals ringing loudly in his ears to indicate how close his pursuers were, he raced for the Dardanelles. He had been warned that, after all, he might not gain immediate entry from the Turks, but so desperate was his plight that he approached anyway. The *Goeben* and *Breslau* anchored off Cape Helles at 5 p.m. on 10 August, and Souchon called for a pilot to guide him through the minefields. A boat immediately complied, and he was soon making his slow and stately way up the Dardanelles to Constantinople.

Within hours the news had been flashed to Milne. He responded predictably for a C.-in-C. who had been given no hint that neutral Turkey could be the enemy's destination, and whose own powers of deduction and conclusion were limited. He put the blame squarely, and equally, on Troubridge for his failure to intercept and the Admiralty for misleading him.

The escape of the *Goeben* was not at first regarded by the general public as a great naval disaster. The effects of the directions and misdirections of the Admiralty, the blinkered vision and lack of clear thinking of Milne, the inadequate performance of his second in command, were transformed by the popular Press and its readers into a characteristic British naval 'sweeping of the seas' operation. It was widely believed that within a few days from the opening of hostilities a powerful German force, arrogantly assuming it could challenge the Royal Navy in the Mediterranean, had scurried for cover, fearful of interfering with French troop movements in the western Mediterranean. When the fact was learned that the *Goeben* and *Breslau* had been cravenly transferred to the Turkish Navy, whose flag now flew from the ships, this led to a further sense of satisfaction.

The implications behind this last act proved to be profound and disturbing. Within days of the loss of two of her dreadnoughts to Britain, Turkey found herself presented with two modern German men o'war. British naval mission officers were replaced by Germans on board Turkish ships, and on 30 October Turkey, under extreme German military and diplomatic pressure, joined the Central Powers in their war against France, Britain, and Russia. The failure of Troubridge's squadron to prevent the *Goeben*'s escape (to damage and slow her, forcing her to seek a neutral port, would have been enough) led directly to the Dardanelles campaign, the isolation of Russia, and a grave loss of British prestige. A steady flow of arms through the Black Sea would have been bound to stiffen Russian resistance morally as well as militarily, and might even have prevented the collapse on the eastern front and the Communist revolution that followed in 1917.

Never has the meaning of sea power been more clearly spelled out than in the Mediterranean during those hectic few days of August 1914, when a single well-aimed heavy shell could have changed the direction of twentieth-century history.

At home the Navy was not deceived for one minute by the popular claims of success. The shock of the failure was expressed by the First Sea Lord. 'Not one of the excuses which Ad. Troubridge gives can be accepted for one moment', charged Battenberg ' . . . The escape of the *Goeben* must ever remain a shameful episode in the war.'

Amongst the better informed there was not a moment of doubt about the identity of the culprits. Fisher, who regarded Milne's ability as nil and thought he was 'a serpent of the lowest order' declared in a letter that 'Personally I should have shot Sir Berkeley Milne.' And to this same friend he added, that Milne 'had no excuse whatever for not surrounding Messina with all his entire force right round the harbour mouth – CLOSE UP! *as if international law mattered a d—n!!* and the Italians would have loved him for ever!'[2]

The Court of Inquiry set up by the Admiralty also had no doubt that Troubridge should have engaged the *Goeben*. His failure was 'deplorable and contrary to the tradition of the British Navy'. The Court judged that he 'had a very fair chance of at least delaying *Goeben* by materially damaging her'. As a result of these findings, a court martial became essential, and this was convened at Portland on board HMS *Bulwark* from 5 to 9 November 1914. Cowardice was not charged. What was to be decided was whether or not Troubridge did 'from negligence or through other default, forbear to pursue the chase of His Imperial German Majesty's ship *Goeben*, being an enemy then flying'.

Troubridge was brilliantly defended by Leslie Scott KC, a future Lord Justice of Appeal, and much advantage for the unfortunate Admiral was gained by citing the clear instructions from the Admiralty not to engage a superior enemy, and from Milne's orders to guard the Adriatic. Troubridge also claimed that the following exchange between himself and his C.-in-C. had taken place at Malta at 2 August:

Troubridge: 'You know, sir, that I consider a battle cruiser a superior force to a cruiser squadron, unless they can get within their range of her.'

Milne: 'That question won't arise as you will have the *Indomitable* and *Indefatigable* with you.'

The Court acquitted Troubridge on the evidence that he was only carrying out orders from the Admiralty via Milne that 'the First Cruiser Squadron and *Gloucester* are not to get seriously engaged with superior force'. The only 'superior force' was the *Goeben*, so by implication Troubridge's claim that he could never hope to sink the German ship was also the Admiralty's view.

Milne felt not a breath of direct or official criticism and the Court 'fully and honourably' acquitted Troubridge. Fawcet Wray gave evidence but was not implicated in any charge. But all three officers were broken. Milne never received the appointment he had been expecting and was left unemployed on half pay until the end of the war. Fisher always referred to him scathingly as 'Sir Berkeley Goeben', and his name was widely vilified. Troubridge, in view of his acquittal, could not be treated so harshly by the Admiralty and was given various commands, all beneath his reasonable expectations, and never served at sea again. Fawcet Wray was, quite simply, ostracized by the entire service and not employed at all for some time, although he later made amends at the Dardanelles and was awarded the DSO.

The Admiralty, which was directly and indirectly the most guilty party in the fiasco, received not a word of official criticism.

A list of guilty men must include Churchill, Troubridge, Wray, and Milne. Churchill had been a brilliant peacetime First Lord for the needs of the Royal Navy between 1912 and 1914. He had made multitudinous enemies, caused massive offence, and thrown his weight about like none of his predecessors, who had not attempted to trespass beyond the accepted role and responsibilities of the political head of the Navy. But he had completed Fisher's reforms, initiated many more, and brought into being the Naval War Staff that was long overdue.

In the highly authoritative judgement of Lieutenant-Commander

Peter Kemp, Churchill should not attract as much blame as he has suffered for his part in the affair.

I suggest it was the Admiralty, rather than Churchill personally, that was one of the chief culprits [he writes], although Churchill in a way must take some of the blame as the political boss of, and therefore responsible for, his department. A lot of the silly signals sent out by the Admiralty did not emanate from Churchill personally. If I had to list the guilty men in order of culpability I would put Milne at the top. He was the C.-in-C. and had the duty to assess the situation on the spot and act accordingly. He had the right and power to ignore Admiralty signals, knowing that the Admiralty would back him up. Every C.-in-C. knows this, it goes automatically with the appointment. Of course the Admiralty has the power of dismissal as the ultimate sanction if the C.-in-C. makes a balls of it. This is one of the recognized risks of the game. Milne's handling of the Fleet, especially after learning that the *Goeben* was at Messina on 5 August, was inept in the extreme.

I would put the Admiralty second in my list of culprits for the silly signals they sent, no doubt some of them drafted by Churchill personally but others coming from the half-baked Naval Staff. But Milne had no right to shelter behind Admiralty signals. His classic remark 'They pay me to be an Admiral; they don't pay me to think', sums him up pretty accurately.

Finally Troubridge. I think his culpability falls into a different category; virtually in sight of the enemy and turning away. Wray was quite entitled to make his representations to Troubridge; the fault lay in Troubridge listening to them and accepting them.[3]

In spite of all that had been accomplished in a decade, the Royal Navy was not suitably equipped, organized, or prepared for modern war when it came. The Staff was deficient in quality and experience and there had been too little thinking. No one had given thought, for example, to the consequences of wireless telegraphy in combination with a Staff. Instead of providing information for the commander on the spot, W/T was used – or misused, like the false Austrian declaration of war signal – to give direct operational orders, often in absurd detail. This was a privilege and right but one that was much abused. In the W/T records of the time there are signals such as, 'Has Herbert Brown, A.B., been discharged to hospital?' from the Admiralty; and 'Permission is requested to issue an extra ration of lime juice' from a ship to the Admiralty.

Although W/T had been in use for ten years, the Admiralty had only recently possessed such wide control over fleets and individual units world-wide. Churchill, with his need to dominate and control everything, rapidly became heady with the power W/T offered, and as he himself wrote, 'I claimed and exercised an unlimited power of suggestion and initiative over the whole field, subject only to the approval and agreement of the First Sea Lord on all operative orders.'[4]

In fact Battenberg was no more than a rubber stamp that Churchill often failed to use anyway and Vice-Admiral Doveton Sturdee, the Chief of Staff, was frequently bypassed. There was, Sturdee later told Jellicoe, 'very little *united* decision'. The transcripts of important operative W/T signals during Churchill's tenure of office sometimes bear the unmistakable style and vocabulary of the First Lord. The woolliness of definition and unprofessional phrasing were Churchill's own. His claim in his war memoirs that the Staff 'arrived at a united action on every matter of consequence' is simply not true. The direction of the war at sea, except on matters of routine detail, was under the control of one man whose military experience extended to the responsibilities of a lieutenant in the 4th Hussars, and whose naval experience was little longer than that of a naval cadet at Osborne.

Churchill's understanding of foreign policy was much more profound and extensive, as his numerous communications to Grey bear witness. Perhaps, therefore, the greatest mystery of the *Goeben* affair is that neither Churchill, who had just given substantial grounds for Turkish hostility, nor Battenberg, who had always been acutely suspicious of Turkey anyway, appear to have thought there was any possibility of the German Squadron seeking shelter in the Bosphorus. (That the Foreign Office failed to pick up any hint of German–Turkish actions is equally extraordinary but outside consideration here.)

There remain two minor but puzzling details. In all discussions on the rights and wrongs of Troubridge's decision at his court martial and elsewhere, every argument rested upon his strength in relation to Souchon's. Not once did Troubridge's defenders point to the vulnerability of his ships to 11-inch plunging shellfire due to their thin armour, and the relative invulnerability of the *Goeben* to British 6-inch, 7.5-inch, and even 9.2-inch shellfire due to her rugged construction and ample armour. The *Defence* was sunk at Jutland after receiving seven hits; at the same battle the *Seydlitz*, similar in construction to the *Goeben*, survived some twenty-two hits from 12-inch, 13.5-inch, and 15-inch shells, each with many times the penetration and destructive power of a 9.2-inch shell.

At the court martial there were one or two references to armour, but only of a passing nature. When Milne was being cross-examined he was asked, 'What are the chief elements that enter into this question of comparative force?' His answer was, 'Gun power, weather and speed. I do not know anything else.' As one naval historian has noted, 'So all the ships, both sides, could have been built of tin plate! But neither the court nor the accused's friend commented on that.'[5]

The last puzzle is a human one. No one appears to have commented on the apparently extraordinary relationship between Troubridge and his flag-captain. Here we have an Admiral of great experience and stature at 3.30 at night taking his squadron towards a dawn engagement with the enemy, the outcome of which – win or lose – must bring further glory to the name of Troubridge and his beloved service; then after no more than a few pleading words from his flag-captain suggesting likely defeat, turning away in order to allow his quarry to escape. Troubridge spoke at his court martial of his 'mental struggle between my natural desire to fight and my sense of duty in view of my orders'. But this did not satisfy his fellow officers, who were tempted to ask, 'Why did he allow himself to be swayed by his subordinate over the most important and critical decision of his life?' That is a question that neither Troubridge nor anyone else has satisfactorily answered.

7

TRAGEDY IN THE PACIFIC

The search for Admiral Spee – His interference with Pacific commerce and troop movements – Admiral Cradock takes up the hunt in the Atlantic, and, later, off the Chilean coast – His inadequate force – Spee at Easter Island, Cradock at the Falkland Islands – The clash off Coronel and defeat of Cradock – Escape of the Glasgow *– The mystery of the* Canopus

THE tide of naval events continued to flow unfavourably in more distant seas, too. At the end of July 1914 there were a number of German men o'war and armed merchantmen in the Atlantic and Pacific. They were not, in total, a very menacing force, even if they had been concentrated. They were, in fact, widely scattered. In the West Indies there were two light cruisers, the *Dresden* and *Karlsruhe*; off the west coast of America the light cruiser *Leipzig*; and on the other side of the Pacific, based on Tsingtao, China, a powerful armoured force, the German East Asiatic Squadron, commanded by Vice-Admiral Count Maximilian von Spee.

Spee was an able, aggressive admiral, a brilliant leader who had brought his force to a high pitch of efficiency. His squadron had won the top gunnery award of the *Kriegsmarine* for two successive years. His two armoured cruisers were the *Gneisenau* and *Scharnhorst* (flag), of similar power to Troubridge's flagship but better protected and with a higher speed. His light cruisers were of recent construction, he was well provided with colliers and supply ships and at the outbreak of war, thanks to German colonizing, had the use of a number of island bases in the Pacific.

On 6 August, the same day that Admiral Souchon departed from Messina with the *Goeben* and *Breslau* on the other side of the world, Spee slipped out of Ponapé in the Caroline Islands with the *Scharnhorst*, *Gneisenau*, and light cruiser *Nürnberg*. For both commanders it was the opening of a pursuit by the enemy, and Spee faced odds as overwhelming as Souchon's. But from this point the parallel ceased. Souchon's task was to fly a few hundred miles to a neutral port to make a politico-military gift of his force. Spee's was to range across the vast expanse of the Pacific as a threat to British trade and shipping movements for as long as his resources and luck lasted and then try to get home. Souchon was a quarry for six days; Spee's pursuit was to last for five anxious and frequently exciting months.

On paper, a couple of light cruisers in the Atlantic and two armoured and three light cruisers in the Pacific did not pose much of a threat when seen against the vast areas and quantity of shipping involved. But even a single raider appearing unexpectedly, making its 'kill' and disappearing over the horizon, can create a degree of nervousness among seamen and shipping insurance companies alike out of all proportion to its real destructive ability. It also requires naval forces of seemingly disproportionate numbers and strength to hunt it down.

Against these widely scattered German men o'war, and possible armed merchantmen, Britain and her allies and empire could call upon a modern dreadnought battle-cruiser, the *Australia*, more than a match alone for Spee's armoured cruisers; some one dozen armoured cruisers; and about twenty light cruisers of widely varying ages and effectiveness. When Japan declared war on Germany she reinforced this strength with a navy already challenging the US Navy, comprising fast, modern, powerful men o'war of all classes.

It could be thought that with this protection, the threat from the German cruisers might safely be ignored. In fact, New Zealand and Australian commerce was at once much disturbed and those Dominions' first troop convoys, bound for the mother country, were forbidden from sailing until adequate protection could be provided. When Spee shrewdly detached to the west his light cruisers *Emden* and *Königsberg*, Indian Ocean shipping came to a standstill after they began their attacks. In three months the *Emden* alone accounted for seventeen merchantmen, while in the Atlantic the *Karlsruhe*, which eluded her pursuers among the West Indies islands to prey on Atlantic shipping, was almost as successful.

But Spee and his two big ships were the Admiralty's greatest worry. While they remained afloat, Britain could not claim complete control of the seas, and must suffer serious commercial loss and – above all – damaging loss of prestige among neutral nations, notably the United States and the republics of South America. Meanwhile Spee began an odyssey among the islands of the Pacific. Wireless which should have been a blessing in an ocean-wide hunt confused the hunters as much as it helped them because its range varied widely according to conditions and poor reception led to misidentification. By destroying the widely spread German wireless stations instead of using them to confuse Spee and assist themselves, the Allies threw away an advantage.

Spee made his slow and tortuous way east, leaving little evidence of his whereabouts. At one point he detached a light cruiser to Honolulu for supplies. On 30 September his squadron appeared off Tahiti's capital and port, Papeeté, shelled the French installations, sank a gunboat and disappeared again, feinting a north-easterly course.

At last, on 4 October, one of the joint British–Australian– French–New Zealand–Japanese forces, with their widely scattered squadrons from Sasebo to Rabaul, intercepted a distant, crackling message from the *Scharnhorst*. The reputation of W/T was redeemed. The German flagship was 'en route Marquesas and Easter Island'. There could no longer be any doubt that Spee was also en route to play havoc with British commerce on the coasts of South America: nitrates, copper, and other vital minerals, beef, lamb, and grain.

The distribution and orders to the numerous Allied scattered forces in the Pacific were rearranged accordingly. In the War Room at the Admiralty Churchill studied the charts covering the vast area of the Pacific, the South Atlantic, and the Caribbean; just as, two months earlier, he had studied the long map of the Mediterranean and with nods of concurrence from Battenberg and Sturdee, drafted telegrams and rearranged dispositions. Nothing gave him a greater sense of power and satisfaction than this tactical masterminding from a distance of thousands of miles. The fact that he was far exceeding his responsibilities no more entered his reckoning than that the *Goeben* had slipped through Milne's fingers partly as a result of these excesses.

In early October 1914 the British squadron most likely to intercept Spee was that of the commander of the South American Station. Rear-Admiral Sir Christopher Cradock, fifty-two years old, was a fine seaman and leader of men who in his native Yorkshire hunted with exceptional dash and was loved and admired by all. 'Kit' Cradock had several times been heard to declare that he hoped when his time came it would be at sea in action or by breaking his neck on the hunting field.

Cradock's responsibility was to 'cover' the Magellan Straits; the River Plate with its important meat and grain trade on the Atlantic side, and the Chilean coastline on the west. He had been told in an Admiralty telegram that, 'There is a strong probability of the *Scharnhorst* and *Gneisenau* arriving in the Magellan Straits or on the West Coast of America . . . Concentrate a squadron strong enough to meet *Scharnhorst* and *Gneisenau*, making Falkland Islands your coaling base.' Cradock was then assured that reinforcements were on their way, the battleship *Canopus*, and armoured cruiser *Defence* from the Mediterranean. 'As soon as you have superior force', continued the telegram, 'search the Magellan Straits with squadron, being ready to return and cover the River Plate, or, according to information search north as far as Valparaiso, break up the German trade and destroy the German cruisers.'

Cradock carried out the first part of his orders in late September and early October under the most stormy and testing conditions, discovering only that a German light cruiser had recently anchored among the inhospitable islands of Tierra del Fuego, and had no doubt subsequently joined forces with Spee in the Pacific.

By early October the operations off South America and the pursuit of the German squadron began to assume a similarity with those in the Mediterranean three months earlier. But the shape of events had a grotesque and fateful quality in this distant southern hemisphere, the pace more laboured, the outcome incomparably more tragic in human terms.

The success of Cradock's operations depended entirely on his reinforcements in order to give him the 'superior strength', a definition the Admiralty might now have learned was as dangerous as it was woolly. His Falkland Islands Squadron consisted of two armoured cruisers dating back to 1902–3, the *Good Hope* (flag) and *Monmouth*, armed mainly with 6-inch guns, most of which were disposed on the main deck in casements so close to the waterline that they could not be worked in any sort of a sea. The flagship also mounted two 9.2-inch guns. The total weight of their broadside, in smooth seas, was some 2,400 pounds, about half that of the German armoured cruisers. These ships were manned almost exclusively by reservists, recently called up, who had worked together for only a few weeks and had undergone almost no gunnery practice.

Cradock's only modern ship was the light cruiser *Glasgow*, with a regular crew, an exceptional commander in Captain John Luce, and a good turn of speed. This heterogeneous squadron was completed by a converted liner the *Otranto* or 'the sardine tin', armed with a few old 4.7s and intended only for hunting down converted ships of her own kind.

With the *Defence* as a reinforcement, Cradock would be greatly strengthened. But she was the equal of only one of Spee's armoured cruisers, and the other could – on paper at least – have sent the rest of the British squadron to the bottom in short order.

Then there was the *Canopus*. A battleship with 12-inch guns, however old, could surely provide the balancing factor. And this was how Churchill saw her, a man o'war that might not be able to outpace Spee, but one that the German Admiral would never dare challenge. In Churchill's judgement, Cradock would always be safe with those big guns to protect him like the fists of a pugilist warding off a hostile crowd. In fact, although Spee could not know it, the usefulness of the *Canopus* was very limited. Her big guns were of an early mark and could not outrange Spee's guns of smaller calibre. The reservist gun crews were led by reservist lieutenants who had never been in a turret before the war, and had not yet had the opportunity of firing them in practice shoots.

The *Canopus*, even though a battleship, was no better protected than the *Scharnhorst* and *Gneisenau*, and had been 'C and M' (under a care and maintenance party only) at Milford Haven for the past two years prior to her scheduled scrapping in 1915. Her reciprocating engines could push her 13,000-ton bulk through the water at some 16 knots; but, as we shall see, things were not as they should have been in her engine-rooms.

So much for the *Canopus*, whose qualities were rated so highly by Churchill that he decided that the *Defence* after all should go to reinforce the cruiser squadron operating farther north in the Atlantic, thus depriving Cradock of the one ship with the speed and power to engage the German squadron.

The key date in the hunt for Admiral von Spee in the South Pacific was 18 October 1914, as 6 August had been in the pursuit of Admiral Souchon in the Mediterranean. On that day Spee sailed from Easter for an even more remote island, Mas-a-Fuera, halfway to the Chilean coast, to rendezvous with his colliers. He had been sheltering at Easter for a week, resting his men, replenishing his supplies and preparing for offensive action. He now had three light cruisers in addition to his two big armoured ships.

Cradock's light cruiser *Glasgow*, under Admiralty instructions, had searched for German shipping and any sign of Spee, and on this same day was proceeding south from Valparaiso down the Chilean coast to rendezvous with C.-in-C. at the little port of Coronel. Spee had heard of British movements by W/T from German agents in Valparaiso, and had high hopes of meeting a force inferior to his squadron.

Also on 18 October Cradock at Port Stanley received a signal from the *Canopus* indicating that she would be a week late and that she could not make anything near 15 knots. Cradock passed on this news to the Admiralty, through Montevideo: 'I fear that strategically the speed of my squadron cannot exceed 12 knots owing to *Canopus*, but shall trust circumstances will enable me to force an action.' He did not explain how his 12-knot squadron could force an over-20-knot squadron to fight, nor speculate on the likely outcome against the crack German gunnery squadron of the German Navy.

Cradock waited impatiently for his old ironclad and then departed for the west coast to concentrate his puny strength and carry out Admiralty orders 'to search and protect trade'. There could be no doubt of Churchill's intention for Cradock urgently to destroy Spee's ships – 'We must not miss them.' But this was on Churchill's assumption that the *Canopus* would be with him, 'a citadel around which all our cruisers in those waters could find absolute security',[1] as he wrote later in justification.

Cradock, the man on the spot, could calculate the real value of this battleship – all that the Admiralty would spare him – and understood what a lumbering handicap she would be. Before leaving Port Stanley, as recounted by Captain Luce, Cradock 'buried all his medals and decorations in the Governor's garden and gave the Governor a large sealed packet to be sent home to the Admiralty as soon as his death was officially confirmed'. It is very doubtful that Cradock expected to survive. But the escape of the *Goeben* was fresh in his memory ('we don't want any more disappointments') as was the fate of Troubridge who had refused battle with what he had regarded as a superior squadron and was now vilified throughout the service.

So the *Canopus* was ordered to complete her refit and, with a convoy of colliers, to follow him through the Magellan Straits and up the west coast of Chile.

The Admiralty remained as confident of the final outcome in the Pacific as they had in the Mediterranean, certain that their dispositions could not be improved upon. Churchill called for an appreciation by his War Staff on 28 October, and this reassured him further. It told how a Japanese battleship and two cruisers were hastening across the northern Pacific and would soon be on the west coast of South America, where they would 'force' Spee onto Cradock's squadron with its 'citadel'. In fact one of the Japanese ships was still at Honolulu. The appreciation failed to explain how this force in the vast reaches of the Pacific would be blessed with the millionth chance of the Japanese even catching sight of Spee, let alone forcing him south; and if it were to do so how it would succeed in directing the enemy into the jaws of Cradock. 'The situation on the West Coast', summed up Churchill's secretary, 'seems safe.'

The *Good Hope* steamed through the narrow channels of Tierra del Fuego, Mount Sarmiento and the countless smaller peaks snow-clad in the summer sun, glaciers glinting, the lowest slopes vivid-bright with summer flowers. Nothing had changed since the early sixteenth century – Magellan's days – neither the naked natives in their dug-outs, nor the spectacular aspect of Cape Desire marking the entrance to the *Mar del Pacifico*. Cradock made one last search among the islands behind Cape Horn, then steered north along the fearsome, tortured shores of southern Chile to rendezvous with his squadron.

At this time – 27 October – it is possible only to speculate on Cradock's thinking and conclusions. He knew that he was in the proximity of a vastly superior homogeneous enemy force; the ether was thick with signals in German code and *en clair*, an ominous chorus in morse; he had been denied reinforcements and had no reason to believe any of the numerous Allied warships in the Pacific were within a thousand miles. We can be reasonably certain that Cradock did not flinch from the prospect of meeting his protagonist with his present pitiably inadequate force. We also know that he was not fool enough to believe he could destroy Spee. He therefore signalled the *Defence* in the Atlantic to join him, and on 26 October gave the news to the Admiralty in a message, mutilated in transmission through Valparaiso, but reading close to this: 'With reference to orders . . . to search for enemy, and our great desire for early success, consider it impracticable, on account of *Canopus*'s slow speed, to find and destroy enemy's squadron. Consequently have ordered *Defence* to join me. *Canopus* will be employed on necessary convoying of colliers . . . '

Churchill was thrown into a state of dismay and perplexity by this message, and was no doubt angered by it. Cradock, it seemed, far from concentrating his squadron, was relegating his 'citadel' to collier convoy work. On the evening of 28 October he signalled, '*Defence* is to remain on East Coast . . . This will leave sufficient force on each side in case the hostile cruisers appear there on the trade routes . . . ' He added what might be thought a fillip concerning the Japanese 'expected on North American coast' but made no reference to, let alone criticism of, Cradock's detaching the *Canopus*, which implied concurrence.

Churchill later claimed that Cradock never received this signal and was therefore not influenced by it in reaching his next bold but suicidal decision within just half-an-hour of its receipt by the *Glasgow*. If the *Glasgow* received it, why not the flagship? One of the *Glasgow*'s officers testified that he was practically certain Cradock read it, and then, 'Tired of protesting his inferiority, the receipt of this telegram would be sufficient spur to Cradock to hoist, as he did half-an-hour later, his signal "Spread twenty miles apart and look for the enemy." '[2]

Cradock sent the *Glasgow* speedily into Coronel to send his last message by land-line, describing his intentions and dispositions, then steamed north, the *Otranto* in close company, the *Canopus* with her colliers some 300 miles to the south. Events now accelerated in pace and assumed the character of dark drama in these Chilean seas.

The *Glasgow* rejoined the squadron at mid-day on 1 November. Captain Luce had important news for his admiral which, for security reasons, he transmitted by lamp rather than wireless. He had picked up ciphered German wireless messages. They were loud and originated from the *Leipzig*. By what seemed like happy chance this cruiser was Spee's slowest; even the *Monmouth* could outpace her, and it occurred to Cradock that he now had a chance of picking her off alone. That afternoon he continued to steam north through the rough, icy seas, his hopes perhaps somewhat raised by this prospect and the consideration that the main German force might be heading north for the recently opened Panama Canal.

It can reasonably be conjectured that Spee's expectations were high, too, and for the same reason. For he had received news from one of the German ships at Coronel that the *Glasgow* had called at Coronel that morning. He therefore headed south in the hope that he might cut off this relatively weak man o'war and destroy her before continuing his search for the two British armoured cruisers.

The moment of truth for both admirals was 4.30 p.m. in high seas, clear weather broken by squalls from the south, fifty miles off the Chilean coast at Coronel. Reports of smoke to the north-east were transmitted by the *Glasgow*; Spee himself on the bridge of the *Gneisenau* could make out the smoke from Cradock's ships to the south-west. The German squadron was widely scattered. Spee closed up and increased speed, as surprised as Cradock but quite confident from the start that he could despatch Cradock's entire force as swiftly as the *Glasgow* alone. He knew at once exactly what to do and his superior speed allowed him to choose his time and range – the privilege Fisher had so loudly claimed for his battle-cruisers.

Until sunset at 7.00 p.m. Spee would be at a disadvantage on the east or shoreline side of Cradock. He manoeuvred accordingly, veering off when the British squadron attempted to close. The moment the sun went down in a stormy western sky, the *Good Hope*, *Monmouth*, *Glasgow* and *Otranto* steaming in neat line ahead, were sharp-etched in silhouette and, later, further illuminated by a near-full moon.

At 12,000 yards with his big ships making heavy weather, Spee ordered his flagship to open fire. It might have been the finale of the German Navy's gunnery championship again. After an 'over' and 'short' salvo, the *Good Hope* was struck forward, losing one of her two big guns before it could fire, and causing a sheet of flame to shoot up into the darkness. The *Gneisenau* was allotted the *Monmouth* as target, and within three minutes this British ship was on fire too.

On the British side, none of the 6-inch main-deck guns could be worked, and the spray from German near misses obscured telescopes. Even the spotters high up could scarcely make out the position of the enemy. Within minutes the German light cruisers were concentrating on the *Glasgow*. The *Otranto*, never intended for action with men o'war, correctly pulled out of line and disappeared, pursued by shell spouts.

Soon the range was down to three miles, and the execution became terrible. Only the *Glasgow* was firing effectively but was herself being hit. Both the *Good Hope* and *Monmouth* had become wallowing funeral pyres by 7.40 p.m., the flames making the German gunnery even more effective. One of Spee's sons commented that 'it was dreadful to have to fire on the poor devil no longer able to defend herself, but her flag was still flying'.[3]

No one saw Cradock's flagship go down. The *Nürnberg* paused alongside the blazing hulk of the *Monmouth*, observed no signs of surrender, and was forced to give her the *coup de grâce*. There was no survivor from either ship. Everyone perished, dying swiftly of their wounds or almost instantly in the freezing, raging seas. Cradock died with them, his wish fulfilled, but surely disappointed that he had not even gained his least objective, to damage the German ships in order to make the task of later pursuers easier. The only one of Cradock's ships to enjoy any luck was the *Glasgow*. Not only was she the single target of two of Spee's light cruisers, but for more than ten minutes she was fired on at point-blank range by the *Gneisenau*, one of whose big shells could have blown her apart. In all the *Glasgow* was hit five times, and three of the shells were duds and a fourth did little damage. Her speed was unimpaired, even her wireless worked as she fled from the scene, first west from the coast and then south, transmitting the dire news and warning to the *Canopus*. Lieutenant Harold Hickling, after witnessing a sudden succession of flashes on the horizon, which could only signal the end of the *Monmouth*, wrote that, 'Utterly dispirited and sick at heart after such a crushing blow I went down to my cabin to snatch a few hours' sleep before going on watch . . . I threw myself onto my bunk, wet clothes and all.'[4]

Leaving two of his cruisers to search for the survivors of Cradock's squadron, Spee proceeded to Valparaiso, where he could be sure of congratulations and a warm welcome from the substantial German colony and the crews of many stranded German merchantmen. 'I am well and almost beside myself with happiness', Able Seaman Hans

Stutterheim wrote home. 'I hope we shall soon confront more of these English and then we'll repeat our success.'[5]

Admiral von Spee was more realistic about his situation. 'I am quite homeless,' he confided to an old friend, a retired naval doctor, who lived in the city. 'I cannot reach Germany; we possess no other secure harbour; I must plough the seas of the world doing as much mischief as I can, till my ammunition is exhausted, or till a foe far superior in power succeeds in catching me.'[6]

In England the news of Cradock's defeat was received with predictable chagrin and popular anger. The Admiralty at first refused to believe the German reports from Valparaiso. Churchill had staked the success of his dispositions and his own reputation on the *Canopus*, and had repeatedly instructed Cradock to act in concert with the battleship. He judged it inconceivable that Cradock would disobey his orders, but conveniently forgot that he had raised no protest when informed by the Admiral that he was leaving the battleship behind. Only when confirmation from the *Glasgow* reached Whitehall was Churchill disposed to believe that the worst had happened.

There is a curious postscript to the tragedy of Coronel, a single dark shadow cast on the bright courage of all who participated and survived or died.

The engineer commander who had for two years been employed as the officer responsible for the *Canopus*'s engines while she was 'C and M' was William Denbow. It may have been a somewhat futile occupation in view of the fact that the ship was due for the scrapyard, but Denbow applied himself to his lonely task sufficiently for the old ship to perform without mechanical trouble when she rejoined the fleet for the July test mobilization. The *Canopus* did 17 knots on the three-hour trial run, not bad for a ship that had done only 18 knots when new. Later, with a new reservist crew but still with Denbow as engineer commander, the *Canopus* was despatched south to the Falklands.

Her senior engineer was Lieutenant Sydney Start, who remained satisfied with the state of the engines for the passage to the Falklands. He was at the same time concerned that he never once saw his senior officer for the entire voyage. 'From now on the Engineer Commander might never have been in the ship', Start wrote later. 'He lived in his cabin . . . The day before we arrived at Port Stanley I sent to the Captain through the Paymaster Commander a written report about the Engineer Commander's strange behaviour.'[7]

This report, it seemed, reached the Captain, Heathcoat Grant, just after he had signalled to Cradock at Port Stanley that, according to his engineer commander, his ship's engines were suffering from faulty condensers and the *Canopus* was capable of only 12 knots. Denbow was fabricating these faults. He had never communicated with his subordinate nor left his cabin for the entire voyage.

By the time Captain Grant discovered that his ship might well be able to exceed the speed he had reported to Cradock, the *Good Hope* had left Port Stanley, and Grant 'did not believe that the Admiral would delay his northward progress so that the battleship could catch up with his faster cruiser'.[8] He therefore said nothing. But it is possible, even likely, that Cradock for all his impetuosity and the provocation he had suffered from his masters in Whitehall, would have waited for the *Canopus* if he had known that she was some 5 knots faster than he had been told earlier.

If Cradock had kept the *Canopus* with him as he had been ordered, would this have affected the outcome of Coronel? Another of the *Canopus*'s officers at the time gave as his opinion 'that had the *Canopus* joined Cradock's flag it would merely have swelled the casualty list and instead of being in the happy position of writing to you at this moment, I, together with the whole ship's company would have died that night'.[9] On paper, and no doubt in a test duel, Spee's two fine big cruisers would have sent the *Canopus* to the bottom. But it is also worth noting Spee's justifiable fear of being damaged, however slightly, when he had no docking and repairing facilities, and when a small loss of speed could prove fatal in any future action. This is always the price the lone raider must pay for the enormous advantage of surprise and flexibility he enjoys. When, weeks later, the *Canopus* had the *Gneisenau* in her sights, two salvoes from her 12-inch guns were enough to send her off in full retreat.

Spee himself, writing a day after the battle and on receiving news that an old 12-inch gun battleship was in the vicinity, declared that 'Against [her] we can hardly do anything. If they had kept their forces together we should, I suppose, have got the worst of it.'[10]

As for poor Commander Denbow, 'On leaving Port Stanley, he was watched by our three doctors and they decided that he was in a bad mental state.'[11] He was sent home from the Chilean coast in a supply ship before Coronel was fought, to be invalided out of the service and never heard from again.

On 3 November 1914 the Board of Admiralty in London, unaware of Cradock's fate, reversed their decision yet again on the armoured cruiser *Defence*. She was, after all, to proceed to the west coast to reinforce Cradock 'with all possible despatch', and Cradock himself was signalled with this news. But, as Churchill wrote, 'We were already talking to the void.'[12] He could have added that it was a different Board talking, for curious and tragic events of an entirely different nature had meanwhile been occurring in Whitehall, and new men were at the helm.

8

TROUBLE IN THE ADMIRALTY, TRIUMPH IN THE SOUTH ATLANTIC

The persecution and resignation of Prince Louis of Battenberg – The reinstatement of Fisher as First Sea Lord against the King's judgement – Countermeasures against Admiral Von Spee – Admiral Sturdee sails with his battle-cruiser squadron – Captain Luce joins him – Spee doubles the Horn – The Canopus *becomes a fortress – Sturdee arrives at the Falkland Islands – Spee decides to attack and faces a surprise British squadron – The pursuit and defeat of Spee – The aftermath of mixed spite and adulation*

THE inability of the Royal Navy to wage war successfully in 1914 had many causes, from unsuitable *matériel* to lack of imaginative leadership, from inadequate preparation to a deep-seated and abiding national arrogance. The reasons were far too numerous and complex for the general public to understand, even if they had been told. Besides, in Britain the months of August, September, and October 1914 were emotionally unsteady. The idea that there was anything inherently wrong with the Navy was unthinkable. What the public was looking for was a sacrificial figure and a fire on which to burn the offering. Clearly, the finger must point to the top – to Winston Churchill and Prince Louis of Battenberg – the only two names the man in the street knew, except Jellicoe and Beatty, and they were heroes.

Jellicoe, as he searched for a safe anchorage for his Grand Fleet, was greatly concerned about Churchill's performance. Beatty, in making comparisons with the Army's record, wrote to his wife: 'If we only had a Kitchener at the Admiralty we could have done so much and the present state of chaos in naval affairs would never have existed.'[1]

In early October Churchill turned his attention to the critical military situation in Belgium, where the imminent loss of Antwerp to the Germans already threatened the left flank of the Franco-British defence line and the Channel ports through which supplies and reinforcements to the Western Front must pass. The Government ordered the Royal Marine Brigade to reinforce the defences of Antwerp, and, encouraged by Kitchener, Churchill personally threw himself into the campaign, crossing the Channel, assuming command, and ordering as further reinforcements raw naval reservists of the 1st and 2nd Naval Brigades to join and form a Royal Naval Division.

There were elements of the romantic and the vainglorious in Churchill's determination to resign his post and lead this modest and mainly untrained division himself, considering it his 'duty to see the matter through'. When read out to the Cabinet, the offer was met with 'roars of incredulous laughter', and he was ordered home without delay.

The expedition put some spine into the Belgian troops, who had been about to surrender, and delayed the fall of the city by a few days – long enough, Churchill later claimed, to secure Dunkirk and Calais. But the naval losses were severe, and some 1,500 ratings were forced to seek shelter in neutral Holland where they were interned. Asquith was furious. 'I can't tell you what I feel of the *wicked* folly of it all',[2] he wrote to his friend Venetia Stanley. Richmond wrote in his diary, 'It is a tragedy that the Navy should be in such lunatic hands at this time.' And from the Battle Cruiser Squadron, Beatty regretted that Churchill had made 'such a darned fool of himself over the Antwerp débâcle. The man must have been mad to have thought he could relieve [Antwerp] . . . by putting 8,000 half-trained troops into it.'[3]

But there was an even more vulnerable figure than Churchill for the sacrificial fire – his professional partner. There was no question that Prince Louis of Battenberg had been a good peacetime First Sea Lord and partner for his swashbuckling and intemperate First Lord. Battenberg the administrator demonstrated a fine intellect and orderly mind. His judgement was beyond criticism, and, rare among his contemporaries, he understood the historical meaning of sea power – no mean achievement for an officer from the land-locked German Grand-Duchy of Hesse, which was renowned for its military rather than naval traditions.

Battenberg was burdened with a handicap which was to prove fatal. He was German-born and suffered from two characteristic German weaknesses: he was over-sensitive to criticism, and lacked imagination. Throughout his long and honourable career in the British Navy, Battenberg had failed to conform to the service's style of conduct, its affected amateurism and disdain for ostentatious success. His royal connections proved a handicap and he possessed too much pride and too little imagination to change his name, and dispense with his title and his German properties which he visited frequently and for long periods. His German accent remained pronounced. In a decade of increasing German hostility and naval competition, Battenberg made no effort to distance himself from his numerous German relations, including his brother-in-law Prince Heinrich of Prussia, High-Admiral in the German Navy and brother to the Kaiser.

When Fisher, his great admirer, told Churchill that Battenberg had only three friends, including Churchill and himself, he was exaggerating as usual. But he did not have many in the Navy. Nor did he have many enemies, though the most bigoted (like Beresford) called him 'the Hun' and did their utmost to retard his promotion. These same officers, all elderly and mostly retired, opened the chorus of defamation the moment criticism could be levelled at the management of naval affairs in wartime. They were supported by the prejudiced, jingoistic, and half-educated middle classes, whose letters poured into the newspaper offices.

'We receive day by day a constantly growing stream of correspondence', ran an editorial in the moderate *Globe*, 'in which the wisdom of having an officer who is of German birth as the professional head of the Navy is assailed in varying terms. We would gladly dismiss all these letters from our mind, but we cannot. They are too numerous, too insistent, and too obviously the expression of a widespread feeling.' Responsible newspapers came to Battenberg's rescue, the gutter Press predictably whipped up the already aroused rumour that a German in the Admiralty was the cause of the Navy's losses and failure to bring about a great victory in the Nelsonian manner. 'Blood is said to be thicker than water,' *John Bull* claimed, 'and we doubt whether all the water in the North Sea could obliterate the blood-ties between the Battenbergs and the Hohenzollerns when it comes to a question of a life and death struggle between Germany and ourselves.'[4]

At the first hints of this sort of criticism, Battenberg's spirit and effort faltered. Where Fisher would have called down the Gods upon his enemies and fought harder, Prince Louis was soon shattered in mind and spirit. His one great act for the Navy in keeping the Fleet mobilized was also his last. He became increasingly inconsolable in his grief. Two days after the sinking of the *Audacious* he wrote to Churchill, 'I beg of you to release me. I am on the verge of breaking down & I cannot use my brain for anything.'[5]

Churchill arranged with Asquith an exchange of letters between himself and Battenberg. Battenberg's began, 'I have lately been driven to the painful conclusion that at this juncture my birth and parentage have the effect of impairing in some respects my usefulness to the Board of Admiralty.' Churchill replied gracefully and generously, expressing 'publicly my deep indebtedness to you, and the pain I feel at the severance of our three years' official association'. Unable to accept that this was the end of his naval career, Battenberg, according to Churchill, wrote 'stating that the Mediterranean was his great desire as the finale of his naval service'[6] after the war, and asked that he be made a Privy Counsellor as confirmation that the nation still trusted him. Churchill recommended that both these requests should be met. PC was added to the long list of initials after Battenberg's name, and he was promoted Admiral of the Fleet, but otherwise he was totally forgotten. He was never even invited to the surrender ceremony of the German Fleet in 1918, and died three years later – one more commander broken by the first few weeks of war.

The departure of Battenberg placated the Admiralty's critics for the time being, and Churchill survived this crisis by a hair's breadth. The choice of a successor to Battenberg taxed the judgement of everyone from Asquith to George V, but not Churchill. He had set his heart on working in harness with Fisher whom he regarded as the perfect partner. Asquith favoured the choice, the King was appalled. George V did not trust or like Fisher and predicted that his return to power would open up old wounds. The King wanted Hedworth Meux or Doveton Sturdee. Churchill told him that he was perfectly prepared to leave the Admiralty and fight in France; and he added, to Asquith, that he would certainly resign if he did not get Fisher. Asquith then told the King that Churchill's 'services in his present position could not be dispensed with or replaced'. That was that. George V had no alternative but to agree, though with all sorts of fears for the future. For the record, he approved the appointment 'with some reluctance and misgivings'.

One or two lowlier admirals expressed their dismay, too. But on the whole the Navy regarded the choice as a welcome one. At least there would now be positive leadership. Beatty wrote to his wife that the choice was 'the best they could have done, but I wish he was ten years younger. [Fisher] still has fine zeal, energy, and determination, coupled with low cunning, which is eminently desirable just now.'[7] *The Times* approved warmly, too – 'undoubtedly the country will benefit'.

The style and pace of the Admiralty's workings changed on 30 October 1914 when Fisher once again pounded into the Admiralty, his heart high, his mind racing with plans. Within hours, heads rolled. Within three days a meeting was held at which a new navy – no less – was planned: 600 ships in all. Submarines was the first item on the agenda. According to Keyes, Fisher 'opened the meeting by telling us his intentions as to future submarine construction, and turning to the Superintendent of contracts, he said that he would make his wife a widow and his house a dunghill, if he brought paper work or red tape into the business; he wanted submarines, not contracts'. He wanted them in eight months (usual time two and a half years) and he would commit *hara-kiri* if he did not get them. When someone muttered, 'Now we know exactly how long he has to live', Fisher fixed Keyes 'with a ferocious glare, and said, "If anyone thwarts me, he had better commit *hara-kiri* too." '[8]

Shipbuilding had been more or less moribund since the start of the war. Now things were to be changed, and at breathtaking (if not life-taking) speed. A new spirit infused naval affairs. The instant despatch of the *Defence* to reinforce Cradock was only the earliest evidence of the new decisiveness controlling naval movements and policy, and the new steadying hand on Churchill's shoulder.

Churchill had wanted to be rid of Battenberg and have Fisher at his side since the first signs of Battenberg's demoralization. Churchill worked better with someone who would stand up to his belligerent ways, someone with the instinct for the positive which he admired all through his life. Fisher, out of office, had taught Churchill nine-tenths of what he knew about naval strategy, tactics and *matériel*. Churchill loved to be with the clever, wily, ruthless old veteran; he warmed to the quips and quotations, the uncompromising judgements, the feeling of pace and accomplishment. For all Churchill's vanity and arrogance, he was much too clever not to allow himself to be overruled or shown to be wrong by someone with Fisher's weight of experience and intellect. At no time was this better illustrated than in Fisher's first days in office.

Within one hour of the receipt of the confirmed news of Cradock's defeat, Fisher and Churchill were planning countermeasures. All evidence pointed to Admiral von Spee proceeding either north or south from the scene of his triumph: north to destroy British trade on the west coast of South America, then through the Panama Canal to create havoc in the West Indies and North Atlantic before attempting to break through the North Sea blockade to home; or south and then north again to prey on British shipping off the Plate, then perhaps east where the effect of his presence would be equally devastating, and would additionally give great support to the German colonial forces fighting the South Africans.

As far as the western and central Pacific areas were concerned, the position had been secured by what were now overwhelming French–Japanese–Australian–New Zealand–British forces. Churchill suggested that the Atlantic could be made equally secure by the despatch of a dreadnought battle-cruiser to reinforce the mid-Atlantic squadron commanded by Admiral Archibald Stoddart, which already included the much-confused, much-abused *Defence* and three more armoured cruisers, his flag flying in the improved County Class *Carnarvon*.

'But', wrote Churchill, 'I found Lord Fisher in a bolder mood.'[9] He proposed that the super-dreadnought 13.5-inch-gunned *Princess Royal* should proceed at once to cover the West Indies, and that two – not one – battle-cruisers should be sent into the South Atlantic. In the tradition of his hero, Nelson, he was seeking instant annihilation of the enemy not just a defeat or partial defeat. Where Churchill was previously content to send an ancient battleship, Fisher successfully persuaded him that three big ships, each alone capable of sending all von Spee's squadron to the bottom, were essential for the task.

And who was to command this massively powerful South Atlantic and South Pacific Squadron – the *Invincible*, *Inflexible*, four armoured cruisers, two light cruisers, and the much maligned *Canopus*? One of those whose head had rolled with Fisher's arrival was the Chief of Staff and one of the King's choices for First Sea Lord. Doveton Sturdee, fifty-five years old, was a fine seaman, and was highly regarded as a tactician and a gunnery officer. Because he read and studied history he was classed as a 'brain', with the result that, after commanding a cruiser squadron, he was appointed to the Admiralty War Staff in August 1914, and perhaps to his own surprise, as Chief. He was not in fact a clever man, and among his attributes that made him unsuitable for the job were inflexibility and inability to listen to advice from members of his Staff, like Richmond, who were markedly cleverer than he was. He enjoyed the power he wielded as Chief of Staff but did not, in principle, approve of the Staff system. He would have much preferred to be away at sea. One young commander on joining his Staff was told, 'My motto is "Damn the staff." ' Ten years after his appointment he wrote, 'One of the disadvantages of the Staff system in the Navy is that there is too great a tendency of Senior Officers to consult their staff on vital questions instead of officers of riper experience holding responsible positions in the Fleet.'[10] The Fleet distribution and dispositions which led to the early disasters and near-disasters recommended to Churchill stemmed from Sturdee. Even after the loss of the *Aboukir*, *Hogue*, and *Cressy*, Sturdee continued to press successfully for regular North Sea cruiser patrols. There is, however, a glimmer of evidence that he earlier proposed the despatch of a battle-cruiser from the Grand Fleet, but had been overruled as a result of Jellicoe's protest.

Sturdee had been well and truly in the Beresford camp in the vendetta against Fisher, and gave evidence in the enquiry that led to Fisher's downfall. He had been Chief of Staff to Beresford, who described him as 'one of the most brilliant, if not the most brilliant, officer of my acquaintance'. Sturdee's rapid advancement was largely due to Beresford's influence.

With the sudden and unexpected arrival of Fisher at the Admiralty, Sturdee knew that he would not last for long in his job, but he put up a gallant fight when Fisher dismissed him. Knowing how politically vulnerable Fisher was and that George V had fought against his appointment and wanted himself as First Sea Lord, he refused to go. 'Sturdee would not listen to Churchill's appeals either, for he knew that his dismissal would be a confession by Churchill that Fisher had forced his hand because affairs had been so mismanaged.'[11] Quick as a flash, Churchill saw the way out of the impasse. Send Sturdee in command of the South Atlantic force!

Fisher agreed at once. It would be hard to bear if Sturdee, that 'pedantic ass, which Sturdee is, has been, and always will be!'[12] were to become a national hero, but there was a measure of justice in the prospect of the ex-Chief of Staff whose 'criminal ineptitude' (in Fisher's view) had resulted in the sinking of Cradock's armoured cruisers, himself becoming responsible for correcting the dangerous situation he had brought about. Sturdee, of course, accepted the challenge with alacrity. His flag would fly in the *Invincible*. It was hoped she would have better hunting this time.

Neither Jellicoe nor Beatty was best pleased at the loss of three battle-cruisers to hunt down two armoured cruisers on the other side of the world. Jellicoe was particularly sore at the loss of the *Princess Royal*, complaining that the *New Zealand* (an earlier 12-inch-gunned ship) should have been sent in her place because she had a more economical coal consumption and could dispose of Spee on her own anyway. He telegraphed and wrote several times to complain at his sudden deprival of strength. It was, he argued, 'specially important not to weaken the Grand Fleet just now . . . I will of course do the best I can with the force at my disposal, but much is expected of the Grand Fleet if the opportunity arises, and I hope I shall not be held responsible if the force is unequal to the task devolving upon it . . . '[13]

Fisher spared the C.-in-C. a soothing word or two before engaging in the task of getting his 'ocean greyhounds' away as rapidly as possible. The *Invincible* and *Inflexible* arrived for coal, stores, and repairs at Devonport on 8 November and the Admiral Superintendent assured the Admiralty they would be away by the 13th – a Friday – 'What a day to choose!' exclaimed Fisher to Churchill, and insisted, against vehement protests, that they must sail not later than the 11th, if necessary with dockyard workers still on board. (They were.)

Once at sea, the urgency of the mission appeared to be forgotten by Sturdee. The two battle-cruisers steamed at their most economical speed of 10 knots, and even hove to several times to check that neutral ships they met were not carrying contraband. He stopped for twenty-four hours at St. Vincente in the Cape Verde islands, lost another twelve hours when a target towing cable wrapped itself round one of the *Invincible*'s propellers, and then diverted from his course on hearing a rumour that a German raider might be not far distant. It took him until 26 November to reach Abrolhos Rocks off the coast of Brazil. Here he rendezvoused with the rest of his squadron, three armoured cruisers and two light cruisers. The crews began to ship stores and coal in a leisurely manner. Sturdee ordered Admiral Stoddart and all the captains to the *Invincible* for a conference. Among them was John Luce of the *Glasgow*.

Since that terrible night when she had fled from the scene of the destruction of her consorts, the racket of jamming German wireless blotting out all other signals, the *Glasgow* had joined the *Canopus* and arrived back at the Falkland Islands on 8 November. At Port Stanley John Luce prepared a full report on the battle while his cruiser was coaled and provisioned and his men took a brief rest. He was then ordered to join Admiral Stoddart at Montevideo, then be repaired and refitted at Rio de Janeiro, and finally steamed north under further orders to meet Sturdee. Among the big cruisers, the 'blooded' *Glasgow* was regarded with some awe and admiration; she was, after all, the only survivor of Spee's impressive gunnery, her crew seasoned in battle, her upper works carrying the scars of Coronel.

Luce was appalled when he heard that Sturdee intended to remain at Abrolhos for three days. The urgency of reaching the Falklands before Spee arrived was incontrovertible in his judgement.

After some consideration and 'in some trepidation', Luce returned from the *Glasgow* to the flagship where he was received again by Sturdee.

'I hope you don't mind me coming over, sir,' he began, 'and please don't imagine I am questioning your orders, but thinking it over I do feel we should sail as soon as possible.'

'But dammit, Luce,' Sturdee replied, 'we're sailing the day after tomorrow, isn't that good enough for you?'

In the end, Sturdee relented, and – not with the best grace – he concluded with, 'Very well, Luce, we'll sail tomorrow . . .'[14]

On the other side of South America, among the giant glaciers of the Gulf of Penas, southern Chile, and in a strongly contrasting temperature to that at Abrolhos, Spee was conducting his decorations ceremony. The Kaiser had telegraphed that 300 iron crosses should be distributed at Spee's discretion. It took the best part of a day to complete the business, the Admiral being ferried in his barge from ship to ship, the cheers echoing back, time and again, from the rocky cliffs and glacier faces.

The squadron then faced the passage round the Horn, which Spee decided would be more likely to conceal their presence than if he passed through the Straits. The weather off the Fuegian islands and the Cape lived up to its reputation, recalling Drake's terrible experiences of 1578. His squadron, like Drake's, was scattered in the moutainous seas, and the light cruisers suffered badly and threatened to capsize as the little *Marigold* had done all those years ago. The commanders were, at one point, obliged to order the deck cargoes of coal, stacked to extend the range of their vessels, to be thrown overboard.

Later, after doubling Cape Horn on 2 December, the weather and visibility improved, revealing a fine four-masted barque. It was flying the British flag, and when it was apprehended and taken in tow by the *Leipzig*, was found to be carrying 3,000 tons of best coal – more than they had lost in the storm.

Spee took his squadron up the spectacular and sheltered waters of the Beagle Channel to tranship this precious find of fuel. In midsummer weather, while some of the men went ashore to dig up young Antarctic beeches and shrubs with berries for the forthcoming Christmas festivities, the coal was transferred to the light cruisers. The storm had lost them at least twenty-four hours, and the coaling occupied a further three days: one more entry in the fine arithmetical calculations of fate and coincidence that governed these critical days of early December 1914.

After performing with such sturdy reliability when believed to be faulty, the engines of the old *Canopus* succumbed to continuous maximum revolutions while escaping south from Spee. Her speed dropped from 16½ knots to a crawl while Lieutenant Start and his men made what repairs they could. On 5 November the *Canopus* limped through the Magellan Straits, past the little township of Punta Arenas observed by the British consul and German agents, and at the low-lying Cape Virgins rendezvoused with the *Glasgow*.

At about this time, the battleship picked up a signal from London via Montevideo and Port Stanley. Captain Grant and his men knew nothing of the changes at the top in London, but recognized from this signal that the fighting power of their ship had been much reduced in

the judgement of the First Lord. Fisher had evidently convinced
Churchill, who called the battleship 'inexpugnable', of the real rather
than the romanticized ability of the *Canopus* to deal with Spee. Now
Grant was ordered (4 November) to 'make the best of your way to join
Defence near Montevideo'. He was told to 'avoid being brought to
action by superior force', and 'if attacked Admiralty is confident ship
will in all circumstances be fought to the last . . . '. Grant's role had,
almost overnight, changed from commander of an impregnable
'citadel' to a latter-day Sir Richard Grenville.

The people of the Falkland Islands were glad enough to see the
battleship with the accompanying *Glasgow*. On the previous day they
had been warned that Spee might raid the islands, and their only
weapons were three pieces of aged light artillery and a few rifles.

On 10 November, an additional signal from the Admiralty ordered
the *Canopus* to remain where she was.

Moor the ship so that the entrance is commanded by your guns. Extemporize
mines outside entrance. Send down your topmasts and be prepared for
bombardment from outside the harbour. Stimulate the Governor to organize
all local forces and make determined defence. Arrange observation station on
shore, by which your fire on ships outside can be directed. Land guns or use
boats' torpedoes to sink a blocking ship before she reaches the Narrows. No
objection to your grounding ship to obtain a good berth.[15]

Like any experienced, responsible captain, Heathcoat Grant
required none of these detailed instructions. He had already
camouflaged his ship, grounded her firmly in mud in a concealed
position, sent ashore his 12-pounders and set them up in protected
batteries, filled old oil barrels with high explosive and strung them
across the outer harbour entrance. At last, now no longer a seagoing
man o'war, the *Canopus* had become a citadel in reality. 'We were
determined to give von Spee a taste of his own medicine', one of her
officers boasted.

Grant also set up observation posts about Port Stanley, each linked
by land-line to the battleship; and it was from one of these that, on the
morning of 7 December, smoke from a number of ships was sighted.
The alarm was sounded, but it did not take more than a few minutes
to identify through a glass the distinctive tripod masts of British
battle-cruisers – two of them, together with the substantial silhouettes
of the three-funnelled armoured cruiser *Carnarvon* and earlier three-
funnelled *Cornwall* and *Kent*, the familiar outline of the *Glasgow* and
another light cruiser, the *Bristol*.

As at Abrolhos Rocks, Admiral Sturdee gave no sign of haste. The
men were given shore leave, and he ordered his captains to attend

another conference in the *Invincible*. Intelligence on the whereabouts of Spee was imprecise and scarce when the ships began coaling. One unconfirmed report suggested that Spee had doubled the Horn two weeks ago, another from Valparaiso suggested he was still on the Chilean coast. Sturdee gave it as his opinion that it would be a long and arduous hunt. It would start, he declared, in two or three days when they were ready, and they would work their way up the west coast of South America, in the tracks of the ill-fated Cradock.

Dawn breaks early in the 50s latitude in midsummer. By 5 a.m. on 8 December it was already a rare clear day, the first for weeks. The civilian look-out on duty on the summit of a small rise outside Port Stanley happened to be a Swede, and thus the honour of first sighting and reporting hostile ships fell upon a neutral. It was just after 7.30 a.m. when he saw through his telescope a smudge of smoke on the south-western horizon. A few minutes later, when he could make out the shape of the ships causing the smoke, he raised the telephone and reported to the *Canopus*, almost accurately, 'A four-funnel and a two-funnel man o'war in sight steering northwards.'

Cape Horn and its islands has been the pivotal point of countless mariners' fortunes over the centuries. For Magellan, after the miseries of becalming, of storm and mutiny in the Atlantic, the Pacific was *mar del Pacifico*. For Admiral von Spee good fortune had sailed with him for thousands of miles in the Pacific, culminating in the triumph of Coronel. Now in South Atlantic waters, fate turned as sharply as the passage round Kipling's 'Blind Horn's hate'.

In his last meeting with his captains, everyone except Spee himself and his Chief of Staff argued for making best speed for the Plate estuary, injuring British trade and then steaming north-east for home. They had ample coal, there was 25,000 tons awaiting them at Pernambuco, a further 15,000 tons would be available from New York after 20 January. And surely, ran the argument, the High Seas Fleet would come to their aid directly or as a diversion when they approached home waters – surely, after what they had accomplished.

Spee argued for a raid on the Falkland Islands, smashing the radio station and harbour installations, setting fire to the coal store, destroying any auxiliary vessels and colliers. The moral effect would be even greater than the material damage and the loss of facilities. Spee discounted his subordinates' argument that they should preserve their remaining ammunition for the almost inevitable clash before they reached Germany – they had used up almost half their supplies sinking the *Monmouth* and *Good Hope*.

Map 3. Relative positions of the Battles of Coronel (1 November 1914) and the Falkland
Islands (8 December 1914)

'We will sail at noon', Spee concluded the proceedings. It was 6 December. They were almost the same distance from Port Stanley as Sturdee coming down from the north. The German Admiralty had known for some time that battle-cruisers had been detached from the Grand Fleet to hunt down Spee. Devonport was thick with German informers, in every pub it was known that tropical kit had been issued to the men of the *Invincible* and *Inflexible* for southern climes. Cruising down the Atlantic, the battle-cruisers had chattered to one another *en clair*. After Coronel, what else could the battle-cruisers' mission be?

The Germans had no difficulty in despatching by cable the critical news to Valparaiso, and from there wireless operators of the German mission made every effort to pass it on to Spee. Their efforts were fruitless and no reply was heard. The massive mountains of the Cape Horn area had temporarily cut off the Admiral from the rest of the world. All that was picked up by the *Scharnhorst*'s wireless operators when the ether was clear of interference came from Punta Arenas. The German consul there assured Spee that, at last report, there were no men o'war at the Falklands.

In accordance with Spee's plan, the *Gneisenau* and *Nürnberg* were detached at 5 a.m. to reconnoitre and then carry out the bombardment. Three hours later, Captain Maerker of the *Gneisenau* and his Commander, Hans Pochhammer, could clearly make out details of their target and the wireless masts on a hill. The *Gneisenau*'s turret guns swung to bear. 'The sea was calm,' Pochhammer recorded, 'the sky was of azure blue . . . Then right ahead of us, where the Pembroke lighthouse, built on a low, thrusting tongue of land, marked the entrance, a slender column of smoke appeared . . .'[16]

The smoke rapidly increased in volume and density. It must be the coal stores being burnt in order that it would not fall into their hands, Pochhammer concluded. Later the *Gneisenau*'s look-out reported masts in Port Stanley harbour, many masts; and, after a few more minutes, he made out through the black smoke the dread sight of twin tripod British Navy-style masts. A few minutes later two almost instantaneous cracks sounded out, and there appeared in the smooth water, uncomfortably close, the tall spouts of exploding heavy shells.

Those heavy shells had not been fired from the *Invincible* or *Inflexible*, nor did they come from the 7.5-inch guns of the *Carnarvon* nor the 6-inch of the other armoured cruisers. They were fired by the *Canopus* from her mud patch, and very creditable shooting it was, too, for raw reservists with a live target for the first time. Captain Grant and the

Canopus's gunnery officer, Lieutenant-Commander Philip Hordern, had had plenty of time to prepare for this moment and had taken full advantage of it with calibration tests and competitive practice 'shoots' between the forward and after turrets, the fall of shot checked at the observer posts. The gun crews had been scheduled to demonstrate their skills to the C.-in-C. that morning, and so keen had been the crew of the after turret to save time and get a start on their rivals that they had 'crept up privily by night' and loaded up with non-exploding practice projectiles. Now there was no time to replace the 850-pound shells. When their 12-inch guns elevated until they were on their 'stops' for maximum range, this gun crew was hoist with its own petard. But their shooting was brilliant. This second salvo struck the water just before the bows of the *Gneisenau*, one of them ricocheting and hitting the base of the first funnel.

Captain Maerker's shock was no less for thinking he had been hit by a 'dud'. First the tripod masts and now accurate 12-inch gunfire. After reporting these uncomfortable facts to Spee, he was ordered to rejoin the squadron at maximum speed. Maerker was shocked beyond measure, and also puzzled. Spee would certainly have been warned if British dreadnought battleships or battle-cruisers had been sent to hunt him down. Then he recalled that the Japanese had recently adopted the British-style masts, the only Navy to do so, and at once concluded that these must be Japanese ships – the *Kawachi* or *Settsu*, or the *Kurama* – all armed with 12-inch guns and known to be searching for them. Spee's only chance was to outpace these Japanese battleships or armoured cruisers and seek again the concealment offered by the innumerable Chilean islands.[17]

Chaos and confusion reigned in Port Stanley harbour. It had begun with the failure to transmit the Swedish spotter's news from the *Canopus*. There was no land-line between the grounded battleship and Sturdee's flagship, and the *Canopus*'s situation precluded visual signalling. Besides, everyone was busy coaling. The *Invincible* had a collier alongside and both she and her sister battle-cruiser lay in a pall of dense coal dust – the dust that Captain Maerker had mistaken for burning coal stocks. Two of the armoured cruisers were either coaling or undergoing repair. The *Kent* had steam up and could leave harbour within an hour, but no less time. The *Glasgow* had providentially coaled and was anchored so that she was in visual contact with the *Canopus* and the *Invincible*.

The *Glasgow*'s officer of the watch attempted to pass on the news of Spee's arrival to Admiral Sturdee, but the coal dust was impenetrable by a standard signal lamp. When Luce heard of the dilemma he snapped, 'Well, for God's sake do something about it – fire a gun, send a boat, don't stand there like a stuffed dummy.'[18] By firing a saluting gun and training a 24-inch searchlight in the direction of the flagship's bridge, the message at last got through. A lieutenant raced down to Sturdee's quarters, found him shaving, and informed him that the enemy was in sight. The Admiral was not in the least rattled. 'I gave orders to raise steam for full speed and go down to a good breakfast.'[19]

The news reached the Admiralty at 5 p.m. Churchill was at his desk. The signal ran: 'Admiral Spee arrived in daylight with all his ships and is now in action with Admiral Sturdee's whole fleet, which was coaling.'

'We had had so many unpleasant surprises that these last words sent a shiver up my spine', wrote Churchill. 'Had we been taken by surprise and, in spite of all our superiority, mauled, unready at anchor? "Can it mean that?" I said to the Chief of the Staff. "I hope not", was all he said.'[20]

Churchill had every reason to be anxious, and Sturdee should have had every reason to be rattled. The squadron's position was a desperately dangerous one. If Spee had not lost his nerve, or if he had thought more swiftly and shrewdly (or was it only his Cape Horn luck again?), he could have brought both his armoured cruisers into comfortable range and shelled Sturdee at leisure. Even a young cadet in the *Canopus* could see that. With justifiable pride in the performance of his ship, he wrote home, 'If we hadn't driven them away until the Fleet got out they would have come across the mouth of the harbour and swept the ships inside with 8″ shell, probably sunk the *Cornwall* and blocked the entrance.'[21]

Be that as it may, Sturdee recorded that Spee 'came at a very convenient time'. It took two hours for the battle-cruisers to get up steam, clear the colliers, clear the decks of coal and complete the numerous and complex preparations for getting these big ships to sea. It was after 10 a.m. when Sturdee's ships, the *Carnarvon* and *Inflexible*, the *Invincible* and *Cornwall*, steamed out in line in that order.

'It was a perfect day,' wrote the *Inflexible*'s captain, '*very rare* in these latitudes, and it was a beautiful sight, the compact line of 5 Germans in line abreast, and the British ships coming round the point and all the flags (we had 5 ensigns flying to make sure all should not be shot away) with the sun on them.'

The *Glasgow* was already ahead, and could observe that the *Gneisenau* and *Nürnberg* had now nearly caught up with Spee. The *Kent* was ahead, too, but she waited for Sturdee's ships and then joined them for the long chase.

Captain Maerker was now able to identify for sure the two big ships which had emerged and were already streaming thick clouds of black smoke as they built up speed. They were not Japanese. The spacing of the three funnels together with the tripod masts told him indisputably that these were British battle-cruisers – ships with a speed of around 26 knots. After the *Gneisenau*'s long cruise without an engine refit and cleaning of her bottom, she could no longer make more than 18 knots, probably still enough to evade those big ships if they had been Japanese. But the simplest calculation told him that only the miracle arrival of Antarctic fog could save them. It was 'a very bitter pill for us to swallow,' wrote Lieutenant-Commander Busche, ' . . . this meant a life and death struggle, or rather a fight ending in honourable death.'[22]

The sea remained calm, the sky clear, the two big British ships sliced through the water after their prey at speeds up to 26 knots. Only the following wind was disadvantageous to the spotters, threatening to obscure the targets with their own smoke, blacker and fouler than ever now that oil was being sprayed onto the coal in the furnaces to gain utmost power. The armoured cruisers were falling astern, the *Bristol*, last to leave, trying to catch up, only the *Glasgow* able to hold this pace and keep up her reporting – as good and as dangerous as that of the *Gloucester* pursuing Souchon.

At a little over nine land miles – 16,500 yards – the *Inflexible* fired the first shots. They fell short. Firing continued intermittently, almost desultorily, from both big ships. It was sloppy work, but at length splashes straddled the trailing *Leipzig*. Then at 1.20 p.m. Spee made the courageous and correct decision to split his forces, to turn and fight with his two big ships, leaving the light cruisers to scatter. They might, perhaps, be capable of outpacing the British armoured cruisers, two of them sister ships to the *Monmouth* and the third almost as old.

In the *Glasgow* doubts were expressed that the *Invincible* and *Inflexible* were ever going to sink the *Gneisenau* and *Scharnhorst*. 'We were all dismayed at the battle cruisers' gunnery', wrote Lieutenant Harold Hickling. 'An occasional shot would fall close to the target while others would be far short or over.' He remarked to another officer, 'At this rate it looks as if Sturdee and not von Spee is going to be sunk.'[23]

'It's certainly damn bad shooting', the officer agreed. There were other reasons for the poor shooting than weak gunnery. The smoke remained a problem throughout the action, making it necessary for the battle-cruisers to form quarter-line. And Sturdee was anxious to keep outside the range of the German 8.2-inch guns and inside the range of his 12-inch guns, which allowed a margin of only about 2,000 yards. He quite rightly recognized the importance of returning his valued battle-cruisers to the Grand Fleet unharmed and with the least delay.

Spee was manoeuvring with great skill, attempting to close the range first down to 14,000 yards when his heavy guns became effective, and then to around 10,000 yards when his numerous 5.9-inch guns could open fire.

For a time in the early part of the action, now on an easterly heading and then north-easterly, Spee was able to fire eight heavy guns from both his ships. By contrast with British shooting, 'The German firing was magnificent to watch', observed one British officer. 'Perfect ripple salvoes all along their sides. A brown-coloured puff with a centre of flame marking each gun as it fired . . . They straddled us time after time.'[24]

The first hit on the *Invincible* led Sturdee to turn away two points to open the range. The smoke problem had also now become so serious that he was forced to put over the helm sharply in order to clear the air for his range-takers and spotters. When the battle-cruisers emerged from their own smoke-screen it was not at first noticed that their protagonists had also made a sharp turn, to the due south, and were now far out of range again. The *Gneisenau* and *Scharnhorst* were still unharmed, and by making efforts in the engine-rooms as valiant as the *Goeben*'s stokers, they sped south with renewed hope that they might escape into bad weather before their pursuers could catch them again. Already there were signs that the weather might close in.

The lull lasted for a full forty minutes of fast pursuit. At 2.50 Sturdee was within range again from dead astern, the *Invincible* and *Inflexible* turning before firing in order to allow a greater number of guns to bear. This time Spee turned sharply across the bows of his enemy in an attempt to 'cross the T'.

For a time the range closed so that the Germans were at last able to open fire with their secondary guns. Hits on the British ships were frequent but did little damage as they descended in their steep trajectory and broke up on the armoured decks. And now at last the British firing was more effective, and the heavy lyddite shells tore through the 2-inch-thick German decks and created havoc deep in the heart of the ships. Soon the *Scharnhorst*'s firing began to fall away as a great fire spread and she assumed a list. Captain Maerker, observing that Spee's flag was no longer flying, managed to get a message of enquiry through to the *Scharnhorst*.

'I am all right so far', Spee replied. By now his ship had been struck by at least forty heavy shells, the upper works were a shambles, most of the casemate guns were out of action and surrounded by the corpses of their crews. Spee's last message was characteristically generous. 'You were right after all', he flashed to his old friend who had opposed this Falklands operation.

Just when the destruction was at its worst, with the British 12-inch guns at a low elevation and putting shell after shell into the German ships, a great sailing ship appeared innocently from the east and ran between the lines of the fighting cruisers 'with all sail set, including stunsails', according to one British officer. 'A truly lovely sight she was with every stitch of canvas drawing as she ran free in the light breeze, for all the world like a herald of peace bidding the two lines of grim warships cease the senseless destruction.'[25]

From the *Invincible*'s spotting top, Lieutenant H. E. Dannreuther (appropriately a godson of Wagner) watched with wonder and awe the dying moments of the German flagship, on fire from end to end and almost stationary. 'She was being torn apart and was blazing and it seemed impossible that anyone could still be alive',[26] he said.

'She heeled gradually over to port,' Commander Pochhammer wrote later, 'and her bows became more and more submerged . . . Then, with her screws still turning, she slid swiftly into the abyss a few thousand yards astern of us.'[27] Like the *Good Hope* and *Monmouth*, she took down everyone with her.

The *Gneisenau* resisted for longer and with equal tenacity, but provided no more than easy target practice for the *Invincible* and *Inflexible*, as well as the smaller *Carnarvon* which had proved too slow to catch any of the escaping light cruisers. Though the *Gneisenau* made a horrible spectacle, the armoured cruiser contrived to continue spasmodic fire with a single intact gun, even after Sturdee hand ordered the cease-fire. And before she would finally go down, she had to be assisted by opening sea cocks and exploding charges against her hull.

Hastily lowered boats managed to drag some 200 of the *Gneisenau*'s men from the sea. Bold and ruthless skuas which had to be beaten off by the living were almost as great a menace as the freezing sea. Thick low cloud and mist had crept up, reducing visibility. It was two hours too late for the *Gneisenau* and *Scharnhorst*, and now the deteriorating weather only obstructed the rescue work and reduced still further the numbers of survivors.

Among those picked up by the *Inflexible* was Commander Pochhammer of the *Gneisenau*, who became the senior survivor and lived to write a book about his experiences. There was a vacant admiral's cabin in the battle-cruiser, and the Commander was treated as a guest of honour, with a hot water bottle and a bottle of wine, later dining with the ship's officers. One of the survivors picked up by the *Carnarvon* was a torpedo lieutenant, who gave his name as the familiar one in this flagship, Stoddart. After further questioning he turned out to be a German relation of the Admiral. The post-battle family reunion concluded with this officer, too, enjoying the best accommodation in the armoured cruiser.[28]

The three German light cruisers were still afloat when the *Gneisenau* went down just after 6 p.m. The *Nürnberg* was all set to complete her escape from the *Kent*, which could only keep her quarry in sight by pressing for such revolutions from her reciprocating engines that the vibration made the use of her range-finders impractical. Then the *Nürnberg*, under equal pressure, blew two of her boilers, the *Kent* closed in as visibility rapidly worsened, and with her 6-inch guns soon sent the little cruiser to the bottom.

Both the *Glasgow* and *Cornwall* had been pursuing the *Leipzig*. The faster *Glasgow* had no difficulty in holding the German cruiser's speed, firing her forward 6-inch gun, forcing the *Leipzig* repeatedly to turn to reply with full broadsides and thus allowing the old *Cornwall* to catch up. But there was squabbling between Captain Ellerton and John Luce before, uneasily sharing the honours, they sent the *Leipzig* to the bottom.[29] Everyone involved in the pursuit of the German light cruisers had suffered from the strain of uncertainty, especially after the *Dresden* showed a clean pair of heels to the *Carnarvon* and disappeared to the south-west. Tempers were not at their best until success was at last assured.

One of the accompanying German colliers escaped, too. But if the action had not been the total annihilation for which they had all hoped, it had been a stunning victory, and, as Beatty later described it, 'the most decisive naval battle of the war'.[30] Letters written home at the time testify to the sense of elation and relief experienced by the crews of Sturdee's squadron, and also praise for the Germans' performance.

As we started our somewhat one-sided battle [wrote one of the *Inflexible*'s company] we were not a little surprised to see what a glorious and plucky fight the two Germans put up. They were 3 or 4 knots slower and were less heavily armoured, indeed they might as well have been made of china when they were concerned with a 12-inch shell. If, therefore, good use was made of our superior speed and range, what hope had they of hitting us? Yes, we all admire those Germans who fought so bravely versus such vastly superior odds.[31]

The loss to Germany of four men o'war and their crews, with some 2,200 dead and the rest made prisoner, was of small account numerically and reduced her naval strength by only a nominal extent. The defeat was, however, a serious moral blow to Germany's pride and reputation, which had been raised high – especially in the Americas – by the earlier victory at Coronel. For Britain, the strategic consequences were profound and gratifying. The threat of dislocation to Atlantic and Pacific trade had been lifted by these few hours of destruction, together with the loss elsewhere of the *Emden* and *Karlsruhe* in early November. The *Dresden* was caught later – by the *Glasgow* it need hardly be added. The numerous ships involved in the hunt (thirty or so in the Pacific alone, excluding the Japanese contribution) could be withdrawn. Troop movements from Canada, Australia, New Zealand, South Africa, and India – 'The Imperial Call' – could be made without fear. The effects on morale in Britain were profound. Everyone felt the better for hearing the news, and the stock of the Navy soared. Churchill was cock-a-hoop. Fisher, in a letter to a friend written nearly three years later, recalled the Nelsonian victory: 'the destruction of Admiral von Spee's Armada off the Falkland Islands . . . And the above accomplished under the sole direction of a Septuagenerian First Sea Lord, who was thought mad for denuding the Grand Fleet of our fastest Battle Cruisers to send them 14,000 miles on a supposed wild goose chase . . . And how I was execrated for inventing the Battle Cruisers! "Monstrous Cruisers", they called them.'[32]

Within the higher echelons of the Navy, the Falkland Islands battle left a bitter taste. Fisher could not forgive Sturdee for failing to bag the *Dresden* too. The escape spoilt the symmetry of the outcome in his mind, and why was the C.-in-C. so long about sinking the German Squadron, and why, he asked, did Sturdee use up almost all his ammunition, firing no fewer than 1,174 shells to sink two inferior and slower ships?

Fisher opened his offensive against the Admiral soon after the despatch of the official Admiralty telegram of congratulation on 10 December. Repeated demands for an explanation of the escape of the last German cruiser were sent to Sturdee, until he felt impelled to retort sharply: 'Their Lordships selected me as Commander-in-Chief to destroy the two hostile Armoured Cruisers and I endeavoured to the best of my ability to carry out their orders. I submit that my being called upon in three separate telegrams to give reasons for my subsequent action was unexpected.'[33]

Fisher snapped back that the nature of this signal was 'improper and such observations must not be repeated . . . '.[34] When Sturdee returned to London to receive public adulation, and later a baronetcy, Churchill – one suspects under pressure – and Fisher gave him a cool five-minute interview during which, according to Sturdee 'neither evinced the slightest interest in the engagement'.[35] Earlier, Fisher had proposed that Sturdee should not be allowed home until he had destroyed the *Dresden* but Churchill would not allow this insult.

Fisher's hates were black hates indeed. He never forgave anyone who had backed Beresford at the height of his vendetta against him in the summer of 1909, and now his tortuous and ageing mind sought every means of denigrating the Admiral who had won a famous victory with Fisher's own beloved 'greyhounds', even to the extent of omitting many names from Sturdee's list of recommendations for honours. It was a thoroughly distasteful business.

Sturdee had certainly been lucky, the arithmetic of his timing working out as favourably for himself as it worked out unfavourably for Spee. If Captain Luce had not prevailed upon him to leave Abrolhos Rocks a day earlier he would have arrived at a smouldering, ruined base, and his prediction of a long search would probably have come true. If Spee had not, most uncharacteristically, panicked on that early morning of 8 December, Sturdee might well have never returned, or at best returned with a ruined reputation and a record of failure which would have deserved all Fisher's coals of fire.

But what did it matter that he fired so many shells? And he could afford to take his time. It was correct judgement to ensure to the best of his ability that his ships were not seriously damaged. The poor shooting of the battle-cruisers was another matter, and one for which he was only partly to blame considering his brief tenure of command. By virtue of being C.-in-C., he also took final credit for the conduct of his captains, which was magnificent, if again tinged with good fortune. To pursue successfully three light cruisers with slow and obsolete armoured cruisers and sink two of them (with the *Glasgow*'s help) was a worthy performance deserving of all the praise heaped upon Captains Walter Etherton and John Allen. As for Captain Luce, the skill and courage he had demonstrated at the Coronel defeat were matched at the Falklands victory. At this time, light-cruiser captains seemed to stand alone in their style and quality and far above the general level of captains of bigger ships. The records of Captain Howard Kelly and Captain John Luce in 1914 shine out brilliantly from the generally indifferent performances of the early days of the war at sea.

9

FIRST CLASH OF THE DREADNOUGHTS

The paramountcy of the battle-cruiser – Defensive German strategy – British intelligence superiority and the creation of Room 40, which predicts a battle-cruiser raid – Poor signalling and sudden poor visibility preclude an interception by Admiral Beatty – Fisher calls the operation 'a hash' – The Dogger Bank pursuit and engagement of Admiral Hipper – The battle a conditional British victory – Beatty's anger and frustration – The controversial aftermath

FISHER's pride in the battle-cruiser was justified. In 1914 it had become the most active, spectacular, and successful class of warship. As a direct result of the Falkland Islands victory, Fisher ordered two more battle-cruisers, the *Repulse* and the *Renown*, which advanced the principles of speed, a hefty punch, and nominal protection to the next logical stage: six 15-inch guns, 6-inch armour belt, and 32 knots: an unprecedented speed to surpass the reported 28 knots of the latest German battle-cruisers. No sooner had he gained authorization for these than he asked for three more, euphemistically calling them 'large light cruisers' (they were 18,000–19,000 tons) as he had been told that no more dreadnoughts were to be laid down as the war would be over before they could be completed. They were the *Courageous*, *Glorious*, and *Furious*, all 35-knotters, in the last case with 18-inch guns. Battle-cruisers with 20-inch guns were in the design stage while Fisher was at the Admiralty.

The German battle-cruisers were equally active, in the North Sea and the Black Sea, where the *Goeben* bombarded Sevastopol and engaged in minelaying, even before Turkey had formally entered the war. In the North Sea, the German high command was tempted into taking advantage of the absence of the several British battle-cruisers out hunting Admiral von Spee to make raids on the English east coast.

The Emperor himself was the most influential policy-maker for the High Seas Fleet, which he regarded as his personal property and responsibility. Admiral von Tirpitz's post as Secretary of the Navy confined him to administration. The conduct of the war at sea was controlled by the *Admiralstab* – the Naval Staff – who translated the Kaiser's wishes and offered him recommendations. German strategy from the outset had been one of restraint and risk avoidance, which was the reason for the Kaiser's fury over the Heligoland Bight débâcle. The High Seas Fleet was seen by the Army General Staff as a shield against Allied landings on the German North Sea coast, and by Russia in the Baltic. In their view any risk to its overall strength was unacceptable. Even attacks on the passage of the British Expeditionary Force to France were ruled out because of the risk of losses, and because the BEF would almost at once be wiped out anyway by the great German Army. This reason was in addition to the strongly-held view of the German Chancellor, Theodore von Bethmann Hollweg, that an intact fleet must be a bargaining asset when the Allies sued for peace (and that could not be long coming).

The German C.-in-C., Admiral Friedrich von Ingenohl, was therefore adjured to sustain a policy of caution, offensive, non-risk attacks being confined to U-boat operations, minelaying, and quick raids which might result in cutting off enemy units or forces so greatly inferior that their destruction would lead to no German losses. This policy was pursued in the teeth of opposition from Tirpitz, without whom the High Seas Fleet would never have come into being, and many seagoing officers who longed to get at the enemy and could not conceal their contempt for their masters.

In fact Jellicoe and Beatty were right in reckoning their sums and viewing reductions in naval strength with anxiety. With the tactical advantage of surprise, the Germans, with generally superior gunnery, far superior shells, mines, and torpedoes, and fighting from tougher ships, would have been very hard to beat in 1914 when for a time they could call on more battle-cruisers, many more destroyers, and an almost equal number of dreadnought battleships.

The German Army General Staff, and even the Kaiser himself, were their own worst enemies in failing to understand the full meaning of sea power. It was an incalculable blessing for the Allies that the Germans, and the Austrians too, saw sea power as no more than an extension of military land power. Aggressively and skilfully handled, the High Seas Fleet could have beaten the Grand Fleet in 1914 in a level fight, and that would have resulted in an end to the war. If Germany had lost her Fleet in doing so, it would have counted for nothing against her at the subsequent peace conference.

British fear was not of a fleet action. There was an ardent longing for all-out battle. As one young lieutenant in the *Lion* expressed it, 'The real tone was one of high expectation that at any moment the enemy might come out and the long-anticipated fight take place.'[1] British fear was for mines and torpedoes, and for being caught napping in their still-vulnerable bases.

In spite of the policy of caution on both sides, Germans and British alike came within a hair's breadth of being irrecoverably crippled during the winter of 1914–15. This uncomfortable truth was brought about by several factors, such as poor British appreciation and signalling, and German failure to recognize the pitfalls of wireless telegraphy and the risks they ran with their tip-and-run raids. In addition, from the outset the British held one trump card which was so confidential that only Jellicoe and Beatty and one or two others knew about it.

By great good chance, two days before the Heligoland Bight skirmish, the Germans lost another cruiser, the *Magdeburg*, which went ashore in the Gulf of Finland and was subsequently destroyed by two Russian men o'war. Among the corpses recovered by the Russians was that of a signalman who had died while still in possession of the German Navy's cipher signal books. It was not until the end of October that these 'sea-stained priceless documents' (as Churchill called them) reached Britain from her ally. By this time, and by another stroke of luck, the British Navy had acquired German confidential charts of the North Sea with the German operational grid used to identify the location of friendly and enemy warships. These had been jettisoned from a sinking German destroyer on 17 October and recovered by chance by an English fishing trawler.

For the purpose of exploiting to the full this double windfall, a secret department was set up in the Admiralty. To the few people who knew of its existence it was called simply 'Room 40'. Its head was a fifty-nine-year-old Scotsman, scientist, and ex-Director of Naval Education, Sir Alfred Ewing – later, and inevitably, to be known as 'the Whitehall Sherlock Holmes'. Ewing was especially strong on electronics, and was an inspired leader. Among those who joined him were Lieutenant William Clarke, RNVR, Lieutenant Herbert Hope and 'professors and dons from the universities, members of the teaching staff at Dartmouth, and men of many other professions', according to Commander James, who later took over Room 40 from Ewing.

For a time, Room 40 was a law unto itself with responsibility to none, not even the Cabinet, the War Staff, or the Naval Intelligence Division (NID). However, Ewing worked closely with Intelligence and its brilliant chief, Captain William Hall ('Blinker' for his mannerism). Hall established wireless direction-finding stations along the east and south-east coasts of Britain, which by taking cross-bearings enabled the position of any ship using wireless to be located with great accuracy. Together with the cipher codes and charts, the Royal Navy possessed a potentially war-winning silent weapon. Messages were deciphered in Room 40, Hope would sift and interpret them, his conclusions went into a red envelope which was then rushed by messenger to the OD.

The Germans soon discovered that the enemy was reading their signals but believed that by frequent code and key changing, they could outwit him. Ewing's department was quite capable of dealing with that German precaution, and was greatly assisted by German unrestrained use of W/T.

Writing many years later as a retired admiral, James recalled the remarkable work of Room 40, Britain's 'principal war-winning weapon' as he termed it, when he was a young commander:

The Germans originally changed their general cypher once a month but soon changed it to every 24 hours, which they no doubt believed would defeat attempts to find the key. They also changed their submarine cypher about (I think) once a week. The certain way of defeating cryptographers was to introduce a new signal book, and this they did from time to time. Shortly after I joined Room 40 the signal book was changed, and it was quite wonderful how the cryptographers slowly, from the wavelengths of signals and the DF [direction finding] bearing of the senders, built up a signal book.

Twice we had the good fortune to obtain the new book. The first time from a sunken submarine; the second time from a Zeppelin. The Zeppelins, being under naval command, used the Navy signal book and ciphers.

The Germans must have known when we were deciphering their signals. They knew that our fleet must have sailed shortly after [actually before] their fleet in order to meet their fleet on the Dogger Bank and off Jutland; and no doubt many other movements of our ships which were evidence that we were reading their signals.

It was the heavy wireless traffic in the Bight that warned us if the High Seas Fleet was sailing: – orders to outposts, orders to open the gate at Wilhelmshaven, orders to minesweepers, etc. And one other very important factor: a single word was sent out on all waves when the HSF was about to operate in the North Sea. Their submarines had to be told.

The Germans towards the end of the war did reduce their wireless traffic, but by this time the clever fellows in Room 40, by studying the wavelengths, length of signals and DF bearing of senders, were able to maintain a steady flow of Intelligence to Operations Division and C.-in-C. Grand Fleet.[2]

German intelligence was skilful and accomplished, too, but British Navy use of W/T was severely restricted and the Germans consequently had much less to chew on. Within the Navy and in Fleet Street, the success in anticipating German movements was ascribed to the British intelligence network in Germany, and to luck.

When the German battle-cruisers under the command of Admiral Franz von Hipper began tip-and-run raiding on 3 November, two days after Coronel, Room 40 was not yet fully operational. This first

raid was a minor affair, a minelaying operation with the bombardment of Lowestoft no more than a brief diversion. A British gunboat
and destroyer were fired at, too, but succeeded in escaping, as Hipper
did after the completion of the minelaying. Fisher judged correctly
that this was no more than a precursor of what was to come. He had
always recognized the likelihood of raids of this kind, using very fast
ships taking advantage of the typical poor visibility in the North Sea.
The War Staff would be heavily dependent on Room 40 for giving
advance warning. On the evening of 14 December, Ewing's secret
machinery went into action successfully for the first time. Using
German ciphers, it built up for the NID a picture of the full strength of
the 1st German Scouting Group of five battle-cruisers, together with
light cruisers and destroyers, clearing the Jade the following morning,
raiding Harwich and the Humber at dawn on the 16th, and then
racing for home.

This was valuable, but like most intelligence, incomplete and not
wholly accurate. The German squadron cleared the Jade early on 15
December, as predicted. The Admiralty's counter-plans were complete. Poised to cut off and destroy Hipper's ships were Beatty's four
battle-cruisers, the 2nd Battle Squadron of six super-dreadnoughts
from the Grand Fleet under Vice-Admiral George Warrender with a
flotilla of destroyers, Rear-Admiral W. C. Pakenham's 3rd Armoured
Cruiser Squadron of four ships, and Commodore William 'Barge'
Goodenough's First Light Cruiser Squadron of six of the fastest and
most modern 6-inch-gunned light cruisers. Keyes with eight of his
submarines off Terschelling, hoped to get a torpedo into one or two of
Hipper's big ships on their way home. Warrender, as the senior
admiral, was in command. Jellicoe's wish to bring down the whole
Grand Fleet was denied by the OD. But he remained in overall
command and selected the rendezvous for Warrender's forces (in spite
of Churchill's subsequent claim that it was the Admiralty's choice),
and it could not have been better. Warrender's destroyers were soon
in touch with German destroyers and light cruisers, and in heavy
weather and darkness began a close-range action.

Reports of the contact were wrongly interpreted by both sides.
Ingenohl deduced that the whole Grand Fleet was out and in close
proximity, and dreaded above all a night destroyer attack. His
initiative in coming this far – half way across the North Sea – had not
been authorized by the High Command, and he turned tail and made
for home at best speed, while ordering Hipper to continue with his
bombardment. Warrender, however, judged that he was in the
presence of only light German forces and set off on an easterly course

at 18 knots, having no idea that he was pursuing the whole High Seas Fleet with his six battleships and Beatty's four battle-cruisers.

For almost one hour, British naval supremacy – and the outcome of the war – were finely balanced. Ingenohl had only to turn west again, and within twenty minutes, and in fine clear weather, he would have had the British Battle Cruiser Squadron and six prized battleships at his mercy. But by 9 a.m. the opportunity had slipped through his fingers. Operating in two groups, Hipper's battle-cruisers had opened a bombardment of Scarborough, Hartlepool, and Whitby. Signals arrived in the *Lion*'s wireless room in quick succession, and just after 9 o'clock confirmation was received from the Admiralty. Beatty and Warrender immediately reversed course. It seemed as if they had the Germans in a trap. For his part, Hipper had no grounds for uneasiness. Ingenohl had told him nothing, not even that he was hastening home. Hipper thought he had a clear line of retreat, and soon after 9.30 a.m. shaped course for Germany.

'Subject to moderate visibility we hoped that a collision would take place about noon', wrote Churchill of this nerve-wracking morning. 'To have this tremendous prize – the German battle cruiser squadron whose loss would fatally mutilate the whole German Navy and could never be repaired – actually within our claws . . . '[3]

From the northern fastness of Scapa Flow, Jellicoe ordered dispositions that would ensure that Hipper would not escape, sent the 3rd Battle Squadron of eight pre-dreadnought battleships down from Rosyth as further reinforcement and ordered out the rest of the Grand Fleet.

The springing of the trap was complicated by minefields and a part of the Dogger Bank which was shallow enough to amount to a navigational hazard. And yet only a glance at the charts suggested the impossibility of Hipper's escape. Even when the weather began to close in after 11 a.m. optimism and excitement in the forces which expected an imminent clash remained high.

At 11.25 a.m. Goodenough in the *Southampton* sighted an enemy light-cruiser and destroyer force which was acting as Hipper's advanced look-out. The Commodore ordered three more of his cruisers to close, and the *Birmingham* as well as the *Southampton* were soon exchanging a sharp fire with the enemy.

At this point, with Hipper only some fifty miles distant, Beatty committed a catastrophic signal error. He was within visual touch with two of Goodenough's light cruisers which were not yet engaged. The enemy had been reported as a single light cruiser with destroyers. Believing that the *Southampton* and *Birmingham* were sufficient to deal with these, and requiring the services of the *Nottingham* and *Falmouth* himself, he signalled by searchlight, 'Light cruisers – resume your position for look-out. Take station ahead five miles.'

As the names of the light cruisers were not included, and the wrong call-sign had been used in any case, Captain C. B. Miller of the *Nottingham* quite properly repeated the signal to his Commodore. Reluctantly, Goodenough obeyed and with the *Birmingham* broke off contact and resumed his screening position ahead of Beatty.

This movement coincided with Hipper's alteration of course from east to south-east in order to support his recently engaged light forces. Still ignorant of the danger he was in, he turned east again at about 12.15. Half an hour later, and in rain squalls and low cloud, he headed north on the first leg of a precautionary detour.

Beatty was furious at Goodenough's loss of contact. 'I do not understand how the Commodore could have thought that the signals made to *Nottingham* and *Falmouth* applied to him',[4] he complained later. But he had not yet given up hope. At 12.25 p.m. Warrender had signalled that he had sighted enemy light forces. Presuming that these were the same ships Goodenough had recently engaged and were a part of Hipper's screen, he turned east to cut him off before he could get too far. But this was a new German light force, widely separated from the German Admiral. If Beatty had continued west he would almost certainly have met Hipper. But his luck was out – or was it? Without Warrender, who could readily be outpaced by the German battle-cruisers anyway, how would Beatty have fared four against five? Certainly, one of the German ships, the *Blücher*, was really a hybrid battle-cruiser with only 8.2-inch guns. But Hipper's other four ships were at least a match for the *Lion*, *Queen Mary*, *New Zealand*, and *Indefatigable*.

Later that day, with the weather now very nasty and visibility right down, it became evident that a great opportunity had been missed earlier when Warrender's and Beatty's forces were close together and within a few minutes of contact.

The abortive operation ended on a sour note, full of recrimination and frustration. 'The more we heard the more bitter was our disappointment at the failure of the previous day', Lieutenant Filson Young of the *Lion* wrote. 'The accounts of the horrible casualites to women and children in the bombarded towns were particularly affecting; the shelling of defenceless towns was something new in naval warfare, and the Admiral's mortification at having been so narrowly thwarted in inflicting punishment on the raiders was intense.'[5]

Beatty blamed Goodenough and wrote to Jellicoe asking that he be removed as Commodore and replaced by Captain Lionel Halsey of the *New Zealand*. Goodenough was 'entirely responsible for the failure'. This conflicts with Beatty's later judgement, which confirms the correctness of Jellicoe in ignoring Beatty's plea. Goodenough was a supremely good commander of light cruisers. The true guilt for the ambivalent signal from the *Lion* points to Beatty's flag-lieutenant, Lieutenant-Commander Ralph Seymour, whose business it was to translate Beatty's intentions. He was the interpreter for his admiral who was deeply engaged in bringing his squadron into successful action and upon whom the whole future of the nation might rest. A flag-lieutenant's job was to select the wording and then the suitable flag, wireless signal, or morse message, to express it. It was Seymour who ought to have been sacked after the Scarborough Raid fiasco, not Goodenough. Instead, he was retained at immeasurable cost to the Navy and the country. 'He lost three battles for me!'[6] glumly confessed Beatty, whose retention of the services of this officer, not even a trained signalman, remains a complete mystery.

Captain John Creswell brings a balanced eye to bear on the subject:

Goodenough was so close to Beatty, [he wrote] that the latter must have seemed to be in tactical command, so to speak, and for all Goodenough knew, Beatty might have had some important reason for ordering the light cruisers to get ahead . . . The whole of this business has been much coloured by the fact that at the time, and for years afterwards, Beatty assumed that the German light cruisers were fairly close ahead of their battle-cruisers, and that if Goodenough had stuck to them, they would have led him to the latter. It is possible that if Goodenough had ridden the Germans off they would not have sighted Warrender and warned Hipper of the danger. But that is by no means certain. I reckon that the fault lay entirely with Beatty and Seymour, but the result would probably have been the same anyway.[7]

At the time, many officers would not have agreed with this final judgement; and it is understandable that a missed opportunity of action against an enemy intent upon avoiding a full-scale fleet action led to so much anger and acrimony. Jellicoe was deeply resentful at being overruled in his wish to throw in the whole Grand Fleet. It is difficult to see how Ingenohl and Hipper could have got clean away if Jellicoe had come down from Scapa Flow in strength – and there was no impediment to this except that the weather was too bad for his destroyers to have kept up.

Fisher agreed with Jellicoe, but for once was sufficiently discreet not to say so to him, although he spoke openly on the subject to others including Maurice Hankey, Secretary of the Committee of Imperial Defence (CID).

'Lord Fisher said that in his opinion a great mistake had been made', Hankey wrote to Balfour. 'He said that he had been overruled, but that the First Lord had afterwards confessed to him that a mistake had been made in not utilising the whole of Jellicoe's Fleet.' He added surprisingly, 'Fisher, I find, frequently disagrees with statements made by the First Lord at our War Council. I wish he would speak up.'[8]

Fisher spoke up elsewhere and to others: 'All concerned made a hash of it.' But to Jellicoe he confined himself to offering cheer, and encouragement, something he felt obliged to do more and more frequently. '*The great thing is not to be downhearted!*' he wrote to him on 17 December. 'Had you heard the Prime Minister last night (at our secret War Council) talking of Beatty missing the German battle cruisers yesterday, you would have thought that England's last hour had arrived! It was bad luck for us to be so very close indeed to all the German ships, and in such immense superiority, and for the thick weather to save them from us *in the very jaws of death*! . . . But the same thing exactly happened to Nelson in the West Indies, and he also did not take the right turn!'[9]

Ironically, the German Navy, too, bewailed lost opportunities. 'On December 16th, Ingenohl had the fate of Germany in his hand', Tirpitz cried. 'I boil with inward emotion whenever I think of it.' Captain Magnus von Levetzow of the battle-cruiser *Moltke* wrote scornfully that Ingenohl had retreated in the face of '11 British destroyers which could easily have been eliminated . . . Under the present leadership we will accomplish nothing.'[10]

When Churchill learned that if Ingenohl had not turned about the High Seas Fleet shortly before it might have made contact with Warrender and Beatty, he declared that the British squadrons had not been at risk because they could always refuse battle against this overwhelming strength and escape with their superior speed. He did not, however, match this hypothetical evasion with Hipper's ability to flee from Warrender's super-dreadnoughts.

The less restrained British Press reflected the public's double anger, at the Germans for perpetrating a crime that contravened all humane considerations and the Hague Agreement to which Germany was a signatory, and at the Navy for allowing them to get away with it. At the Scarborough inquest on the dead – and there were 86 fatalities and 424 wounded in that town – the Coroner asked, 'Where was the Navy?' Newpaper headlines echoed this question, and followed up with words that would have been even harsher if they had known how precisely informed the Admiralty had been about German movements leading up to the raids. The more responsible Press, like the *Observer*, took a steadier view of the raid: 'The best police force may firmly preserve general order, but cannot prevent some cases of murder, arson and burglary.'[11]

As a sop to public opinion, the Admiralty moved Beatty's battle-cruisers from Cromarty south to Rosyth in order supposedly to improve the chances of catching 'baby-killer' Hipper (his new soubriquet) next time. And it was from this anchorage on the Forth, again guided by the sure ears and eyes of Room 40, that Beatty emerged and shaped course south-east again in pursuit of his adversary. This time he was not to be deprived of success.

Admiral of the Fleet Sir Arthur 'old 'ard 'eart' Wilson had been asked to return to serve on the Naval War Staff as a supernumerary at the time of Fisher's reappointment. Everyone, even Churchill, recognized the irreplaceable value of his knowledge and experience. For his part, this selfless old man was only too willing to serve in any way useful to the Navy, which had been his whole life (he had never married), and he looked for no position nor pay for his services. He just got on with his work, and operated well with Oliver, who wasted as few words as he did, and no lighthearted ones. They made a dour couple. But there could have been the shadow of a smile on their faces when at around midday on 23 January 1915 they entered Churchill's office with important news. 'First Lord,' said Wilson, 'those fellows are coming out again.'

'When?' asked Churchill.

'Tonight. We have just got time to get Beatty there.'[12]

Churchill had been visiting Fisher who was laid up with a cold. How he would have loved to be present to hear this news!

A signal was flashed to Beatty at Rosyth: 'Get ready to sail at once with all battle cruisers and light cruisers and sea-going destroyers. Further orders follow.'

Jellicoe had recently been appealing to the Admiralty to return Beatty's 'Cat Squad' to Cromarty in order that it would work more closely with the rest of the Grand Fleet, and in order to provide opportunities for combined gunnery exercises, Jellicoe being profoundly suspicious of the accuracy and discipline of the Battle Cruiser Squadron's gunnery. But it was as well that he had not got his way. As Wilson explained, from 'the conclusions which we had formed from the intercepted German message which our cryptographers had translated', it was clear that it was going to be a very close race.

'Those fellows', of course, were Hipper's battle-cruisers, towards which the Grand Fleet and the general public felt a special antagonism. This time there were only four of them. On Christmas Day seven Royal Navy seaplanes had made a daring bombing and reconnaissance raid on the Cuxhaven Zeppelin sheds. They were frustrated by fog and dropped their bombs on various targets, including a German cruiser. Their presence over Schillig roads on the way home had an important result. Seven battleships and three battle-cruisers were among the vessels spotted, and the presence of the aircraft created so much alarm that anchors were weighed and the ships made for the open sea in such haste that there was a serious collision between the *von der Tann* and another cruiser. The damage was the first in naval history to be caused by air power, albeit indirectly.

Hipper, then, was without this important unit and had to make do with only the *Seydlitz* (flag), *Moltke*, *Derfflinger*, and the smaller *Blücher*. The newest, *Derfflinger*, was armed with eight 12-inch guns all on the centre line; the *Seydlitz* and *Moltke* had ten 11-inch guns, all of which could be fired, two of them through a relatively narrow arc, on either beam.

The purpose of the operation was not evident from the intercepted signals. But it was clear that Hipper would leave the Jade at 5.45 p.m. on 23 January to reconnoitre at least as far as the Dogger Bank. Churchill later claimed that the Admiralty reading of the situation was that another coastal raid could be expected, but does not explain how this conclusion was reached. No cryptographic nor other intelligence had been received to suggest this. But dispositions were made and orders given just as if this was to be a repeat Scarborough raid. The shortsightedness was compounded by making the same errors as before, too. Again, it was reasoned that Hipper's battle-cruisers would be unsupported by the main High Seas Fleet. Again, Jellicoe was not ordered to sea at once as a back-up to Beatty to ensure the destruction of the enemy battle-cruisers if they were alone, or as protection to Beatty if the High Seas Fleet was out and sprung the surprise it had come so near to achieving during the Scarborough raid. Later on the 23rd the Admiralty appears to have changed its mind, for it suddenly ordered Jellicoe to sea. In the event, Jellicoe weighed at 9 p.m., his three battle squadrons clearing Scapa Flow and speeding south to a rendezvous with Beatty.

Beatty had reorganized his force into two squadrons, his 13.5-inch-gunned newer ships forming the 1st Battle Cruiser Squadron, and Rear-Admiral Archibald Moore, with his flag in the older *New Zealand*, with the *Indomitable*. When Jellicoe proceeded to sea, Beatty, with his earlier news and prompter orders, had already been out for three hours. Filson Young recalled the sense of expectation and the drama on board the flagship that night.

I had the first watch; very quiet, as wireless was practically unused while we were at sea on an operation of this kind, and nothing likely to come in. As his custom was, the Admiral [Beatty] looked in upon his way to his windy sea cabin, and we talked over the chart and the possibilities of to-morrow. For some curious reason we were confident on this occasion, in a way we had never been before, that we should meet the enemy on the morrow. No one had any doubts about it and there was an air of suppressed excitement which was very exhilarating . . . The ship drove on calmly and stiffly through the dark surges. Midnight came, and with it the brief commotion incident on the changes of the watch; a slight aroma of cocoa was added to the other perfumes below deck, and I departed to turn in. In my cabin I stowed away everything movable and breakable, saw that the door was hooked back, that my swimming waistcoat was on the bed, looked at my watch . . . and fell asleep.[13]

Beatty, accompanied by Goodenough's First Light Cruiser Squadron, was due to meet Commodore Reginald Tyrwhitt's Harwich force of light cruisers and destroyers at 7 a.m. 24 January. It was still dark, but the rendezvous was completed with precision. The first light confirmed the unusual calmness of the sea and perfect visibility. 'The day was so clear,' Goodenough recalled, 'that only the shape of the earth prevented one from seeing everything on it.'

Twenty minutes later, gun flashes suddenly lit in spasms the south-eastern horizon, and at almost the same time the light cruiser *Aurora* signalled, 'Am in action with High Seas Fleet.' Beatty and his Staff had a good laugh. If this had been the case, it would almost certainly have been the ship's last signal, and Beatty would have been forced to reverse course and fall back until Jellicoe arrived. In fact the cruiser's contact was with the port wing of Hipper's screening cruisers, as became evident when, with the improvement in light, first Goodenough and then Beatty himself made out Hipper's squadron.

Admiral Drax, then a thirty-four-year-old commander on Beatty's Staff, recorded in his diary his impressions of this first-ever meeting of dreadnoughts:

Climbing to the bridge I found that they [Hipper's force] were running for home, while we were working up to full speed as quickly as possible. On the horizon ahead could be seen indistinctly a number of smaller vessels and beside them 4 dark patches with a mass of smoke overhead. These 4 patches, each containing more than 1,000 men, were our long-destined prey, but alas they were on such a bearing that to cut off their retreat was quite impossible.[14]

Instead the operation now rapidly developed into a stern pursuit and running battle. Beatty had not, as the Admiralty hoped, got between Hipper and his base, but there still remained a good chance of catching him before he reached safety. There was a breeze from the north-east, which promised Beatty the advantage of relative freedom from smoke, and there was good reason to believe that Hipper could be outstripped, especially as he had brought along the slower *Blücher*. Moreover, unlike Scarborough, the advantage of five to four this time lay in Beatty's favour.

Progressively the speed of the battle-cruisers built up, from 24 to 25, then to 26 knots, and finally, just before 9 a.m. Beatty ordered 29 knots, but only as confirmation that the utmost was required. None of his ships had ever made this speed.

As Drax's narrative continues:

We discussed on the bridge the best moment for opening fire, the Admiral sagely remarking that if we started too soon it might make them fly the faster. For an hour and a half we chased, greatly hampered by the urgent necessity of never crossing the track of our enemy. Occasionally he altered course and at times his destroyers or cruisers hauled out on his starboard bow. As any of these might have been laying mines, we had to use the utmost care to avoid 'treading on the tail of his coat'.[15]

Hipper's intelligence from intercepted W/T call-signs was that his adversary was the British 2nd Battle Squadron, over which he had a wide margin of speed, and, like von Spee in retreat, he had therefore not hurried until he saw to his dismay the big ships rapidly gaining on him. He immediately ordered full speed, which was around 27 knots for the newer ships but only 23 knots for the *Blücher*. Hipper flew his flag in the *Seydlitz* as before, and behind him in loose line ahead steamed the *Moltke*, *Derfflinger*, and *Blücher*, in that order.

At last, at 8.52 a.m., Beatty decided to try a ranging shot. Commander Drax recorded:

We fired the B turret at 20,000 yards and it fell short. A second, fired 2 minutes later at 20,200 appeared to fall over. This fortunate occurrence gave us the range pretty accurately and we continued firing very slowly, 1 gun at a time. Our 3rd or 4th shot produced a very faint cloud of yellowish smoke and seemed evidently, by peculiar luck, to have scored a hit, certainly the longest range at which a hit has ever been made between 2 ships in action. The *Tiger* then commenced slow firing and *Lion*'s rate of fire was slightly increased, time being 9.10 a.m.[16]

Almost a year earlier, Beatty had ordered experimental firing at the then unprecedented range of 16,000 yards. Now, within ten minutes of that first shot, and while still at 20,000 yards, Beatty signalled his other ships, 'Open fire and engage the enemy.' Like the older *Blücher*, Beatty's rearmost ship, the *Indomitable*, was no longer able to hold the pace and was dropping astern. But the other four battle-cruisers were soon in action. 'By this time others of the German ships had opened fire; the sea between the two forces was becoming alive with spouting columns which were now coming very near, and as the *Lion* had apparently straddled her target, the duel would at any moment develop into a general action.'[17]

It did so, shortly after 9.30 a.m., when the British flagship made another signal whose ambiguity was to have a serious bearing on the outcome of the battle. 'Engage the corresponding ships in the enemy's line', it ran. The ships were not identified by name, and this signal took no account of the fact that there were five British heavy ships and only four of the enemy. Beatty intended that his *Lion* would fire on the *Seydlitz*, the *Tiger* on the *Moltke*, the *Princess Royal* on the *Derfflinger*, and the *New Zealand* on the *Blücher*, the *Indomitable* not yet being within range. But in part because of the loose wording of the signal, and in part because the captain of the *Tiger*, Henry Pelly, believed that the whole squadron was now in action, he concluded that his ship *and* the *Lion* were to concentrate on the German leading ship, this being correct practice, leaving the three rearmost ships to engage their opposite numbers.

This interpretation led to the *Moltke* becoming free of enemy fire at a crucial time when hits were being made by both sides. Clear of 'splashes', unapprehensive of being struck, the *Moltke* made highly effective practice with her 11-inch guns on the *Lion*. Both the *Derfflinger* and the *Seydlitz* were also concentrating on the *Lion* in accordance with the age-old principle of going for the head of the line.

Soon after 10 a.m. the *Lion* began to suffer grievously from accurate enemy shooting, and at 10.18 a.m. was struck simultaneously by two 12-inch shells from the *Derfflinger*. One of these drove in the (insufficiently thick) water-line armour plate, letting water into the feed tank of the port condenser. Unlike other hits, the damage was not at once evident:

The *Lion* here received a blow so violent that we thought we had been torpedoed [wrote Filson Young of his experience in the fore-top]. The ship seemed to stop, and the mast, to which the fore-top was secured, rocked and waved like a tree in a storm, and the ship seemed to be shaking herself to bits. We looked at one another and prepared to alight from our small cage into whatever part of the sea destiny might send us; but nothing happened, and the old *Lion* seemed to pick herself up and go on again.

Below on the bridge, Beatty awaited news of the damage. 'We had a shell in our submerged torpedo tube', recalled Signal Boatswain Edwin Downing. 'The next that happened was that the Engineer Commander appeared on the bridge and reported he would have to draw fires from the boilers as a shell had got into the condenser, letting salt water in. So we had to stop, with an 11-degree list.'[18]

Beatty's Staff commander described vividly these minutes when three of the enemy battle-cruisers were concentrating on the *Lion* and all three had got the range:

From 10.30 to 10.50 the *Lion* received heavy damage . . . the whole ship seemed to lift and shake violently as the projectiles struck us. From these reports, of armour belt pierced on the waterline in several places, switchboard room flooded, port engine reducing speed and shortly to stop, 'A' turret magazine on fire, ship making water heavily along port side, all lights gone out, it was clear that we could not long continue in action, while it was more than possible that within a few minutes we should be projected heavenwards by the magazine exploding.

The Admiral gave the order to flood it and turned to me saying, 'I wonder what we should do next?' Not liking to suggest hauling out of the line, but feeling that we ought to do so, I replied, 'Reduce speed and repair our damage, get the fires put out, and then resume our place in the line.' The Captain was accordingly ordered to do this and we slowly dropped back, still wondering when the magazine was going to explode. It was a great relief to see the enemy's shells gradually falling further away, and then, finding us no longer in range, being all directed at the *Tiger* . . . [19]

In the short time since the opening of the duel, the *Lion* had been hit by no fewer than fifteen heavy shells, which says much for the German shooting and also for the resistance and strength of the British battle-cruisers, which were to be so severely dealt with by future historians. Hits numbers five and fourteen had done the worst damage. The heavy-shell hit below the water-line had put the dynamos out of action from 10.01 a.m. until 10.50 a.m., depriving the flagship of all light and electric power. Temporary light and power was regained at 11 o'clock, but it was this single hit which had knocked the *Lion* out of the battle. Earlier, a single 8.2-inch shell from the *Blücher* on the *Lion*'s 'A' turret had put the left-hand 13.5-inch gun out of action.

The *Lion* had fired in all 235 rounds of heavy shell, 'A' and 'B' turrets being in action from 8.52 a.m. until 10.50 a.m., 'Q' and 'X' turrets from 9.25 a.m. until the same cease fire time. Chatfield reported later in his 'Remarks on the Action' that a mistake was made in firing too slowly during earlier stages, one reason being an order of

3 September 1914 warning of extravagance and what Chatfield described as 'a general impression that ammunition expenditure must not be excessive'.

It was the end of the chase, and the end of the battle for the *Lion*. 'Close the enemy as rapidly as possible consistent with all guns bearing', Beatty signalled as the *Tiger*, *Princess Royal*, and *New Zealand* tore past, leaving the slower *Blücher* to be dealt with by the trailing *Indomitable*.

In the German line, the first and last ships had been worst hit. The *Blücher*, down to 17 knots now and falling far behind, had been hit in her ammunition supply system. Her foremost turrets were set on fire, and her upper works and steering gear were also damaged. The *Seydlitz* was struck by a 13.5-inch shell from the *Lion* at 9.50 a.m. It penetrated the quarterdeck and the 9-inch armour protecting the barbette of the aftermost turret. Waiting charges in the working chamber were set on fire and the flames raced into the ammunition chamber. A few survivors struggled to open the door into the adjoining ammunition chamber for the superimposed turret farther forward, allowing the flames to spread. Flames from this second turret reached up high into the sky. Some 160 men, the entire gun crews of the two turrets, perished in the fire and explosion. The 'great glowing mass of fire' was seen, with mixed awe and satisfaction, from all the British ships, and seemed to spell the end of the German flagship. This grave injury certainly cut down the volume of enemy fire but did not affect the *Seydlitz*'s speed, nor Hipper's ability to handle his squadron.

By 10.45 a.m. it appeared possible that the Germans would lose all their heavy ships. There were still 200 miles of clear sea with clear weather ahead for the five British battle-cruisers to deal with Hipper's three surviving ships, the *Blücher* now clearly doomed. Then came the disabling blow on the *Lion*, followed by two highly questionable decisions by Beatty, which together would deprive him of the annihilating victory he had felt in his grasp. 'I had made up my mind that we were going to get four, the lot,' Beatty wrote soon after the battle, 'and four we ought to have got. There is no blinking it, we had them beat.'[20]

As the mighty *Lion* lost way and assumed a list shortly before 11 a.m., a lookout reported a periscope on the starboard bow. 'I personally observed the wash of a periscope 2 points on our starboard bow', wrote Beatty in his dispatch. As Captain Creswell has commented, 'Only a badly handled submarine would have allowed its periscope to be sighted before it was quite close to its target. And a well-handled one would never been seen at all.'[21] Periscopeitis, that nervous ailment which had dogged many commanders since the outbreak of war, had struck again. Beatty believed that Hipper had sprung his trap, that his ships had been lured onto a shoal of submarines, as he had so often feared. He at once ordered all his battle-cruisers, 'Turn together eight points to port.'

A 90-degree turn at this juncture served to open the range, and at the same time unknowingly foiled a German destroyer attack which Hipper had just ordered in desperation, and now cancelled. The German C.-in-C. was at once mystified and relieved on observing this manoeuvre by the enemy, and sped on south-east, thankful to have left only the *Blücher* to her fate.

The turn, which aroused hot controversy later, was strictly in conformity with Grand Fleet principles of turning away from a torpedo attack rather than heading towards the enemy. 'If, for instance, the enemy battlefleet were to turn away from an advancing Fleet,' Jellicoe had stated, 'I should assume that the intention was to lead us over mines or submarines, and should decline to be so drawn. I desire particularly to draw the attention of Their Lordships to this point, since it may be deemed a refusal of battle, and indeed, might possibly result in failure to bring the enemy to action as soon as is expected and hoped.'[22]

In making this sudden turn, Beatty was also taking into anxious consideration the possibility of minelaying by the German destroyers, and having evaded the threatened submarine attack, intended that Admiral Moore should haul round to starboard and re-engage the fleeing enemy, this time on their starboard ,bow. The fact that there was not a U-boat within sixty miles on that day, and that none of Hipper's ships was equipped for minelaying does not affect the argument – adding only a note of irony – as to whether or not Beatty should have ordered the turn. He had been frequently warned by his C.-in-C. of the dire threat mines and torpedoes from U-boats posed to dreadnoughts. His own flagship was crippled and at best, if she could be towed home, would be under repair for some time. If mines or torpedoes claimed even one of his battle-cruisers, the Grand Fleet, with a heavy scouting force inferior to the enemy's, would be severely handicapped, and further raids on the east coast could be carried out by Hipper with relative impunity. Beatty could not forget how a single mine sent to the bottom the relatively stronger *Audacious*, and how only three torpedoes were needed to despatch three armoured cruisers.

If the question of Beatty's guilt in causing the escape of Hipper's prized ships leads to a not-proven verdict, the finger of guilt points steadily at him over the signals he made subsequently. Four minutes after his 8-point turn order, Beatty modified it by directing Moore onto 'Course NE', which brought the *Princess Royal*, *Tiger*, and *New Zealand* between the sinking *Blücher* and the rear of Hipper's line. This second signal was still flying when Beatty ordered another hoist: 'Attack the rear of the enemy.' When these signals were hauled down simultaneously, making them executive, they were correctly interpreted by all who could read them as, 'Attack the rear of the enemy bearing NE'. The *Blücher* was the only enemy bearing NE; she was also 'rear of the enemy'. Moore had not been informed of the threatened U-boat attack, and had interpreted the unexpected 90-degree turn as a preliminary to the combined destruction of the *Blücher*, whose dire condition could not be observed clearly from his bridge. He reasonably assumed that with his flagship disabled, Beatty had given up the chase, contenting himself with this single victim. Beatty's next signal, which was simply 'Keep nearer the enemy', was invisible due to poor visibility. Beatty could not use one of his undamaged searchlights instead of relying upon his signal halliards, of which all but two had been shot away, because of the *Lion*'s loss of electric power.

The *New Zealand* and *Indomitable* had reduced their distance from the *Tiger* and *Princess Royal* by cutting off the angle of the 8-point turn. The two bigger ships 'now proceeded to circle round the *Blücher*, firing all the time, and the other two ships fell into line astern of them', Filson Young described this phase of the engagement.

The doomed *Blücher*, already shot to pieces and in the act of dissolution, might well have been left to the squadron of light cruisers and flotillas of destroyers which were rapidly closing her; but her actual destruction seems to have been a kind of obsession with the captains of the two British battle cruisers. The psychological effects attendant upon 'the blooding of the pack' must not be ignored. Yet Admiral Beatty's idea had been so very simple. The 'cats' were to continue the chase of their living prey, while to the gallant but slower *Indomitable* was to be allotted a fine fat mouse . . .

Lieutenant Young, a great Beatty admirer, was quite correct in his interpretation of Beatty's intentions. But a well-reasoned plan, a simple plan, is valueless if orders are not communicated clearly to the participants.

Beatty was appalled when he saw Hipper disappearing towards the southerly horizon, while Moore and his four battle-cruisers did no more than expedite the end of the *Blücher*. 'The disappointment of that day is more than I can bear to think of', he lamented later.

'Everybody thinks it was a great success, when in reality it was a terrible failure.'[23]

Like the *Gneisenau* and *Scharnhorst*, the *Blücher* fought to the end, her moment of capsizing being recorded in a series of photographs seen with appropriate satisfaction by millions of readers of the *Daily Mail* and *Illustrated London News*. 'It will be some time before they go baby-killing again', observed the *Globe* of Hipper's surviving ships. Nearly 800 men went down in the German ship: 234 were saved by the British, and the number would have been much higher but for a final stroke of ill-fortune which struck their ship. A German seaplane at 12.30 p.m. spotted the boats pulling men out of the water, assumed they were British, and bombed and machine-gunned them in the water. The pilot killed a number, but more seriously the boats were instantly recalled, leaving many more struggling in the icy seas.

Beatty transferred his flag to the *Princess Royal*. He was in a dreadful rage, and for a time contemplated taking up the pursuit again. But it was clearly too late. Brokenhearted, he ordered the *Lion* to be towed home with a strong screen against U-boats. His state of mind was not improved when he learned that Jellicoe was only 140 miles north during the heat of the action, so that if the Admiralty had ordered steam up in the morning instead of the afternoon, the Grand Fleet's massive strength would have been present at the point of rendezvous. As at Scarborough, even with his advantage of higher speed, Hipper would have been extremely fortunate to have escaped.

Both Moore, and Pelly of the *Tiger*, came in for some heavy criticism from the Navy's hierarchy. Beatty told Jellicoe that Moore had not got the right sort of temperament for a battle-cruiser admiral. 'Moore had a chance which most fellows wd have given [the] eyes in the head for, and did nothing . . . It is inconceivable that anybody should have thought it necessary for 4 BCs 3 of them untouched to have turned on the *Blücher* which was obviously a defeated ship and couldn't steam while 3 others also badly hammered should have been allowed to escape.'[24] Fisher called Pelly 'a poltroon' for misunderstanding Beatty's signal allotting targets and leaving the *Moltke* unmolested. But to contravene Jellicoe's General Fleet Instructions, which laid emphasis on the importance of knocking out the enemy's vanguard, was asking too much of a captain under these circumstances. As Hipper by doing just that was to demonstrate, to knock out the leading enemy ship could swing the tide of battle. Fisher also considered that Pelly should have taken the initiative after the *Lion* was knocked out. Pelly 'was a long way ahead, he ought to have gone on, had he the slightest Nelsonic temperament in him regardless of signals! Like Nelson at Copenhagen and St. Vicent! In war the first principle is to disobey orders. *Any fool can obey orders!*'[25]

Admiral Moore's appointment was terminated, and as a slap in the face, but not too heavy a one, he was appointed in command of a cruiser squadron responsible for the Canary Islands area. Pelly got away scot-free, thanks to Beatty who took into account this captain's blameless record to date and the Battle Cruiser Squadron's morale, which was never improved by the removal of senior officers.

Heads rolled in Germany, too. Hipper's reputation as a clever, successful and dashing battle-cruiser commander was enhanced, if anything, as a result of his escape. It was Ingenohl who was blamed for not bringing out the High Seas Fleet in support of him, and he was relieved on 2 February. His replacement had previously been an excellent squadron commander, and more recently Chief of the Naval Staff. Admiral Hugo von Pohl was fifty-nine years old, a short, slim man who 'gives the impression of ability, quickness of decision and force of character', according to one estimate. 'A very taciturn fellow who looks as if he had lost ½ a crown and found 6d.'[26] He was just the admiral the Kaiser needed to keep the High Seas Fleet safe, although his poor state of health was a consideration.

The Battle of the Dogger Bank was hailed by the British Press as a great victory, with 'baby-killer' Hipper being put to flight and losing a ship on the way while also suffering considerable damage to his other ships. 'After yesterday's action, it will not be easy for the loud-mouthed boasters of Berlin to keep up the pretence that the British Fleet is hiding in terror', was the satisfied conclusion of the *Pall Mall Gazette*. By contrast, the German Press had nothing to crow about. There was no denying that they had lost a heavy armoured ship (even if it was not quite a battle-cruiser) and over a thousand men. The German Fleet felt the loss of pride more than the loss of the *Blücher*, which had, all said and done, indirectly saved Hipper's force from likely catastrophe.

The engagement also led to a profound material advantage for the German Navy. All the battle-cruisers present had been designed at a time when predictions pointed to relatively short-range actions. Even in the stronger German ships insufficient emphasis had been paid to horizontal protection, which was the reason why the *Seydlitz*'s deck had been pierced by a shell fired from around 17,000 yards, and therefore on a steeply plunging stage of its trajectory. The subsequent fire was spread by instant 'flash', and failed to reach down to the magazines (which would have been an end of the flagship) only as a result of the heroic flooding of these magazines by an officer. The men who had succumbed in the terrible inferno had not died in vain. The need for further protection between turrets and magazines was recognized by the German naval authorities, and urgent work was put in hand for all dreadnoughts, battle-cruisers and battleships.

Both sides had been heavily handicapped by poor visibility in spite of the clearness of the day. As at the Falkland Islands, funnel and cordite smoke, combined with spray from bursting shells, made life a nightmare for layers and spotters alike. German destroyers added to the confusion by putting down a smokescreen at one point, the first time this protective device had been used in a naval battle. Because of the wind, German smoke was particularly troublesome, but that does not excuse the relatively poor shooting of the British battle-cruisers, especially the *Tiger*'s which made only one hit out of 355 heavy shells fired. Beatty's ships fired in all 1,150 heavy shells and scored only 6 hits, or ½ per cent – excluding the *Blücher* from the calculations, and most of the shooting at her was short-range target practice.

Hipper's ships (again excluding the *Blücher*) fired 976 rounds and scored 22 hits, or 2.1 per cent. Jellicoe thought the German fire was markedly superior, 'thus confirming my suspicion that the gunnery of our Battle Cruiser Squadron was in great need of improvement, a fact which I very frequently urged upon Sir David Beatty'.[27]

In mitigation, two factors should be taken into consideration. First, it was the battle-cruisers' first experience of firing while proceeding at a speed of around 28 knots, which led to an immense amount of spray and vibration, obscuring lenses and adding to the difficulties of spotting. There were periods when the enemy, because of smoke and spray, were invisible and the guns were firing 'blind'. To make matters worse, the enemy tended to fire 'shorts', creeping up 'the ladder system' to hitting range rather than straddling with 'shorts' and 'overs'. These enemy 'shorts' added to the relative invisibility of the German ships, which in any case were half shrouded, and sometimes wholly shrouded by funnel smoke and the smoke-screens laid by German destroyers. The gunlayers and spotters suffered a very hard time of it at the Dogger Bank. In the north-east wind, the Germans were much less affected by smoke.

It might also be added in extenuation of the relatively poor British gunnery that they had never done gunnery practice at these extreme ranges. But of course they should have done, just as they should have practised firing at full speed in unfavourable smoke and spray conditions.

As so frequently happens, exaggerated claims were made by both sides. Hipper claimed that he had sunk the *Tiger*. Beatty thought he had badly damaged the *Derfflinger* as well as almost crippling the *Seydlitz*. In fact, the *Derfflinger* was hit three times, and suffered a fire which was subsequently extinguished without much harm. The *Moltke* was untouched by so much as a splinter. Only the *Seydlitz*, from that single hit from the *Lion*, was gravely damaged.

Faults could be found in the conduct of almost every aspect of the Dogger Bank engagement from the British point of view. But judgements should not be too harsh. Britain was without experience of a major action for more than one hundred years, since when tactical, strategical, and *matériel* factors had experienced greater changes than in the previous five centuries. *Everything* was new. All the peacetime experiments and exercises could not simulate the reality of a running fight at eight to ten miles range and more between 25,000-ton dreadnought battle-cruisers travelling at up to 35 m.p.h.

In an ideal naval world, Moore would have seized the opportunity, disregarded Beatty's signal (as he interpreted it), and gone after Hipper. But under centralized control, brought about by W/T and other electronic novelties, Nelsonian initiative had perforce shrivelled. Over the years, so much emphasis had been placed, by the service, Press, and public alike, on the vast size, vast cost, and vast value of the individual dreadnought, that even Beatty ('If I lose one of these valuable ships the country will never forgive me') was affected by it. The spirit, the style, all the tactical thinking in the Navy tended towards preservation rather than aggression, because the price of loss was considered too high. The first reason why Beatty had not destroyed more of the enemy was the sight of a supposed periscope. The torpedo had given everyone the jitters. By contrast with the torpedo, the gun was to become a little-used and relatively innocuous weapon.

If the Battle Cruiser Squadron's shooting was generally weak, the *Tiger*'s shooting was appalling, in spite of the fact that she was the only ship fitted with director firing: Beatty should have taken greater pains to ensure that it was better. She had joined his squadron on 6 November, and in that time had never fired her guns at a moving target. Moreover, her company was a mixed one, including a large number of recovered deserters, whom, one can presume, were not the most eager for battle. Morale was poor in spite of heroic efforts by Captain Pelly. Why this newest and most formidable battle-cruiser was assigned such a motley bunch is a complete puzzle.

Whatever mixed opinions there were about most aspects of this first-ever dreadnought-to-dreadnought action, there were two things against which it was impossible to find fault. Room 40 and NID had worked superbly well. No commander could have been better served.

To know when, where, and in what strength you would meet the enemy was a priceless asset. The second was the performance of the ships themselves. For the duration of that long pursuit, not a turbine faltered under sustained and mostly maximum pressure. It was a proud day for British engineering.

For the *Lion*, it was a long, slow, cold passage back home, towed by the *Indomitable*. To be without heat or artificial light in the middle of the North Sea in January was an uncomfortable experience with uncanny overtones – no sound of water against the hull, no beat of turbines, only the stale, sharp smell of spilt oil and chloroform.

Beatty had wanted to save time and distance by sending her at once into the Tyne for repairs but her increased draught due to the quantity of water she had taken in precluded this. Nor did the Admiralty wish to advertise too widely the extent of her damage and the urgent need for repairs by sending her to a southern dockyard. As she proceeded slowly up the Forth, her list and damage were plain for all to see, and people gathered in groups on the bank and cheered her on.

Here the *Lion* received temporary repairs and then 'we were escorted to the Tyne,' wrote one of her company, 'where they hadn't a dock big enough to take us. They put us on the mud off "Pelau" where they tilted the ship over on her starboard side and put on eight new 4-inch armoured plates. We were there about 6 weeks and so we had a nice spot of leave, the first since war broke out . . .'[28]

10

THE DARDANELLES FIASCO AND ITS CONSEQUENCES

The need to assist Russia and the search for a diversion – The Baltic project and associated island-seizing enterprises – The Fisher-Hankey amphibious Gallipoli plan – Churchill embraces the Navy-only solution – The record unfavourable to naval attacks on forts – Early Gallipoli bombardments confirm the historical view – Air support shunned by gunnery officers – The mine menace and heavy battleship losses – The War Council authorizes landings – Fisher's growing disenchantment and resentment – The final rift, Fisher's resignation and the fall of Churchill

THERE can be no doubt that Winston Churchill's influence on the early course of the war was, by a wide margin, greater than that of anyone else – greater than Jellicoe's or Beatty's, more powerful than that of the Board of Admiralty. His self-claimed responsibility for directing the affairs of every department combined with his capacity for work increased even further under the pressure of war. As the supreme authority, Churchill was not exceeding his powers in taking so much upon himself; but he was certainly breaking with custom and common practice. The consequent diminution of the First Sea Lord's powers and responsibilities had deeply depressed Prince Louis, who had been too demoralized to fight back. With Fisher it was a different story.

Admiral Beatty was one of the first to catch the whiff of discord. 'The situation is curious', he wrote to his wife, 'two very strong and clever men, one old, wily and of vast experience, one young, self-assertive, with a great self-satisfaction but unstable. They cannot work together', he predicted. 'They cannot both run the show.'[1]

Admiral Jellicoe had his doubts too, especially on the relatively frequent days when he received a letter ('BURN THIS!!!') from Fisher about what was going on down in Whitehall:

Winston has so monopolized all initiative in the Admiralty [he wrote on 20 December 1914] and fires off such a multitude of purely departmental memos (*his power of work is absolutely amazing!*) that my colleagues are no longer '*superintending Lords*'. but only '*the First Lord's Registry*'! I told Winston this yesterday and he did not like it at all, but *it is true*! and the consequence is that the Sea Lords are atrophied and their departments run really by the

Private Office, and I find it a Herculean task to get back to the right
procedure . . . [2]

The relationship between Churchill and Fisher makes a strange,
awesome, but finally tragic story. The two men had so much in
common. No one can deny the fierce patriotism and love of the Navy
that fired them. But their egocentricity was on an heroic scale, too. So
much in these two brilliant men was compatible, but too much was
incompatible. After receiving the news from the Falkland Islands,
Churchill writes, 'This was your show and your luck . . . Your *flair*
was quite true. Let us have some more victories together and
confound all our foes abroad – and (don't forget) at home.'[3] But one
month later a note of asperity creeps in here and there: 'You seem to
have altered your views, since taking office,' writes Churchill, 'about
the relative strengths of the British and German Grand and High Sea
Fleets . . . '[4]

For the first weeks their prolific exchange of letters, notes and
memoranda reflected an alert, restless, creative, and emphatic united
front. But there were other disruptive factors at work, seemingly
trivial and stemming from contrasting life styles. Fisher arrived at his
office 'before the cleaners', customarily took a brief, spartan lunch and
returned home relatively early to dinner and bed around 9 p.m. When
Churchill arrived at the Admiralty Fisher had already been at work
for four hours: he would often take a leisurely luncheon, enjoy a brief
nap, and work through until dinner. After a sociable and intellectually
amusing and stimulating evening, he would retire and, full of good
food, wine, and brandy, work through from 10 p.m. until one or two in
the morning, 'starting the nightly strafe of memoranda, full of brilliant
ideas that seldom could be taken seriously in the mornings', as Fisher's
naval assistant described the activity.[5]

Fisher was already working his way through these midnight
emanations from Churchill, the great majority of them frivolous or
irresponsible, when Churchill awoke at around 8 a.m. One admiral
who witnessed the extended breakfast scene in Churchill's bedroom,
wrote that 'he presented a most extraordinary spectacle, perched up
in a huge bed, and the whole of the counterpane littered with dispatch
boxes, red and all colours, and a stenographer sitting at the foot – Mr
Churchill himself with an enormous Corona Corona in his mouth, a
glass of warm water on the table by his side and a writing-pad on his
knee!'[6]

At the time of the Falkland Islands victory, with its mellow
exchange of felicitations between the two men, the fuse was already

burning. Five months were to pass before the explosion disabled the careers of both men, one of them permanently.

The Dardanelles catastrophe stemmed from a strategical need for a diversion and an easing of Turkish pressure on Russia, a political need for the Navy 'to make a splash', and from Churchill's lack of appreciation of the meaning of sea power. Every shred of bad news from the sea, every day that passed without the expected modern Trafalgar, further weakened Churchill's position. He was very conscious of this and also by temperament allergic to the passive role. He was not satisfied with an armada swinging on its anchors, no matter that harbours all over the world contained hundreds of German ships that would not move for another four years. As Captain Richmond wrote: 'We have the game in our hands if we sit tight, but this Churchill cannot see. He must see something tangible and can't understand that naval warfare acts in a wholly different way from war on shore. That [Grand] Fleet in the north dominates the position. It's no business of ours to go trying to pluck occasional, small indifferent fruits in the south.'[7]

Richmond and the rest of the Staff recognized clearly that the Grand Fleet might never experience a battle with the High Seas Fleet. They did not view this as a disaster or as a reflection on the C.-in-C. While the High Seas Fleet remained behind its minefields and batteries it posed no threat. Britain continued to control the trade routes of the world; not an ounce of steel, not a single grain of wheat nor pound of Argentine beef could reach Hamburg from New York or Buenos Aires. Communications by sea with her widespread empire were severed for Germany on 4 August 1914. The public, and especially the men of the Grand Fleet, dearly longed for a great decisive battle in the North Sea. But first the enemy had to come out of his corner – and then, everyone fully believed, one round would suffice for the knock-out. The blockade of Napoleon had tested to the full the patience of Nelson and Collingwood. They had their day in the end but it was a long time coming.

A great number of Churchill's depth-of-night memoranda concerned alternatives to what he regarded as the deadlock at sea as well as on land. Amphibious raids and operations were foremost in his mind, and the first to be considered was the possibility of wresting control of the Baltic from Germany and making a landing on the north German coast. The Baltic Project had been nursed by Fisher since 1908 when he had visited Russia with Edward VII prior to the formation of the Triple Entente. As with most of his concepts, he had no difficulty in infecting Churchill with his enthusiasm. The project was nothing less than the transportation of an invasion fleet into the Baltic and landing large numbers of troops in a surprise side-swipe at Germany's heart.

'The Baltic Project', Fisher once wrote, 'meant victory by land and sea. It was simply history repeating itself. Frederick the Great, for the only time in his life (on hearing [incorrectly] the Russians had landed), was frightened, and sent for poison. Geography has not altered since his time. The Pomeranian coast has not shifted, and a million Russian soldiers could have been landed within eighty-two miles of Berlin.'[8]

As early as 19 August 1914, Churchill sounded out the C.-in-C. of the Russian Army, the Grand-Duke Nicholas, on the possibility of a combined Baltic operation. Its success, he suggested to the Russian, would depend on either defeating the High Seas Fleet in open battle first, or blocking the Kiel Canal, which permitted the rapid transfer of this fleet from the North Sea to the Baltic. Churchill desired 'the Russian General Staff to tell us what military use they would think it worth while to make of that command assuming we were able to get it'. Churchill believed that it was possible to send a British fleet through the Belts – the islands between Denmark and Sweden – 'if the main strategic situation was satisfactory'.

With the command of the Baltic, Churchill continued, it would be possible to land a Russian army either (1) to turn the flank of the German armies holding the Danzig–Thorn line against the Russians; or (2) to attack Berlin from the north; or (3) to attack Kiel and its canal in order to force the High Seas Fleet to sea. The Russian reply was favourable – 'We therefore gratefully accept in principle the First Lord's offer . . . '[9]

After further lengthy consideration, and discussions with the C.-in-C. and officers of the Grand Fleet, and in Cabinet, Churchill elaborated the plan, and the Director of Operations (Division) (DOD) came up with schemes which were intended to cause dismay and bring out the enemy. The storming and capture of islands close to the German coastline was one, even Heligoland itself, which was bristling with artillery and surrounded by minefields. As alternatives, the DOD offered an attack on the great lock gates at the western end of the Kiel Canal, or a raid up the Elbe River, or even a raid on Hamburg harbour. Commodore Keyes wanted to carry out a submarine raid on Kiel harbour. Several other hotheads had other schemes of daring up their sleeves and now produced them.

The one Churchill liked best was an assault on Borkhum, which had been devised by a very positive admiral, Lewis Bayly, before the war. It involved racing past the island's forts at night with transports lashed to the protected side of the warships, the use of smoke-screens, guiding gas buoys, minesweeping, a bombardment and the landing of 10,000 troops. It was all very G. A. Henty, and that was what especially commended it to Churchill. Norwegian, Danish and Dutch islands were also considered as fair alternative game.

By the time Fisher joined him, Churchill was still as strong as ever on offensive action in the Baltic, but had reluctantly accepted that it was not feasible to send the fleet through the Belts without preliminary action elsewhere. In answer to an anxious enquiry from Fisher about the future of 'his' Baltic project, Churchill answered that he was wholly with him. 'But you must close up this side first. You must take an island and block them in, *à la Wilson*; or you must break the Canal or the locks, or you must cripple their fleet in a general action . . . The Baltic is the only theatre in which naval action can appreciably shorten the war . . . '[10]

All these island-seizing proposals were listed as non-feasible by the experts who studied them. It was one thing to seize them (risky though that must be), but quite another to hold them, keep them supplied, the vessels operating from them protected, all at considerable distance from England and very short distance from the enemy. Churchill pooh-poohed all these supposed difficulties and dangers: he knew better than the experts. His first ally was Fisher. He also had Wilson – of all people – on his side, and Wilson was the strongest advocate for Heligoland. There were other fire-eaters, too, like Bayly and Keyes.

The strongest need for a side-show came from the situation on the Western Front which by December was already committed to what seemed like a hopeless and expensive war of attrition: a deadlock on land *and* sea. New British armies were rapidly being formed and trained. The question was asked by Churchill himself: 'Are there not other alternatives than sending our Armies to chew barbed wire in Flanders?' The Balkans situation was critical. Lloyd George proposed using a part of these new armies for an assault on Austria from Salonika. Hankey was less specific and proposed that they be used in 'conquests beyond the seas'. Churchill still pressed for the Baltic project in some form: Sylt was yet another island for which contingency planning went ahead. Fisher put in hand his enormous new building programme, all designed with combined operations against the German coast in mind – from his 'large light cruisers' to hundreds of landing craft.

An attack on the Dardanelles, the seizure of the forts and the Gallipoli peninsula, was far removed geographically and strategically from the multitudinous islands off northern shores which had so far been considered. And yet in the contingency planning carried out by the CID in the years leading to war, 'The possibility of a Joint Naval and Military Attack upon the Dardanelles' was the subject of a memorandum prepared in 1906. Now, eight years later, Britain was at war with Turkey, which posed a threat to the eastern Mediterranean, to Egypt and the Suez Canal, as well as to the Balkans. This 1906 appreciation summarized its conclusions with the advice that a landing on Gallipoli 'would involve a great risk, and should not be undertaken if other means of bringing pressure to bear on Turkey were available'.[11] No consideration was given to the idea of a naval attack unsupported by any landing for the excellent reason that an attack on strong forts by men o'war alone had for long been considered unproductive. 'Any sailor who attacked a fort was a fool', Nelson once said with feeling and with memories of a rebuff and a lost arm at Tenerife after he had boasted 'I shall destroy Santa Cruz, and the other towns in the island, by a bombardment.' Examples of success were few, of failure many. In 1882 a day-long bombardment at point-blank range of the forts at Alexandria by a powerful British fleet had resulted in only some 30 of 293 guns being put out of action. Twenty-two years later the Japanese had little success bombarding forts from the sea in the war against Russia.

The earlier record against the Dardanelles forts themselves was just as discouraging. In 1807 Admiral Sir John Duckworth with seven ships-of-the-line forced the Dardanelles against weak defences and reached the Sea of Marmora. But when he tried to get out again, the Sultan had reinforced the guns and Duckworth sustained grievous damage. Admiral Phipps Hornby, C.-in-C. Mediterranean Fleet in 1895, sent a long reasoned report on why he should not be asked to force the Dardanelles as part of the Salisbury Government's offensive plan during the Armenian massacres. It made convincing reading and the plan was abandoned. It would appear that there was less all-round wisdom at the Admiralty twenty years later.

There were general and there were particular reasons for the relative failure of ships' guns against forts. A ship can never be as steady a platform as a fixed fort. As one senior gunnery expert explained:

The fortress gunner can easily see the ship he is firing at and a great column of water marks the position of his shot, short or over. The fortress gun, on the other hand, merges into the landscape and at long ranges only betrays itself by an occasional flash. Observation of fire is also very difficult unless a forward observer can be used. The sailor has the further disadvantage that the whole of his ship is vulnerable to attack, whereas only a direct hit puts his opponent out of action.[12]

Churchill was under the misapprehension that modern warfare and modern artillery had changed all this. He had been at the siege of Antwerp and had noted what the German guns had done against the forts here and at Liège and Namur. He came back with graphic accounts which the Admiralty War Staff believed without making further enquiries. The fact was that the German heavy guns were *howitzers*, firing at easily-observed short-range targets and with the high trajectory which characterizes this breed of gun intended for this sort of work. Oliver later admitted that the success of the German fire on the Allied forts 'influenced me to some extent' when the Dardanelles forts were being discussed at the Admiralty. The Dardanelles bombardments had to be conducted by heavy ship-based naval guns intended for long-range action against moving targets at sea, firing with a relatively low trajectory to conform with the maximum elevation of the 12-inch and 15-inch guns – 15 and 20 degrees respectively. And to hit a gun or its mounting, measuring a few feet, is a different proposition to hitting a ship 500 feet long.

The Dardanelles adventure first came up for discussion at a War Council meeting on 25 November 1914. With the Baltic project and associated operations still undeveloped and unauthorized, Churchill proposed a *joint* land and sea operation on Gallipoli. This was instantly blocked by Kitchener who declared that no troops were available. The subject of action of some sort in the east was raised again in January because of the worsening situation in Serbia and the increasing menace of Turkey, now even more strongly supported by German military authorities and *matériel*. It had become urgently necessary to accomplish some military success in the Balkans in order to deter Bulgaria from becoming another German ally, impressing neutral Balkan nations to take some of the German pressure off Russia, and open up communications with Russia through the Black Sea.

Gallipoli remained a dormant subject on the War Council's agenda until 2 January 1915 when an appeal for help, 'either military or naval', to relieve Turkish pressure on Russian forces in the Caucasus came up for discussion. A Foreign Office telegram despatched the next day assured Grand Duke Nicholas that something would be done. On the same day, Fisher and Hankey presented to Churchill a dramatic joint plan for an attack on Gallipoli by Greek and Bulgarian forces backed by Indian troops and 75,000 seasoned troops from France – an international force indeed, on a mission which presupposed that Bulgaria and Greece, both at present still neutral, would join in and present a united front against the common enemy.

At the tail of this proposal, almost as a postscript, came the suggestion that the Navy should force the Dardanelles with old pre-dreadnought battleships. In typical Fisher style, there was exhortation and threat, too: 'But as the Great Napoleon said, "CELERITY" – without it, "FAILURE".'[13]

Churchill, dismissing all the Army considerations which were thick with hindrances and complications, seized upon the last item: a bombardment followed by a purely naval assault, up the Narrows, into the Sea of Marmora, onward to Constantinople! Here was the panacea, here was glory! A naval 'splash', a naval offensive which they had all been seeking.

The C.-in-C. on the spot was Vice-Admiral Sackville Hamilton Carden, aged fifty-seven, of an old Anglo-Irish family, who had commanded the Eastern Mediterranean Squadrons since the *Goeben* fiasco. His brief had been to 'watch' Turkey and counter any moves against Egypt. On the day Churchill received the Fisher–Hankey plan, he telegraphed Carden, 'Do you think it is a practicable operation to force the Dardanelles by the use of ships alone? It is assumed older battleships would be employed . . . The importance of the results would justify severe loss.'[14]

Carden, not one of the Navy's greatest 'brains' and also suffering from an ulcer, but a fair all-rounder, replied that he did not think the Dardanelles could be rushed 'but they might be forced by extended operations with a large number of ships'.[15] He followed up with 'more detailed proposals', declaring that he would bombard first the entrance forts, then the inner forts, reducing them in turn; then he would destroy the defences in the Narrows, clear the minefields, and steam into the Sea of Marmora. Churchill presented this plan which, he claimed, 'made a great impression'. It was, he said, 'an entirely novel proposition'. What happened after that no one knew or enquired about.

So deep was the sense of frustration, so strong the apparent need to do *something*, and so infectiously enthusiastic Churchill's presentation, that a great number of those who heard it for the first time – including Fisher – fell for its novelty, conciseness, and simplicity. Hankey described later the occasion when Churchill spoke of the plan for the first time at the War Council on 13 January:

At this point, events took a dramatic turn, for Churchill suddenly revealed his well-kept secret of a naval attack on the Dardanelles! The idea caught on at once. The whole atmosphere changed. Fatigue was forgotten. The War Council turned eagerly from the dreary vista of a 'slogging match' on the Western Front to brighter prospects, as they seemed, in the Mediterranean. The Navy, in whom everyone had implicit confidence and whose opportunities had so far been few and far between, was to come into the front line.[16]

The immediate excitement and relief are understandable. The Turkish forts were, it was believed, armed mainly with old guns, which would easily be outranged by heavy naval guns, and the ships, therefore, would be secure from their fire. With the forts reduced, the minefields would rapidly be cleared, the battleships would sail up in line ahead to Constantinople, sinking the *Goeben* and putting Turkey out of the war. As Jellicoe was to write later, 'Has anyone who wants to push battleships through the Dardanelles said what they propose they should do when through and how their communications are to be maintained and from what base they are to work?'[17] Nonetheless, the War Council enthusiastically gave its approval.

The unqualified enthusiasm was as short-lived as that of children who, told of a treat, soon realize that there is some penalty attached to it. Fisher was among the first to awake to the realities of the prospect, writing to Jellicoe in near despair on 19 January:

And now the Cabinet have decided on taking the Dardanelles solely with the Navy, using 15 battleships and 32 other vessels, and keeping out there three battle cruisers and a flotilla of destroyers – *all urgently required at the decisive theatre at home! . . . I don't agree with one single step taken . . . The way the war is conducted both ashore and afloat is chaotic! We have a new plan every week! . . .* [18]

Fisher had earlier agreed with several steps taken, but how reluctantly it is impossible to judge. At the time it seemed that few people were immune to Churchill's persuasiveness. Lloyd George once wrote that when Churchill had 'a scheme agitating his powerful mind . . . he is indefatigable in pressing it upon the acceptance of everyone who matters in the decision'.[19] Blunt, prescient Richmond was an exception. 'Winston, very, very ignorant,' he confided to his diary, 'believes he can capture the Dardanelles without troops . . .'[20] The next day (10 February) Hankey wrote to Balfour that he was still in favour of an attack on the Dardanelles, 'the only extraneous operation worth trying', but, from Lord Fisher downwards every naval officer in the Admiralty who is in the secret believes that the Navy cannot take the Dardanelles position without troops. The First Lord still professes to believe that they can do it with ships, but I have warned the Prime Minister that we cannot trust to this. I understand, though, that there are only 12,000 reserve Turkish troops in the Gallipoli peninsula, and less than 3 Army Corps, mostly reservists, in this part of Turkey. A relatively small force therefore will suffice.[21]

Balfour himself, however, claimed that he always favoured a naval-only attack and feared for the fate of a joint operation. 'Nobody was so keen as myself upon forcing the Straits as long as there seemed a reasonable prospect of doing it by means of the Fleet alone, even though the operation might cost us a few antiquated battleships', he wrote to Churchill. 'But a military attack upon a position so inherently difficult and so carefully prepared, is a different proposition: and if it fails we shall not only suffer casualties in men and still more in prestige, but we may upset our whole diplomacy in the Near East . . . '[22]

Churchill later stated to the Dardanelles Commission investigating the campaign that he would never have ordered the Navy-only assault if he had known that substantial land forces would after all be available to make the operation an amphibious one. This was a hypothesis and therefore can never be resolved. In the event, authority was given on 28 January for the naval bombardment to commence on 19 February. For this purpose, Carden had under his command numerous auxiliary craft, a swarm of minesweepers; and for the bombardment fourteen pre-dreadnoughts, including the two newest, completed after the *Dreadnought* herself, four old French battleships, the battle-cruiser *Inflexible*, and (the star of the show) the *Queen Elizabeth* super-dreadnought. To the fury of Jellicoe who had expected her to join the Grand Fleet shortly, Churchill had seized this brand new vessel, the largest, fastest and most heavily gunned (15-inch) battleship in the world. He also had the Navy's only seaplane-carrier, the *Ark Royal*, equipped with six aircraft for spotting purposes.

The fleet base was Mudros Bay in Lemnos, fifty miles west of the Dardanelles. Carden and his Staff planned the destruction of the forts in three stages, a long-range bombardment out of range of the biggest Turkish guns (about 12,000 yards), a medium-range and much heavier bombardment using secondary armament as well as the heavy guns at about 8,000 yards, and finally 'an overwhelming fire at decisive ranges of from 3,000 to 4,000 yards'. Two French and three British battleships, and the *Inflexible* (flag) were to take part in the first day's shooting. 'It was at 9.51 on the morning of February 19 that the first shot heralded the opening of the unparalleled operations which', as Corbett, the official naval historian, appropriately described them, 'were destined to attain such vast proportions, to consume so much heroism, resource and tragic effort, and to end with so glorious a failure.'[23]

The second in command of the *Ark Royal*, Flight Lieutenant Hugh A. Williamson, who acted as a seaplane spotting observer with one-way wireless that day, has left an account of that first bombardment.

It was a glorious day of brilliant sunshine, and from my seat in the nose of our seaplane, I had an ideal view of the bombardment. It was like watching a theatre scene from the front row of the dress circle. Beneath us lay the Dardanelles: on the European side one could see over the Gallipoli peninsula and as far as the Sea of Marmora; while on the Asiatic side the Plains of Troy were visible in the distance.

Immediately beneath us were the ships of the Fleet, under-way and steaming up and down and banging off at the forts. It was a rare spectacle such as few have had the opportunity of witnessing.[24]

Unfortunately the ship to which the aircraft was assigned, HMS *Cornwallis*, shot so badly that Carden ordered it to cease fire. But generally the Admiral was delighted with the result of the first stage of the bombardment, and gave the order that at 2 p.m. the second and closer-range bombardment should commence. But Williamson, with his bird's eye view, flew low over the targets, and formed a different impression. 'After checking the condition of each fort, and finding that in no case had any damage been done to the guns, we returned to the *Ark Royal*.' He took the despatch boat to give his verbal report. 'I had an interview with the Flag Commander and the Chief-of-Staff, Commodore Keyes. I was not well received. Being annoyed over the *Cornwallis* episode, I made no bones about telling them that their ships had not hit a thing, which was strictly true. This made Roger Keyes very indignant, much to my amusement.'[25]

The seaplanes' spotting, which was enterprising and novel, was not a success. The gunnery officers took little or no notice of the observers' reports under the misapprehension that they could see better themselves. 'Most of the gunnery officers', wrote Captain H. C. B. Pipon, 'thought that the airmen knew so little about gunnery that their spotting corrections were merely misleading.'[26] Also, there were many days when the sea was too choppy for the machines to get off the water. Indeed, inclement weather and poor visibility had not been taken into account. For the next five days low visibility and gales made any follow-up bombardment impractical. But when conditions allowed, Carden continued the attack. There was so much smoke, such dense clouds of dust, so much rubble evident when it cleared, that it seemed impossible that all the forts and guns had not been destroyed. Carden's reports to the Admiralty continued on an optimistic note so that Churchill was convinced that the efforts of the Navy alone would be successful. 'Our affairs in the Dardanelles are prospering, though we have not yet cracked the nut', he told Jellicoe on 9 March. 'The ship of war has proved superior to the fort', crowed the *Naval and Military Record* on 3 March, and *The Observer* believed that 'one of the memorable efforts of all history will be steadily carried to success'.

Churchill, looking into the imminent future, wrote to Grey on 28 February, 'Should we get through Dardanelles as is now likely, we cannot be content with anything less than the surrender of everything Turkish in Europe. I shall tell the Admiral after destroying the Turco-German fleet to push in at once to attack Bosphorus, and thus cut off the retreat of the army. Their capitulation is then only a matter of time. The terms of an armistice might be . . . '[27] And he proceeded to list them as if the Dardanelles operation was virtually a *fait accompli*. His confidence, as so often, spread to the War Council, which at its meeting on 10 March planned what to do after the fall of Constantinople.

The outer forts had been silenced, and the results of the *Queen Elizabeth*'s firing with her 15-inch guns were awe-inspiring. The troubles began when the ships tackled the next stage, the intermediate defences, which could only be fired at from inside the narrow straits. Churchill, when fully informed after the excitement had cooled, put the Navy's problem in a nutshell. Minefields were the major stumbling block.

The defences with which our Fleet was confronted after the fall of the Outer Forts . . . consisted of four factors – forts, mobile howitzers, minefield batteries and minefields – all well combined but all mutually dependent. The minefields blocked the passage of the Straits and kept the Fleet beyond their limits. The minefield batteries prevented the sweeping of the minefields. The forts protected the minefield batteries by keeping battleships at a distance with their long guns. The mobile howitzers kept the battleships on the move and increased the difficulty of overcoming the forts.[28]

But other reasons for the impasse were, first, the conduct of Carden, who remained barren of ideas and drive from the beginning and until he belatedly resigned, and, second, the poor standard of shooting. One officer thought this was because the gunnery officers 'were not thinkers; they were used to shooting at floating targets and could not adapt themselves to shooting at targets on shore'. Nor, it seemed, could they adapt themselves to 'blind' firing with another ship spotting. This occurred when the *Irresistible* inside the straits was spotting for the *Queen Elizabeth* firing over the peninsula. 'Q.E. fired one round (15-inch) which landed about 3,000 yards beyond the target (a fort); *Irresistible* signalled '3,000 over'; presently Q.E. fired again; again the shot landed about 3,000 yards beyond the target. The same thing happened to every one of the many rounds fired by Q.E. (except one); no attention was paid to *Irresistible*'s corrections and all the rounds missed the target by the same amount.'[29]

On the same day when the War Council met to consider the Turkish surrender terms, Carden was drawing up his first pessimistic report. 'We are for the present checked by absence of efficient air reconnaissance,' he began shamelessly, 'the necessity of clearing the minefield, and the presence of a large number of movable howitzers on both sides of the Straits, whose positions up to the present we have not been able to locate. Meanwhile, every effort will be made to clear the minefields by night with two battleships in support . . . Our experience shows that gunfire alone will not render the forts innocuous . . . '[30] The truth was at last being driven home.

The minesweepers were adapted North Sea trawlers manned by their regular peacetime crews turned almost overnight into reservist ratings. They were as intrepid and stalwart as fishermen anywhere but they had had no disciplinary training and no experience of being under fire. Seven of these vessels were ordered out on the night of 10 March to steam against the strong (4-knot) current to a point above the main minefield and sweep back again, supported by the gunfire of the *Canopus*, now withdrawn from the mud of the distant Falklands, a light cruiser, and destroyers. It was a fiasco. It was found impossible to shoot out the Turkish searchlights, which spotlit the trawlers and subjected them to an intolerable hail of fire from mobile howitzers. One was sunk, the others hastily retired.

Carden tried the next night, using stealth, with the trawlers going in alone. 'To put it briefly,' wrote Keyes, 'the sweepers turned tail and fled directly they were fired upon.'[31] When Churchill heard he sent a sharply worded telegram to Carden telling him that caution must be thrown to the winds and casualties and losses expected. He then detailed how the forts in the Narrows must be overwhelmed 'at decisive range' while 'landing parties might destroy the guns of the forts'. Commenting on this, a captain wrote, 'It is one of those peculiarly objectionable messages, in which the man on the spot is not only urged to attack but told how to do it ... In its easy and superficial reference to very difficult or impracticable tasks, it bears the unmistakable impress of the First Lord's hand.'[32]

Further efforts by the trawler crews, now strengthened by a number of regular ratings, were equally futile. If the minesweepers' gear was not shot to pieces first, it was virtually impossible to get it out under the intense fire. The courage of the men was sublime. Churchill believed they were lacking in spirit. Carden resigned on 16 March, ill, sick at heart, and close to a nervous breakdown. He was replaced by Admiral John De Robeck, 'worth a dozen of Carden' judged General William Birdwood, commander of the Australian and New Zealand Corps (Anzacs) newly arrived in Egypt.

Intent on silencing the guns, and the armchair critics in London, in one supreme effort on 18 March, De Robeck sent his four most powerful ships, the *Queen Elizabeth*, *Inflexible*, *Lord Nelson*, and *Agamemnon* six miles up the Straits to silence the Narrows forts. Two battleships engaged the intermediate defence batteries, while six more bombarded the Narrows batteries at point-blank range. The plan was to send in the minesweepers as soon as all the batteries had been silenced.

The ear-splitting and sustained thunder of the guns continued almost without a pause from 11.25 a.m. until 4 p.m., and the peninsula and adjoining mainland was covered by a vast pall of smoke and dust. Shortly before 2 p.m. a single explosion of even greater volume caused eyes to turn towards the French battleship *Bouvet*. She had struck a mine, her magazine had blown up and she sank in a few minutes with almost all her crew of 640 men.

The trawlers then went in once more and were met with undiminished fire from the howitzers. All six of them were forced to retire. That was not an end to De Robeck's catastrophes. At 4.11 the *Inflexible* struck a mine, leaving her out of action for six weeks. Then the *Irresistible* struck another mine, drifted towards the Asiatic shore and foundered during the night. The same fate befell the *Ocean* when she went to the battleship's aid. At this point the C.-in-C. withdrew and cancelled the operation.

One man was credited with causing these casualties, and with saving Constantinople, for the forts were down to their last few rounds when De Robeck withdrew. Lieutenant-Colonel Geehl was a Turkish mine expert. 'He had observed warships manoeuvring just inside the slack water parallel to the Asiatic shore, and thought it worth trying to lay mines there.' Flight-Lieutenant Williamson continues: 'On the night of March 8th from a small steamer, the *Nousret*, he laid a line of

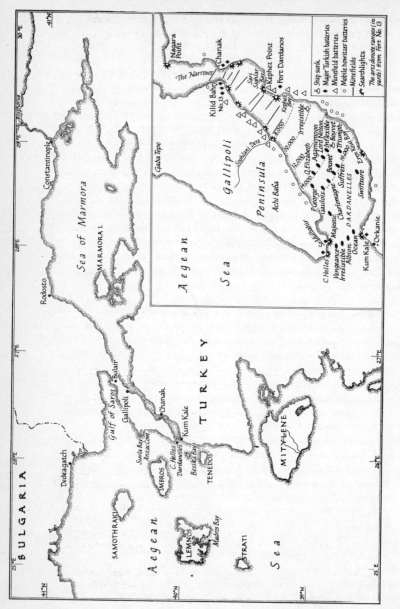

Map 4. The Sea of Marmora and approaches. The Dardanelles, 18 March 1915

20 mines in this position. It was these mines that did all the damage. It was a perfect modern version of the David and Goliath story; with the British Fleet as Goliath, and Geehl as David, with the *Nousret* as his sling, and the mines as his pebbles.'[33]

The minefields were intact, missing only those which had served their purpose. And, as was learned later, the sum total of that gigantic bombardment was the loss to Turkey of two 14-inch guns and a few smaller ones. The Dardanelles was as impenetrable as ever. And it was not learned until later that the dire Russian crisis in the Caucasus against the Turkish Army, the *raison d'être* of the Dardanelles operation, had been resolved by a resounding Turkish defeat at Sarikamish in Armenia before a gun had been fired at Gallipoli. But the Russians told their allies nothing.

Some time before this expensive and memorable repulse and even before the first bombardment, the use of supporting troops was being considered, in spite of Churchill's belief that the Navy could do it alone. Inside the Admiralty, Jackson made the firm statement that a naval bombardment made sense only if 'a strong military force is ready to assist in the operation, or, at least, follow it up immediately the forts are silenced'.[34] Fisher agreed with Richmond when he declared that 'the bombardment of the Dardanelles, even if all the forts are destroyed, can be nothing but a local success'.[35]

Army opinion, at home and on the spot, was that there would have to be a landing. General Sir William Birdwood was despatched by Kitchener to give his judgement and returned with the same verdict. From a diplomatic point of view, it was thought essential that an army should be ready to land if the Navy failed in order to prevent a severe loss of Allied prestige. Kitchener told the War Council on 24 February that he 'felt that if the Fleet would not get through the Straits unaided, the Army ought to see the business through'.[36]

At an informal meeting of the War Council on 16 February, decisions were made that were to change the course of the war, lead to ruined reputations and the deaths of more than 100,000 men. Hankey recounted what occurred in a 'most secret and strictly personal' letter to Balfour the following day:

Yesterday decisions of the very first importance were arrived at . . . I was not present, but I have received a full account of what happened from Mr Lloyd George, Lord Fisher and the Prime Minister, who asked me to communicate the following decisions to you:—

1. The XXIXth Division, now forming part of Sir John French's army [in France] to be despatched to Lemnos at the earliest possible date. It is hoped that it may be able to sail within 9 or 10 days.

2. Arrangements to be made for a force to be despatched from England, if required.

3. The above forces, in conjunction with the 4 batallions of Royal Marines already despatched, to be available in case of necessity to support the naval attack on the Dardanelles.

4. Horse boats to be taken out with the XXIXth Division, and the Admiralty to make arrangements to collect small craft and lighters in the Levant.

The Naval Attack on the Dardanelles forts begins on Friday morning, and it is agreed by all naval officers that sooner or later troops will be required . . . I am immensely relieved by this decision, though I fear it has been made rather late, and I should like more men. This is a decisive operation against the decisive front of the Turkish Empire, and, if undertaken at all we ought to throw in every man we have . . . [37]

Three days later, Kitchener made the decision not to release the XXIXth Division after all, citing as the excuse that recent Russian defeats might lead to Germany transferring troops from her eastern to western fronts. Churchill testified to the Dardanelles Commission later that, although he had every confidence that the Navy could break through on its own, he wanted troops 'to reap the fruits or to help the Navy through if we were checked'. Now his voice was loudest in protest at Kitchener's decision, which was not reversed until 10 March.

If this Division had gone as was decided [Churchill said later] on the 16th February and in the transports we had collected, we could have begun to embark it from the 22nd; it would have reached the Dardanelles about the same time as the Naval attack culminated . . . In that event if we had met with success the Army would have been able to reap the fruits. And confronted as we were with a check, the Army would have been strong enough in the opinion of Generals to begin an immediate attack upon the Gallipoli Peninsula . . .

If the decisions of 16 February had been implemented with speed and efficiency, there is little doubt that the single weak Turkish Division could have been overwhelmed with relatively few casualties. Instead, the operation was conducted without any sense of urgency, procrastination governed every step before the fatal landings were made, and blunders abounded at all command levels during the subsequent fighting. On the credit side, the Dardanelles campaign showed up so many weaknesses in planning and execution, and scarred its main conceiver so badly, that when Churchill faced the giant amphibious task of invading the Continent thirty years later, he created a whole new amphibious command with priority powers to prepare for it.

Those who landed in Normandy with such relatively few casualties in 1944 owed their lives in part to those who fell on the beaches of Gallipoli.

The naval contribution was limited to an auxiliary level as soon as the Army arrived in strength. But before then Churchill refused to be dismayed by the disasters of 18 March. 'I regarded it as only the first of several days' fighting,' he testified, 'though the loss in ships sunk or disabled was unpleasant. It never occurred to me for a moment that we should not go on.'[38] With this in view, he sent out more old battleships and more encouraging telegrams to De Robeck. For a while the Admiral played along with his chief and gave signs that a new attack would soon be launched. Then on the morning of 22 March he appeared after all to have tamely accepted defeat. There was a conference on board the *Queen Elizabeth* attended by both military and naval commanders. The recently appointed Army General, Sir Ian Hamilton, recorded in his diary: 'The moment we sat down De Robeck told us *he was now quite clear he could not get through without the help of all my troops.*'

On the following day De Robeck sent a long telegram of explanation and justification to the Admiralty, referring to the mine menace and the numerous guns 'not more than a small proportion [of which] can be put out of action by gunfire'. It could have been a Staff contingency report prepared a month earlier showing why the first naval attack should not take place. He proposed now to wait until 14 April, when Hamilton had told him the Army would be ready, and then conduct a combined assault. Nor would the Admiral, in the teeth of the most strenuous opposition from Churchill, change his mind. On 24 March Churchill telegraphed a final entreaty – 'the forts are short of ammunition', 'it is probable they have not got many mines'. The message could not be an order because, 'for the first time since the war began,' as Churchill himself described the occasion, 'high words were used',[39] and he was opposed by Oliver, Wilson, Jackson, and Fisher when he proposed to make his telegram a demand rather than a plea. In spite of this near-unanimity of opposition (Churchill's secretary, Charles Bartolomé, stuck by his chief), the telegram when it was sent made no reference to the opposition of his confederates. But the response from De Robeck was still as if he had been deafened by the cacophony of that last bombardment. The Straits remained silent, while the Germans reorganized and strengthened many times over the defences, and the Turks poured in more troops and hundreds more guns from the Austrian Skoda works.

If ever clear-cut evidence were needed that underwater weaponry now dominated sea warfare and that the big gun was only of secondary importance, the naval opening of the Dardanelles campaign provides it. The Straits were already littered with the wrecks of men o'war sunk by a few cheap mines. Ashore, the forts and batteries were virtually intact. And now a single torpedo explosion was to lead to the fall of both Fisher and Churchill.

Fisher always subsequently claimed that he had supported the Dardanelles naval operations at the outset with reluctance and in order not to disturb the unanimity governing the conduct of Admiralty affairs. During February and March he observed with growing disquiet the draining of naval strength from home waters – 'the vital area'. 'To dispatch any more fighting ships of any kind to the Dardanelles operations', he told Churchill (31 March 1915) 'would be to court serious losses at home.'[40] In this view he was of course solidly backed by Jellicoe and Beatty, and, with increasing vehemence, by all the Sea Lords.

Fisher was convinced that large-scale action in the North Sea was imminent. It was known during March that severe pressure was being imposed on Holland to declare war on Germany's side, and that if this happened the High Seas Fleet was certain to make a demonstration. Meanwhile, Churchill had 'collared' sixteen battleships, twenty-four destroyers, the only seaplane carrier, and countless auxiliary craft. The one-way stream was still flowing to swell the numbers, which included Jellicoe's best battleship, a sorely needed battle-cruiser (*hors de combat* from a mine) and the two best pre-dreadnoughts.

Fisher and the Sea Lords were feeling more strongly than ever that they were no longer taking any part in naval affairs. Fisher's predecessor had been nicknamed Prince 'I concur' Battenberg. And now the time for concurrence had passed. By 9 May, the Army which had landed on the beaches of Gallipoli in strength on 25 April was completely deadlocked. Churchill started to raise again the now-discredited notion of a Navy-only operation – not of course on the previous scale, 'a limited operation' as he defined it. But Fisher knew that if there was even a partial success, it would rapidly grow to a size beyond control. Meanwhile the warships all remained at risk, and U-boats were reported to be on the way. Then on the night of 11–12 May a German-manned Turkish destroyer succeeded in sending a torpedo into the battleship *Goliath*. It sank instantly with the loss of 570 lives. It could as easily have been the *Queen Elizabeth*. The following day, Fisher insisted that this super-dreadnought be brought home. Churchill was forced to agree but insisted upon her replacement with two pre-dreadnought battleships and two monitors.

When Kitchener learned at a conference that this great battleship, with its dominant silhouette and unmatched power, which from the beginning had symbolized the Navy's participation in the operations, was to be withdrawn, he called it a 'desertion' and expressed great unhappiness. Fisher then stood up, exuding all the pent-up resentment and frustration he had suffered over many weeks, and said excitedly that if the battleship did not come home that night at full speed he would resign instantly. He got his way.

The next day, 14 May, at a meeting of the War Council, the need for further naval reinforcements for the Dardanelles was discussed. Fisher was appalled. Monitors, shallow landing craft, all the *matériel* he had been authorized to build for his Baltic project were being sucked into the bottomless pit of the Dardanelles. Everyone present at that meeting described the mood as gloomy and totally pessimistic. A new offensive on the Western Front was already faltering. The shell shortage was critical, and what was worse, *The Times* had that day exposed the scandal it had started.

That evening Fisher went to bed with the new agreed figures for naval reinforcements engraved on his mind. While he slept, Churchill was busy with new calculations, and before dawn had completed an extensive memorandum demanding additional ships, aircraft, guns, and other *matériel*: nine new heavy monitors in all, two out of five of the newest submarines being delivered to the Navy, and the latest seaplanes. The memorandum was couched in the peremptory tone of a C.-in-C. to a junior captain which had become so depressingly familiar to all members of the Board. This time it was to prove his undoing. 'They cannot both run the show', Beatty had said.

Fisher received the memorandum at his usual early hour of awakening, and his outrage knew no bounds. Churchill later wrote in his memoirs of this moment, 'The old Admiral, waking in the early morning, saw himself confronted again with the minutes proposing the reinforcements . . . '[41] This was untrue, and Churchill knew it. These were *additional* reinforcements. It was in order to conceal from his readers the fact that the figures had been greatly increased overnight that Churchill wrote 'again'.

Considering the pressure under which he was suffering and the natural volatility of his temperament, Fisher's reply was mild as well as firm. He was leaving his partner and one-time friend. 'After further anxious reflection I have come to the regretted conclusion I am unable to remain any longer as your colleague . . . I find it increasingly difficult to adjust myself to the increasing daily requirements of the Dardanelles to meet your views . . . This is not fair to you besides being extremely distasteful to me . . . '.

Fisher had threatened to resign eight times already in 1915. Churchill took as little notice of this note as earlier threats. But Fisher was not to be found at the Admiralty that morning, and Churchill, increasingly alarmed, could get no answer from his house. Fisher was at the Treasury telling Lloyd George of his decision. Lloyd George thought he meant it this time, unlike Asquith who commented, 'Fisher's always resigning.'

Churchill wrote a long letter of appeal, knowing that his own future was at stake.

Admiralty, Whitehall
May 15th, 1915

Private and Confidential

My dear Fisher,

The only thing to think of now is what is best for the country and for the brave men who are fighting. Anything which does injury to those interests will be very harshly judged by history, on whose stage we now are.

I do not understand what is the specific cause which had led you to resign. If I did, I might cure it. When we parted last night I thought we were in agreement. The proposals I made to you by minute were, I thought, in general accord with your views, and in any case were for discussion between us. Our personal friendship is and I trust will remain unimpaired.

It is true the moment is anxious and our difficulties grave. But I am sure that with loyalty and courage we shall come through safely and successfully. You could not let it be said that you had thrown me over because things were for the time being going badly at the Dardanelles.

In every way I have tried to work in the closest sympathy with you. The men you wanted in the places you wanted them, the ships you designed, every proposal you have formally made for naval action, I have agreed to. My own responsibilities are great, and also I am the one who gets the blame for anything that goes wrong. But I have scrupulously adhered to our original agreement that we should do nothing important without consulting each other. If you think this is not so, surely you should tell me in what respect.

In order to bring you back to the Admiralty I took my political life in my hands with the King and the Prime Minister, as you know well. You then promised to stand by me and see me through. If you now go at this bad moment and thereby let loose upon me the spite and malice of those who are your enemies even more than they are mine, it will be a melancholy ending to our six months of successful war and administration. The discussions which will arise will strike a cruel blow at the fortunes of the Army now struggling on the Gallipoli Peninsula, and cannot fail to invest with an air of disaster a mighty enterprise, which, with patience, can and will certainly be carried to success.

Many of the anxieties of the winter are past – the harbours are protected, the great flow of new construction is arriving. We are far stronger at home than we have ever been, and the great reinforcement is now at hand.

I hope you will come to see me to-morrow afternoon. I have a proposition to make to you, with the assent of the Prime Minister, which may resolve some of the anxieties and difficulties which you feel about the measures necessary to support the Army at the Dardanelles.

Though I shall stand to my post until relieved, it will be a very great grief to me to part from you; and our rupture will be profoundly injurious to every public interest.

Yours ever,
W.[42]

Fisher's whereabouts remained a mystery until a messenger succeeded in tracking him down to a private room at the Charing Cross Hotel. The messenger delivered an order from Asquith that in the King's name he must remain at his post. As the news filtered through the corridors of Whitehall and the royal palaces, the appeals for him to stay fell about Fisher. '*Stick* to your *Post* like *Nelson!*' wrote Queen Alexandra: 'The Nation and we all have such full confidence in you and *I* and they will not suffer you to go. You are the Nation's hope and we trust you!'[43] Jellicoe telegraphed, 'I would far sooner lose some ships than see you leave the Admiralty.'[44] Beatty followed with another agonized appeal: 'If it is of any value to you to know it, the Fleet is numbed with the thought of the possibility. Please God it is NOT possible for we absolutely refuse to believe it.'[45]

Churchill wrote a further long letter of appeal the next day, pointing to the effects his resignation would have on the whole Dardanelles venture, encouraging the enemy and perhaps leading to Italy ('trembling on the brink') to draw back from joining the Allies. Fisher was offered a seat in the Cabinet if he would withdraw his resignation – 'I rejected the 30 pieces of silver to betray my country', he responded.

Fleet Street soon had wind of what was up. 'LORD FISHER MUST NOT GO' headlined the *Globe*: 'Lord Fisher or Mr Churchill?' began their main story. 'Expert or amateur?': *The Times* wanted Fisher to replace Churchill as First Lord. The stories brought a new flood of appeals to him to stay. Asquith's political framework was cracking from pressures from all sides. The Conservative Press was after him almost as fiercely as after Churchill. On 17 May

Asquith decided that the only way to survive was by forming a coalition.

Fisher, for all his vanity, was surprised at the outcry and the strength of the appeals he had caused. Among the numerous letters he received was one from his old friend and admirer, Lord Esher, whose influence in affairs was still very powerful: '*My dear, dear Jackie,*' it began, 'You will never *permanently* paper up these quarrels. The only thing to be done is to revive the office of Lord High Admiral and take it yourself. Otherwise we are beaten presently at sea.'[46] This was the only communication that shook Fisher's resolve. 'Lord High Admiral' had the right ring. And if the Conservatives came into the Government, Churchill stood no chance of survival after all the attacks he had suffered and with his enterprise at Gallipoli in a shambles.

In too great haste and guided by vaingloriousness and too little judgement, Fisher drew up a document which he despatched precipitately to Asquith. He would withdraw his resignation, he wrote, if it was agreed that Churchill would be dismissed and 'is not in the Cabinet'; that he could have 'an entirely new Board of Admiralty'; that Churchill's successor 'should be absolutely restricted to policy and parliamentary procedure'; that 'I should have the sole absolute authority for all new construction' and 'complete professional charge of the war at sea . . . '[47]

Everything was wrong with this document, most especially its timing. While the crisis raged in Whitehall, Room 40 at the Admiralty was busy decoding German intercepts which strongly suggested that the High Seas Fleet was coming out. Fisher, alternately plotting and sulking in his room, evinced little interest when he heard. He was no longer needed, he told those who informed him. A decisive sea battle, a new Trafalgar, appeared imminent, and Jacky Fisher, still the supreme commander, refused to participate!

When this word of Fisher's dereliction of duty got about in the Admiralty and through the higher echelons of Whitehall, there was an instant reversal of feeling about the old Admiral. Asquith thought he ought to be shot. The King, who had predicted trouble from the start, was outraged: he should be court-martialled and hanged. The closest of his friends thought he had temporarily lost his reason under stress, and for his own sake, the sooner he went away the better. His enemies regarded his behaviour as characteristic. A great many people simply thought he had gone mad. He was, without doubt, temporarily unhinged.

Fisher's resignation had still not been accepted when he left for

Scotland by train on 22 May. The acceptance caught him up by telegraph at Crewe junction. The uproar and outrage he had created no longer sounded sweet in his ears, and he wanted peace and privacy 'absolutely out of reach of interviews and snapshotters!' He acquired both at Dungavel in Lanarkshire, the home of the Duke and Duchess of Hamilton. The Duke had for long been an invalid, the Duchess had been Fisher's closest woman friend for over six years.

By this time the pressure on Churchill had become too strong, and he was forced to resign. In spite of all his fears, he thought he might survive. When the blow fell it left, according to his private secretary, Eddie Marsh, 'a horrible wound and mutilation . . . it's like Beethoven deaf'. For a man who savoured power with so much relish, it was a bitter time. As always, he was wonderfully supported by his wife, and the encouragement of his friends. J. L. Garvin, alone among newspaper editors, afforded him some consolation. 'He is young,' he wrote in the *Observer*, 'he has lion-hearted courage. No number of enemies can fight down his ability and force. His hour of triumph will come.'

Churchill, who described his situation as experiencing 'the austerity of changing fortune', was observed by the Prime Minister's daughter, Cynthia. 'He looks unhappy but is very dignified and un-bitter. I have never liked him so much. Clemmie said she had always known it would happen from the day Fisher was appointed, and Winston said that, if he could do things over again, he would do just the same with regard to appointing Fisher as he says he has done really great organising work.'[48]

The Navy was thankful to see the back of the First Lord. Jellicoe said that he had for a long time 'thoroughly distrusted Mr Churchill'. Beatty spoke for the Grand Fleet when he wrote to his wife, 'The Navy breathes freer now it is rid of the succubus Churchill'. There was little comfort for Churchill in the public utterances of Fleet Street with the single exception of Garvin.

The cause of fair judgement is not served by regarding Churchill's first term at the Admiralty as a mere shadow of his later achievements or their preface. It must be seen in the context of the times, unrelated to the period 1940–45. It was good for the Navy and the country that he should have been appointed First Lord in 1912. He brought with him into the Admiralty a breath of fresh air, and his presence with his enthusiasm, drive, eagerness, and transparent relish in his work and love of the Navy, inspired many more officers than those to whom his overbearing and tactless style gave offence. It needed a dominant and ruthless figure to battle through the Fisher–Wilson defences against the formation of a War Staff. While he succumbed all too swiftly to the Navy's obsession with the dreadnought, the big gun, and the offensive spirit, to the neglect of 'back-up' in the shape of properly protected bases, mines and torpedoes, the material benefits introduced during his time and the numerous reforms proved valuable. Far more valuable was the quality of youthful zest and joy which he brought to the Admiralty, and, by virtue of his unsurpassed power to inspire those about him, spread throughout the Navy, blowing away the last of the Victorian cobwebs. Churchill was responsible for a process of reform and improvement of spirit that complemented and rounded off Fisher's administrative and *matériel* reforms of 1904–10, and was equally valuable. There is no question that the Navy was a service of higher quality in every department in 1914 than in 1894. The achievement was less visibly spectacular than the parallel achievement of Germany's creation of a great fleet from scratch, but it was at least as great in its own way and it was to save the nation from defeat.

Churchill should have gone with Battenberg at the outset of war. For quite different reasons, his term of office should have been limited to peacetime. His leadership in war had very few redeeming features. He failed to draw on the advice of his Board because he either knew the answers or did not want to hear them if they were contrary to his own. He was divisive and impatient, and, as so many complained, ran the show from top to bottom. He took advantage of his superiority in rank to abuse his powers; this shrank the inspiration and initiative of his Board members just as much as his personal and insistent control of distant commanders reduced their instinct for initiative. For this reason he failed to gain the confidence of the commanders at sea as completely as he failed with his advisers. Mistakes that can be traced to others were numerous, but in many cases they would not have occurred if Churchill had not been there, fussing over everyone and everything, causing dismay and resentment. The system had enough faults already; it was no better for being abused by him.

Before his youthful self-confidence and arrogance had matured and mellowed, Churchill was an almost impossible leader for sailors to work with. The influence with which Churchill invigorated the Navy before the fighting began was almost wholly baleful after August 1914.

The difficulty that Asquith faced in May 1915, among the multitudinous problems demanding his attention, was to find a successor. There was as grave a dearth of candidates for the office of First Lord of the Admiralty to succeed Churchill as there was for a First Sea Lord to succeed Fisher.

11

THE UNDERSEA WAR

The opening of U-boat warfare – Strong internal division in Germany on the breaking of international law and the pursuit of unrestricted U-boat warfare against merchantmen – The 'hawks' prevail – The Lusitania *torpedoing and hostile American reaction – Early German U-boat losses – Fisher and the founding of the British submarine force – Hazardous and productive operations in the Baltic – The Dardanelles campaign and the equal daring and skill of British submarine crews in the Straits and Sea of Marmora – The development of the RNAS and early operations at Gallipoli*

ON 20 October 1914, fourteen miles off the coast of Norway, the 866-ton British steamer, SS *Glitra* was apprehended by *U-17*, Lieutenant-Commander Feldkircher. The crew were given time to lower and board their boats, the *Glitra*'s sea cocks were opened and she at once went to the bottom. It was a very correct and non-violent overture to a bloody campaign, even though the boarding party tore up the ship's flag. The operation was carried out in accordance with international law governing commerce warfare which held that everyone on board must be 'placed in safety, with their goods and chattels if possible'. The commonplace little *Glitra* had only one distinction: she was the first merchantman ever to be sunk by a submarine.

This relatively trivial incident was formally noted by the Admiralty but aroused no comment. Four months later, the commander of the Fourth Battle Squadron, Rear-Admiral Alexander Duff, wrote in his diary: 'With submarines alone she [Germany] cannot hope to inflict any serious damage on our merchant shipping.'[1] Most authorities would have agreed with Admiral Duff, one of the most respected 'brains' in the service. In the first six months of war ten merchantmen totalling 20,000 tons were sent to the bottom as a result of U-boat attack, mostly in a gentlemanly manner and at trivial cost to the Germans who did not at that stage of the war waste torpedoes.

When the subject came up for discussion in 1901, Tirpitz had told the Reichstag that the new Navy had no need for submersibles. 'We have no money to waste on experimental vessels. We must leave such luxuries to wealthier states like France and England.'

The German U-boat branch had, ironically, come into being as a result of Russian encouragement during the Russo-Japanese War.

The Russians ordered from Krupps three submarines propelled by a combination of internal combustion engines, dynamos, and electric motors for use when submerged. The little boats were designed with a double hull, the fuel being stowed between. There was a single torpedo tube set into the bows, and three 17.7-inch torpedoes were carried. The crew, who suffered the most cramped and unhealthy conditions numbered about fifteen. The boats, the *Karp*, *Karas*, and *Kambala*, worked successfully and were delivered to the Russian port of Libau under their own power. What happened to them after that no one knows. But these Russian boats caused Tirpitz to change his mind, and in the 1905–6 naval estimates, some £70,000 was set aside 'for experiments connected with submarines'. *U-1* was a qualified success on its sea trials in July 1908. She was all right for coastal operations but, ran the report, 'her employment in the high seas is attended with danger'.

By this time, France had already completed sixty submarines, and Britain rather more. German progress remained cautious, especially after the accidental sinking of *U-3* in Kiel harbour. But between May 1908 and May 1910 the first serious, non-experimental boats were put in hand, fourteen in all, with a surface displacement of 500 tons, armed with four torpedo tubes, six mines and a single small gun. They were supposed to manage 15 knots on the surface but never achieved that speed. Suitable engines were the limiting factor, and the answer lay in the diesel engine. The diesel, an all-German invention, had been in production since 1893. The Wright brothers had experienced the problem of inadequate power/weight ratio with their flying machines and had not solved it until they produced their own engine in 1903. Krupps experienced the same problem with the diesel. It was the rival firm of MAN (Maschinen-fabrik Augsburg-Nürnberg AG) that produced the power units for the first Krupps-built submarine, the *U-19*, in 1913. Krupps followed up with an engine of their own, and by the outbreak of war all the most modern craft were diesel powered, a form of propulsion which endured in all navies until the advent of nuclear power. The diesel engine produced no 'spark', the heavy oil was far safer than petroleum, and it was a reliable, long-lasting unit. The newest German submarines, the *U-23* to *U-30*, were armed with two 12-pounders and a pair of light anti-aircraft guns, a pointer to the potential threat of another new weapon. But the most significant item in the specification was their endurance, which ran up to 5,000 miles. Clearly they were ocean-going men o'war intended for operation in the Atlantic. Their numbers were still small, but seen with the advantage of hindsight, the destructive potential of these modern U-boats was formidable – much more formidable than the German Navy appreciated.

While the main body of the High Seas Fleet, which had been off the Norwegian coast in late July, returned to the Elbe and the Jade, the U-boat flotillas were in operation from almost the first day of war, and remained so until the last day, the most active as well as the most destructive of all classes of warship. At this early stage, the U-boats' task was to reconnoitre the North Sea to discover what blockade patrols were being set up by the British and to discover the whereabouts of enemy squadrons and fleets. It was the U-boats which brought back the first evidence of the unexpected absence of a close blockade.

The activities of Commander H. Bauer, who was later to become Commodore of the High Seas Fleet submarines, were typical of these early days, which included no specific orders to attack merchant shipping. Bauer commanded ten U-boats, *U-5, 7, 8, 9* and *U-13* to *18*, which left their base at Heligoland early on the morning of 6 August and proceeded northwards widely spread out and expecting shortly to meet the first British patrols. But it was not until the 9th that *U-18* sighted the first British warship, a cruiser. A destroyer was reported a few minutes later. The flotilla had spotted not a patrol but the outer screen of the Grand Fleet, and very quickly paid the price for it. The light cruiser *Birmingham*, Captain Arthur Duff, spotted a periscope and turned so swiftly and accurately that he succeeded in ramming and sinking *U-15* with all hands. It was an achievement which gave the Fleet great encouragement, although unfortunately this all too rapidly turned to 'periscopeitis' and Jellicoe jitters.

The U-boats took their revenge four weeks later when Lieutenant-Commander Otto Hersing, later to become one of the great 'aces', spotted the British flotilla leader *Pathfinder* after he had ventured as far as St Abb's Head. Hersing took aim at just short of one mile range, considered a great distance. His accuracy was as good with the torpedo as Spee's with the gun. He struck the ship fair and square, and the *Pathfinder* went down with almost all hands.

Although she was a new ship the effect of her loss was out of all proportion to her value. After 5 September 1914 fear of the submarine was no longer theoretical. Jellicoe's 'First Battle of Scapa' and the pursuit of the seal, was followed by the Battle Cruiser Squadron's 'Battle of Jemimaville'. As Beatty's battle-cruisers steamed slowly into the main anchorage at Cromarty, a destroyer's bow wave was misidentified as the wake of a U-boat's periscope. Fire was at once opened on it, causing damage to the roofs of the nearby village of

Jemimaville, where a baby was also slightly hurt. One of the ship's doctors was summoned, and the flag-lieutenant, Ralph Seymour, who accompanied the surgeon, assured the parents that two if not three U-boats had been sunk, and there were no survivors.

The loss of the *Aboukir*, *Hogue*, and *Cressy* froze any laughter at these diversions. But while the U-boat service was delighted with its early successes, the German command had no idea of the serious effect it was having on the dispositions and strategy of the Grand Fleet. One British admiral exclaimed in chagrin, 'It is the German Fleet that now controls the North Sea!' Admiral Sir Percy Scott later recalled saying good-night to Jellicoe at Scapa before the base's protection was complete, the C.-in-C. laconically replying, 'I wonder.'[2] Scott puzzled over the continuing failure of the German command to take advantage of the situation brought about by the U-boat flotillas. Was it that the German submarine commanders 'lacked pluck', or as Jellicoe later surmised, 'the German mind could not believe that we would be such fools as to place our Fleet in a position where it was open to submarine or destroyer attack . . . If the Germans had had half a dozen men of the stamp of our submarine commanders, we should now be a German colony.'[3]

Although the submarine had a profound effect on the conduct of the surface fleet, it did not in fact sink a great number of warships on either side. It was the merchant fleets that were to suffer. This was due to a decision reached in Germany at about the time Admiral Duff was making his prediction. Influenced by the destruction of von Spee's squadron, the disappointing performance of the other surface raiders, and especially of their fast armed merchantmen of which much had been expected, the German high command began to press for an unrestricted U-boat campaign against Allied shipping. This flouted international law and the traditional code of conduct at sea honoured for centuries by all but pirates. On 4 February 1915, Germany declared a war zone round the British Isles in which ships would be sunk without warning. All the old formalities of 'visit and search' were to be dispensed with, and neutrals were warned that their shipping was equally at risk.

When this had first been proposed, Bethmann Hollweg opposed the plan, not out of any fastidious feelings but because of the bad effect it would have on neutrals, especially the United States and Italy. The Chancellor eventually gave way under the pressure of the admirals and the Kaiser showed no hesitation in approving. The German pretext was that Britain had already broken international law by abolishing the distinction between conditional and absolute contraband in her blockade. The German plan was for an up-to-date version of the old *guerre de course* operated by men o'war which, if obliged to abide by the rules and operate on the surface giving fair warning, sacrificed their one advantage, their *raison d'être*, their invisibility.

In order to blunt the effects of international calumny after the war and provide an alibi for the *Kriegsmarine*, German historians put it about that no peacetime plans had been prepared for a U-boat campaign against Allied shipping, and it was resorted to only after illegalities in the Allied blockade of Germany became evident. 'The thought of cutting England off from her sea supply by means of submarines', wrote Admiral Hermann Bauer, 'had in no manner been considered, since such a submarine war against English sea trade would not have been in conformity with the [1909] London Declaration.'[4] Statements like this had the desired effect of temporarily distorting the record. But a Staff study had been prepared by Kapitänleutnant Ulrich-Eberhard Blum on a U-boat campaign against British shipping on behalf of the Submarine Inspectorate at Kiel in May 1914.[5] It envisaged a fleet of 222 U-boats, and was sent for approval to Tirpitz the following month. Then again, Kapitän A. Gayer wrote, 'Before the outbreak of the war one of the best technical experts in this weapon, Lieutenant-Commander Blum, had calculated the number of submarines necessary to conduct cruiser warfare against England, and had placed this number at 200.'[6]

By early October 1914, Bauer himself was already pressing for an all-out submarine war against British shipping. There is evidence that he was strongly influenced by reports from his commanders who were searching for warships of the volume of merchant shipping entering British west-coast ports. Another favourable factor was evident British anxiety about the depredations the submarine could create, including a widely-read article by Arthur Conan Doyle in the *Strand Magazine*, and the more violent outbursts of Jacky Fisher: as long before as 1903, Fisher had written an eulogy of the submarine and its power to revolutionize war at sea: 'Death near – momentarily – sudden – awful – invisible – unavoidable! Nothing conceivably more demoralising!'[7] Lord Esher was among those who were influenced by the more carefully reasoned passages from Fisher's paper. 'If he is right,' Esher wrote, 'and his argument appears unanswerable, it is difficult to exaggerate the vast impending revolution in naval warfare and naval strategy that the submarine will accomplish.'[8]

Ten years later, out of office, Fisher was still energetically proclaiming the cause of the submarine, and pressing Churchill, 'Build more submarines!' Still unsatisfied with progress, he wrote to

Churchill, 13 December 1913, 'I note by examining the Navy List there have been no less than 21 removals of Submarines since I was First Sea Lord and only *12* additions. *Do you think this is satisfactory?* and the remainder of "A" and "B" classes are now approaching 10 years of age and there are 19 of them which figure in our totals. *We are falling behind Germany in large submarines.*'9

Fisher held strongly to the view that the Germans in war would confirm his often-expressed belief that 'War has no amenities' and that as far as rules were concerned 'You might as well talk of humanizing Hell!' In 1913 he greatly shocked Battenberg and Churchill with a paper on submarines, which Churchill thought was 'brilliant and most valuable'. But there were 'a few points on which I am not convinced'. He continued: 'Of these the greatest is the question of the use of submarines to sink merchant vessels. I do not believe this would ever be done by a civilized Power.'10

Fisher later came in for heavy criticism for indirectly drawing the attention of the *Kriegsmarine* to the merits of the submarine, and thus helping to create the U-boat flotillas.

At the outset of the unrestricted war against enemy shipping the German Navy could call on only about twenty U-boats or one tenth the number called for in the Staff Study. A number of these were small and obsolescent, fit only for coastal work ('U.B.') and minelaying boats ('U.C.'). Moreover they could work only in three relays owing to the need for proper maintenance and rest for the crews. Allowing for the long and time-consuming voyage to the rich hunting-grounds of the Western Approaches, Irish Sea, and the western end of the English Channel, only two or three U-boats were operating at any one time in the west while another handful of smaller craft combed the east coast and eastern Channel approaches.

In less than two and a half months this tiny and inexperienced force had accounted for thirty-nine ships, almost all destroyed without warning and often with heavy loss of life. The worst of Fisher's fears seemed to be well founded. More than this number were lost in the single month of August 1915. There was a special significance to the attack on a large American oil tanker in April. Although the ship was towed into Scilly the captain was killed. The United States was outraged, and those who had fought against Fisher's conversion of the Fleet to oil instead of home-produced coal nodded sagely.

The one ship whose name signified the barbarity and revulsion felt for this new form of warfare was the *Lusitania*. She was the largest and fastest liner on the Atlantic run, and had completed five round trips, relying on her speed as the best protection against U-boat attack. The

13. Rear-Admiral the Hon. Horace Hood, Commanding
3rd Battle Cruiser Squadron

14. Rear-Admiral W. C. Pakenham,
Commanding 2nd Battle Cruiser Squadron

15. (*right*) Commodore Reginald Tyrwhitt, Commanding Harwich Force December 1913–May 1919

16. (*below*) Commodore William Goodenough (*left*), Commanding 1st (later 2nd) Light Cruiser Squadron July 1913–December 1916, talking to Acting Vice-Admiral Sir John De Robeck (*right*), C.-in-C. Eastern Mediterranean Squadron March 1915–June 1916

17. Early days of air sea power: HMS *Ark Royal* hoisting out a seaplane

18. Submarine *E11* cheered home after her successful cruise

19 *and* 20. German commanders at the Battle of Jutland: Vice-Admiral
Reinhard Scheer (*left*); Vice-Admiral Franz Hipper (*right*), Commanding
the High Seas Fleet's Scouting Forces

21. SMS *Blücher* going down at the Battle of Dogger Bank

22. Rear-Admiral Hugh Evan-Thomas, Commanding 5th Battle Squadron [*Drawing by Francis Dodd*]

23. Captain (later Rear-Admiral) Reginald Hall, Director of Naval Intelligence October 1914–January 1919 [*Drawing by Francis Dodd*]

24. Acting Vice-Admiral Sir Henry Oliver, Chief of Admiralty War Staff November 1914–May 1917 [*Drawing by Francis Dodd*]

25. Admiral Sir Henry Jackson, First Sea Lord May 1915–December 1916 [*Drawing by Francis Dodd*]

26. Seaplane Carrier HMS *Engadine*

27. A 15-inch shell, HMS *Queen Elizabeth*

28. *HMS Iron Duke*, Jellicoe's flagship at Jutland

29. Battle Cruiser SMS *Seydlitz*

Lusitania was almost home safely when at 2.15 p.m. on 7 May 1915 Lieutenant-Commander Schweiger in *U-20* held this massive target in his sights. A single torpedo was enough, although some survivors spoke of a second explosion. The liner took on a sharp list, and in twenty minutes was at the bottom with 1,198 of her passengers (many children) and crew, including 128 Americans.

Germany brushed aside American protests, justifying the attacks because full published warnings had been given in New York and the liner was carrying arms, and when the U-boat captain had seen how many people there were on board he had forborn from firing a second torpedo. The second explosion, claimed Schweiger, came from the ammunition. The authorities had been unwise enough to stow 173 tons of rifle cartridges and shrapnel before she sailed from New York. 'Never had there been such a war loss at sea,' wrote the official historian, 'never one which so violently outraged the laws of war and dictates of humanity.'[11]

Other sinkings during May were, however, so few that a feeling of complacency overcame the Admiralty, and Churchill boasted that 'the failure of the German submarine campaign'[12] was evident to the whole world. Defensive measures – nets, patrols, sweeps carrying explosive charges – were taking their toll of the small force of U-boats, and early experiments with submerged acoustics and depth charges were already showing favourable results by May 1915. Seven U-boats had been lost before the unrestricted campaign opened. Then March 1915 turned out to be a good month for U-boat killings. *U-8* was caught and sunk in the Dover nets. On 18 March the Fourth Battle Squadron, exercising off the Pentland Firth spotted a hostile submarine, and by brilliant manoeuvring the *Dreadnought* herself succeeded in ramming her. She revealed her identity when her bows rose high out of the water before her fatal plunge. It was *U-12*, commanded by Korvetten-Kapitän Weddigen, who had sunk the *Aboukir*, *Hogue*, and *Cressy*. The *Dreadnought* wore the flag of Doveton Sturdee, the luckiest admiral of the war. Another U-boat was rammed and sunk by HMS *Ariel*.

There is no evidence that the Germans were discouraged by these losses, or that they could not have been made good by new construction, which was going ahead so fast in German yards that sixty-one new craft had been completed by the end of 1915. The reason for cancelling this first unrestricted campaign was not military but diplomatic. On 19 August *U-24* sighted and torpedoed the liner *Arabic* off Ireland. Again there was heavy loss of life, including three Americans. The United States protest was so sharp that the German

Navy was ordered to modify its campaign. From 30 August U-boats were prohibited from attacking passenger liners of any nationality without giving prior warning and ensuring the safety of the passengers. This virtually ruled out as too risky any attacks on liners; and, still fearful of offending American opinion and bringing that country onto the side of the Allies, Germany later withdrew all her U-boats from western waters. For a time she concentrated on minelaying in the North Sea and a campaign in the Mediterranean where few American ships plied.

Unknown to the Allies, the U-boat war had now deteriorated into internecine conflict involving the Naval High Command, the German Chancellor, the Foreign Minister, and the Kaiser. It was a contest the 'hawks' were certain to win, but it was a long and anxious one in which American neutrality figured most prominently. By this time (winter 1915–16) the confidence of the naval high command in the effectiveness of the U-boat knew no bounds. The force was now an enthusiastic, substantial one, and it was straining at the leash. 'If after the Winter season, that is to say under suitable weather conditions,' claimed the German Chief of Naval Staff, 'the economic war by submarines be begun again with every means available and without restrictions which from the outset must cripple its effectiveness, a definite prospect may be held out that, judged by previous experience, British resistance will be broken in six months at the outside.'[13]

Admiral Henning von Holtzendorff failed to get his way at once. Still terrified of American intervention, the new campaign announced on 11 February 1916 was a conditional one, only enemy merchantmen inside the war zone being fair game without restriction. Outside the zone they could only be sunk without warning if they were armed, and passenger steamers were not to be touched. As many senior German naval officers predicted, including Admiral Reinhard Scheer, the new C.-in-C. of the High Seas Fleet, the campaign could not be successful with restrictions. Either U-boat commanders would be carried away by zeal or excitement when a vessel came into the sights and fail to check the target in detail, or, over-anxious to stay within the rules, would allow the enemy to escape.

On 24 March 1916 *U(B)-29* torpedoed the French passenger steamer *Sussex*, *en route* from Dieppe to Folkestone. She was carrying 380 passengers, and although the ship remained afloat a number of people, including Americans, were killed or injured. This time Washington issued an ultimatum with its protest: Germany must abandon 'its present methods of submarine warfare against passenger and freight-carrying vessels' or face a break in diplomatic relations.

The German alarm was so great that the Government ordered the Naval Staff to prohibit all attacks outside the prize law regulations, which provided a code of conduct – warning the ship to stop, examining papers and cargo, ensuring the safety of the crew, etc.

Angry and exasperated, the two naval commanders operating the flotillas, Scheer and the C.-in-C. Flanders Flotilla, recalled all their U-boats. This marked the end of the second and very brief campaign. Neutral revulsion and threat had won again. The U-boats would be back, but for the present trade flowed freely to and from Allied ports and the Admiralty relaxed its counter measures.

Fisher's prophetic eye had led to the founding of a British submarine service before Tirpitz had been converted to its cause. Its first inspecting captain of submarines was Fisher's friend and ally Captain Reginald H. Bacon, with his headquarters in HMS *Dolphin*, a hulk at Fort Blockhouse Gosport, the submarine depot. Keyes's appointment in 1910 was a surprise one, for this valiant and dashing figure was not renowned for his outstanding intellect nor technical facility, both qualities that were essential in these formative years. But Keyes did have sound common sense and an ability to impart enthusiasm to those serving under him.

British submarine development stemmed from the American Holland design built under licence by the huge shipbuilding firm of Vickers Maxim at Barrow-in-Furness. The early British Hollands were indistinguishable from the American vessels, but in subsequent classes improvements were made until in 1907, with the D-class, the Royal Navy possessed a true ocean-going vessel of 500 tons, diesel-powered and with a surface speed close to 15 knots. The E-class which followed formed the basis on which most of the subsequent wartime submarines were designed. They had broadside as well as bow torpedo tubes. The submarine had become a potent ocean-going man o'war capable of working with the fleet and at long distances from its base. It was superior in all respects to the contemporary U-boats except in its fuel capacity and range of operation, and proved its potential in early operations, notably at the Heligoland Bight skirmish.

One of Keyes's early tasks in 1910 was to break the Vickers monopoly which that company had legitimately acquired from the Admiralty. He also made himself more widely unpopular by going abroad for some experimental vessels, and for periscopes which were superior to the home product. The British service, like the German, attracted the young enthusiast, the natural risk-taker, and a fair proportion of eccentrics. Morale was high, dress standards shocking. The typical 1914 submariner was depicted with oil-stained hands, a mad gleam in his eye, and the appearance of a Grimsby trawlerman who has been at sea too long.

The total number of British submarines at the outbreak of war was seventy-four, the great majority old coastal operating vessels. By contrast, the smaller German force, because of Tirpitz's late start, was more modern. There were three British submarines each at Malta, Gibraltar and in China. The cream of Keyes's force based at Harwich was the 8th Flotilla of D- and E-class boats. He also had five flotillas of older B- and C-class and three more flotillas of the small and now obsolete A-class which were attached to the Local Defence Flotillas. The whole force was nominally under the overall command of Jellicoe, but like Tyrwhitt's 1st and 3rd Destroyer Flotillas also at Harwich, led a somewhat rakish life of its own for much of the time.

Owing to the submarine's inherent restricted range of vision, even in clear weather, Keyes acquired two modern fast (32-knot) destroyers to scout ahead of his flotillas. With his commodore's pennant flying in the *Lurcher*, Keyes personally led a number of early operations, much to Admiralty disapproval. The first of these was a scouting operation deep into the Heligoland Bight while thirteen of his submarines covered the passage of the BEF to France spread out on a line from the North Goodwin Sands to Ruytingen Shoals. On 18 August Keyes borrowed four of Tyrwhitt's destroyers, and towing three of his submarines to save their fuel, made another, deeper penetration into the Bight with the *Lurcher* and the *Firedrake*. He returned safely, without having drawn blood but with much useful information which led to his issuing a warning to withdraw the old armoured cruiser patrol. No one acted in time to prevent the destruction of the *Aboukir*, *Hogue*, and *Cressy*.

Keyes maintained his aggressive policy which culminated in the Heligoland Bight battle. One of his E-class boats scored the force's first major success on 12 September when Lieutenant-Commander Max Horton fired two torpedoes at a range of 600 yards at the German cruiser *Hela*. Horton was forced to submerge speedily when fire was opened on him, but when he later ventured to surface he saw only some trawlers apparently searching for survivors.

Although the results were abortive, there was no clearer example of how the bigger submarines now had a tactical role to play in fleet operations than in the December Scarborough raid. With his pennant in the *Lurcher* again, and with the *Firedrake* and submarines *E2, 7, 8, 10, 11, 12, 15*, and the French *Archimède*, Keyes spread his force off

Terschelling ready to pounce on Hipper if he attempted a southerly raid. When it became clear that this was not going to take place, Keyes received at 10.30 a.m. on 16 December a W/T order from the Admiralty to take his force into the Heligoland Bight in the hope of intercepting the German force on its return to base.

Unfortunately, most of his craft were submerged and unable to pick up the new orders. By 5 p.m. he had managed to collect only four, including the *Archimède*. In spite of the worsening weather and a reduction in numbers, the correctness of the dispositions was shown early the following morning. At 7 a.m. Lieutenant-Commander Martin Nasmith in *E11*, the southernmost of the line, observed first a number of destroyers and then two heavy ships proceeding towards the Jade and zig-zagging defensively. He had intercepted the head of the High Seas Fleet's 2nd Division of dreadnoughts and succeeded in manoeuving himself so that he was within range of the flagship *Posen*. He fired at 400 yards at 8.10 a.m. His aim was perfect, but the torpedo under-ran the battleship. Nasmith now turned to get within range of the third ship, the *Nassau*, but her zig-zagging saved her as she turned and steered straight towards the *E11* as if to ram her. Nasmith carried out a rapid dive, unfortunately disturbing the submarine's trim so that when she again came up to periscope depth, she unwittingly surfaced. This should have been her end, but her sudden appearance seemed to strike panic in the German force, which scattered and made off before Nasmith could follow up his attack.

In these early months of war, the alarm and destruction which one or two submarines could cause was demonstrated just as forcefully by the British as the Germans. Their most effective hunting-grounds were the Baltic and (in connection with the Dardanelles operation) the Sea of Marmora. At a meeting with Jellicoe in October 1914, Keyes discussed the possibility of sending one or two of his E-class boats into the Baltic. The High Seas Fleet frequently used this sea for exercises and manoeuvres, usually between Bornholm Island and the southern entrance to the Sound. The passage through the Belts was certain to be hazardous and was probably mined, but for the advantage of a sunk dreadnought or two this seemed a small risk to take.

Three submarines were selected, commanded by Keyes's most daring and able commanders, Noel Laurence in *E1*, Max Horton in *E9*, and Martin Nasmith in *E11*. They were to pass through at night to give them a better chance of escaping the German patrol between Rügen and the Swedish coast, search for and attack the High Seas Fleet, and then head for the Russian port of Libau.

E1 got through on the night of 17–18 October, almost at once sighted a German cruiser and fired at a range of 500 yards. The torpedo ran under the ship. This under-running was a perennial problem in the Royal Navy and, according to one ex-submariner, 'was probably caused by the initial dive that all torpedoes make on firing before the hydrostatic valve can operate to bring them up to their set depth.'[14] If this was the case, as seems likely, it was the consequence of the age-old Navy tradition of closing the range to hit the enemy harder and with greater accuracy – and to demonstrate fighting zeal.

The *E9*, too, got through safely, although Horton could not make it in one night and was forced to lie on the bottom all of one day before proceeding again at nightfall. He, too, had immediate evidence of the rich pickings to be had in the Baltic. Both submarines were escorted into Libau, which was intended to be their base. But the Russians, in anticipation of a German attack, had virtually destroyed the dockyard facilities, and Horton and Laurence eventually proceeded to an anchorage in the Gulf of Finland where they placed themselves under the command of the Russian C.-in-C., an officer who proved to be both amiable and able.

The *E11* did not share the same luck. Her presence was already suspected when she mistook a Danish boat for a German submarine, and fired a torpedo. Later, while on the surface recharging her batteries, she was spotted by a seaplane. Next she was harried by destroyers, in daylight and through the hours of darkness, 'and on the 22nd [October] she decided to return to her base and wait for the hue and cry to die down'.[15]

All through that winter of 1914–15 Noel Laurence and Max Horton with their two small submarines performed the part of indestructible killer sharks in the confines of the Baltic, and in conditions which froze conning tower hatches, torpedo tube caps, and periscopes alike. There were two main German forces operating against them. Both German squadrons were made up of cruisers and destroyers, one from Kiel and the second from Neufahrwasser. Rear-Admiral Jasper with the Kiel squadron, unaware that the Russians had evacuated Libau, made a strong attack on the base, losing his flagship on a mine. The Russians had learned a lot about mines in the war with Japan, in which they had once claimed two of four modern Japanese battleships on one small field. They claimed another modern 4,350-ton German cruiser off Bornholm that winter and a number of patrol vessels. The Germans suspected that the British submarines were the real culprits. Then Horton torpedoed a destroyer, the first of eight, off the Danish coast. 'I consider the destruction of a Russian submarine will be a great success', proclaimed Grand Admiral Prince Heinrich. 'But I regard the destruction of a British submarine as being at least as valuable as that of a Russian armoured cruiser.'

With periods for rest, replenishment, and refit, the two submarines continued to survive and operate through the spring and early summer. Horton fell in with a convoy of transports, heavily escorted, and with two torpedoes, while under heavy attack, sent one of the transports to the bottom. A collier and destroyer fell to him on 4 June. A month later the redoubtable and tireless Horton found himself involved in an intense battle between Russian and German cruisers and destroyers. He succeeded in intercepting two reinforcing German battleships and sent two torpedoes into one of them, disabling it.

The Russians were now being hard-pressed and appealed to their ally for further submarine support. *E8* and *E13* were despatched from Harwich on 14 August 1915. *E13* was soon in trouble. Compass failure led to her running aground on one of the numerous sandbanks between Malmö and Copenhagen. At daybreak she was still there, and now a Danish torpedo boat was in attendance, to inform Lieutenant-Commander Geoffrey Layton that he had twenty-four hours in which to leave and that no assistance could be given under international law. A few hours later several German destroyers appeared, and with rather less concern for the law torpedoed and opened fire on the submarine and her crew with shrapnel and machine guns, killing fifteen men and wounding many more as they leapt from the submarine's deck and sought protection under the sea. A steady fire was kept up until the Danish torpedo boat steamed between the German ships and their victim.

During this unpleasant business and at some distance to the east, Noel Laurence in *E1* was observing the richest target any submarine commander could pray for – the entire German battle-cruiser squadron steaming in line abreast at the perfect angle for imminent attack. In ten minutes the nearest big ship was within easy range. Laurence fired once amidst a flurry of maddened destroyers, and was forced to crash-dive within seconds of seeing an explosion forward on his target, now identified as the *Moltke*, a part of the German force in the combined attack on Riga. Thickening fog, and the defensive efforts of the destroyer screen precluded another attack. But to Laurence, who was to be awarded a DSO and bar, there also was now accorded the honour of being the first to torpedo a dreadnought. This same attack was believed to have led to the calling off of the assault, thus 'saving Riga and probably Russia too'.[6]

As for Max Horton, he became a popular submarine legend, the

Baltic became known as 'Horton's Sea', and the Germans actually put a price on his head. When he was at last ordered home at the end of 1915 the Russians, who adored him, were grief-stricken.

There was a curious similarity between the operations of British submarines in the Baltic and the Dardanelles. Both had as their first purpose to establish contact with the Russians and to commit as much damage to the enemy as a handful of small submarines could hope to do. The straits of the Dardanelles and the Belts between Sweden and Denmark were both necks of the richly rewarding bottles of the Baltic and Marmora Seas. The commanders and men who succeeded, or who tried and failed to negotiate these narrow, hazard-strewn bottle-necks, proved a fundamental truth. It was this: no matter how incompetent, misguided, and unimaginative the naval high command could be; no matter how dependent on orders and guidance from above most commanders had now become; whenever initiative was granted, the British sailor's old cunning and daring remained as powerful as ever.

Any submariner would accept that the dangers and difficulties of the Dardanelles straits were even greater than those of the northern passage into the Baltic. The passage from the Aegean to the Sea of Marmora is twenty-seven miles long. For three and a half miles the width is less than a mile. Map 4 shows the sharp changes of direction, at the Narrows between Kilid Bahr and Chanak, and at Nagara. The currents run up to 4 knots and there is a 10-fathom-deep stratum of fresh water pouring down at a varying depth and unpredictable course which has the power to throw any submarine about like a twig in a mill race.

To these natural hazards were added the skilfully laid Turkish defences. Anti-submarine nets were laid across the Narrows, there were numerous minefields, the finger beams of searchlights played over the waters all night, and there were ever-alert gunners ashore and on gunboats and other men o'war.

The first attempt to penetrate the straits predated the naval bombardment by many weeks. It was made by Lieutenant Holbrook on 13 December 1914 in the small, old, and relatively primitive *B11*. Holbrook entered the straits between Cape Helles and Kum Kale, worked his way up on the surface unobserved by the batteries, and submerged to attempt to navigate under the five known minefields before Chanak. His B-class submarine had a very short submerged endurance and a speed little more than that of the contrary current. It took him four hours of bumping and scraping to reach the relatively open water beyond. Holbrook brought his boat up to periscope depth and was rewarded with the sight of the 10,000-ton Turkish battleship *Messudieh* at a range of no more than 800 yards. He fired a single torpedo, lost trim in doing so, submerged and felt the concussion of a mighty explosion. When he next rose to the surface, the *Messudieh* was sinking. But her gunners opened fire as she went down, and the shore batteries joined in. *B-11* crash-dived, and now lost the use of her compass.

The passage home was a nightmare of blind groping, bumping and boring, flooding tanks, and near asphixiation for the crew. At one moment the submarine was stranded on a shoal, the target for every Turkish gun within range. Holbrook never understood why they were not blown to pieces there and then. But he managed to get her off, and he blindly continued his passage through and under the five minefields.

'*B11* arrived at the entrance to the Dardanelles at 2.10 p.m., [runs one account] and here she came to the surface. She had been diving for just over nine hours – nine of the most crowded hours which have ever fallen to the lot of man. So foul was the air in the tiny submarine that a match would not burn in her. Even the engine refused to start until the boat had been ventilated.'[17]

The Navy loved this unprecedented feat, which did much to balance the damaging effects on the service caused by the Scarborough raid, Holbrook was given the immediate award of a VC, his second in command received a DSO and the rest of the crew received a DSC or DSM according to rank.

Later, with the failure of naval bombardments, thoughts turned again to more ambitious raids up the straits, even as far as the Sea of Marmora, with the more modern E-class submarines which had now arrived from Britain. The first attempt ended in tragedy. *E15*, Lieutenant-Commander Theodore Brodie, used a novel and enterprising approach, penetrating on the surface, keeping the centre of the channel, and relying on a succession of seaplanes armed with small bombs to scout ahead and divert the attention of the gunners with sporadic attacks. But the current beat the *E15*, and she was thrown onto a shoal where Brodie and a number of his men were killed and the boat destroyed.

The Australian submarine *AE2* was the next to try. With Lieutenant-Commander Henry Stoker in command, she succeeded in getting under all the minefields while the first landings were in progress, and to his own astonishment made it all the way to the Sea of Marmora, where he transmitted news of his success. After sinking a

Turkish gunboat, his submarine developed a fault which forced him to remain on the surface. You could not expect to survive long in those waters deprived of the advantage of concealment, and a torpedo boat soon despatched her with gunfire.

Lieutenant-Commander Edward Boyle was the next volunteer to run the gauntlet of minefields and gunfire. According to an officer who served under him, 'Boyle was tall and dark, with slightly greying hair, very reserved and immensely self-contained. Off duty, you would find him immersed in some technical book . . . He had a sense of humour, but it never ran away with him.'[18] In short, a typical submariner, with none of the flamboyance and all the sublime courage of a Francis Drake.

Boyle took *E14* past Cape Helles as soon as it was dark on the evening of 26 April 1915, remaining on the surface until gunfire and searchlights forced him to dive. It took *E14* six hours before she was past Chanak and at last emerged into the comparatively open sea beyond. On the way she had come up once, observed a large Turkish gunboat and torpedoed her. 'I just had time to see a great column of water shoot as high as the gunboat's mast,' Boyle wrote in his report, 'when I had to dive again as some men in a small steamboat were leaning over the side trying to catch hold of my periscope. We dived,' he concluded formally this part of his account, 'and proceeded as requisite.'

For three weeks, Boyle led a charmed life in the Sea of Marmora, chased and harried night and day and himself creating disorder and dismay. After he sent the Turkish transport *Gul Djemal* to the bottom, with 2,000 troops and a battery of artillery destined for the front line on board, all further Turkish sailings ceased. When the submarine's torpedoes were exhausted, she held up small boats with the only armament left to her, .303 rifles.

Boyle was recalled on 17 May. The return passage was as incident-filled as the rest of the voyage. 'Diving under the first barrier near Nagara,' wrote the same fellow officer, 'she rose to periscope depth again off Chanak, followed the wake of any enemy patrol through the minefields, passed a yacht, a battleship, and a number of tramps, ran through the Narrows under the fire of the Chanak forts, dived under the Kephez minefields as before, and came to the surface near a French battleship.'[19] Asked to identify himself, Boyle gave his name, and received a huge accolade. He also received a VC. 'It really is a great feat of persistent gallantry',[20] Keyes wrote home proudly to his wife.

Martin Nasmith now proceeded to carry out two of the most successful and daring of all the Gallipoli operations in the same boat,

E11. Nasmith was less reserved than his fellow submariner, Boyle, who possessed 'a delicate sense of the incongruous and an almost ferocious insistence on efficiency'. These two characteristics were exhibited at one stage in his astonishing three-month-long stay in the Sea of Marmora when supplies of torpedoes ran low and he set them to float at the end of their run if they should fail to hit their target. Then, like a wasp replacing its sting, he swam out recovered it, unscrewed the firing pistol (an operation as delicate as defusing a bomb), and with the aid of a working party of swimmers, reloaded it into the tube and reprimed it.

Another ruse omitted from the book of instructions was the capture of a sailing dhow and its use as a camouflage for *E11*'s conning tower to which it was securely lashed. Nasmith captured at rifle point a store ship with great quantities of ammunition on board and sent her to the bottom with a demolition charge. He even went through the straits into the Golden Horn, the first enemy ship to do so for five hundred years, firing two torpedoes at Constantinople harbour (one circled madly, adding to the panic) and calmly taking a snapshot through the periscope of a munition ship blowing up.

Not satisfied with the paralysis of shipping he had created, Nasmith set about halting the railways. On this second operation he had the advantage of a 12-pounder gun, and a fresh supply of ammunition brought up by another submarine. He bombarded a railway viaduct in the Gulf of Ismid, and later put his second in command ashore on a one-man demolition enterprise. Lieutenant Guy D'Oyly-Hughes had already learned the art of defusing spent torpedoes in the water from his captain, and now, armed with a bayonet and pistol, pushed ashore a raft heavy with explosive. The night's work included cliff-climbing, pursuit by armed guards and the final successful explosion of his charge under the railway line. By the end of this second voyage, Nasmith had added a battleship to his list of ships sunk, making up a total achievement worthy of being described as 'a modern tale of the Arabian Nights'.

Boyle and Nasmith are the most memorable names in the roll of Dardanelles submariner heroes, but there were others whose score and record of courage were almost as great. With the benefit of experience, the E-boats were able to make the passage up the straits with relative safety and regularity. By the time the last was recalled on 2 January 1916 the seven boats participating in the operations had run up a score of two battleships, a destroyer, five gunboats, seven ammunition ships, nine transports, and more than 200 steamers and sailing ships; all at a cost of three submarines.

If the skill, efficiency, and devotion to duty of these few submariners had been matched in the land operations and Admiral Carden's early bombardments, the toll of lives of the Gallipoli fiasco need never have occurred.

The presence of one or two submarines halted all sea traffic in the Sea of Marmora, even more effectively than Max Horton and his fellow commanders dislocated communications in the Baltic. The first months of the war confirmed the most extravagant claims of the submarine proponents. But a second and even newer sea weapon was also gaining its wings. The Gallipoli campaign provided a marvellous opportunity for enterprise, novelty, and experiment because of the unusual problems facing the attackers and the relatively small geographical dimensions to which the fighting was restricted.

When the decision was made to send out, first a submarine force from Britain, and then a seaplane-carrier, with all their youthful and zestful crews, it became certain that their presence would lead to adventurous and pioneering events. Flight Commander Williamson and Lieutenant-Commander Boyle were only two of the bright and fearless figures who brought fame and distinction to their relatively new branches of the Royal Navy.

No *Ark Royal*s had served in the Fleet since the Armada ship of that name of 1588. It scarcely seemed appropriate that such an honoured and historical name should be perpetuated by a half-completed tramp steamer late in 1913. Nor was she to carry the distinction of being the Royal Navy's first seaplane-carrier. She was, however, the first vessel to be commissioned in any navy that could be called an aircraft-carrier because she was equipped with a flight deck from which machines could take off, although the deck was not large enough for them to land on again. They were expected to fly to an aerodrome and only land in the sea alongside *in extremis*.

When the *Ark Royal* was ordered out to the eastern Mediterranean within a few weeks of commissioning, she carried six seaplanes and four land-planes in her hangar, the former with wings folded. The process of launching was elaborate and not very quick. A crane hoisted up a seaplane, swung it round and placed it on the ship's forecastle. Here its wings would be spread, its engine started and warmed up. Then, with engine switched off, the machine swung out and lowered into the water, where the pilot took over.

The 7,500-ton *Ark Royal* arrived off the Dardanelles two days before the first bombardment. The ship had behaved impeccably on the voyage out from Harwich, but, to say the least, her ship's crew and flight crews were raw and quite untrained for the operations assigned to them. They were further handicapped by their aircraft which, with the exception of the single two-seater Short seaplane flown by Williamson, were quite inadequate. The other seaplanes could not cope with the prevailing choppy seas, and when the wind from time to time died, they could not get enough lift to become airborne. However, in the words of the official historian, 'In view of the disadvantages under which the carrier worked, her achievement was a remarkable one.'[21]

During March further aircraft of a more suitable kind were shipped out, and No. 3 Naval Squadron established an airfield on the island of Tenedos. Besides spotting for the guns and reconnaissance work, the *Ark Royal*'s seaplanes and the land-based squadron, reinforced by a French squadron, carried out much useful and effective bombing work, spotted minefields and guided submarines. A German airfield at Chanak was bombed and knocked out on 18 April, and for several months the Allies had complete control of the air. A second and faster carrier, the *Ben-My-Chree*, arrived on 12 June, and the air contribution to the operations became substantial. Names like Squadron Commander Richard Bell Davies, Flight Commanders C. R. Samson and Hugh Williamson became as closely associated with daring achievement in the air during those early days of hope and enterprise in the Dardanelles operations as Noel Laurence and Edward Boyle under the waters of the straits and Sea of Marmora.

The primitiveness of the equipment with which these early Naval Air Service pilots flew can be judged by some of the instructions Samson, now a wing commander, issued to No. 3 Squadron:

Pilots always to be armed with a revolver or pistol; to carry binoculars; some safety device, either waistcoat, patent life-belt or petrol can.
Observers always to carry rifle; proper charts for journey; binoculars; life-saving device or petrol can; watch if not fitted to the aeroplane.
At all times the pilot should carry out independent observations and note down what he sees (noting the time). Nail a pad of paper on the instrument board for this purpose.

On several occasions the role of the aircraft in the Dardanelles operations closely resembled that of the submarines, and co-operation between the two branches was close. At one time, learning of a submarine's need for a spare periscope, arrangements were made for a seaplane to fly one in to the Sea of Marmora. Unfortunately, at the last minute it was discovered there were no spares. Adaptation combined with initiative led to more fruitful and long-lasting results early in August. Several ingenious members of the *Ben-My-Chree*'s crew, notably a warrant officer (Carpenter) and a senior torpedo rating working under Lieutenant-Commander Barber, a navigator, rigged up a device for carrying a 14-inch torpedo under the belly of a Short seaplane. On 14 August 1915 Flight Commander C. H. K. Edmonds succeeded in taking off with his 'tin fish'.

I climbed to 1500 feet [ran Edmonds's report] and crossing the Isthmus of Bulair over the low land one mile to the East of Bulair, arrived over the Sea of Marmora and shaped course along the coast towards the North East . . .

Approaching Injeh Burnu, I glided down and fired my torpedo from a height of about 14 feet and range of some 300 yards, with the sun astern of me. I noticed some flashes from a tug so presumed she was firing at me and therefore kept on a westerly course, climbing rapidly. Looking back, I observed the track of the torpedo, which struck the ship abreast the mainmast, the starboard side. The explosion sent a column of water and large fragments of the ship almost as high as her masthead.

Edmonds repeated this feat three days later, while a fellow pilot, adapting further this exercise, actually torpedoed a ship successfully while taxying on the water after his engine had lost power. Pursued by defensive fire, Flight Lieutenant G. B. Dacre taxied out of range, when, relieved of his burden and discovering that his engine was running better, took off and flew close enough to the *Ben-My-Chree* to glide alongside when his engine finally packed up.

In his report on these first-ever torpedo-bomber sorties, Squadron Commander C. L'E. Malone, commanding the seaplane carrier *Ben-My-Chree*, wrote that 'One cannot help looking on this operation as being the forerunner of a line of development which will tend to revolutionize warfare.'

These early torpedo attacks were only one contribution to the portentous operations of the Naval Air Service. Already, by the autumn of 1915, the bombing offensive was having a marked influence on the campaign. A more urgent and substantial effort by seaplanes and land-planes at the earliest stages could have swung the outcome of the whole campaign. Instead, as the official historian recorded, the RNAS carried out successfully the crucial task of covering the Army's retreat and disembarkation. 'There is, perhaps, something of pathos in the fact that the air service, as the year wore on, became so strong that it was able to deny to the enemy any sight of an intention to withdraw from the peninsula.'[22]

Considering the primitiveness of the aircraft employed, casualties were relatively light and mostly from accidents. Only in the very last days of the campaign were any aircraft shot down by enemy pilots, three being accounted for by a newly arrived flight of German Fokker monoplanes. The *Ben-My-Chree* was sunk by Turkish shellfire during the last days of the campaign, the *Ark Royal* survived into the Second World War as the *Pegasus*, her service spanning that epochal period of naval history when the aircraft-carrier displaced the battleship as the Fleet's capital ship.

Considering the remarkable promise, and achievement, of air power at the Dardanelles it is a poor reflection on Admiralty policy that the Royal Navy Air Service was not more urgently developed and exploited in 1916. It was almost as if the distance of the events and the fog of shame that developed about the whole Gallipoli operation obscured the vision of the Naval War Staff. The Air Department was reorganized in the spring of 1916, and divided into two, but the first preoccupations were administration and discipline. 'From the very beginning,' wrote the official historian, 'the Naval Air Service had set their heart on the fitting out of big bombing raids against distant German centres.'[23]

In a secret Joint War Air Committee paper on 3 March 1916, there was a clearly identifiable note of disdain in references to RNAS personnel who 'will have a naval training and will be attached only to the Royal Navy Air Service for certain periods, returning to their sea duties at intervals. Thus close touch will be kept with naval customs and methods and the latest developments in naval warfare.' The list of duties laid down for the RNAS was drawn up as if no one had informed the committee that bombs as heavy as 500 pounds had been successfully used against Turkish ships, that ships had been *sunk* by airborne torpedoes.

1. To attack the enemy's fleets, dockyards, arsenals, factories, air sheds, &c., from the *coasts*, whether the coasts be the enemy's or our own (i.e. long-distance bombing).
2. To patrol our own coasts to look out for enemy's ships and submarines, and to meet and repel enemy's aircraft. Possibly also to discover minefields.
3. Observation of fire during ship's bombardments of enemy's coasts. Destruction of enemy's coast batteries, means of communication thereto, and material in connection therewith.
4. Scouting for the fleet and reconnaissance work from ships.
5. To assist the Army whenever and wherever required.

12

THE SEARCH FOR DECISIVE ACTION

The new team at the Admiralty – Less inspiration, greater steadiness – Jellicoe's concern for his Fleet's strength, his personal health and the health of his admirals – Restlessness for action among both belligerents – The new German C.-in-C. provides a response – The Lowestoft raid – Consequent agitation for swifter defence and counter-action – British and German efforts to trap the enemy with similar plans – Jellicoe's operation pre-empted – The Fleets sail – Their quality compared

ASQUITH approached the problem of the succession at the Admiralty with caution, and with a desire for calm in this storm-battered seat of the naval war. He had quite enough on his mind politically and on the Western Front, to say nothing of the Dardanelles, to risk further internecine warfare. At the same time, his options were severely restricted in number. The civil post of First Lord of the Admiralty was more easily filled than that of the professional appointment of First Sea Lord. Arthur James Balfour had already been Prime Minister for three years (1902–5) and knew the political and defence scenes as well as anyone. With Churchill, who warmly approved of his appointment, he had 'a complete understanding'.

Balfour had been born in East Lothian in 1848, a nephew of Lord Salisbury, who later had no difficulty in attracting him to politics. His father had died young, and the influence of his charming, vivacious, and brilliant mother was all-consuming during his childhood. He adored her and never married, though he grew up as attractive to women – tall, handsome, elegant in style and manners, amusing, morally and physically courageous, and renowned as a conversationalist. He performed brilliantly at Oxford and Cambridge, became an essayist and philosopher. His rise as a Conservative politician was predictably exceptional and not by any means dependent upon the influence of his uncle. He was in the Cabinet at thirty-eight, and sixteen years later succeeded Lord Salisbury as Premier.

To many there appeared no limit to Balfour's qualities. F. E. Smith, the first Earl Birkenhead, once said that 'Balfour gave to politics the finest mind of his generation.' His manner was calm and 'unflappable', his mind keen and understanding, he appeared cheerfully ready to listen to all sides and to all men. By 1915, partly thanks to Churchill who took him into his closest confidence, Balfour had become an expert on the Navy. Graham Greene, the Secretary of the

Admiralty when Balfour came to office, wrote that 'in his presence all men seemed rather small and inferior, and this placed him as First Lord in an unrivalled position for settling differences of opinion or deciding important questions. Naval officers knew that he would give what they had to say the closest consideration and would support loyally his official colleagues and advisers, and would never attempt to influence them to do what, as practical seamen, they might consider unwise.'[1]

Here, then, was a change from Churchill. Unfortunately, the differences extended into another sphere, that of working tempo. Balfour gave an impression of perennial lethargy. His style was the measured one of the patrician. As a philosopher, he cared about contemplation. His long and arduous studies of metaphysics did not tend towards haste and snap decisions, nor was he at his best in a crisis. He knew this and therefore did his utmost to avoid them. Lloyd George thought he was a 'dawdler'. Arthur Balfour was not a man of the people, nor a man of the lower deck, and least of all a reformer. 'His appeal', it has been written, 'was essentially to the few, and not the many, to the salon and to the senate rather than to the street.'[2] If it was Asquith's intention to reverse trends at the Admiralty, Balfour was the man to change the gear.

The same might be said of his professional partner. Admiral Sir Henry Jackson was sixty at the time he succeeded Fisher. He was the complete technician, with numerous achievements behind him, a Fellow of the Royal Society, author of technical papers. Like many of the Navy's 'brains', Jackson had early specialized in the torpedo branch. By virtue of his own experiments and his work in conjunction with Marconi, he was instrumental in introducing W/T into the Royal Navy in 1900. As Third Sea Lord and Controller (responsible for the design and construction of ships) at the time of the *Dreadnought* he had been a brilliant member of Fisher's special committee.

Jackson was a man of Yorkshire, the son of a farmer, dour of manner, parsimonious of words, sombre of outlook, infertile of all but scientific imagination. The least inspired of men, he drew out nothing from his juniors and was not much liked by them, though grudgingly admired. His eyes were ever on the dark side of things. 'He does nothing but groan and sigh and be miserably pessimistic', wrote one of his Sea Lords. 'I fear he will not last long.'[3] His part in the pre-Coronel dispositions was not widely acknowledged and had scarred his reputation among only a handful (including Richmond) at the Admiralty.

Jackson's qualities were those of the level-headed scientist, steady in approach, weighing and balancing before deciding. Although he remained throughout on polite and gentlemanly terms with Balfour, he did not mix well with politicians and was something of a problem at War Council meetings. He was also a problem to his subordinates, being a great man for paperwork and red tape and at the same time finding difficulty in delegating even the most trivial tasks.

As a result of these top appointments, a profound change overcame the Admiralty. Solemn lethargy took over from exuberant and sometimes inspired activity. 'The Admiralty jumped from one extreme to the other', commented Hankey. 'In place of two men of driving power, initiative and resource, but occasionally lacking in judgement, there were now in charge two men of philosophic temperament and first-rate judgement, but less dynamic than their predecessors.'[4]

The Board of Admiralty as a body had scarcely counted during Churchill's wartime administration. With heads down in their offices, the members were rarely called to meetings, Churchill experiencing no urgent need for their advice on anything. Balfour now received an appeal from Lord Selborne, that wisest of ex-First Lords: 'Do at the Board all the business which possibly can be done at the Board. Churchill has almost killed it. You can give it fresh life.'[5]

The Board lacked neither interest nor variety. The Second Sea Lord was Sir Frederick Hamilton, much loved by the Fleet, though better known for his Court associations than for his dynamism. More competent and professional was Vice-Admiral Sir Frederick Tudor, the Third Sea Lord. The role of the Fourth Sea Lord – the 'Junior' Lord – had traditionally been that of a dogsbody. The man who filled that post from 1913–16, Captain Cecil Foley Lambert, subsequently suffered unfavourable comment, no doubt because his tasks were so wide and so many of them attracted unpopularity. He was nominally responsible for Transport and Supplies, including in 1914 and 1915 the passage of the armies to France and the Dardanelles, and the provision of all kinds of stores (except armaments – Third Sea Lord) to a rapidly expanding Fleet. Additionally, he was asked to form an armed Yacht Patrol at the outbreak of war, to take charge of the boom defences at refuges like Loch Ewe to which the Grand Fleet retreated from Scapa Flow while that anchorage was being secured, to supervise measures to deal with the menace from mines and U-boats (a formidable enough undertaking in itself), and to co-ordinate precautionary defences in the Fleet and at shore stations against poison gas attack when the Germans introduced this new weapon in 1915.

When Fisher was still vacillating about the Dardanelles, Lambert joined with Tudor and Hamilton in sending him a memorandum (7 April 1915) expressing their grave doubts about the naval participation in the operation, and subsequently Fisher proposed the removal of all three members. In fact, Lambert was at this time doing all he could to find means of reconciling Churchill and Fisher, recognizing the cataclysmic consequences of a final split, and working late at his desk, a break with his usually precise timetable.

'No one could call Capt. Lambert genial', wrote his private secretary. ' "Dour" and "Sardonic" would be more appropriate epithets, but when his primary responsibilities were increasing and new ones thrust upon him he never lost his composure or his temper. He possessed the great secret of good administration – of knowing when and to whom to delegate work. Much of his business was done by word of mouth; his minutes on official papers were brief, lucid and to the point and by 7 his table was clear of papers.'[6]

Oliver remained as Chief of Staff, an able and very nearly brilliant 'brain'; but with serious shortcomings, as we shall see. Richmond remained too, cranky, curmudgeonly, his brilliance unqualified; and Wilson, too, like some oak with its ancient roots entwined through every department. In all, then, the demerits of Jackson were more than offset by the merits of the rest of the Board and Staff, if Balfour followed Selborne's advice and used them. He was sagacious enough to do so, with the consequence that the Admiralty could now be likened to a stately dreadnought with an alert and cautious ship's company steaming at best economical speed rather than a battle-cruiser at 27 knots racing through minefields and hoisting a series of imprecise signals. It did, however, labour under a considerable handicap – a burden which it shared with the C.-in-C. of the Grand Fleet.

Jellicoe had been quite capable of standing up to the barrage of vituperative, malicious, and not always true accusations about his recent associates – especially Wilson and Churchill – with which Fisher assailed him immediately following his resignation, and of drawing his own conclusions. Jellicoe kept his counsel about the new administration. He had strongly regretted Fisher's departure, much less so the enforced resignation of Churchill.

With Scapa Flow now relatively safe from torpedo attack by destroyers or submarines, one of Jellicoe's first causes for complaint was removed. Many others remained. The new administration reached the conclusion that destroyers were the best antidote to submarines, and was soon attempting to coerce Jellicoe into dispensing with some of his seventy boats. The efforts were not successful. Jellicoe believed he was already at risk at sea, and with insufficient destroyers. Mines remained for Jellicoe an abiding anxiety. A further advantage possessed by the enemy was his Zeppelin force. When the day of the decisive fleet action came, Jellicoe feared that the High Seas Fleet with its Zeppelins scouting ahead, invulnerable and all-seeing, would know in advance the course, speed, and strength confronting it. Seaplanes were not the answer. 'All my experiments with seaplanes in the north have shown that the chances are about a hundred to one against it being suitable for them to rise from *the water*', he wrote to Beatty. He had by this time a carrier of sorts in the *Campania*, from which he 'got one up yesterday, the first that has risen from a ship under way. It is not a nice job for the pilot,' he went on, 'as he has to get up a speed of 45 miles an hour before he leaves the deck . . . Therefore if there is any hitch, he comes a purler . . . '[7]

It was a small example of Jellicoe's attitude and philosophy as C.-in-C. that he has no sooner achieved a very considerable 'first' with a weapon that will one day revolutionize sea warfare than he contemplates with dismay what could happen if there is a mishap.

It was right and proper for Jellicoe to communicate his concerns to his chiefs, to defend his Fleet against attempts to weaken it and to fight for its strengthening. But, like Jackson, he was a born complainer, and a querulous one at that, and lacked the virtues of positivism and optimism which are two of the most important attributes of a great leader.

In a revealing message to Beatty 'as a reminder of the possible difficulties of the situation', he wrote:

The Admiralty and country's attitude would certainly be one of great praise and laudation in case of success, and one of exactly the opposite should you have ill luck over such a venture [an offensive operation]. One need not worry about the attitude of others, possibly, but one must concern one's self very seriously with the result to the country of a piece of real bad luck culminating in a serious decrease in *relative* strength. Of course the whole thing is a question of the game being worth the candle, and only the man on the spot can decide. If the game looks worth the candle the risks can well be taken. If not, then however distasteful, I think one's duty is to be cautious.[8]

The burden which the Board of Admiralty shared with the C.-in-C. Grand Fleet, and others, was that of ill health, a condition which has lost battles and wars. The strain of running the Navy at war, whether from Whitehall or Scapa Flow, was great enough to tax the strength of the fittest men. Churchill and Fisher in office in 1914, for all their follies and their age difference of thirty-three years, were extremely fit and strong, and always had been. Churchill, watching Fisher 'narrowly to judge his physical strength and mental alertness' when considering him as a partner, was given 'the impression of a terrific engine of mental and physical power burning and throbbing in that aged frame'.[9]

Jackson, however, had always suffered from poor health, and when in one of his quite frequent bad phases, was unable to prevent himself from discourteous and even rude behaviour. Balfour, in spite of his strong and handsome looks, suffered from bad health all his life, too, and his eyesight was particularly poor. No doubt the impression of lethargy he left with everyone who worked with him stemmed from his weak health, leading Lloyd George to write of him: 'He lacked the physical energy and fertility of resource, and untiring industry for the administration of the Admiralty.'[10]

Although a keen 'keep-fit' man and presenting to the officers and men of the Grand Fleet an impression of rude health, Jellicoe had never been 100 per cent fit from his earliest days in the Navy. Like Nelson, he suffered greatly from tropical diseases when he was a young officer and he never quite threw off their effect on his constitution. Dysentery and Malta fever struck him down and left their scars. A burst eardrum while at Whale Island caused permanent slight deafness. At Scapa Flow he was much troubled by piles and pyrrhoea, and on several occasions had to leave the flagship for attention. On 29 January 1915, he wrote to his old friend, Hamilton, at the Admiralty: 'I am laid up for a bit. It is of course due to the worry of trying to get things done which ought to be done without my having to step in. I hope to be right early next week, but the doctor says at present it is dangerous to move out of bed. A nice look out if [Admiral] Ingenohl comes out . . . '

Nine months later, Jellicoe writes to the commander of the 3rd Battle Squadron, 'I have not been well lately. Partly strain, partly the result of the fashionable complaint of pyrrhoea, which I have succeeded in developing and which has affected me in the way of rheumatism, neuralgia, etc. I've sacrificed several teeth but it has not yet stopped and a rest is suggested.'[11]

Even if it is reluctantly accepted that the C.-in-C. Grand Fleet was a hypochondriac, the question remains: Should Jellicoe be sending to his subordinates discouraging bulletins on the state of his health? An officer suffering from piles, pyrrhoea, and exhaustion, they might well consider, is perhaps not the man to instil confidence in his fleet, nor lead it into a modern Trafalgar. The 'quiet spell' caused by Beatty's victory at the Dogger Bank enabled him to have his piles operated on but he remained off and on below his best in health, which led to worry, which in turn led to further stress-derived maladies and his own expressions of dismay at them.

It sometimes seemed that poor health was the norm in this vital service which relied so much on the alertness, keenness, and decision-making facility of the top commanders. The younger light-cruiser commanders like Tyrwhitt and Goodenough kept well, and no one could survive long in destroyers or submarines unless he was fighting fit. Amongst the admirals it was a different story. 'My Vice-Admirals are always a little shaky', Jellicoe himself complained to the First Sea Lord (16 June 1915). 'Warrender gets awfully deaf at times and is inclined to be absent-minded . . . I am not always quite happy about him. Burney is first rate when in good health, which unfortunately is not always the case.' Again on Burney, upon whom would devolve the supreme command if Jellicoe were stricken down by illness or incapacitated in battle: 'He suffers from bad rheumatism in his joints, especially his wrists. His depression is inclined to make him pessimistic and over cautious. It is not possible to say how he will stand the winter . . .'[12] And of other of his squadron commanders: 'Bayly is I fear occasionally a little mad. Sturdee is full of fads. Warrender is too deaf. Jerram has not the experience . . .'[13]

As for his own health and fitness to command, Jellicoe let his condition be known in detail to the Admiralty: 'I had two teeth out last week as I was having a real bad go of neuralgia. My own opinion is that the strain is telling a bit on me. One can't go on like this for ever without feeling it a bit. But there is nothing for it but to stick it out.'[14] He stuck it out for another eight months before facing the greatest test of his life.

The spirit of the lower deck in both the Grand Fleet and High Seas Fleet remained remarkably high after eighteen months of war. There was a good deal of cynical grumbling about the enemy avoiding a show-down – 'Another bloody sweep!' was the usual comment in Jellicoe's Fleet when they put to sea, with the chances of meeting the enemy predictably low. The German sailor was equally convinced, first that he was superior to his opposite number in an equal battle, and, second, that Jack Tar had lost his nerve. Only when the odds against him were overwhelming, claimed the average German rating, as at the Heligoland Bight skirmish and the Falkland Islands, could the German be beaten at sea. Outnumbered at the Dogger Bank, the

Germans believed they had knocked out the British flagship and sunk the enemy's newest and most powerful battle-cruiser, the *Tiger*, for the loss of their slowest and oldest ship. (German intelligence reported after Dogger Bank that the *Tiger* was now only a three-funnelled cruiser acting as a dummy substitute.)

The German sailor had a softer time of it than his British counterpart. He spent the greater part of his time in barracks ashore at Kiel or Wilhelmshaven. The climate there in winter was more agreeable than at Scapa Flow where there were almost constant gales, squalls, low cloud, freezing rain, or snow. At Scapa Flow in December and January it was dark before four in the afternoon and scarcely light again by 9 a.m. Jellicoe sought to break the monotony and keep his men fit and occupied by encouraging every sort of inter-ship and inter-squadron competition. Football pitches were laid down ashore and a golf course for the officers. Training and practice shoots were frequent, and the men were never allowed to forget that they might be faced with the decisive battle the next day.

The British sailor's impatience about the Fleet's inaction was mitigated by his knowledge that they 'had the Hun bottled in'. While they thirsted for battle, they all knew that they were meanwhile fulfilling the time-honoured British tradition of ruling the waves. The average civilian, and especially the average newspaperman, had no conception of this truism nor of the meaning of sea power. He wanted action, and by the winter of 1915–16, was becoming more discontented and impatient than the sailors who were being held responsible for the lack of it. Nearly a year had passed since the Dogger Bank victory, and a blockade was a silent, invisible business. In peacetime the Navy, by frequent appearances of men o'war off ports and resorts and coasts, ensured that the people who paid for them saw value for their money, and felt pride in the Navy's strength. In wartime all that show ceased, and the Navy's role, except in victorious battles, became an increasingly negative one with every Allied merchantman and liner reported sunk, with every announced loss of a British warship, with every enemy claim of success. Even the Zeppelin raids on British towns and cities, which were particularly damaging and tiresome that winter, were blamed on the Admiralty, which was responsible for air raid defence until late in February 1916.

The same wartime hysteria which had driven Battenberg from the Admiralty in 1914 exaggerated the depredations caused by the German surface raider *Moewe*, which ranged the Atlantic with apparent impunity, laying a minefield which caught the battleship *King Edward VII*, and sinking or capturing a number of merchantmen.

Then there was great excitement about the rumour that the Germans had almost ready for action new battle-cruisers armed with 17-inch guns, outranging and outclassing the pride of the Grand Fleet, the 15-inch gunned *Queen Elizabeth* class. Even the solid *Manchester Guardian* gave credence to these mighty and terrible men o'war, obliging Balfour to deny their existence with authority and circumlocution: 'I have seen in the Press mention of guns of 17-inch calibre', he stated in the House of Commons on 26 January. 'We have no evidence that such exist . . . The most diverse conjectures about German shipbuilding may be made by the ingenious; and speaking for myself, I am by no means sure that of these conjectures the one to which I have just referred is the most plausible.'

The rumble of discontent was rearoused by the thunder of enemy gunfire off the east coast early on the morning of 25 April 1916. The German battle-cruisers were at it again, destroying hundreds of houses and causing civilian casualties in Lowestoft and Yarmouth. Tyrwhitt with the Harwich light force was the only commander to make contact, and by valiant and brilliant manoeuvring caused first the battle-cruisers, then the main body of the High Seas Fleet backing them up, to turn tail. At the cost of two damaged light cruisers and a lost submarine, the commodore threw back the whole enemy Fleet before its scheduled time and before it could do much harm to Yarmouth.

In the course of this brief operation, the Germans lost two U-boats and the battle-cruiser *Seydlitz* was put out of action by a mine. The British public knew nothing of this, nor, thankfully, that the Admiralty through Room 40 knew the precise timing of the raid and its target. All they knew was that once again the *Kriegsmarine* had destroyed British property on British soil and killed and maimed British civilians. 'Where was the Navy?' the demand re-echoed.

The answer which was not publicly uttered was that the Navy was again too late, in spite of the early warning. Both the battle-cruisers from the Forth and Jellicoe's squadrons from Scapa had been tipped off and had struggled south against mountainous seas. Beatty got within forty-five miles of the enemy, then, according to the official Naval Staff Monograph on the raid, 'There was nothing in sight, all hope of cutting off the enemy had vanished, and the battle cruisers turned back at half-past twelve [p.m. 25 April].' The Admiral was, rightly and predictably, furious at the OD's gross mismanagement which had, once again, led to the enemy's escape.

The raid was also unfortunate for the Navy because it suggested that only the Germans were possessed of the offensive spirit, with the

Royal Navy on the defensive, and unsuccessfully on the defensive at that. Yet again, the problem of bases for the Grand Fleet was aired in the Admiralty and in the Fleet. The controversial subject had never been deeply submerged, but the Lowestoft raid brought it sharply to the surface again. The selection of east-coast bases was a political more than a strategic problem. From a strictly military point of view, the destruction of houses and the deaths of their occupants was of no consequence. When he had been in power, and impelled by political needs, Churchill had frequently pressed for Jellicoe to move his squadrons farther south to prevent these raids. Balfour faced now the same outcry as his predecessor had suffered, especially from the mayors of Yorkshire and Norfolk coastal towns.

Jellicoe hated, as much as anyone, the idea of the High Seas Fleet being able to move relatively freely if only for brief spells in the southern part of the North Sea. He did not much care for Scapa Flow either, even since it had been made safe. Ideally, the whole Grand Fleet should be based on the Forth, with Beatty. But for the present the dangers there were too great. At Rosyth, above the bridge, the battle-cruisers were safe, and there were berths for twenty big ships. But by early spring 1916 Jellicoe had some twenty-nine dreadnoughts in addition to Beatty's growing force, which could not be berthed below the bridge until this outer anchorage was made safe against U-boats and destroyer raids.

Additional arguments against the Forth were first the sometimes crippling handicap of fogs, winter and summer. This applied to the Humber and other possible bases farther south, while at Scapa it was, except occasionally in the summer, too windy for fogs to form. Then while the Forth gave a fleet an approximate and theoretical four-hour advantage over Scapa Flow in the time required to reach the likely battle area, some of this time was lost in the technical handicap at the Forth created by overcrowding and inferior facilities for putting to sea swiftly. All the same, if Jellicoe had arrived three hours earlier on only one of several critical occasions, a great deal of damage to the enemy might have resulted.

In February 1916 Beatty suggested a compromise solution. Send the fast 15-inch gunned *Queen Elizabeth* class, the 5th Battle Squadron, to support him in the Forth in place of the pre-dreadnought 3rd Battle Squadron, which was too slow and old to be of any use in a fleet action anyway. Jellicoe turned this down because these prized big new ships had always been intended to form a fast special wing to work independently of the battle line and to intervene as required. Besides, as Jellicoe wrote to Jackson, 'The stronger I make Beatty, the greater is the temptation for him to get involved in an independent action.' It was a cornerstone of Jellicoe's tactical policy that the Grand Fleet should be operated as one cohesive unit with Beatty's squadrons as a powerful force intended to scout and destroy the enemy battle-cruisers. This was sound reasoning. The fear of Beatty being separated, cut off, and destroyed piecemeal at too great a distance for the dreadnought squadrons to intervene was an abiding one, reinforced by Beatty's near shave during the Scarborough raid.

After the Lowestoft outcry, Jellicoe proposed a compromise disposition, moving the old 3rd Battle Squadron with the *Dreadnought* as flagship to the Thames estuary under able and steady Vice-Admiral Sir Edward Bradford. If not quite a 'live bait' squadron, this force of seven (eight before the *King Edward VII* was sunk) obsolete battleships and one obsolescent dreadnought was intended to draw on and hold a superior enemy force until Beatty and Jellicoe arrived, or deter it. At least, with Room 40's accurate predictions, it could be off any east-coast town before Hipper arrived and no doubt would send him swiftly over the horizon before he could do any damage. With a total broadside of thirty-eight 12-inch guns, about the same weight as Hipper's, they might even do him some damage.

It was not in the nature of Jellicoe, and less still in Beatty's character, to allow defensive measures to preoccupy their calcula-tions. They were in constant communication with one another, and offensive possibilities figured as prominently in their considerations as defensive activities. Two random examples, the second actually being the genesis of Jutland:

JELLICOE TO BEATTY

HMS *Iron Duke*
20th February 1916

I am proposing a movement for Saturday . . . I am proposing you should have the 1st Flotilla (I don't mean to bring out the 3rd BS [Battle Squadron]). Incidentally you may of course stumble on some German patrols during the night. Saturday night is a favourite night for them to be out . . . The meeting will be useful even if we don't pick up any Germans . . .[15]

BEATTY TO JELLICOE

Lion
7th April 1916

In view therefore of your recent excursion [in the northern part of the North Sea] indicating that the enemy can now be drawn, and of the desirability of ascertaining whether they have taken the opportunity of having the North Sea under complete and undisturbed observation [by Zeppelin] . . . I submit that the moment is opportune for sweeping operations on a large scale strongly supported . . . [16]

Since the earliest days of the war and the Ingenohl regime, every sort of ruse and stratagem had been considered that might lead to drawing out the High Seas Fleet or a substantial part of it. The chances of finding a solution fell further with Ingenohl's replacement by the even less adventurous Pohl. Pohl was, moreover, a sick man who became so ill in the early days of 1916 that the new C.-in-C. took over. Scheer, fifty-two years old, had commanded the 2nd Battle Squadron at the outset of war. Reinhard Scheer was one of the ablest and fastest-thinking flag-officers in the *Kriegsmarine*, much admired by his subordinates and fellow flag-officers. His vigorous and offensive spirit was well known in the British Admiralty, and it was recognized that a bolder policy was now likely to be pursued in the North Sea.

This was soon confirmed by an increase in activity in Room 40 reflecting the movements of German ships and future plans. No one at the Admiralty expected Scheer's appointment to lead to the sudden exodus of the entire High Seas Fleet seeking a decisive action with the Grand Fleet, as was indeed the case. But Scheer had the brief to apply 'systematic and constant pressure' on the British Fleet to provoke Jellicoe into greater activity in the hope of isolating and destroying units or squadrons of inferior strength.

Seventeen days after taking over, Scheer ordered a destroyer sweep east of the Dogger Bank. This interrupted a British minesweeping exercise and led to the destruction of the new sloop *Arabis* after a gallant fight against hopeless odds. There was a further, more serious loss that night when Tyrwhitt was returning from the abortive rescue mission and his flagship struck a German mine in a newly laid field. The *Arethusa*, which had led such a bold and eventful war, was driven onto a shoal and broke in two. This German exercise was, according to Corbett, no more than 'part of the method by which Admiral Scheer was tuning up his fleet for the part he was determined to see it play'.[17]

Three weeks later Scheer took out the entire High Seas Fleet and brought it farther south towards the entrance to the English Channel than on any previous occasion in the hope of netting larger game. Two fishing smacks was all it picked up. But here was certain proof that the offensive spirit was being activated by Scheer as never before.

The appointment of Scheer was echoed in the Grand Fleet by a new intensification in the search for a break in the stalemate. After the war

Churchill asked the rhetorical question, 'What was there that we could do which would force the German Navy to fight us at our own selected moment and on our own terms?' To which Jellicoe appended the marginal comment, 'Plans were constantly carried out to tempt the [High Seas Fleet] out with portions of the Grand Fleet as a bait.'[18]

A few days before the Lowestoft raid, Scheer's next offensive exercise, Jellicoe wrote to Beatty that, 'There is a feeling at the Admiralty which I think may lead to their trying to persuade me into what is called a 'more active policy'. After reciting the difficulties of supporting, for example, a seaplane raid with the entire Grand Fleet, he told Beatty, 'I am still trying to devise a means of drawing them further out.'[19]

Beatty agreed that an air raid was not the whole answer, though it might, at some risk, lead to a portion of the enemy force being 'snapped up'. He then proceeded to define the problem with characteristic economy and precision:

I am not arguing against air raids. Anything that we can do to harass and annoy has great advantages. And there is always the possibility that they may be tempted to overstep themselves, go too far with an inferior force, etc., which could be punished severely before it got back; and such operations fairly frequently may produce something which will be worth the risks. They would also have the advantage of denying [the enemy] the initiative, and so prevent him from bringing off any of his Set Pieces. But it is certain that he will not come out in *Grand Force* when we set the tune, i.e. to fight the Great Battle we are all waiting for.[20]

This Great Battle could not be delayed for ever, and was in fact only some seven weeks away. Suddenly, after twenty-two months of war, it seemed as if the need had become so sharp and urgent that, allied with fate, fair weather, and coincident timing, it must lead to the massive clash so ardently prepared for.

In the early days of May 1916, Admiral Scheer and his Staff drew up a plan which would answer the demand for more positive action, one of 'greater boldness than anything he had yet ventured'.[21] He intended to bombard Sunderland with Hipper's battle-cruisers after placing sixteen of his U-boats, withdrawn from commerce warfare, off Cromarty, Rosyth, and Scapa Flow. To safeguard his own bases, more U-boats would be stationed in suitable defensive positions. Beatty would be bound to come out in pursuit of Hipper's battle-cruisers and light cruisers, and any that escaped the U-boats' torpedoes would be lured south-east onto Scheer's battle squadrons and destroyed. The High Seas Fleet would then rapidly retire before

Jellicoe's squadrons – those that escaped the U-boat trap – could come within range. In order to ensure that Jellicoe did not surprise him on one of his frequent sweeps, Scheer's Zeppelins were to scout ahead in search of the enemy battle fleet. The U-boats sailed on 15 May, initiating the long-drawn-out series of movements by some 274 men o'war that would culminate in the clash of arms sixteen days later.

Jellicoe's plan, devised some three weeks after Scheer's, was also, according to Corbett, 'beyond anything we had yet hazarded'.[22] It called for two squadrons of light cruisers to arrive off the northern-most tip of Denmark, deep in the Skagerrak, by daylight on 2 June, and then sweep provocatively south down the Kattegat with a single squadron of dreadnoughts penetrating the Skagerrak in support. The seaplane-carrier *Engadine*, escorted by light cruisers and destroyers, would send up machines to scout ahead, while east of the Dogger Bank submarines would lie in wait to spring the trap. Beatty, and Jellicoe with his remaining battle squadrons, would station them-selves close to the entrance to the Skagerrak ready to fall on the vanguard of the High Seas Fleet as it sped north.

The similarity between the two plans demonstrated the limited options open to commanders intent on doing as much damage to the enemy while taking as few risks as possible and avoiding a full-scale gun duel against the total enemy forces. They also reflected the new face of sea warfare, introducing the two elements of air power and submarine power for the first time. The last-ever battle with the gun totally and exclusively resolving the outcome had been on 8 December 1914, south of the Falkland Islands.

But war is not a tidy business, and sea warfare in the North Sea, as in the days of sail, was still partly governed by visibility and the vagaries of the wind. In Scheer, boldness was tempered by a reasonable caution, and he was not going to leave the Jade for the middle of the North Sea with his Fleet, both flanks exposed, until his Zeppelin commanders had reported all clear. The days passed, with the U-boats completing their reconnaissance patrols and heading for their stations off Rosyth and Scapa, with orders to remain on station until 1 June. After the *Seydlitz* had completed her repairs, poor visibility, and contrary winds especially for May, continued to prohibit the use of Zeppelins. The last practicable day on which to sail was 30 May. When haze and low cloud and north-east winds still precluded the use of his Zeppelins, Scheer implemented his alter-native plan.

Plan Two was a good deal less ambitious, and much safer. Hipper would proceed with his full scouting force north to as far as the Norwegian southern coast, which would ensure his detection, while Scheer would follow some sixty miles behind and taking every precaution not to be detected. With the Danish coast protecting his starboard flank, his own light scouting forces could ensure that he was not taken by surprise from the west; and the first part of Plan One, the drawing of Beatty at Rosyth, Jerram at Cromarty, and Jellicoe at Scapa into the U-boat traps, would still operate.

Hipper sailed from the Jade at 1 a.m. on 31 May, his flag in the High Seas Fleet's newest battle-cruiser, the *Lützow*. Never had the risks been greater, the hopes higher. This was no tip-and-run raid. It was an offensive operation that could hardly fail to bring out the enemy. If he met light forces, he was to destroy them. If he met equal or superior forces he was to use every endeavour to lure them south onto the main battle squadrons, which would never be far behind.

At the Admiralty Ewing and his men had interpreted signals relating to Scheer's operation as early as 16–17 May, the night of the U-boats' departure, and recognized that Jellicoe's own offensive plan was likely to be pre-empted. Little more came in until the morning of 30 May when they read that the High Seas Fleet was ordered to assemble in the Jade roadstead by 7 p.m. that evening. The deduction was clear enough for the Admiralty to warn Jellicoe at midday 30 May that a major operation was in the offing and that the High Seas Fleet was likely to sail during the early hours of the morning of 31 May.

By 5 p.m. 30 May, Hall knew that Scheer had issued an operational signal at 3.40 p.m. Two hours later, Jellicoe learned that the 'Germans intend some operations commencing tomorrow'. By 11 o'clock that evening, two hours before Hipper sailed, the full might of the Grand Fleet was at sea and already heading for a rendezvous with Beatty's Battle Cruiser Fleet that would lead to a meeting with the enemy.

It was a dark and relatively warm night with no more than a slight swell in the North Sea. Sunrise was 4.50 a.m. but in this high latitude within three weeks of midsummer there would be light in the east long before then. Fine weather was forecast for the last day of May with some low cloud and the likelihood of mist. The wind, which had so persistently been from the east and north had backed north-west, and would later back further to the south-west, one of the numerous factors the commanders on both sides noted for the smoke factor in any gunnery action. Not that many officers or men on either side felt that there was any greater likelihood of a clash now than on any earlier operation. Hopes had, by May 1916, been so often dashed that most men had adjusted to a fatalistic expectation of disappointment. Only a favoured few at the top recognized that there was a greater chance of action than ever before.

There was no precedent in all the centuries of sea warfare for this titanic, half-blind race in the darkness of the ocean, trailing unseen clouds of black smoke as the Grand Fleet steered east; the Germans, thundering north, a new Navy without experience or tradition in fighting but rich and enthusiastic in technology. Sixty-four great battleships and battle-cruisers in all, manned by some 70,000 men, the population of a fair-sized town, every one with his specialized skill, age ranging from fourteen to the mid-fifties, from new recruits to men who had served a lifetime and boasted of roots in the Navy going back for generations.

Of the thirty-seven British dreadnoughts, six mounted 15-inch guns, one 14-inch, fifteen 13.5-inch and fifteen 12-inch. Although the 15-inch gun was already in use in the *Kriegsmarine*, the new battleship armed with eight of them was not yet worked up, and Scheer could bring to bear only 12-inch and 11-inch guns. Of his twenty-seven battleships and battle-cruisers fourteen were armed with 12-inch and thirteen with 11-inch guns. On the other hand, the German big ships were equipped with heavier secondary armament, all of them mounting between ten and fourteen 5.9-inch guns, while only the most recently completed British dreadnoughts were armed with 6-inch guns. None of these secondary guns would count seriously against armoured ships but might be important in countering destroyer attacks.

Because of the larger average calibre of Jellicoe's heavy guns, the total weight of broadside of his fleet was very considerably higher than Scheer's, 332,000 pounds against 134,000 pounds, discounting secondary armament. The Germans consoled themselves with the belief that the rate of fire of their guns was higher than the British, giving less of a disparity in pounds fired per minute, but this did not work out in practice. At maximum rate, the big guns on either side, whether 11-inch or 15-inch, could be fired every 20 to 50 seconds approximately, but this was not sustained for more than about 15 minutes as the physical effort involved was very considerable.

All but two of the British dreadnoughts were equipped for director firing for their main armament. German dreadnoughts were similarly equipped although the system was somewhat different. A periscope, electrically linked with every turret and operated from the conning tower, was kept on the target and electrically indicated the lateral movements of the target on a Director Pointer, or *Richtungsweiser*, to each heavy gun. Zeiss range-finders operated on the steroscopic principle in preference to the British coincidence principle. In the *Derfflinger*, one of the newest German battle-cruisers, there were seven large range-finders, and the average reading was electrically transmitted to each gun and indicated by a Range-Pointer.

'All the guns are kept dead on the enemy without anyone working the guns needing to see the target at all!' wrote the *Derfflinger*'s chief gunnery officer. 'The enemy may be near or distant. He may be far ahead or far astern. The ships may be travelling in parallel or on opposite courses. As long as the periscope is on the target, and as long as the proper range from the enemy has been established, every gun is aiming dead at that part of the hostile ship at which the periscope is pointing.'[23]

The German range-finder's stereoscopic principle demanded exceptional eyesight in the operator, with identical power for both eyes. The disadvantage of the British coincidence range-finder was that it was more light-absorbing and was markedly less efficient in poor visibility.

For their bigger guns and heavier broadsides, the British dreadnoughts paid the price of lighter protection. This was well known throughout both Fleets, and recognized (with some pride) by the British sailor as deliberate risk-taking. It was not only the weight of the gun that had to be provided for, but also the turret and its mounting and all the associated equipment and machinery. The four turrets and eight guns of the *Warspite*, for example, weighed about the same as the five turrets and ten 13.5-inch guns of her immediate predecessors. As well, the *Warspite*'s 15-inch shells in her magazines weighed almost three times that of, say, the *von der Tann*'s 11-inch shell.

As far as the comparable weight of armour is concerned, Jellicoe's figures in his account in *The Grand Fleet* tell their own story:

Battleships	Displacement	Wt. armour tons	Wt. deck protection tons	Total tons
HMS *Monarch*	22,500	4,560	2,010	6,570
SMS *Kaiser*	24,410	5,430	3,130	8,560
Battle Cruisers				
HMS *Queen Mary*	27,000	3,900	2,300	6,200
SMS *Seydlitz*	24,610	5,200	2,400	7,600

These figures show a German advantage of 33 per cent in the case of the battleships, and 25 per cent for the battle-cruisers; and that German battle-cruisers were as strong and well protected as British battleships while possessing a speed advantage of around 6 knots (except over the 5th Battle Squadron). On the other hand the British ships' superiority in weight of broadside was roughly comparable to the German ships' superiority in weight of protection. Given gunnery of equal quality, then, there would appear to be no doubt of the outcome of a ship-to-ship gunnery duel *if the quality of shell had also been equal*. But the quality of shell was not equal. As Jellicoe himself ruefully noted, 'We thus lost the advantage we ought to have enjoyed in *offensive* power due to the greater weight of our projectiles, while suffering the accepted disadvantage in the protection of our ships due to the heavy weight available for armour plating.'[24]

Paradoxically, German and British flotillas reflected reverse philosophies. The *Kriegsmarine*'s torpedo boats were smaller than their British counterparts, fitted with more torpedo tubes and smaller guns. The British boats were called torpedo boat *destroyers*, carried a heavier armament and fewer torpedoes, the emphasis of their function being to defend the battle line, i.e. the big gun, against German torpedoes, and to attack the German line as a secondary role.

For both Jellicoe and Scheer their constant concern was for the flotillas' ability to keep up with the fleet in heavy weather, and with their endurance which perforce was much more limited than that of the bigger vessels.

Jellicoe put to sea with twenty-six light cruisers, Scheer with thirteen. There was little to choose between them, although the newer British cruisers boasted 6-inch against German 4.1-inch main armament. All in all, they were fine modern vessels.

There were anomalies on both sides. Jellicoe incomprehensibly included no fewer than eight relatively old, armoured cruisers which, in accordance with a Fisher aphorism, had 'neither the guns to fight nor the speed to run away'. Armoured cruisers' guns had shown their ineffectiveness at the Falkland Islands, where the German 8·2-inch shells were little more effective than bricks against the battle-cruisers' armour, and at the Dogger Bank engagement where the *Blücher* was helpless in the face of 12-inch British shells. As to their ability to stand up to underwater attack, the *Aboukir*, *Hogue*, and *Cressy* had told their own melancholy story.

Even more surprising – at least to Jellicoe who in his Grand Fleet Battle Orders (GFBOs) wrote that 'it is doubtful whether these ships could take part in action . . . owing to their inferior speed' – Scheer brought his pre-dreadnoughts with him. There were six of them, the earliest laid down in 1902, armed with four 11-inch guns and capable of 18 knots when new, probably no more than 15 knots after twelve years' or so service, which would restrict the whole battle fleet to that speed. They were dubbed 'the five-minute ships' in the High Seas Fleet for the likely time they would last against British dreadnoughts. Scheer claimed later that he agreed to take them with him at the last moment because of the pleas of the 2nd Battle Squadron's flag-officer, Rear-Admiral Franz Mauve. But there is also evidence that he had in mind a contingency suicide role for them in an emergency.

Because of the virtual dissolution of the German Navy and dispersal of its personnel following the 1918 mutinies and the subsequent surrender and scuttling at Scapa Flow, relatively little is known of the true quality of the officers. The Versailles Treaty ensured that the *Kriegsmarine* returned to the size and strength it had been before the Kaiser/Tirpitz expansion of the early years of the century. All that is known, of a general nature, is that in its heyday the quality and *esprit de corps* of the High Seas Fleet's officers was extremely high and that ships' captains were less hide-bound and less concerned with tradition and protocol than their British opposite numbers.

Reinhard Scheer was a very different man to John Jellicoe. All that they had in common was a swift brain. But while Jellicoe was also a non-delegating, detail-obsessed plodder when haste was not urgently required, Scheer liked everything done in a hurry. 'He was impatient and always had to act quickly', said his Chief of Staff, Admiral Adolf von Trotha. 'He would expect his staff to have the plans and orders for an operation or manoeuvre worked out exactly to the last detail, and he would then come on the bridge and turn everything upside down. He was a commander of instinct and instant decision who liked to have all options presented to him, and then as often as not chose a course of action no one had previously considered.' In action 'he was absolutely cool and clear', von Trotha added, 'Jutland showed his great gifts, and a man like that must be allowed to drive his subordinates mad.'[25]

Scheer was fortunate as a C.-in-C. to have inherited the Navy's greatest admiral as battle-cruiser commander – by the *Kriegsmarine*'s definition, 'The Commander-in-Chief, Scouting Forces'. Hipper's appointment dated from before the war; he knew the job inside out, knew his men, knew his ships and their capabilities. His men had complete confidence in him and he was admired by them quite as much as Beatty by his men of the Battle Cruiser Fleet. Hipper possessed an element of the buccaneer which was unusual in a senior German officer. He never took a Staff College course. He disliked paperwork and theoretical speculation; was a man of action, 'an energetic and impulsive individual, with quick perception and a keen "seaman's eye" ',[26] according to his Chief of Staff.

Both Hipper and Beatty were, in both temperament and appearance, marvellously matched to their commands. Beatty was the more flamboyant, but he affected his sharp-tilted cap and non-regulation three-button monkey jacket as the distinctive and readily recognizable marks of his leadership and not as a cover for an inadequate brain. One of his staff officers, who later became his biographer, wrote that he had a 'phenomenally quick brain and he can take in all he wants to know in one glance'.[27] He spoke with the patrician voice fashionable at the time and in short, staccato sentences without a wasted word. This same officer also revelled in Beatty's sense of humour and the way he got 'a great deal of fun out of his staff officers, especially when they take themselves too seriously'.

Beatty's sureness of judgement is shown in his writing, especially in his frequent communications with Jellicoe, for whom at this time he had nothing but admiration and affection. What debarred him from being a great commander was his lack of imagination. He was acute and swift at anticipating what the enemy was likely to do and what he should do in reply; but he was less capable of imagining how others viewed what was happening. An admiral on his bridge should know what is likely to be going through the minds of other commanders who might be viewing and interpreting events quite differently. If Beatty had tried to understand the dilemma of his subordinates at the Dogger Bank engagement when the *Lion* was knocked out instead of condemning them for inaction, he would have been better equipped to face the next major action against the High Seas Fleet.

Beatty not only had the cream command in the Grand Fleet, he also had the cream of the flag-officers. The Hon. Horace Hood, his flag in the *Invincible*, was highly competent and renowned for his intellect. Sir William Pakenham (2nd BCS) possessed a high reputation as a wit, eccentric, and dandy. As an observer with the Japanese Navy in the war with Russia he had taken notes in action from a deck chair on the exposed quarterdeck of the flagship, evincing wonder among his hosts. When he descended below, to their delayed satisfaction, it was only to reappear in a fresh uniform after being spattered with blood from a nearby casualty. Flying his flag in the Princess Royal was Osmond de Beauvoir Brock, another of the Navy's few 'brains', as steady as he was clever.

Of Beatty's four light-cruiser commanders, two were exceptional. They were William Goodenough, the epitome of the bluff and intrepid mariner, and Edwyn Alexander-Sinclair, a red-haired Scot who could have fought at Bannockburn. All in all, the light-cruiser and destroyer officers were a fine bunch, by contrast with the battleship squadron commanders and ships' captains who, with certain exceptions, were sterile of intellect and imagination and lacking in initiative. On the other hand, the Royal Navy had always laid great emphasis on ship-handling, and where it counted most – among the flotillas – it was matchless.

JUTLAND: BATTLE-CRUISER ACTION

Dearth of intelligence in British and German Fleets – Misleading Admiralty signal to Jellicoe – And his failure to bring his aircraft-carrier – The importance, and belated arrival, of the 15-inch-gunned battleships – 'Enemy in sight' – More signalling failures in the Battle Cruiser Fleet – Germans open fire with singular light advantage – The fierce artillery duel in 'the run to the south' – The first British catastrophes – The flotillas go in – Commodore Goodenough's brilliant scouting – The appearance of the High Seas Fleet – Beatty reverses his course – 5th Battle Squadron takes a beating but gives as good as it receives

EQUIPPED as they were with such technically advanced equipment and machinery, it seems anachronistic that these men o'war of the Grand and High Seas Fleets knew so little about each other's whereabouts as they steamed silently through the night to their involuntary rendezvous. For all the computer-like director systems that enabled them, at a range of fourteen miles, to land a ton projectile squarely onto a 100-foot wide deck constantly moving laterally and forward; for all their hydraulic and electric power systems, their brilliantly engineered turbines, their wireless telegraphy and long-range searchlights; for all these, and countless more modern wonders of their age, neither side knew for sure that the other's scouting forces were out, nor their strength nor heading. And neither side had any idea that the other's main battle fleet was *even at sea*.

Radar was scarcely a generation away, efficient aerial reconnaissance closer still in time. But on the night of 30–31 May 1916 only speculation and contingency planning governed the calculations of the commanders, and ignorance was as dark as the night outside the chart-room, the ether undisturbed by a single note of information. And yet, had it not been for the wonders of wireless telegraphy and electronics, the British Fleet would still be in its bases, Admiral Hipper leading Admiral Scheer northwards into an empty sea instead of a *Nordsee* already occupied by an enemy of almost twice his own strength. What had gone right, and what had gone wrong to bring about this extraordinary overture of a twentieth-centure naval battle?

As part of the German moves against the unnerving way in which the British Admiralty seemed to keep track of German movements, intelligence had devised a simple ruse. When Scheer put to sea in his flagship he changed his call-sign from DK, the code letters for

Wilhelmshaven itself. Room 40 had rumbled this long ago but the OD remained unaware. Relations between the two departments had never been cordial, communication minimal. OD suspected that Room 40, with all its brainy fellows, some of them mere civilians, and with all its special hush-hush privileges, was encroaching on their territory.

For reasons never explained, at 12.30 p.m. on 31 May, when Jellicoe was already far out to sea, Rear-Admiral Thomas Jackson, the DOD, asked Room 40 where it placed the German call sign DK. The short answer: in Wilhelmshaven. Acting without the knowledge of Room 40, the DOD proceeded to transmit a telegram to Jellicoe informing him that the German flagship was still in the Jade at 11.10 a.m. 'Apparently they have been unable to carry out air reconnaissance which has delayed them.'

The message was all the more dangerous for being half true. The air reconnaissance for which Scheer had patiently waited for so many days, and was finally denied, depended upon the speed of the wind outside the Zeppelin sheds. Without mooring masts, the giant machines could not be manhandled out into the open if it was above 12 m.p.h., and for at least a week it had been blowing too strongly. But Scheer had in fact proceeded to sea *without air reconnaissance*.

This German deprival of air reconnaissance was matched by a British mishap reminiscent of the *Canopus* affair. Jellicoe possessed a single carrier with a complement of ten planes and fitted with a flying-off deck. She was a converted 20,000-ton Cunard liner, and was therefore fast, well able to keep up with the fleet. Due to some administrative slip rather than the fantasies of a Commander Denbow, Jellicoe had been informed that the *Campania* could do only 19 knots rather than her actual 21½ knots. Her anchorage in Scapa Flow was a remote one, and following a further mishap, her captain never received the signal at 8.10 p.m. on 30 May ordering the fleet to leave harbour at 9.30.

The *Campania* at length weighed two hours late. Jellicoe, ever mindful of the smallest detail in the dispositions of his ships, calculated that at 19 knots she would never arrive in time for her aircraft to be of any use, and at 4.37 a.m. she was ordered to return to Scapa rather than continue unescorted as a U-boat risk. In fact the carrier was rapidly gaining on the battle fleet and would have been with Jellicoe for some three hours before the enemy was sighted.

As the sun rose ahead of these numerous British ships steaming across the North Sea, Admiral Beatty's Battle Cruiser Fleet was approximately 120 miles east of the Firth of Forth on an almost due easterly heading, cruising at an easy 19 knots. His flag flew, as always, in the *Lion*, and he had with him the 1st Battle Cruiser Squadron, the 'Cat Squad' of three 13.5-inch gunned ships, *Princess Royal*, *Queen Mary*, and *Tiger*, the 2nd Battle Cruiser Squadron of two 12-inch gunned ships, *New Zealand* and *Indefatigable*, the 1st, 2nd and 3rd Light Cruiser Squadrons totalling thirteen ships, and twenty-nine destroyers; also the carrier *Engadine*, 'no more than a floating hangar' with three seaplanes in it, the sum total of aerial contribution to the pending battle.

Beatty was lacking four of his oldest and slowest battle-cruisers, the *Australia* which was in dockyard hands, and his 3rd Battle Cruiser Squadron, *Invincible*, *Indomitable*, and *Inflexible*. The absence of these ships was offset several times over by four of the five battleships of the 5th Battle Squadron. He had for long coveted and for long been denied these magnificent 15-inch-gunned battleships which were almost as fast (24½ knots) as the 'I-class' battle-cruisers, packed double their punch and were immensely stronger. Moreover, they had had the benefit of the superior facilities for gunnery practice provided for Scapa Flow-based ships to those in the confined area of the Forth and had a first-class squadron commander in Rear-Admiral Hugh Evan-Thomas. By ironic chance, Hood with the 3rd Battle Cruiser Squadron had been ordered to Scapa to provide his gunners with this much needed practice, and Jellicoe had temporarily detached the 15-inch-gunned ships in exchange. As a pointer to Beatty's hell-for-leather reputation among his flag-officers, Hood himself on hearing the news remarked, 'I think this is a great mistake. If David has these ships with him, nothing will stop him from taking on the whole German Fleet if he gets the chance.'

Beatty's orders were to proceed east to a rendezvous with Jellicoe's combined Grand Fleet at 2 p.m. 31 May 240 miles from Scapa Flow and approximately 90 miles west of the entrance to Skagerrak. But in order to reach this rendezvous he was to take his fleet a further 20 miles, and if he had by that point still had no news of the enemy, was to join Jellicoe.

Jellicoe at dawn was approximately 100 miles east of Scapa Flow on an easterly heading, his course soon to be altered to south-east-by-east, speed 15 knots, the most economical speed of his destroyers. With him were the 1st and 4th Battle Squadrons, sixteen battleships in all, Hood's three battle-cruisers, four armoured cruisers of the 2nd Cruiser Squadron, obsolete and armed with mixed batteries of 6-, 7.5-, and 9.2-inch guns, commanded by Rear-Admiral Herbert Heath, and the 4th Light Cruiser Squadron.

This force was due to link up with the 2nd Battle Squadron of eight more battleships, commanded by Vice-Admiral Sir Martyn Jerram, at noon. Jerram also had with him the 1st Cruiser Squadron of armoured cruisers, four more big ships which were little better than encumbrances. In command was Rear-Admiral Sir Robert Arbuthnot, Bt., a rabid disciplinarian and (not only for this reason) an unpopular officer, though an extremely able one. Finally, Jerram's force was screened by eleven destroyers of the most modern M-class, several of which had exceeded 37 knots on their trials.

At about this time, Hipper had left Heligoland behind on his starboard beam, and was steaming due north, his five battle-cruisers, screened by the 2nd Scouting Group of six light cruisers, and his destroyers. Scheer, some sixty miles behind, had combined his forces from the Elbe and the Jade and was proceeding on an identical course with his sixteen dreadnought and six pre-dreadnought battleships in three squadrons, escorted by the 4th Scouting Group of light cruisers.

Nine hours later, at 2 p.m., with the vanguard of both fleets now only 120 miles apart, neither C.-in-C. was any better informed of the whereabouts of the other, or knew for certain that any enemy ships at all were roaming the North Sea. The carefully stationed U-boats had all failed to damage any British ship as they passed through their 'traps'. Nor had they given to Scheer any clue to the fact that the entire Grand Fleet was at sea and heading in his direction. So far, then, the new weapons, the submarine and aircraft, had either failed in their task or been given no opportunity to exercise their skill. The only positive news Jellicoe had received was the dangerously misleading message from the Admiralty that at just before noon Scheer was still in the Jade. Jellicoe and Scheer were therefore equally ignorant of the singular stroke fate had played them, with the enemy falling unknowingly into a similar trap each side had prepared for the other.

In accordance with his instructions, Beatty ordered a signal to his fleet to alter course to N by E at 2.15 p.m., at the same time warning Evan-Thomas's 5th Battle Squadron, which was five miles to the north-west of him, to watch for the vanguard of Jellicoe's battle fleet with which they were soon to join forces. Five minutes earlier, the *Galatea*, Alexander-Sinclair's light cruiser and the easternmost British ship, sighted a stationary Danish merchantman, a modest little vessel blowing off steam as if nervously aware of the formidable forces closing about her. This sighting by a sharp-eyed look-out at a range of twelve miles was made just in time before Beatty's entire force, driving north, began to distance itself from the unseen enemy.

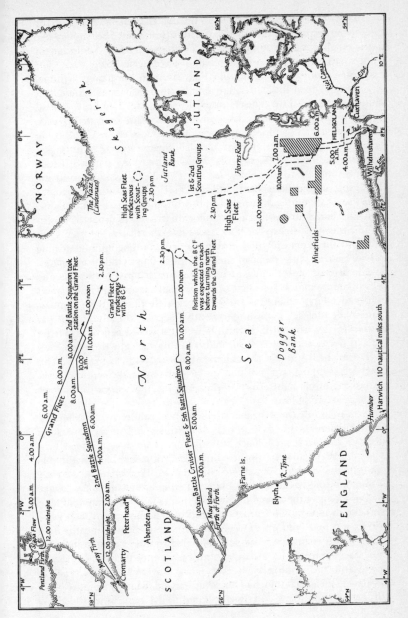

Map 5. The Battle of Jutland, 31 May–1 June 1916: the Fleets' approach

Hipper, fifty miles to the east of Beatty, and still heading for the Norwegian coast, learned that two of his destroyers had sighted the same suspicious-looking Danish vessel, the catalyst of the imminent battle, had turned to investigate, and ordered her to stop.

The *Galatea* at full speed, with the *Phaeton* in company, identified the German men o'war, though incorrectly, and at once signalled, 'Enemy in sight. Two cruisers probably hostile in sight bearing ESE course unknown.' Both British cruisers opened fire with their 6-inch guns at 2.28 p.m., and four minutes later as more enemy ships could be made out in the already variable visibility, a German light cruiser returned the fire at 15,000 yards, at once straddling the two British cruisers, and then hitting the *Galatea*. The shell was a dud; but the Battle of Jutland had been joined. On sighting more smoke to the north-east and east indicating considerable enemy forces, Alexander-Sinclair led his two swift cruisers to the north-west to draw the enemy on in order that Beatty's heavy forces could cut them off from their bases, at the same time performing his primary function of reporting range, bearing, and course of enemy ships as they could be made out.

The second movement was made by Beatty's battle-cruisers and was precisely matched to that of the two light cruisers. The *Galatea*'s report of 'a large amount of smoke as from a fleet bearing ENE at 2.35 p.m. made it clear', according to Beatty's report, 'that the enemy was to the Northward and Eastward, and that it would be impossible for him to round the Horns Reef without being brought to action.'[1] At 2.32 p.m. Beatty made the general signal by flags to turn SSE, his destroyers taking up position as a submarine screen, and the remainder of his light cruisers spreading out to the east forming an advance scouting force.

At 2.40 p.m., the battle-cruisers in two columns with the *New Zealand* leading the *Indefatigable* three miles to the north-east of Beatty's *Lion* were on a south-easterly course and heading for Horns Reef, confident now and for the first time in the war of being able to cut off any enemy vessels to the north. Word spread rapidly throughout the Battle Cruiser Fleet, from the bridge of the *Lion* to the engine rooms of the racing destroyers, that action was imminent, and that this was to be no fruitless pursuit of a fleeing enemy. After the frustration and failure at Dogger Bank, among Beatty and his Staff there was a rising sense of determination and expectancy that this time they were going 'to bag the lot'. Certainly Beatty's heart was high, and the same elation and relief that this was the day of reckoning for which they had been waiting for so long was reflected in all the battle-cruisers. Beatty calculated that Hipper would have six battle-cruisers this time, including the recently complete *Hindenburg*. Ship for ship, he felt more than equal. But in addition, and by happy chance, he had the 5th Battle Squadron whose guns far outranged the enemy's and whose combined broadside weight alone was greater.

Unhappily, the same belief that battle would soon be joined did not yet prevail amongst these super-dreadnoughts of the 5th Battle Squadron. Evan-Thomas's ships were still on a northerly course and heading in the opposite direction to that of the two battle-cruiser squadrons. Once again Beatty's signalling arrangements had broken down. At 2.25 p.m. the *Barham* and her consorts, to the north-west of the *Lion*, were following the turn to the north to join Jellicoe. The signal by flags from the *Lion* seven minutes later was not taken in by the *Barham* and the repeated signal to turn by searchlight five minutes later was either not seen or simply not recorded in the *Barham*'s signal log. More minutes were lost because the *Tiger* as repeating ship failed to pass on Beatty's signal and when it was taken in there was no indication as to when the order was made executive, which is normally when a signal is hauled down. According to the *Barham*'s captain, Arthur Craig, the flagship was on a SSE course by 2.38, but only 'in consequence of 1st LCS [Alexander-Sinclair] reporting enemy cruiser SSE at 2.35 p.m.'[2]

By this time the 5th Battle Squadron with its decisive gunnery capability was ten miles from the battle-cruisers and out of their sight. *Barham*'s speed was 22 knots, with 2½ knots in reserve; the *Lion*'s speed 19½ knots with 8½ knots in reserve.

Between the time of this crucial signal to turn south-east and 3 p.m., Beatty made several turns to port until he was steering due east, directed by Alexander-Sinclair who had now succeeded in drawing the distant enemy force to the north-west. The commodore was continuing his brilliant and dangerous work in accordance with the finest traditions of fleet scouting, and drawing Hipper and Beatty together. Then, at 3.35 p.m., Alexander-Sinclair observed the enemy light-cruiser screen suddenly reverse course to the south-east. Ten minutes later he observed the distant flickers of yellow light on the south-eastern horizon which could only mean the firing of heavy guns. It was 3.45 p.m., the battle-cruisers were engaged, and there were still at least five hours of daylight in which to conclude a successful fleet action.

The German cruiser which had scored that first hit on the *Galatea* was the *Elbing*, 4,500 tons, a fine, modern, fast (28 knots) cruiser armed with 5.9-inch guns. With three destroyers in company, she pursued the *Galatea* and *Phaeton* to the north-west. Little more than a mile astern of the *Elbing* raced the 2nd Scouting Group's flagship, *Frankfurt*, Rear-Admiral Friedrich Bödicker, and at varying distances the rest of Hipper's light cruisers and destroyers. The battle-cruisers in line ahead were on the same north-westerly course, to the left of their screen. They were therefore unprotected and without scouting benefit to the west from which any enemy was likely to appear, an inexplicable tactical weakness.

The enemy did appear from the west at 3.20 p.m. when Hipper's look-outs discerned six grey shapes streaming black smoke hull down at fourteen miles. They were at once presumed to be Beatty's battle-cruisers although at first no details of their funnels or rig could be made out. They appeared to be in two groups, two ships leading four more, steering north-west on a south-west bearing and coming straight towards them. Evan-Thomas's squadron was not yet in sight, but the presence of Beatty's battle-cruisers alone was sufficient to cause Hipper to cut short his drive north, turn without more ado, and hope to draw his adversary onto Scheer's battle squadrons. With his own speed at its maximum of 26 knots, and Scheer's at 15 knots, it should be no more than an hour before the overwhelming gunpower of the High Seas Fleet would reinforce the battle-cruisers and the long-planned trap be sprung.

At 3.28, then, the five German battle-cruisers swung through 180 degrees in succession, just as the Japanese Admiral Togo had boldly reversed the course of his battle fleet at Tsu-Shima against the Russians in 1905. Hipper, however, was still safely out of range as the last of his ships, the *von der Tann*, completed her turn at 3.33 p.m. and the *Lützow* led the Group south.

In the fore-top of the second in line, the *Derfflinger*, the chief gunnery officer, Georg von Hase, still had not learned that the British Battle Cruiser Fleet in its full strength was closing in on them. He believed that they had sighted only light enemy forces. 'Suddenly my periscope revealed some big ships. Black monsters; six tall, broad-beamed giants steaming in two columns', he wrote of this moment (3.35 p.m.). Then he watched Beatty turn south-east on a converging course with his own battle line. 'Heavy guns armour-piercing shell!' van Hase ordered. 'Direction on second battle-cruiser from left [*Princess Royal*] 102 degrees! Ship making 26 knots, course ESE! 17,000! Our target has two masts and two funnels, as well as a narrow funnel close to the foremast! Deflection 19 left! Rate 100 minus! 16,400! Still no permission to open fire from the flagship!'[3]

The order came a few minutes later. Although visibility conditions were favourable, with the bright afternoon light behind the British, and Hipper was 4,000 yards inside the maximum range of his 11-inch guns, all the German ships overestimated the range, the first salvoes falling on the far side of the British line. With the range already closing, and the first sparkles of fire rippling along the line of six British ships as they returned the fire, the *Derfflinger*'s next salvo was an 'over' too. And the next. It was four minutes before this crack gunnery ship recorded a straddle on the *Princess Royal*.

'I explain the serious error of calculation as follows', wrote von Hase. 'The B.g. men [Basis Gerät, or range-finder operators] were completely overwelmed by the first view of the enemy monsters. Each one saw the enemy ship magnified twenty-three times in his instrument! Their minds were at first concentrated on the appearance of the enemy.'[4] So, for all the years of training and practice, for all the optical and mechanical skills lavished on the instruments of these modern miracles of war, the sight of the enemy proved too much, and many rounds from all the German ships were wasted before the German guns began to find the range.

A few seconds after 3.52 p.m., von Hase ordered '*Gut schnell Wirkung*', which meant the 12-inch main batteries were to fire in salvoes every twenty seconds, with the secondary 5.9s, now within range, firing two salvoes in rapid succession in the intervals.

Then began an ear-splitting, stupefying din. Including the secondary armament we were firing on an average one mighty salvo every seven seconds . . . Dense masses of smoke accumulated round the muzzles of the guns, growing into clouds as high as houses, which stood for seconds in front of us like an impenetrable wall and were then driven by the wind and the weigh over the ship. In this way we often could see nothing of the enemy for seconds at a time as our fore-top was completely enveloped in thick smoke.[5]

Finding that the 'splashes' from the two calibres of guns were confusing him – the first reason for the introduction of the all-big-gun dreadnought – von Hase ordered the secondary guns to cease fire. This reduced the visibility problem at once, and the *Derfflinger* settled down to a steadier rate of fire in the much improved visibility, with the range closing, and with the additional advantage that no fountains of water, a hundred feet high and surrounded by spray, interrupted the view of the enemy through range-finder or periscope. For some mysterious reason, not one of the more numerous British battle-cruisers was firing at the German second in line.

Beatty might bless that little Danish steamer for bringing him into contact at last with his adversary. And he was gratified that he had caught him so far from his base and with no chance of falling back onto it without a battle. But already it was evident that a delayed meeting, when Jellicoe would have been nearer and Hipper closer to the Norwegian coast, would have been much more advantageous, and might well have allowed Beatty to get round to the east of the German battle-cruisers. Now, from the very outset, he had lost one of his greatest advantages, his longer-ranging guns. A situation that Hipper had always feared most was the one in which he was outranged and helpless to reply, as von Spee had been at the Falkland Islands. On this last afternoon of May, North Sea weather saved him. Beatty's biographer, who was on the *Lion*'s bridge at the time, described conditions as 'one of those typical North Sea summer days with a thin white mist varying in intensity and having too much humidity for the sun to break up.'[6]

The German ships were diffuse grey shapes against a dark background, the British line etched clear against the afternoon sky. In reverse positions, Beatty could have opened fire at 23,000 yards and held that range at which Hipper could not have replied. On the *Lion*'s bridge the range-receiver showed 20,000 yards and rapidly closing at 3.40 p.m., speed 25 knots. The flag-captain, Ernle Chatfield, was on the compass platform with his navigator, Commander the Hon. Arthur Strutt, and the chief gunnery officer, Gerald Longhurst, and his Staff. Beatty was on his own bridge below with his secretary and Staff and the unfortunate flag-lieutenant, Ralph Seymour. 'I wanted Beatty to come on the compass platform,' wrote Chatfield, 'and sent a message to Seymour, telling him to advise Beatty that the range was closing rapidly and that we ought almost at once to be opening fire. But Beatty was too busy getting a message through to Jellicoe. And every second that passed reduced the advantage of the 13.5-inch guns of the flagship and the other 'big cats'. Still the coincidence range-finders gave no certain reading, and it was Hipper with his 12-inch guns who opened fire first. 'I could wait no longer,' said Chatfield, 'and told Longhurst to open fire.'[7]

Beatty thought he had opened fire at 18,500 yards, his flag-captain thought it was 16,000 yards, the reality was around 15,000 yards. Every shot was therefore an 'over', and it took much longer than the Germans' five minutes or so to adjust the range. As soon as Beatty saw that he was much closer to the enemy than he had thought, he opened the range by altering course to SSE. Hipper in reply turned onto a southerly heading, and a steady gunnery duel, the most destructive in history, developed on parallel courses.

The *Lion* was hit twice within the first five minutes. 'On the bridge', wrote Lieutenant William Chalmers, 'we were blissfully ignorant of the fact that two large shells had exploded in the ship: the rush of wind and other noises caused by the high speed at which we were travelling, together with the roar of our own guns as they fired, four at a time, completely drowned the noise of bursting shell.'[8]

After the signalling fiascos at the Dogger Bank, it seems remarkable that there could have been confusion again about the distribution of fire as ordered by Beatty at 3.46 p.m. But this is just what happened. To gain maximum advantage from his numerical superiority, Beatty ordered his own ship and the next in line, *Princess Royal*, to concentrate on Hipper's flagship, *Lützow*, and the others to engage ship for ship. The *Queen Mary* missed the signal, as transmitted *by flags only*, and fired at her opposite number, the third in the German line, *Seydlitz*, leaving von Hase in the *Derfflinger* to fire unimpeded for ten precious minutes.

This error was compounded by the *Tiger* which also failed to see the *Lion*'s signal. This resulted in her and the *New Zealand* both firing at the *Moltke*. Meanwhile, at the end of the line, the two oldest battle-cruisers present, the *von der Tann* and *Indefatigable*, fought their own private duel.

The effect of the cannonade intensified as both sides warmed to the work, nerves steadied and spotters and range-takers corrected, and the complex sequence of directing and laying and reloading assumed a desperate rhythm amidst the cacophony of sound that reached to every quarter of every vessel. Already the Dogger Bank engagement seemed a relatively tame business. No amount of gunnery practice could simulate these conditions. 'All round us huge columns of water, higher than the funnels, were being thrown up as the enemy shells plunged into the sea', wrote Lieutenant Chalmers of this period on the *Lion*'s bridge. 'Some of these gigantic splashes curled over and deluged us with water. Occasionally, above the noise of battle, we heard the ominous hum of a shell fragment and caught a glimpse of polished steel as it flashed past the bridge.'[9]

After the battle, many other eyewitnesses were puzzled that a serious explosion elsewhere on a ship was not even noticed. When the *Lion* received its most serious hit soon after 4 p.m., many of the officers on the bridge felt nothing at all, and the first news was delivered by a Royal Marines sergeant, groggy from shock, his face black, hair singed and clothes burnt. He managed to stagger up to the flagship's bridge, stand to attention, salute, and report in a dull voice, ' "Q" turret knocked out, sir. All the crew are killed, and we have flooded the magazines.' He was, in fact, the only survivor from this holocaust.

A heavy German shell had penetrated the front armour plate of the

turret at its joint with the roof plate, blowing half the roof into the air.
The cordite in the loading cages was ignited and half the men had
been killed or mortally wounded. Major F. J. W. Harvey did not die
instantly. He managed to reach a voice pipe and ordered the handing
room crew to close the magazine doors and flood the magazines to
prevent the flames reaching the magazine itself. He was later awarded
a posthumous VC.

No such opportunity for courageous and instant reaction was
granted to Beatty's last ship. The *Indefatigable* had been firing
accurately and steadily at the *von der Tann*, and hitting the German
ship several times, when a salvo of three 11-inch shells fell onto the
upper deck at 4.02 p.m. The German AP (armour-piercing) shell had
only an inch of steel to pierce. All the shells appeared to explode deep
inside the battle-cruiser. She hauled out of line, already sinking by the
stern. Like a vicious kick at a dying dog, the next salvo caught the big
ship near the fore 12-inch 'A' turret. There was another gigantic
explosion and she heeled over and disappeared from sight.

Seconds later, Chalmers went out on the *Lion*'s bridge and looked
down the line of firing ships. 'How magnificent they looked with their
huge bow waves and flashing broadsides', he recorded. But astern of
the last of them he saw only an enormous pall of grey smoke. 'I gazed
at this in amazement, and at the same time tumbled to the fact that
there were only five battle cruisers in our line . . . I glanced quickly
towards the enemy. How many of them were afloat? Still five.'[10]

No matter how accurately the British guns fired, at no matter what
range, and while certainly scoring hits, the enemy's ships remained
afloat, with the rate and destructive capacity of their fire seemingly
undiminished.

The Germans thought they had done for the *Lion*, too, and the lucky
few who could see what was happening experienced a great sense of
elation at the way they seemed to be mastering the enemy. The huge
explosion on the enemy flagship was followed by a steadily burning
fire, and when Chatfield ordered a 5-degree turn to starboard to open
up the range, Hipper thought she was hauling out of line like the
Indefatigable before her. But a few minutes later, Hipper recognized the
harsh reality of his position. He made two more observations, as well,
both of which added to the certain truth that no matter what losses he
had caused the enemy he still had a fight on his hands.

Beatty had sent in the 9th Destroyer Flotilla to take some of the
pressure off his ships, and at almost the same time, he observed even
taller shell splashes falling among the German ships. Evan-Thomas's
5th Battle Squadron was at last in range, and his 15-inch shells were

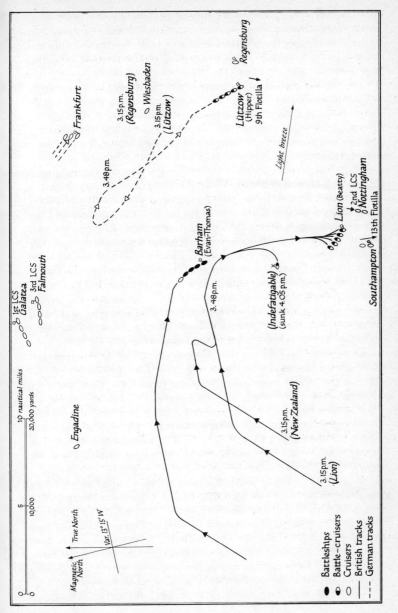

Map 6. The Battle of Jutland. Situation at 4.10 p.m.

Battleships
Battle-cruisers
Cruisers
British tracks
German tracks

Magnetic North
True North
Var. 13° 15′ W

Engadine

1st LCS
Galatea
3rd LCS
Falmouth

Frankfurt

3.15 p.m.
(Regensburg)
Wiesbaden
3.15 p.m.
(Lützow)

3.48 p.m.

Regensburg

Lützow
(Hipper)
9th Flotilla

Light breeze

Barham
(Evan-Thomas)

3.48 p.m.

(Indefatigable)
(sunk 4.05 p.m.)

3.15 p.m.
(New Zealand)

3.15 p.m.
(Lion)

Lion (Beatty)

2nd LCS
Nottingham

Southampton
13th Flotilla

10 nautical miles
20,000 yards
10,000
5

now adding a new dimension to the destructive gunnery duel which had already blown up one ship and severely damaged others. 'As many-headed as a Hydra,' the German Official History describes this moment, 'the British Navy thus produced four more powerful opponents to take the place of the destroyed *Indefatigable*.'

The officers and men in the fore-top of the *Derfflinger* continued to enjoy an uninterrupted view of the enemy line. For them, it might have been peacetime target practice in the Baltic. Through his periscope the chief gunnery officer could make out the bearing of the turrets and gun barrels of the *Queen Mary*, and confirm that they were directed at the *Seydlitz*.

This peace was short-lived. Von Hase observed the distant fingers of the 13.5-inch barrels swinging onto his ship, and the stab of muzzle flash as they fired. What astonished him, and so many of those few on both sides who were above decks during this engagement, was the clarity with which they could observe the enemy shells racing towards them, one more feature of modern sea warfare that no manoeuvres nor gunnery practice could prepare them for.

'With each salvo fired by the enemy,' von Hase recalled, 'I was able to see distinctly four or five shells coming through the air. They looked like elongated black spots. Gradually they grew bigger, and then – crash! they were here. They exploded on striking the water or the ship with a terrific roar. After a bit I could tell from watching the shells fairly accurately whether they would fall short or over.'[11]

The *Queen Mary* was shooting superbly, the Germans reported, and was scoring hits on the *Derfflinger*. When the *Lion* appeared to fall out of line, burning fiercely, the *Derfflinger* turned her guns from the *Princess Royal* onto a new target. With the loss of the *Indefatigable*, the *Seydlitz*, too, concentrated her fire on the *Queen Mary*, which was firing full eight-gun broadsides but also taking a lot of hits, each one momentarily marked by a dull glow. The range was about 15,000 yards, and for the German gunners the target remained sharply outlined against the western sky.

At 4.26 p.m., after receiving a number of hits from the 11-inch-gunned *Seydlitz*, the *Queen Mary* took a full salvo – four 12-inch shells – forward. This caused a massive explosion, which was at once followed by an even greater explosion amidships. The 26,000-ton battle-cruiser broke up as if crushed underfoot. Her bows disappeared, her stern for a moment rose high in the air, and as the *Tiger* and *New Zealand* raced past, littered by hot falling debris, the propellers were seen to be still turning as if to accelerate mercifully her descent to the bottom.

Von Hase described the dying moment of his victim, with black debris flying, 'and immediately afterwards the whole ship blew up with a terrific explosion. A gigantic cloud of smoke rose, the masts collapsed inwards, the smoke hid everything and rose higher and higher'[12]; to a height, he estimated, of 300 to 400 metres.

Captain Percy Oram, in the destroyer *Obdurate*, thought 'the stark reality too stupendous to take in. One felt involved in the occult, a trick in which a conjuror's black pall lifted to reveal – nothing.'[13] A gunlayer in the *Tiger* described how the German shells had been straddling the *Queen Mary*, 'when suddenly a most remarkable thing happened. Every shell that the Germans threw seemed suddenly to strike the battle cruiser at once. It was as if a whirlwind was smashing a forest down, and reminded me very much of the rending that is heard when a big vessel is launched and the stays are being smashed.' The *Queen Mary*'s launch had taken place on the Clyde four years and two months earlier. Hall had been her first captain, and by sensible and liberal treatment of his men had made her the happiest ship in the Fleet. Now 'she seemed to roll slowly to starboard, her masts and funnels gone, and with a huge hole in her side. She listed again, the hole disappeared beneath the water, which rushed into her and turned her completely over. A minute and a half, and all that could be seen of the *Queen Mary* was her keel, and then that disappeared.'[14] A midshipman and a rating were later picked up by a German vessel, and a handful more survivors by the British destroyer *Laurel* – that was all of a total complement of 1,266.

The battle-cruiser fight was now at its most savage, its sound and fury increased by a close-fought contest between the destroyers. Hipper had ordered his destroyers into the shell-torn seas between the two lines of big ships at the same time as Beatty. Here, for some fifteen minutes the German light cruiser *Regensburg* (4,900 tons, twelve 4.1-inch) with fifteen destroyers fought a tumultuous gun and torpedo duel with twelve of Beatty's destroyers led by the light cruiser *Champion* (3,800 tons, three 6-inch, six 4-inch) at ranges down to less than two miles. According to Corbett,

It was a wild scene of groups of long low forms vomiting heavy trails of smoke and dashing hither and thither at thirty knots or more through the smother and splashes, and all in a rain of shell from the secondary armament of the German battle cruisers, as well as from the *Regensburg* and the destroyers, with the heavy shell of the contending squadrons screaming overhead. Gradually a pall of gun and funnel smoke almost hid the shell-tormented sea, and beyond the fact that the German torpedo attack was crushed, little could be told of what was happening.[15]

On the British side, there were several reckless charges to close range against the German battle-cruisers, which threw over their helms to dodge the torpedoes. Only one of them struck home, doing relatively little damage, on the *Seydlitz*. Two destroyers on each side were sunk in this mêlée before Beatty called off the attack at 4.40 p.m.

On the *Lion*'s bridge, Captain Chatfield, assuming the temporary mantle of a naval Boswell, reported on Beatty's comments as the battle entered its climax and the second loss, the second disaster, struck his fleet. 'The thought of my friends in [the *Queen Mary*] flashed through my mind', wrote Chatfield. 'I thought also how lucky we had evidently been in the *Lion*. Beatty turned to me and said, "There seems to be something wrong with our bloody ships to-day", a remark which needed neither comment nor answer.'

For the present, however, there was nothing wrong with the giants of the 5th Battle Squadron, nor with their shooting. Still at their maximum speed of 24–25 knots, the *Barham* led the *Valiant*, *Warspite*, and *Malaya* south until they were as close to the German line as Beatty's surviving battle-cruisers. *Barham* had opened fire on the *von der Tann*, and had shifted to the second to last ship when, *Moltke* came within range. 'The Germans saw the salvoes falling absolutely together and closely concentrated,' according to Corbett, 'and were full of admiration for the remarkable fire direction it revealed.'[16]

Hipper's concern about this new accretion of enemy power and his need for relief was as great as the need for reinforcement Beatty had felt and which Evan-Thomas had provided. It was a characteristic of this ding-dong 'run to the south', as it will always be called and which had proved so tragically destructive, that each side, when pressed to the limit, was relieved in the nick of time. No G. A. Henty would have dared to construct a plot so pat as this battle was formulating. In spite of the loss of one of his best ships, and another of relatively small value, Beatty still had three of his 'big cats' battleworthy, the 12-inch-gunned *New Zealand*, which seemed to bear a charmed life (it was said later because her captain always wore a good-luck Maori skirt in battle, which had been presented to the ship for that purpose), and the 5th Battle Squadron.

Beatty's tactical situation to the west of his adversary remained disadvantageous, but he could still cut him off from his base, and with his overwhelming superiority in gun power must destroy him before darkness set in.

Everything appeared set for this last triumphant strike against his old adversary, when Beatty's flagship took in a W/T signal from his most advanced scouting cruiser: 'Have sighted enemy battle fleet bearing approximately SE, course of enemy N . . . '

Light-cruiser commanders are as different in temperament and outlook from battleship commanders, as destroyer men, with their own unique and dashing style, are different again. Goodenough was typical of the cruiser breed – the successors to Nelson's frigate men – and combined all the best attributes: a burning need to search out the enemy and learn his strength and likely intentions, the tenacity to hold on like a terrier, the coolness and precision of expression to communicate swiftly to his C.-in-C. all the intelligence he could offer.

The task of complementing the earlier work of Alexander-Sinclair in bringing the battle-cruiser forces into contact appropriately fell upon 'Barge' Goodenough, whose performance in the past had not always met with Beatty's approval, but should have done. At 4.30 p.m., as the furious destroyer action opened up, Goodenough in the *Southampton*, with the *Birmingham*, *Nottingham*, and *Dublin*, was on a south-easterly course, two and a half miles ahead of the *Lion*. He had resisted the temptation of throwing his squadron into the destroyer attack, which would have suited his temperament admirably, and correctly stuck to his first duty of scouting ahead.

Suddenly, dead ahead, there came into sight a great black pall of distant smoke, and then almost at once the masts, funnels and upper-works of battleships. Arthur Peters, the flag-lieutenant, spoke for all those on the bridge of the racing *Southampton*. 'Look, sir, this is the day of a light cruiser's lifetime. The whole of the High Seas Fleet is before you.'

The look-out filled in the details: sixteen battleships, with a destroyer screen disposed around them on each bow, in single line ahead, with six more battleships taking up the rearguard – the entire strength of Scheer's battle fleet. The range, rapidly closing, was about 13,000 yards, little more than seven land miles. Peters was ready to send the news to Beatty. Edward Rushton, 'efficient and cool' according to his commodore, remarked laconically, 'If you're going to make that signal, you'd better make it now, sir. You may never make another.'

There were other remarks from the officers present, 'some acid, some ribald'; but Peters had already got off the signal. 'I held on a little longer,' recalled Goodenough, 'and [Rushton] laughed and said, half to himself, "This is madness." It was curious that I said to him, "No, no, Commander, I can do no wrong today, whatever stupidities I may have committed on other days." '[17]

The *Southampton* was brought in to within 12,000 yards of the enemy's vanguard, the battleship *König*, flying the flag of Rear-Admiral Paul Behncke. Any one of more than fifty heavy guns could have blown the little cruiser out of the water with one hit. Not one opened fire, while Goodenough completed his examination. The German gunnery officers had seen him before he had made his first report, but with only a hazy end-on view of his ship failed at first to identify the *Southampton* for certain. When fire was finally opened, the *Southampton* turned on full helm, heeling hard over until her rails were close to brushing the water. Zig-zagging at 25 knots, she made off with her consorts, signalling by searchlight as the shells fell about her and the tall fountains of water from near misses fell like trees across the cruiser, soaking everyone above decks.

'Damn, how I hate this wet!' complained Lieutenant Ralph Ireland, navigating officer. Another officer claimed that he had never before known how much protection there was in a canvas screen.

Sensitive to the criticism he had attracted after the Scarborough raid eighteen months earlier, Goodenough was not going to let go of the High Seas Fleet now that he had found it. 'If ever I see another German ship,' the Commodore had declared, 'I won't lose sight of her until one or other of us is sunk.'[18]

The speedy, evasive little cruisers made a difficult target for the German gunners, streaming smoke from their four funnels, zig-zagging unpredictably. Lieutenant Stephen King-Hall reckoned that forty large shells fell within 75 yards of the *Southampton*, and many more almost as close. 'We seemed to bear a charmed life . . . How we escaped for an hour, amazes everyone from the Commodore downwards . . . I can truthfully say that I thought each succeeding minute would be our last . . . Needless to say we could not fire a shot in return as the range was about 16,000 yards.'[19]

This cruiser's navigator, Lieutenant Ralph 'Paddy' Ireland, had worked out a plan for just this desperate situation which any scouting force was likely to find itself in. He 'steered the ship in the direction of the last splash, with the notion that the enemy having registered an "over" would reduce the range for the next salvo, by which time our range would, in fact, have increased. Thus we were enabled, without damage, to continue making enemy reports so long as we maintained touch with the enemy.'[20]

The navigator of the *Nottingham*, who was to survive, too, found the experience stirring. 'Salvo after salvo we were able to dodge in this way,' he wrote, 'and although I think one may say that the man who says he enjoys a naval battle on the whole is well, – not exactly accurate, I must confess that I never had a more interesting and, in a way, really amusing half hour than I had conning the ship at that time.'[21]

By contrast, the *Lion* had been severely battered although not as disabled as at the Dogger Bank. Two of her eight heavy guns were out of action, there were many wounded and dying about the ship. Her electrics had gone for the time being and she was reduced to using the *Princess Royal* as signalling ship as she had only short-range W/T left to her.

On receipt of Goodenough's first sighting signal, Beatty ordered the *Lion* to alter course slightly in her direction. Almost at once he had visual confirmation that the High Seas Fleet, far from still being in the Jade, as the Admiralty had insisted, was less than twelve miles away, deployed in a single line for action, and already firing heavily on his light cruisers. He told Seymour to make a general signal to turn in succession 16 points to starboard thus reversing his fleet's course, with the intention of drawing Scheer towards Jellicoe as rapidly as possible. If he had been surprised by the sudden appearance of the German battle squadrons, he was also quite certain now that Scheer had no idea that Jellicoe with his battle squadrons was in close proximity, too. The duty of his battle-cruisers, like those of his own light scouting squadrons earlier, was to report on and to lure on the superior enemy force. The fact that he had lost two of his 'bloody ships' was merely a regrettable statistic which in no way affected his duty or his decisions.

Evan-Thomas's 5th Battle Squadron was eight miles behind Beatty's rearmost ship, the *New Zealand*, when the *Southampton* sighted the German Fleet. The enemy battle-cruisers at that time were almost abeam, and the *Barham* was firing at the *Moltke*. 'The enemy presented a fair target at a range of 18,000–17,000 yards, and was frequently straddled', reported the flag-captain. 'Three certain hits only were seen, but after we started using AP Lyddite, hits could not be seen. This would naturally be the case, however, and it was noted that the enemy hits on *Barham*, though doing great internal damage, did not show outside the ship.'[22]

The *Lion*'s flag signals were too distant to be read by the *Barham*. Visibility had suddenly deteriorated, according to Captain Craig, and the British battle-cruisers themselves were evidently half-obscured because, when they reversed course, he thought they had turned to port onto their northerly direction instead of to starboard. What he could see – but only just – was that the German battle-cruisers had turned north, too. For a moment, Evan-Thomas and his Staff were

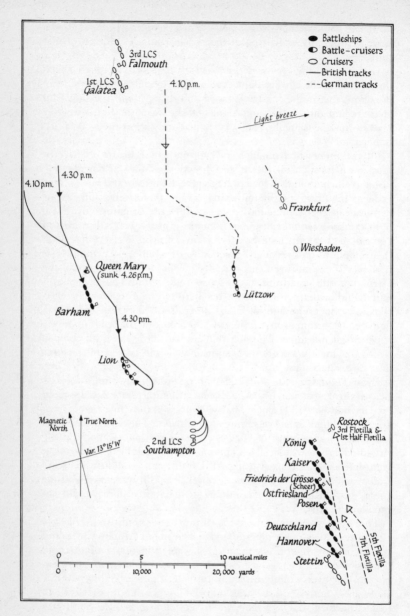

Map 7. The Battle of Jutland. Situation at 4.48 p.m.

puzzled by this new development. Why this turn? Was Hipper pursuing Beatty north, or were the Germans in retreat, heading perhaps for the Skagerrak and the safety of the Baltic? The flagship's W/T office had not taken in the *Southampton*'s sighting report, nor had the distant morse searchlight signal been readable. Beatty had not repeated either the sighting report from the *Southampton* by search-light, or the order to the Battle Cruiser Fleet to turn 16 points. It was not until the *Barham* herself sighted the vanguard of the German line that Evan-Thomas recognized the reason why both German and British battle-cruisers were now driving north through the deterio-rating visibility, firing intermittently at one another.

And so it came about that at 4.48 p.m. Evan-Thomas with his four super-dreadnoughts still steaming south, was approaching Beatty steaming north at a combined closing speed of 50 knots, 26 knots by Beatty, 24 by Evan-Thomas. Just before the 5th Battle Squadron thundered past on the *Lion*'s port beam, Beatty hoisted a flag signal ordering it to turn through 16 points to conform to his own northerly course – the turn to be made in succession (ship by ship) to starboard. However, the signal was not executive until it was hauled down. By then five more minutes had been lost, and as a consequence and because Beatty had ordered a starboard turn, Evan-Thomas was almost out of touch with Beatty's rear and dangerously close to Scheer's battle squadrons.

Two of the leading German battleships opened fire on the *Barham* as she completed her turn and, assisted by the favourable light conditions, scored a hit almost at once, wrecking the flagship's medical store and Auxiliary W/T office, causing casualties among the medical and wireless staffs. 'Large pieces of the shell also penetrated the middle deck,' the Captain reported, 'and a piece entered the lower conning tower mortally wounding Lieutenant Blyth, assistant navigat-ing officer. The Platform deck, forming the roof of the forward 6-in. magazine was also pierced, and the 6-in. magazine and shell room filled with smoke. There were three other heavy hits during this part of the action.'[23]

The *Valiant* and *Warspite*, turning on the same point in succession, were luckier and although straddled frequently and with hundreds of gallons of water streaming across their decks from near misses, emerged unscathed. For the last in the line, the *Malaya*, the German gunners seemed to have reserved all their pent-up fury at their failure to sink the others. For the five minutes occupied by the turn and for some fifty minutes after as she shaped course due north again, the *Malaya* was the target of the 12-inch guns of most of the crack ships of

Behncke's 3rd Squadron. At one time, six salvoes a minute were
falling around the super-dreadnought. The battleship's strength and
armour, together with the skilful evasive tactics of her captain,
Algernon Boyle, saved the ship. By sudden changes of course, the
Malaya made herself a difficult target, and at one point the chief
gunnery officer, Archibald Domville, order the starboard battery of
6-inch guns to fire rapidly into the sea at close range to provide a
moving screen of waterspouts. But two heavy shells in rapid
succession at 5.30 knocked out this battery and caused a fire before a
single gun could be fired. Five hits were suffered between 5.20 and
5.35 p.m. One heavy shell struck the roof of 'X' turret aft but failed to
penetrate the one-foot-thick hardened steel. Two more struck below
the water-line, and the water that came pouring in caused the *Malaya*
to assume a 4-degree list, which in turn restricted the elevation of her
own big guns.

In spite of this handicap, the heavy odds against her (Hipper's
battle-cruisers plus four to seven battleships), a hundred casualties,
and the intermittent shudders from hits, the *Malaya* kept up a steady
and accurate return fire. Conditions were difficult for all the 5th Battle
Squadron ships. 'I simply could not see in what direction we were
travelling,' recounted one gunner rating, 'for we were shaping course
and zig-zagging all the time. For a good part of the battle the sun
made it difficult to sight our guns on their ships. They could see us but
we could hardly see them.'[24] Four of Hipper's five battle-cruisers and
two of Behncke's battleships were hit by 1,900-pound 15-inch shells.
Five hits were made on the *Seydlitz* alone, one of them tearing a 10 by
13-foot hole which let in such vast quantities of water that she came
close to sinking. By this time the *von der Tann* did not have a single
heavy gun working, but Captain Wilhelm Zenker decided to keep his
ship in the line to take her share of the punishment.

Towards the end of this 'run to the north' the light advantage
changed in favour of the British ships – if intermittent smoke-
shrouded glimpses of the enemy at 16,000 yards may be called
advantageous. But the German gunners now had the low sun straight
in their eyes, making both ranging and spotting difficult. At 5.35
Beatty altered course from NNW to NNE to effect his meeting with
Jellicoe, and five minutes later he as able to reopen fire on Hipper's
hard-pressed ships on their converging course with his own.

All four captains of the surviving Battle Cruiser Fleet – Chatfield
Walter Cowan (a real fire-eater) of the *Princess Royal*, Henry Pelly of
the *Tiger*, and John Green of the *New Zealand* – had every reason to feel
exhilarated by the fighting and confident of the outcome. In cricket

jargon, after losing two of their leading batsmen, they were now playing themselves in. In all only two turrets were out of action and all the ships were capable of full speed. Jellicoe's squadrons were not far distant, and as Walter Cowan was shortly to remark, 'We felt like throwing our caps in the air, it looked a certainty we had them.' Certainly the spirit of the men was as high as ever, only a handful of observers above deck having witnessed the destruction of the *Indefatigable* and *Queen Mary*; and Captain Cowan's feeling that 'we had them' was shared by all.

At 5.30 p.m. the battle had been raging, with scarcely a break, for two hours, the tide flowing implacably from one side and then from the other. The initiative now lay firmly in the hands of Beatty, tactically and in terms of gunfire, now that the 5th Battle Squadron was out of range of the German Battle Fleet's vanguard, by a margin of forty-six heavy guns to twenty-four. The *Derfflinger* had been badly hit several times. Von Hase found that he could not answer the very long-range fire of the 5th Battle Squadron, which he found 'highly depressing, nerve-wracking and exasperating. Our only means of defence', he wrote, 'was to leave the line for a short time, when we saw that the enemy had our range.'[25]

Beatty's tactical intiative was emphasized when he began altering course to the east while ahead of, and easily outpacing, Hipper. It was a masterly move which forced the German battle-cruisers onto an easterly course, like a wrestler overpowering backwards his opponent. Then at 5.35 p.m. there came the sound of medium-calibre gunfire from a new and more distant quarter – towards the north, where the horizon was lit by the flashes of a sharp engagement. Hipper now suspected that this gunfire was only the precursor to heavier intervention, that the whole Grand Fleet was not far distant, that he in his turn was being driven into a trap. A few minutes before 6 o'clock, 12-inch shells began to fall among his ships from the north-east. They could not come from Beatty's battle-cruisers, which were on a NNW bearing. The hydra had produced one more head – or three more battle-cruisers to add new problems and new dangers faced by the German battle-cruiser commander.

One by one the squadrons on both sides had been drawn into the tumult and fury of this greatest sea engagement of all time, first the light cruisers as an overture to the Beatty and Hipper duel, then Evan-Thomas, next the vanguard of the High Seas Battle Fleet, now the British 3rd Battle Cruiser Squadron; and soon, under this quiet evening sky washed by swirling mists and lit by a dying sun, the full might of both battle fleets must now inevitably collide.

At 6 p.m. Jellicoe was 80 miles SSE of Lindesnes, the south-eastern tip of Norway, and just 100 miles west of the north Danish coast. Over an hour had passed since he had signalled the Admiralty 'Fleet action is imminent'. Not a word had he heard from Beatty since. Now he despatched an impatient appeal to him. 'Where is enemy battle fleet?'

Hipper's battle-cruisers were only eight and a half miles to the south-east, flashes lit the horizon and the gunfire was like the riffle of a thousand drums. But still Jellicoe could see nothing of the enemy, and still his numerous scouting forces told him nothing.

14

JUTLAND: BATTLE FLEETS IN ACTION

The Grand Fleet's deployment dilemma and Jellicoe's decisiveness – Admiral Hood engages the enemy – Hipper's shock at discovering more of the enemy offset by further successes – The end of the Defence *and* Invincible *a preliminary to the main fleets' contact – Scheer's first turn-about and retreat – The manoeuvre repeated – Hipper's 'death ride' – Brief renewed contact – The blind ride to the south – Night actions – Chances missed by the Grand Fleet before the High Seas Fleet reaches safety at dawn*

ADMIRAL JELLICOE's signal 'Fleet action is imminent' sent a tremor of excitement through the Admiralty unequalled since the first news of the Dogger Bank engagement had been received sixteen months earlier, in Churchill's time. Since then, the Admiralty's sense of urgency had declined into a state of relative torpor. Every department got on with its own work and it sometimes seemed as if the maintenance of the bureaucratic machinery of the Royal Navy was the only consideration of importance, and warfare – certainly offensive warfare – of no consideration at all. Now a growing awareness that something big was afoot, stemming from Room 40's first hint that the German Fleet intended a major enterprise, percolated along every corridor.

Jacky Fisher, the officer who was more responsible than anyone else for bringing into being the dreadnought, creating the Grand Fleet with all its merits and defects, who had long before sponsored Jellicoe as C.-in-C. and anticipated this modern Trafalgar, knew nothing of the inevitable coming clash of arms. Fisher, who could still have been here in command of events, and was wanted back by so many ('Destiny has not done with you yet' – Winston Churchill[1]) was at his office at the Board of Inventions at 36, Berkeley Square, Mayfair.

For others, there was much to be done, contingencies to be prepared for, messages to be decoded, the King, members of the Cabinet and War Council to be informed. Hospitals had to be warned of imminent casualties, forts put on alert, the Army informed in case the operation was only the overture to an invasion. 'Dockyards all round the coast were astir,' wrote Corbett, 'and tugs were getting up steam to assist crippled ships, and nowhere was the tension higher than in the squadrons that were still chafing in port.' The life of the nation and empire, the fate of the Allies, the course of the war and of history itself, rested upon the slender shoulders of one man out there in the middle of the North Sea, and on the performance of his subordinates.

At the Admiralty it was known when the battle-cruisers came into action. Of the progress or outcome of this battle, as of everything else beyond Jellicoe's signal, the OD and the members of the Board, Jackson and Wilson and the Chief of Staff, knew little more.

Imagine two giant tridents, aimed south-east from Scotland towards Denmark and the Baltic. There are six parallel columns, each made up of four battleships. The right hand, or most westerly spearhead of this double trident is the *Marlborough* flying the 1st Battle Squadron's flag of Vice-Admiral Sir Cecil Burney. His 2nd Division is commanded by Rear-Admiral Ernest Gaunt. Leading the 4th Battle Squadron with his flag in the *Benbow* is the ubiquitous Doveton Sturdee; on his port beam the C.-in-C. himself in the *Iron Duke*, then Rear-Admiral Arthur Leveson with his flag in the *Orion* leading her 13.5-inch-gunned sister ships *Monarch*, *Conqueror*, and *Thunderer*; and finally, on the extreme east wing, Vice-Admiral Sir Martyn Jerram's flagship *King George V*.

This cruising formation of six parallel columns was standard for the Grand Fleet and had been practised interminably in peace and war. An aerial observer poised above the fleet could attest to the precise handling of the big ships in geometric pattern, and two and a half cables (500 yards) between the ships in line ahead and four cables between the columns. Although now called dreadnoughts, these great turbine-driven, 20,000-ton-plus men o'war were still ships-of-the-line like Nelson's, and it was for the rapid formation of this single line that this arrangement had been devised. No matter from what quarter the enemy might appear, the columns could, within fifteen minutes, be transferred into a single line, turning (or deploying) to port or starboard in a form of follow-my-leader. Two critical deployment decisions had perforce to be made. The first related to timing. Deploy too soon and the long line of twenty-four ships might be left steaming away in the wrong direction, allowing the enemy to escape, if so he wished, or to 'cross his T', with the full broadsides of the enemy line concentrating on the vulnerable van. Deploy too late and the enemy might find himself able to concentrate the full weight of all his batteries on a part of the fleet in the throes of an evolution, deprived of co-ordination and the ability to make full use of its guns.

The second decision related to direction; whether to deploy to port or to starboard, or, much more awkwardly, on the centre, which required all but the chosen lead column making two 90-degree turns to fall into line behind.

Deployment success depended on accurate knowledge of the enemy's whereabouts, course, and speed, and on the C.-in-C.'s interpretation of this knowledge. Jellicoe had made every possible provision for learning well in advance this vital information, with the exception of bringing along his only aircraft-carrier. His heavy scouting force (Beatty) had its own three light-cruiser squadrons scouting ahead of it. His main battle fleet had its own heavy scouting force in the three I-class battle-cruisers of the splendidly able Horace Hood, two armoured cruiser squadrons of doubtful value but with as keen-eyed look-outs as any other ships and a turn of speed marginally better than his own, the five fast cruisers of the 4th Light Cruiser Squadron, the best of their class in the Fleet, and four more cruisers, one assigned to each battleship squadron. Spread out on both sides were some fifty destroyers, primarily as a screen against torpedo attack but also acting as eyes of the Fleet.

Finally, Jellicoe had the Admiralty. It was the secret ears of the OD through Room 40 which had brought the Grand Fleet out of its bases even before the German Fleet had sailed. This was of incalculable value, as it had been in the past. But past performance also tended to show that, once at sea, the information provided, via the direction-finding coastal stations, Room 40, and OD was by no means reliable, and even misleading. After being misinformed at 2 p.m. that Scheer was still in the Jade at 11.10 a.m. three hours later Jellicoe heard: 'At 4.9 p.m. Enemy Battle Fleet Lat. 56.27′ N Long. 6.18′ E. Course NW 15 knots'. Admiral Scheer had therefore covered 200 miles in five hours, according to Admiralty intelligence, which also failed to correct the earlier, now clearly false, information. No wonder that Jellicoe, from now onwards, took any Admiralty signals with a pinch of salt!

At 5.30 p.m. Jellicoe noted the cessation of fire to the south, and waited in vain for some reports of the engagement and of the enemy's position. He received neither. Hood, with the 3rd Battle Cruiser Squadron, the light cruisers *Chester* and *Canterbury* and four destroyers, was twenty-one miles ahead. Between them and the *Iron Duke* were seven armoured cruisers, eight miles apart, with one, the *Hampshire*, as linking ship. The four squadron light cruisers covered the battle fleet's flanks.

This great spread of scouting ships, designed to provide a visual warning screen forty miles wide had been obliged gradually to draw in to conform with the reducing visibility, so that by the critical hour of 6 p.m. it was only twenty-five miles wide.

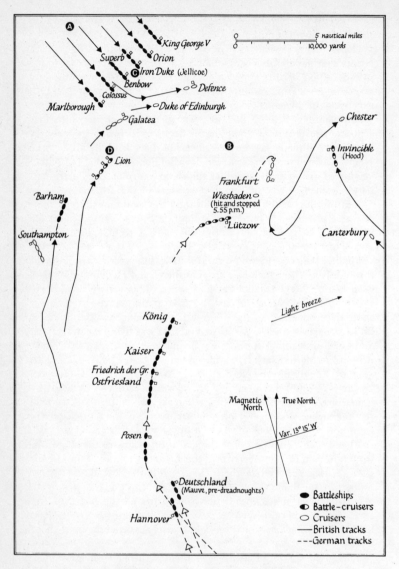

Map 8. The Battle of Jutland. Situation at 6.00 p.m.

Author's Note: (based on Diagram 16 in the Admiralty Narrative)

The first visual contact between the Battle Fleet and the Battle Cruiser Fleet was made shortly before 6.00 p.m., when the *Marlborough* sighted the *Lion*. Jellicoe had supposed that at 6.00 p.m. he was at A and Beatty at B, nearly right ahead of the *Iron Duke* and 12 miles away. In fact he was at C and Beatty at D, 65° on the *Iron Duke*'s starboard bow and 5½ miles away, relative positions which were now revealed by the *Marlborough*'s report and confirmed by his own sighting of the *Lion* a minute later.

Other mischances and mishaps served to conceal events from the *Iron Duke*. Because of the relatively slow speed of the old armoured cruisers, and of Jellicoe's acceleration to 20 knots; and also because one of their duties was to stop and search suspicious merchantmen in case they were acting as enemy scouts, the armoured cruisers were only six instead of sixteen miles ahead. An even worse handicap which had developed gradually through the day was the consequence of the errors in the dead reckoning calculations of both Beatty's and Jellicoe's flagships. Jellicoe claimed that he took into account the likely inaccuracy of Beatty's dead reckoning position in view of the *Lion*'s severe shocks from enemy hits and their effect on the compasses, the numerous changes of course, to say nothing of zig-zagging, which had been necessary in two hours of action.[2]

In fact, the *Iron Duke*'s dead reckoning calculations, in spite of Jellicoe's later claims to the contrary, were inaccurate, too, due to the long run from Scapa at varying speeds through tides and currents. He was four and three-quarter miles ahead of his dead reckoning position, and Beatty almost seven miles west of where Jellicoe calculated he was. Jellicoe expected to sight Beatty to the south-east (visibility permitting) at twelve miles at 6 p.m., the enemy battle fleet half an hour later dead ahead. Instead, he learned from the *Marlborough* on the extreme starboard wing that Burney had identified the *Lion* a mere five and a half miles distant to the south-west. Now he had to be prepared for action twenty minutes earlier with the enemy appearing from a different bearing. Deployment could not therefore be delayed, and he had to decide in seconds whether he should turn his fleet into a single line to the east, or to the west and towards the assumed course of the enemy. No martial decision was more critical, no order from one commander's lips more influential on the outcome of a battle, and a war.

We see John Jellicoe, fifty-six years old, uncertain in health and endurance, confident in his intellectual powers and decisions, less confident in his admirals and his ships, standing on the *Iron Duke*'s compass platform. He is dressed in a much-worn blue raincoat, white muffler round his neck, old cap with tarnished brass on his head – an unpretentious, rather plain figure, below average in height and standing erect. At 6.01 p.m. Jellicoe sights the *Lion* at a distance of about five miles to the south-west. She is moving fast, turning on an easterly heading, and bears evidence of the fierce battle she has been fighting since 4 o'clock.

The *Iron Duke*'s flag-captain recalled this moment: 'Beatty in the *Lion* appeared out of the mist on our starboard bow, leading his splendid battle cruisers, which were engaged to starboard with an enemy invisible to us. I noted smoke pouring from a shell-hole on the port side of the *Lion*'s forecastle and grey, ghost-like columns of water thrown up by heavy enemy shells pitching amongst these great ships.'[3]

Jellicoe at once ordered the signal, by searchlight: 'Where is enemy's battle fleet?'

The answer was not satisfactory, and the C.-in-C. was not pleased by it. 'Enemy battle cruisers bearing SE.' But Goodenough, ten minutes earlier, had reported that Scheer had altered to a northerly course, with Hipper's battle-cruisers bearing south-west from him. Could there have been yet another signalling error? Jellicoe repeated the signal to Beatty. This time he got an almost immediate answer. Jellicoe was not to know that Beatty had been out of touch for a long time with the main enemy battle fleet lumbering up from the south but by happy chance had, that minute, just caught a glimpse of the head of Scheer's line, dimly through the mist. 'Have sighted enemy's battle fleet bearing SSW', the *Lion* flashed in reply: no indication of heading, speed, or distance, but it was something to go on.

Jellicoe had earlier worked out the position of Scheer's battle fleet from a combination of the *Barham*'s sighting at 6.10 p.m. and that of the *Lion* four minutes later. He did this by taking the point of intersection of the two bearings adjusted for the time difference. Under all the circumstances, it is very creditable that the actual position was only two and three-quarter miles south of the calculated position. Now Jellicoe worked out that his enemy must be double the distance away of the *Lion*, or ten miles, on the speculative assumption of similar visibility to the south-east.

Five miles at 18 knots, plus his own 18 knots. Perhaps a shade less if they were closing obliquely. Was it already too late to deploy at all? To be caught by an enemy in battle formation while still himself in cruising formation, after all these years of training and dashed hopes! Such a calamity did not bear thinking about.

Nothing of the strain or anxiety showed on Jellicoe's face as his flag-captain watched him and waited for the order.

He stepped quickly on to the platform round the compasses and looked in silence at the magnetic compass card for about twenty seconds. I watched his keen, brown, weather-beaten face with tremendous interest, wondering what he would do.

With iron nerve he had pressed on through the mist . . . until the last possible moment, so as to get into effective range and make the best tactical manoeuvre after obtaining news of the position of the enemy battle fleet. I realised as I watched him that he was as cool and unmoved as ever. Then he looked up and broke the silence with the order in his crisp, clear-cut voice to Commander A. R. W. Woods, the Fleet Signal Officer, who was standing a little abaft me: 'Hoist equal-speed pendant SE.'[4]

It was his decision, and his alone, without consultation with his flag-captain or his Staff. This was not a situation for debate, even if there had been time. Already the ships were answering the signal, the *Orion*, *Monarch*, *Conqueror*, and *Thunderer* to port, the *Benbow*, *Bellerophon*, *Temeraire*, and *Vanguard* the nearest dreadnoughts to starboard. Jellicoe emphasized the order to his flag-captain: 'Dreyer, commence the deployment'; and Dreyer blew the two short siren blasts indicating a deployment to port, which was taken up by the other ships in rapid turn, creating a mournful chorus echoing across the water.

The Hon. Horace Hood was the beau ideal of a naval officer, spirited in manner, lively of mind, enterprising, courageous, handsome, and youthful in appearance. The gods had given him everything, including a beautiful wife and two sons. His lineage was pure Royal Navy, at its most gallant. Hood at forty-five was one of the youngest flag-officers in the fleet, and had come out with top marks from the earliest days of his training in the *Britannia*. In his naval career he had contrived to be in troublesome places – in the Sudan Expedition, at Omdurman, in the Somaliland Expedition in 1903 when he won a DSO. After Churchill had been First Lord for two and a half years, he chose Horace Hood as his naval secretary for the same reasons that he had earlier selected Beatty. The two officers had much in common, including their fighting record. In October 1914 he accompanied Churchill to Antwerp, and was then placed in command of the Dover Patrol during the most critical days of that month when the Allies were attempting to hold the Belgian coast.

A year before Jutland he was given command of the 3rd Battle Cruiser Squadron, with his flag in that active progenitor of the battle-cruiser, HMS *Invincible*. 'He drew from all of us our love and respect', one of his captains once remarked.

At 5.35 p.m. on 31 May Hood was leading the *Indomitable* and *Inflexible* on a SSE course, and was – unknowingly – only ten miles from Hipper's 2nd Scouting Group of light cruisers headed by the *Frankfurt* on an opposite course. Hipper himself was four miles farther west behind this screen. Hood's order at 3.11 p.m. had been to reinforce Beatty. He was now steaming at his best speed of 25 knots – the actuality of Fisher's dreams of his 'ocean greyhounds' racing into battle. He had a screen of four destroyers ahead, the *Canterbury* a further two miles ahead of them, the *Chester* six and a half miles to the west acting as linking ship to pass signals visually to the armoured cruisers.

The sound of firing was renewed and at a much closer range this time, with yellow flashes lighting the western horizon. Hood led his squadron round through 160 degrees to starboard and made for the scene of action. A few minutes later, out of the haze to the west there emerged his light cruiser *Chester*, zig-zagging frantically at 26 knots through a forest of shell bursts. Outgunned by the four German cruisers, she made it just in time after being under fire for nineteen minutes. Several of her own guns were knocked out, dead and wounded lay about her decks. At one 5.5-inch gun, Boy First Class Jack Cornwell, sixteen-year-old sight-setter, was found manning his gun, though mortally wounded, the rest of the crew lying dead about him. He died within a few minutes, earning a posthumous VC.

As the *Chester* raced across the *Invincible*'s bows, still the target of enemy fire, Commander Dannreuther in the fore control ordered his 12-inch guns to turn onto the German cruisers just visible in the mist and firing their torpedoes as their only effective defence. It was one more example of rapid tit-for-tat against this massive assault. Hood's 12-inch shells tore into the German cruisers, reducing the *Wiesbaden* to a wreck and severely damaging the *Pillau* and *Frankfurt*. Then Hood was forced to put over the helm to comb the tracks of the approaching torpedoes.

Now it came the turn of Hood's destroyers to charge gloriously and pay the price. The *Shark*, Commander Loftus Jones, *Acasta*, *Ophelia*, and *Christopher* had turned to conform with their flagship, and when the German cruisers were seen fleeing west, followed them in the hope of launching a torpedo attack. It was Commander Loftus Jones who had earlier played a gallant part in the Scarborough raid. Now as he raced in he also spotted through the mist a developing German destroyer attack against Hood's battle-cruisers. His sudden appearance frustrated this attack, and as Loftus Jones lunged at the German cruisers his four destroyers were subjected to a hail of fire during which the *Shark* succeeded in despatching a torpedo at one of his assailants.

Again in this battle, just as one side appeared doomed, 'spared and blest by time', rescue appeared. For Jones and his tiny battered ships, salvation appeared out of the south in the form of the cruiser *Canterbury*, which had doubled back on Hood's orders and now lured the German cruisers away from their mauled prey. The relief was brief. Hipper's destroyers in overwhelming numbers chanced on the crippled enemy. The *Shark* took the main brunt. 'In a moment her after gun was hit, and its crew killed, and Commander Jones, who was himself controlling its fire, had a leg shot away at the knee', Corbett wrote. 'Yet he continued to encourage his men to fight the only gun he had left . . . So, maintaining to the last the finest traditions of the Service, she came to her end, and it was in the heart of the battle she found it.'[5]

The unexpected appearance of heavy ships from the east, followed by the savaging of the German light cruisers and the development of an enemy destroyer attack, had come as an unpleasant shock to the hard-pressed Hipper, already suffering badly in a renewed gunnery duel with Beatty and the 5th Battle Squadron. His immediate conclusion was that he was faced with the full might of Jellicoe's battle squadrons, and this seemed confirmed by the thunder and flash of heavy gunfire dead ahead. His first order, therefore, was to turn through 180 degrees and double back on to Scheer behind him. At the same time, he recalled a full-scale destroyer attack which he had just launched against Beatty to the north, and diverted it against this new force to the east, which he mistakenly believed to be the Grand Fleet. Rightly, his first thought was for Scheer. It was, he knew, no part of his C.-in-C.'s plans to become involved in a gunnery duel with a fully deployed Grand Fleet in an overwhelmingly superior tactical situation across the 'T' of the High Seas Fleet.

Although they were frequently and inaccurately to lament later that providence was denied them at the Battle of Jutland, Jellicoe and Beatty now (6–6.15 p.m.) experienced it in full measure. Hood was the magician who pulled off the trick; the dying Loftus Jones applied the finishing touches. But for this intervention from the east, Beatty would have been forced to turn away from Hipper's destroyers, exposing the Grand Fleet both to German eyes and German gunfire. Its real position and its state of vulnerability in the full throes of deployment, would have been revealed to Hipper and to Scheer. Appalling devastation would have fallen upon Jellicoe's fleet at a moment when it had scant means to defend itself, allowing the German Admiral to withdraw at leisure with his fleet intact and the British Fleet broken. As one German admiral recalled: 'Shortly before his death, Admiral Scheer told me that the thought of how Providence had given them opportunities for a complete annihilation of the British fleet still robbed him of sleep.'[6]

Instead, Jellicoe was allowed time to complete his majestic

deployment, ship following ship, division following division, squadron following squadron, like an uncoiling cobra. Appropriately, but by chance, the leader of this long line of dreadnoughts was the *King George V*, not only reigning monarch but an Admiral of the Fleet; the *Iron Duke* ninth in line; and last the proud *Agincourt*, 'the gin palace', armed with more heavy guns than any battleship in the world. There was, inevitably in view of its scale, some bunching during this complex evolution; but it was worthy of a Fleet Review. By 6.30, the twenty-four battleships were on an easterly heading ready to face the enemy coming up from the south. From a potentially disastrous tactical situation, Jellicoe was now poised ready to coil his great cobra about his enemy and crush him to extinction.

How many men had died, how many ships had already gone to the bottom, before the main fleets clashed in this long-drawn-out overture? There can never be an accurate answer. Over 1,000 in the *Indefatigable*, nearer 1,300 in the *Queen Mary*, some 600 in the *Wiesbaden*, several hundred in all in the German battle-cruisers and Evan-Thomas's squadron, 85 in the *Shark* besides her gallant commander, and many more in other sunk destroyers on both sides. But nearly 2,000 more were to disappear in sheets of flame, billowing clouds of smoke and disintegrating men o'war before Scheer and Jellicoe were finally matched against one another.

Robert Arbuthnot in his obsolete armoured cruiser *Defence* had indicated to one or two of his close friends what he would do in a fleet action. Now, he was stationed on the starboard wing of the battle fleet prior to deployment, at the rear of the line after deployment. In order to take up this position he could, he said, either do this by passing down the disengaged side of the battle fleet, protected from the enemy, which would, he felt, be 'a dull performance', or he could pass down on the engaged side between the two opposing fleets. Captain Dreyer, reporting this conversation, said he thought he ought to go down the disengaged side, that if he went between the fleets it would be highly dangerous and, anyway, his smoke might interfere with the battle fleet's shooting. 'He was inclined to pooh-pooh both these objections.'[7]

By unhappy chance, Arbuthnot had caught an early glimpse of German light cruisers to the south, had opened fire out of range, and when the mist closed about them, set off in pursuit with the *Warrior* at full speed. His hell-bent course took him across the bows of the *Lion*, forcing Beatty to swerve to port to avoid a collision. Arbuthnot's movement also obscured Beatty's view of the enemy and forced him to break off contact.

Arbuthnot pressed on, trailing a huge cloud of smoke and paused to pour several salvoes into the luckless *Wiesbaden*. A moment later the dark silhouettes of towering superstructures, turrets, and great hulls of German battle-cruisers and battleships loomed up out of the mist. The *Defence* and *Warrior* were four and a half miles distant from the batteries of 11-inch and 12-inch guns when they opened fire, the first salvoes tearing into the vitals of the two thinly-armoured vessels. The *Warrior* was reduced to a wreck in seconds, the *Defence* blew up, 'suddenly disappearing completely in an immense column of smoke and flame, hundreds of feet high', reported one observer. 'It appeared to be an absolutely instantaneous destruction, the ship seeming to be dismembered at once.'[8] And thus perished the bold Arbuthnot and his 856 officers and men. As he had wished, it had not been 'a dull performance'.

The *Warrior* would have gone the same way but for the *Warspite* of the 5th Battle Squadron, which suffered a jammed helm from its being put hard over at 25 knots, and was forced into two successive complete circles, the second of which brought the battleship within 10,000 yards of the head of Scheer's line. The target was irresistible, and within a minute the *Warspite* had suffered thirteen heavy hits. She was better able to sustain them than the *Warrior*, which limped away during this diversion only to sink later with the loss of some seventy of her crew.

Intermittently through the mist and against the dark sky of the north-east, Hipper and his captains, von Egidy, von Karpf, Hartog, and Zenker with the gunless *von der Tann*, perceived the parallel enemy Battle Cruiser Fleet. It was impossible to count them all at once, but by careful calculation through their powerful Zeiss binoculars there could be no doubt of the number. Four hours ago this now battered, weary German First Scouting Group had faced a superiority of six to five. Two of the enemy had been eliminated – of that there could be no doubt, either – and now there were seven. This was the arithmetic of madness, or were they overwrought from the cacophony of their own guns and the shock of enemy hits? At that moment – 6.30 p.m. – the leading British ships opened fire at a range of five miles, the salvoes coming swiftly and at once straddling the German battle-cruisers.

After causing Admiral Hipper the worst shock of his life, and shattering his light-cruiser squadron, Admiral Hood had completed his mission by locating Beatty's line, turning his ships in succession onto the *Lion*'s heading and forming the Battle Cruiser Fleet's

vanguard. The 3rd Battle Cruiser Squadron had not undergone the
agony and frustration experienced by Beatty's surviving battle-
cruisers of firing at an enemy painted dim dull grey against a grey sky.
For Dannreuther of the *Invincible* and the gunnery officers of the
Indomitable and *Inflexible*, Lachlan MacKinnon and Ronald Oldham,
their targets, when clear of mist, were sharply outlined against the
bright western sky. Fresh from their gunnery practice at Scapa Flow,
their shooting was superb. Beatty watched them with proud
excitement, and one of his officers on the bridge recalled, 'Hood
pressed home his attack, and it was an inspiring sight to see this
squadron of battle cruisers dashing towards the enemy with every gun
in action. On the *Lion*'s bridge we felt like cheering them on, for it
seemed that the decisive moment of the battle had come.'[9] It also
seemed, ironically, that Hood was assuming the role he had feared for
Beatty, that of 'taking on the whole German Fleet'.

Then for one fatal minute, and probably no longer, the ever-shifting
low cloud and mist parted like a net curtain before the *Invincible*. Von
Hase of the *Derfflinger* and the other gunnery officers who still had
guns to fight, including those of the leading German battleships,
seized their chance with the speed and opportunism acquired by their
long training. Turrets steadied on the *Invincible*'s bearing, gun barrels
hovered in their elevation, steadied in accordance with the fine optical
calculations, needles swung, electric buttons were firmly pressed and
the broadsides blasted out.

Dannreuther, standing high up in the *Invincible*'s foretop, had hit
the *Derfflinger* two or three times, and also struck some heavy blows at
the *Lützow*. 'Your fire is very good.' It was Admiral Hood calling to
Dannreuther and his party through the voice pipe. 'Keep at it as
quickly as you can. Every shot is telling.'

But suddenly, at 6.33 p.m., every enemy shot began to tell on the
flagship in their turn. Time and time again she was hit, a heavy shell
struck and pierced the 7-inch armour of 'Q' turret amidships. It
detonated inside, hurled the roof into the sky, ignited the charges, the
'flash' simultaneously thrusting down with the speed of light to the
magazines. The subsequent explosion, like those in the *Indefatigable*,
Queen Mary, and *Defence*, was all-consuming.

'Flames shot up from the gallant flagship,' wrote Corbett, 'and
there came again the awful spectacle of a fiery burst, followed by a
huge column of dark smoke which, mottled with blackened debris,
swelled up hundreds of feet in the air, and the mother of all battle
cruisers had gone to join the other two that were no more.'[10]

The North Sea is relatively shallow here, with the result that the poor *Invincible* created her own tombstones for her 1,026 dead. She blew up exactly in half, observed one of Beatty's Staff Officers. 'The two ends then subsided, resting on the bottom, so that they stood up almost vertically with the stem and stern standing an appreciable distance out of the water.'[11]

Most of the handful of men who escaped from this holocaust were in the foretop. The senior survivor was Dannreuther himself. 'I just waited for the water to come and meet me', he recalled in later years. 'Then I stepped out and began swimming. The water was quite warm and there was no shortage of wreckage to hold on to.'[12] 'Within half an hour the survivors had been picked up by the *Badger*, detached by Beatty. There were six in all. The destroyer's commander, Charles Fremantle, was the first to remark on Dannreuther's *sang froid* as he stepped on board, wet from the sea but showing no other evidence that this was any different from a courtesy visit to another ship.

The destruction of the *Invincible* marked the opening of the next phase in the Battle of Jutland, a phase which Jellicoe had reason to believe and Scheer even stronger reason to fear, would lead to a decisive British victory. By 6.30 p.m. Scheer's position had become highly dangerous. Hipper had reported heavy ships from the east, and later from the north-east. Advanced destroyers reported that they had seen battleships on a south-easterly course. The 5th Battle Squadron had been last seen to the north-west. The realization that, far from having trapped the British Battle Cruiser Fleet, the High Seas Fleet was already poised at the jaws of a much superior enemy in an overwhelmingly superior tactical position, struck the German C.-in-C. with uncomfortable force at this time.

'It was now quite obvious that we were confronted by a large portion of the English Fleet,' Scheer remembered, 'and a few minutes later, their presence was indicated on the horizon directly ahead of us by firing from heavy calibre guns. The entire arc stretching from north to east was a sea of fire. The muzzle flashes were clearly seen through the mist and smoke on the horizon, though there was still no sign of the ships themselves.'[13]

Jellicoe's battleships, still in the last phase of straightening out their line after the deployment, were, however, quite able to see Scheer's vanguard: Hipper's battle-cruisers, and then the *König*, *Grosser Kurfürst*, *Markgraf*, *Kronprinz*, *Prinzregent Luitpold*, the *Kaiser* and *Kaiserin* – all the newest and most powerful dreadnoughts of the Third Battle Squadron, and with names like the opening pages from the *Almanac de Gotha*. But the ever-varying visibility caused by smoke and

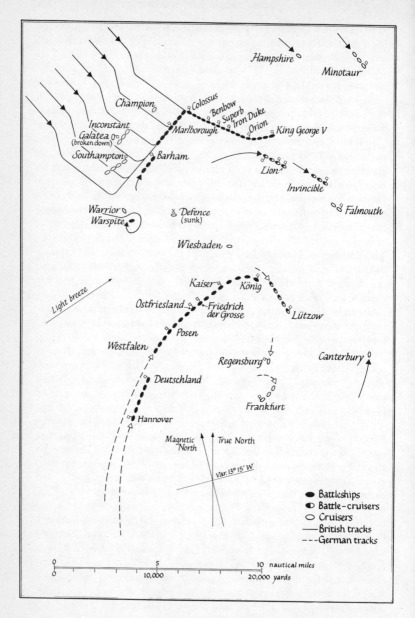

Map 9. The Battle of Jutland. Situation at 6.30 p.m.

mist and low cloud, like threads of gossamer, prohibited a continuous view of all the ships, and it was tantalizing to observe a target through the range-finder fading to invisibility before a reading could be obtained.

There was not an officer or a rating of the Grand Fleet who had not imagined this moment of contact, had not prepared themselves for it, feared it or relished it in their minds, prayed perhaps that they would survive or not flinch, perform their duties punctiliously regardless of enemy fire, do credit to their ships and their mates. Everyone had their own picture of what it would be like – the line of distant ships, the thunder of gunfire, the shuddering of the ship, the scream of enemy shells. No one who spoke or wrote of the battle afterwards had predicted this reality: the confusion and blindness, the exasperation, the impossibility of keeping eyes and sights on an enemy for more than a few moments. Nobody could have known that when they met the enemy they would learn so little of his numbers, course, speed, or identity; that haze, cloud, mist, and smoke – smoke from burning ships, smoke from funnels, smoke from gun muzzles and deliberately created smoke to conceal and preserve – would blind and confuse and cause such instant confusion.

To many the end of the *Invincible* was seen as a German catastrophe, and cheers went up as the wreckage was passed. 'We were quite certain we had sunk a German battleship or battle-cruiser,' one officer recalls, 'and were very cheered by the sight.'[14] 'At 6.40 p.m. the second *König* [class] was seen to be heavily hit and to be ablaze fore and aft', ran the *Official Despatch* hopefully. '. . . The ship settled by the stern and was observed to blow up.'[15] Numerous witnesses attested to this sinking. Of the *Derfflinger*, ' . . . on fire after being hit by a salvo. Water came up to quarter deck, then over funnels, and [Boatswain Charles Trenchard] saw the water close over her.'[16] Others saw enemy ships disappear without an explosion. Jellicoe's flag-captain himself wrote of opening fire on a *König*-class battleship just after 6.30 p.m. 'Range 12,000. The 2nd, 3rd and 4th salvoes hitting her, with a total of at least 6 hits.'[17]

In fact, while several *König*-class battleships were hit, and knocked about, none was sunk and only the *König* herself had serious casualties (45 killed out of a complement of 1,100). The sinking of the *Derfflinger* was another piece of wishful thinking under the stress of combat and lack of clear vision. Like all the German battle-cruisers she was severely mauled and had over 150 dead but was never near sinking. And it is equally doubtful that the *Iron Duke* made six hits in three salvoes at a range of 12,000 yards.

While the *Official Despatches* were grossly inaccurate in many of their reported observations, passage after passage faithfully reflects the difficulties of seeing the enemy, holding him, and firing on him, let alone hitting and sinking him and bringing about a conclusion to this battle. 'We opened fire at her at a range of about 16,000 yards . . . by the time deflection was corrected, and about four salvoes fired, she had disappeared in the mist', runs one typically laconic report. 'Shortly afterwards another battleship came into sight, but before fire could be opened on her, she was obscured by smoke.'[18]

Admiral Burney's observations in the *Marlborough* in the minutes before she was torpedoed recount this flagship's difficulties, and she was the closest ship to the German battle fleet prior to the deployment:

As the battle cruisers [Beatty] drew ahead and their smoke cleared, the German line could be more easily seen and 4 *Kaisers* and 4 *Helgolands* could be dimly made out. *Marlborough* opened fire at 6.17 p.m. at a battleship of the *Kaiser* class . . . Owing to haze and the enemy's smoke, organised distribution of fire was out of the question; individual ships selected their own targets. As the action developed and disabled ships of both sides passed down between the lines, great difficulty was experienced in distinguishing the enemy's from our own ships.[19]

James Ley, Captain of the *Collingwood*, suffered the same experience:

The flashes of the guns of the enemy's ships beyond the cruiser were observed, but insufficiently clearly to lay the director or guns on, and at no time could the enemy's hulls be seen from the fore conning tower or director tower. An officer in the after director tower informed me afterwards that, on one occasion for a few moments, he was able to make out dimly the hulls of three or four ships and later he saw the enemy's line, or some ships of them, turn away apparently together.[20]

The only German ship that every British battleship could see, stopped and battered and on fire, was the *Wiesbaden*, which received an uncounted number of heavy shells of every calibre as the deployed battle line passed her at short range. But unlike larger and more heavily protected British ships, she never blew up and remained afloat until about 7 p.m. when, full of water, she turned over like the *Blücher* at the Dogger Bank and went to the bottom with all 570 of her crew.

While the British suffered only aggravation and gall at the frustration of their efforts to destroy Scheer's battle fleet, the German position became more and more critical as they continued north-east and were

'bent' more to the east by the weight and proximity of their enemy –
an enemy still seen only as a continuous line of muzzle flashes against
the evening sky. Scheer claimed afterwards, with outrageous hypoc-
risy, that the thought of retreat never entered his calculations; 'There
was never any question of our line veering round to avoid an
encounter', he wrote. 'The resolve to do battle with the enemy stood
firm from the start.'[21] In fact his mind was preoccupied by a single,
decisive problem: how to extricate himself from the noose tightening
about his neck. There was, he quickly accepted, only one answer,
and that was to turn tail and flee, praying all the while that his luck
would be better than Admiral von Spee's and that the night would
close about him before the Grand Fleet's heavy guns sent every one of
his ships to the bottom. In the German tactical manuals there was a
manoeuvre called the *Gefechtskehrtwendung*, or battle turn-away, in
which every ship simultaneously turned through 180 degrees,
reversing both the order and the heading of the line. The High Seas
Fleet had often practised this turn. It was a difficult manoeuvre to
counter although Jellicoe had prepared contingency plans within the
limitations imposed by torpedo and mine risk.

Scheer gave the signal for the turn-away at 6.35, the same moment
when the *Invincible* blew up, and ordered a simultaneous destroyer
attack with torpedoes and smoke. It was the beginning of this turn
that the *Collingwood*'s officer, and a number of others, had observed,
although some minutes passed before Jellicoe realized that his enemy
was extricating himself from the trap. Although it was an extremely
difficult manoeuvre requiring the highest standards of seamanship,
Scheer's captains carried it out successfully, without a collision or
even losing the symmetry of the line to any serious degree. And the
reward was more than worth the risk. 'The effect was all he could
desire', wrote Corbett. 'In two or three minutes his fleet, already only
visible from the British ships by glimpses, had disappeared, and all
firing ceased.'

Jellicoe was neither dismayed nor even surprised by Scheer's
turn-away; only determined not to fall into what he regarded as a
probable trap. He knew the dangers of conforming to the enemy's
'invited direction'. Back in October 1914 he exemplified this in a
memorandum directed to and approved by the Admiralty: 'If, for
instance, the enemy were to turn away from an advancing fleet, I
should assume the intention was to lead us over mines and
submarines, and should decline to be so drawn.' It was not yet
7 o'clock. Sunset was at 8.24 p.m. Although visibility continued to
deteriorate, there would be sufficient light in the sky for gunnery

action for two more hours at least. By turning south, Jellicoe planned
(6.44 p.m.) 'to place himself as soon as possible athwart [the enemy's]
line of retreat to the Bight, for along that line, sooner or later, they
were almost certain to be discovered.'[22]

At 7 p.m., then, the brief clash – no more than a brush – was over.
The two flagships were some thirteen miles apart, Scheer steering
west, his battle fleet spread out in echelon, the old pre-dreadnoughts
now in the van, Hipper's battle-cruisers to his east; Jellicoe on a
southerly heading with his battle fleet more or less back into
pre-deployment divisions, Beatty's battle-cruisers five miles in the van
to the south-east. Beatty would have been farther ahead but for a
mishap with the *Lion*'s gyro compass which had been so shaken about
that it led the navigator to extend a turn to the south so far that it was
quicker to complete it through 360 degrees than do an 'S' turn back.
Beatty was always sensitive about this incident, with its hint that he
was turning his stern on the enemy, and refused to allow it to be
recorded in the official narrative.

The last stage of the daylight battle is the most interesting and most
controversial, the intentions of the two C.-in-C.s as grey and
uncertain as the dusk light under which they were effected.

What happened, in broad definition, was that Scheer carried out a
second 16-point turn, reversing his course to the east, found himself
facing again the full might of the Grand Fleet like an echo of the
earlier shock, carried out a second *Gefechtskehrtwendung* and for a
second time escaped the noose. Then, by a series of British mishaps,
the relatively lightly damaged German Fleet escaped into the night.

Pride demanded that Scheer and his Staff should ever after claim
that this second thrust was an attack – 'to deal the enemy a second
blow by again advancing regardless of consequences', as the C.-in-C.
reported to his Emperor. If you accept this entirely unconvincing
claim, then by the same token you deny to Scheer any claim to the
most elementary tactical skill. Having had his 'T' crossed once and
barely escaping with his life, why would he come back for more
punishment? As Jellicoe's biographer has written, 'If Admiral Scheer
really intended to give a formidable thrust at the battleships of the
Grand Fleet it is incomprehensible that he should have stationed his
battle cruisers in the van . . . To charge with his ships in line ahead at
the broadside of the enemy's line of battle was, as it proved to be,
futile; but to take the shock with his battle cruisers in the van was an
incomprehensible manoeuvre.'[23]

Scheer's plan was to escape round the rear of the Grand Fleet and make for the Skagerrak and the Baltic, or Horns Reef and the safe passage inside the minefields off the Danish coast, if possible picking up any survivors of the *Wiesbaden* on the way. But he had miscalculated his antagonist's position. Reports from his scouting forces told him that Jellicoe was on a southerly heading, intent on cutting him off, but he gave him credit for a higher speed than Jellicoe was in fact steaming. The result was that Scheer for the second time 'found himself enveloped in a flaming arc of gun-flashes, and now they were so near that his predicament was more critical than ever'.[24]

Scheer's 'advance regardless of consequences' was rapidly halted by the hail of shellfire from ranges of 11,000 to 14,000 yards which opened up between 7.10 and 7.15 p.m. Scheer countered in the only manner open to him. In quick succession he ordered (7.13) his battle-cruisers to go straight for the enemy – *ran an den Feind, voll einsetzen*, 'give it everything'. Two minutes later he ordered his flotillas to carry out an equally reckless but essential torpedo attack and lay smoke. And then at 7.18 he signalled his fleet to turn about.

The German destroyers discharged a large number of torpedoes in spite of the severe fire from their opposite numbers and from the battleships' secondary batteries, scored no hits, and suffered one boat lost and two more badly damaged. They did, however, again force Jellicoe to turn away from the attack, taking two 2-point turns to port until his battle fleet was for a while steering SE. Hipper's already severely mauled ships took a further battering on their 'death ride', as it was romantically called, to within a lethal range of 7,700 yards of the nearest British battleships. Then, observing Scheer's vanguard turning through 180 degrees, he led away his ships first to the south and then south-west, and mercifully out of sight.

The battle fleet's second *Gefechtskehrtwendung* was a great deal less orderly than the first, many of the lead ships having already slowed down under the intense fire, and the whole manoeuvre taking on a disordered appearance, with a touch of panic evident here and there. By 7.30 the firing had died to spasmodic salvoes, and ten minutes later the German High Seas Fleet was making best speed to the west. The gun crews were able to relax, casualties dealt with – there were, amazingly, only 108 dead in the battleships – and temporary damage repairs carried out. Sunset was still half an hour away, but so deep was the dusk, so thick the mist and low cloud, that Scheer felt a renewal of confidence that he would succeed in gathering about him his great flock and steal his way home in the darkness. He was also confident that he had sunk more ships than he had lost; and that on 1 June he could proudly report a victory to his Emperor.

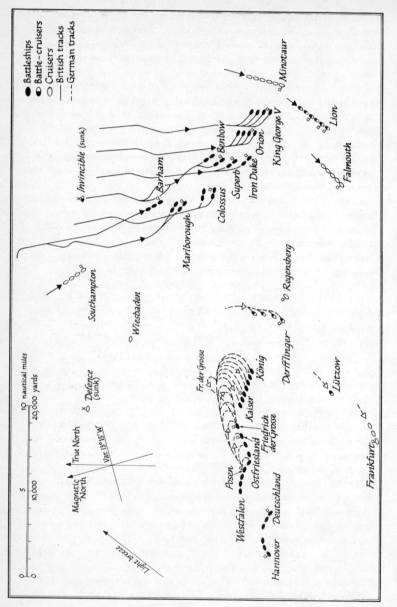

Map 10 The Battle of Jutland, c.1835

At 7.30 p.m. it was as if a cease-fire had been sounded, the contestants withdrawn from the ring to prepare for the night during the last hour before the sun set. Repair parties went into action, hot cocoa was served to the men at the guns who took off their scarves and gauntlets and took the cotton waste from their ears. In the aftermath of the noise and danger and excitement, everyone wanted to talk – of what they had seen, of what might have been. News which had been silenced by the thunder of the guns, began to circulate from deck to deck as it always circulates on board a ship at sea, but now with twice the note of drama and at twice the speed. Where there had been casualties, these were the first topic, and as always after a battle the details were recounted with a touch of relish or hilarity to cover the fear and horror.

In the worst hit British ships – all three of 'the big cats' and the *Barham* and *Malaya* – there was a lot of activity in the sick bays, often under difficult conditions. There were twenty-six dead and thirty-seven wounded in the *Barham*, as many wounded and nearly twice as many dead in the *Malaya*. In the *Lion*, Chatfield took advantage of the lull to go below to check on the damage.

Passing down the gangway to the lower deck [he wrote] I found the gallant Fleet Surgeon, Maclean, and his only remaining surgeon, Horace Stevens, a highly skilled officer standing up to their ankles in water, dressing the wounded who were lying on the mess-tables. The mess-deck was flooded by the fire mains being damaged by shellfire . . . As the ship surged in the swell the water swept unpleasantly from one side of the mess deck to the other. The electric light was out, and only the candle fighting lights illuminated a rather grim scene. The dead still lay here and there, and some fifty men, many seriously wounded or burnt, were awaiting treatment.[25]

In the *Warspite*, left far behind by her involuntary complete circle and the battering she suffered with it, there were thirty dead and wounded. A cordite fire had broken out in the starboard 6-inch battery, and many were burnt. 'Father Pollen, the Roman Catholic Chaplain,' according to one report, 'did very well with the wounded, although badly burnt himself.'[26]

Jellicoe had turned the battle fleet away from the torpedo attack and Scheer's retreating fleet until it was steering SE. But at 7.35 p.m. he ordered course to be altered to starboard to continue the pursuit on a SW heading, and at 8 p.m. the Grand Fleet in orderly single line ahead was steering across what everyone believed was Scheer's line of retreat. Beatty, some six miles ahead, had already (7.47 p.m.) signalled Jellicoe. 'Submit van of battleships follow battle cruisers.

We can then cut off whole of enemy's fleet.' This reached Jellicoe, after transmission and decoding at 7.59. From the *Lion*, the rear of Scheer's ships had briefly been glimpsed some ten to eleven miles ahead, and while Beatty was as enthusiastic as ever to get at the enemy, he rightly judged it as rash to brush seriously with the High Seas Fleet – even if it was in full retreat – with his now much depleted force. What he wanted was the immediate support of Admiral Jerram's powerful squadron, headed by the *King George V*, in lieu of Evan-Thomas's 5th Battle Squadron which (less the *Warspite* which was *hors de combat*) had now taken station at the rear of the line of battle. But Jerram's ships were 20-knot battleships, some 4 knots slower than Evan-Thomas's, whose high speed had been such a godsend to Beatty earlier in the battle. At 8.15, therefore, when Beatty once again sighted Hipper's battle-cruisers and opened fire minutes before the sun went down, he was alone and without support.

The disposition of the two fleets was a repeat in reverse of their relative positions two hours earlier. The German battle fleet was in line ahead on a southerly heading with Hipper's battle-cruisers (as Beatty's had been earlier) between his C.-in-C. and the enemy. And this time it was Jellicoe's battle squadrons which were heading straight for the centre of the German line and the theoretically disadvantageous position of having their 'T' crossed. The differences were that for Jellicoe a meeting would be not a surprise but a relief; and that the poor visibility must now restrict if not prohibit a full-scale gunnery duel.

As Hipper had sighted the Grand Fleet in line at 6.15 and opened fire, so it now fell to Beatty to sight and open fire on the leading German ships at the close range of 10,000 yards. It was 8.23 p.m. He at once began to score hits, and within a few minutes inflicted severe damage on the *Seydlitz* and *Lützow*, while himself remaining immune from German fire because of the lack of any light behind him.

'The leading ship was hit repeatedly by *Lion* and turned away 8 points,' claimed the *Official Despatch*, 'emitting very high flames and with a heavy list to port. *Princess Royal* set fire to a 3-funnelled battleship; *New Zealand* and *Indomitable* report that the 3rd ship, which they both engaged, hauled out of the line heeling over and on fire.'

Once more, the heat of combat expanded the claims, but the *Seydlitz* and the *Derfflinger* lost the use of their last guns, and there were fires burning in both ships. The élite First Scouting Group was now a spent force deprived of its teeth. The *von der Tann* was still without a heavy gun. The *Moltke* was the least devastated by shellfire, and it was to her that Hipper later, at 10.50 p.m., shifted his flag from the *Lützow*, left wallowing and almost ready to sink far astern. In a few minutes all four surviving battle-cruisers would certainly have been brought to a standstill or sunk by the combined fire of Jerram's battleships and Beatty's battle-cruisers.

It was at this moment (8.30 p.m.) that Scheer made the decision to use his old pre-dreadnoughts, whose loss would not seriously deplete the strength of the High Seas Fleet, as a screen against further attack. Up to now their presence, which had further limited his speed by 3 to 4 knots, had been an embarrassment. Now the time had come for the old ships to prove themselves, even it it was only to fulfil their contingency 'suicide' role. As a result of the repeated turn-abouts, they were at the head of Scheer's line. He now ordered them to the rear by allowing Hipper's battle-cruisers to make off to the west under cover of a smoke-screen while they held their southerly heading. In this way the gallant Admiral Mauve, who had been so keen to sail with the rest of the fleet, found himself leading his men o'war of another era in front of the guns of the enemy at a range of 8,000 yards. Gunnery was by now a highly speculative business but shots were exchanged with Beatty before the British Commander ordered a cease-fire, and Admiral Mauve successfully escaped to the west. Beatty had succeeded in forcing the High Seas Fleet some eight miles to the west and away from its bases but had been robbed of his ambition to 'bag the lot' – of Hipper's battle-cruisers – by half a dozen old ships which in more favourable circumstances he could have blown out of the water in their estimated five-minute survival time.

At 9 p.m. the leading battleships of both sides, the *Westfalen* and the *King George V*, were a mere six miles apart, and on converging courses, but neither knew of the other's proximity, and the last shots between dreadnoughts in the Great War at sea had been fired.

Darkness, which was complete soon after 9 p.m., did not however mean the end of contact or the end of fighting. In the vanguard and on both flanks of the two fleets light forces sped about their business, groping in the dark for one another then suddenly finding themselves in a fearful fairyland of flitting searchlight beams and yellow spatters of gunfire. It was even more nerve-testing than the slugging matches between the dreadnoughts of the daylight hours, with the mysteries of mist and smoke of daylight increased many times over as shapes loomed up out of the blackness – friend or foe? – and were gone with a dull murmur of engines, a whisper of bow wave and wash, or the shatter of point-blank gunfire.

It is impossible to recount in any tidy detail the happenings of the night of 31 May–1 June. No one at the time was able to record much

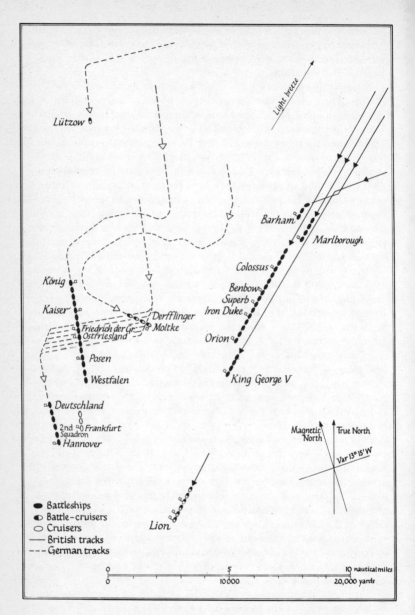

Map 11. The Battle of Jutland. Situation at 9.00 p.m.

more than the sequence of events as seen from their own ship, and that was mostly confusing and limited, with the problem of correct identification always foremost. All that can be coherently reconstructed are the encounters, more or less definable but sometimes almost fused into a continuous linked engagement.

The first contact between the light forces occurred little more than an hour after Beatty 'lost' Hipper's battle-cruisers. The two fleets were still converging but on almost identical southerly courses, their tracks forming the two sides of a very narrow 'V'. If a reconnaissance Zeppelin had been out, the crew must have judged that the protagonists were certain to meet within two hours at the most, the light forces fanned about the British rear and the Germans' vanguard even sooner. This latter clash occurred at 9.50 p.m. in almost total darkness. German destroyers fired torpedoes at the British 4th Flotilla. The *Garland* replied and, with no damage on either side, the Germans made off. A few minutes later, there was a sharp and confused exchange between the light cruiser *Castor* and her flotilla (the 11th) and part of the German 4th Scouting Group. The *Castor* was heavily hit by German gunfire directed by searchlights, and there was shooting elsewhere, which would have been heavier if certain identification had been possible. One British destroyer captain was convinced that he had been fired on by his own side until, in daylight, shell fragments with German markings were found among the debris.

The next action occurred at 10.30 p.m. between Goodenough's light cruisers and the German 4th Scouting Group, and was a much more frenzied and damaging business. Goodenough had sustained his splendid record of scouting and reporting which had marked the 'run to the south' whenever opportunity occurred. Now, outnumbered by a determined enemy, the light cruisers fought back. The *Southampton* succeeded in torpedoing and sinking the *Frauenlob* at close range, but not before she herself had been severely damaged, including the loss of her W/T which had played such a significant part in the operation so far. At one point, recounts Corbett, a shell from the *Dublin* 'could be seen to tear a hole in the side of one of the strangers; instantaneously a dozen searchlights were switched on to her and the *Southampton*, and they were smothered with rapid fire by the whole enemy squadron. In a moment all was a roar of passing and exploding shell and a wild confusion of gun-flashes, dazzling searchlight beams, and rapid changes of course.'[27]

Then, for fifty minutes, between 11.30 p.m. and 12.20 a.m., the British 4th Flotilla was again in action, this time with Scheer's battleships, and as a result was scattered and badly mauled, and ceased any longer to be in the reckoning. Although it lost five destroyers in all (and that any survived after attacking battleships at 1,000 yards was a miracle) they damaged and reduced the speed of the dreadnought *Nassau* (by ramming), and accounted also for the light cruisers *Rostock* (torpedo) and *Elbing* (collision).

A few minutes later, three more British flotillas, led by the light cruiser *Lydiard*, also brushed against the German battle fleet but in the course of a much less determined action, which did the enemy no damage, and lost one destroyer.

The sixth encounter, at 1.45 a.m., was the most effective. There was already a trace of light in the sky, which was to his advantage, when Captain Anselan Stirling in the *Faulknor* led the 12th Flotilla against a line of six great dark shapes spotted on his starboard bow and on a south-easterly course. He was correctly positioned for the classic destroyer attack as they went in through a forest of exploding shells. He and five of his flotilla succeeded in discharging seventeen torpedoes in all, and were rewarded by the sound of a rending explosion and the sight of a yellow flash that lit the sea and sky. Recovered from the temporary blinding, Stirling could see that the symmetry of the line had been broken by a gap. A single torpedo had struck the pre-dreadnought battleship *Pommern* in a vital and vulnerable part, and the ship had instantly disintegrated without trace. No sinking could be more decisive, or horrifying.

Of greater potential importance than the destruction of this battleship, the only one to be sunk, was the message which Captain Stirling managed to transmit at 1.56 a.m.: 'Urgent. Priority. Enemy battleships in sight. My position 10 miles astern of 1st Battle Squadron.'

The end of another British armoured ship was as spectacular as that of the *Pommern*. Ever since Admiral Arbuthnot's doomed charge at the German line, one of the survivors, *Black Prince*, had been searching for the battle fleet like some lame lost animal seeking its herd. It was typical of the luck of the 1st Cruiser Squadron that she found the wrong fleet, and that it was in the few hours of total darkness which gave her no warning of her fate. It was the dreadnought *Thüringen* that spotted her first, illuminated her with her searchlights, opened fire, and blasted her into torn wreckage in minutes. The armoured cruiser became a blazing furnace which was extinguished only when her magazines blew up with the same decisive and terrible result which had demolished her sister ship.

The last encounters of that night did not match up to 'The Glorious First of June' 122 years earlier – something that everyone was hoping for. The participants were the light cruiser *Champion*, Captain James Farie, and four destroyers of the 12th and 13th Flotillas. Farie was drawn towards the scene of Stirling's skirmish and successful attack, and at 2.30 a.m. made out the shapes of Admiral Mauve's pre-dreadnoughts. One of his destroyers fired a torpedo which sank an enemy destroyer. But that was all. The *Champion* made no attack, and made no attempt to report this sighting to the C.-in-C. In this way, the surviving five 'five-minute ships', followed by the crippled *von der Tann* and *Derfflinger*, made their way safely across the rear line of the Grand Fleet.

The final encounter took place at 3.30 a.m. when the *Champion* sighted four German destroyers on an opposite course at a range of 3,000 yards. The *Champion* opened fire briefly, and one of her destroyers fired two torpedoes, one of which made a hit. But no turn was made, nor attempt to close the greatly inferior enemy, which was also handicapped by being crowded with 1,250 survivors from the sunk *Lützow* – who, as twice-escapers, can be regarded as the luckiest ship's company to survive the battle.

It was in keeping with the whole nature of the operation that it should peter out in this inglorious manner twelve hours after it had begun. It was as if the British were too tired to act or care. Numerous sightings of units of the German battle fleet were made during the night by destroyers scattered about the Grand Fleet. Not a word reached Jellicoe. Evan-Thomas's three surviving super-dreadnoughts, taking up Jellicoe's rearguard, all made sightings of what could have been, or were, German heavy ships, but neither the Admiral nor his captains bothered to report to Jellicoe.

Two of Hipper's mauled battle-cruisers, the *Moltke* and *Seydlitz*, which had become separated from the main fleet, had remarkable escapes when they were sighted, the first by the *Thunderer* at 10.30 p.m., the second by the *Agincourt* (fourteen heavy guns against two or three) at 11.45 p.m. Both were allowed to slip away into the darkness, unreported.

The main body of the High Seas Fleet, the sixteen dreadnoughts and Admiral Mauve's surviving five pre-dreadnoughts, reached the safety of Horns Reef by 3 a.m. A heavy mist had formed with the first touch of light from the east. There were still some gun crews whose elation at earlier successes kept alive their enthusiasm for a renewal of battle. But in the commanding echelons there was profound relief that they were safe now, with only the Amrum Bank to negotiate behind minefields which the British would never enter. Many officers had not slept for thirty-six hours, none for the past twenty-four hours. They were without a heavy scouting force, they were depleted in numbers in light cruisers and destroyers, whose ammunition and torpedoes were low, the battleships of the 3rd Battle Squadron had been knocked about and were not fully fit for battle, while the older dreadnoughts of the First Battle Squadron, like the relatively early *von der Tann*, had experienced various troubles, including jamming, with their earlier mark of 12-inch gun.

All in all, the High Seas Fleet was in no condition to face a fleet action against an enemy which, in spite of its losses, was far superior in gunpower and possessed a Battle Cruiser Fleet as powerful as it had been twenty-four hours earlier. As Scheer's Chief of Staff later wrote to Tirpitz on the subject of a renewal of battle, 'Perhaps it was just as well we didn't.'[28]

And Jellicoe? 'At 2.47 a.m., as dawn was breaking,' he wrote, 'the Fleet altered course to north and formed single line ahead . . . The weather was misty and the visibility even less than on May 31st, being only some three or four miles, and I considered it desirable under these conditions, and in view of the fact that I was not in touch with either my cruisers or destroyers, to form a single line, accepting the danger of submarine attack on a long line in order to be ready for the enemy's Battle Fleet, if suddenly sighted.'[29]

Jellicoe had never for one moment contemplated a night action. It was not a contingency planned for or trained for in the Grand Fleet. There had been occasional night firing practices before the war but the results had been near-chaotic. Besides, Jellicoe believed (quite rightly) that German searchlights and searchlight control were far superior to his own. 'Nothing would make me fight a night action with heavy ships in these days of T.B.D.s [torpedo boat destroyers] and long range torpedoes. I might well lose the fight. It would be far too risky an affair.'[30] During the long haul south during the night, it had been Jellicoe's intention to close Horn Reefs in daylight if he had not then made contact with Scheer. But now, the lack of a proper screen 'rendered it undesirable'. 'It was obviously necessary to concentrate the Battle Fleet and destroyers before renewing action.'[31]

At the critical dawn hour of 3 a.m. then, the German fleet had eluded its foe and was safe, and the British fleet (or at least its C.-in-C.) had no wish yet for a renewal of action. No situation could be more negative than this. And yet at 3.30 a.m. Jellicoe was still hopeful of a renewal of the battle when he was ready for it, believing that Scheer was still to the west, in spite of the flashes of gunfire which had intermittently lit up the northern horizon during the short night.

Above the two fleets in the North Sea on that night a wireless battle took place, controlled by the W/T operators in every one of those blind warships, and by the transmitting and D/F stations in Germany and Britain. It was not only the British who had refined the art of direction-finding from ships' transmissions. The Germans, too, were good at it, and moreover had set up a special department devoted exclusively to jamming enemy signals. Time and again the Germans succeeded in frustrating the passage of important messages to Jellicoe's flagship, especially from the lower-powered and relatively primitive destroyers' transmitters. The Germans' 'Room 40' was able to part-read British coded messages, just as Ewing and his men were able to intercept, de-code and pass to OD German coded messages, and more comprehensively and efficiently than the Germans could.

Jellicoe was not, therefore, kept entirely in the dark about German movements in spite of the failure of some of his ships to pass on sighting intelligence and in others the failure to get the message through. As early as 10.41 p.m. the Admiralty transmitted this vital piece of news, which if acted upon even an hour or two later could have brought the Grand Fleet round to meet the High Seas Fleet off Horns Reef at dawn:

German Battle Fleet ordered home at 9.14 p.m.
Battle Cruisers in rear. Course SSE. ¾ E.
Speed 16 knots.

Plotted from Scheer's presumed (and at that time correctly presumed) position at 9 p.m., this order could only mean that the High Seas Fleet was heading for Horns Reef, bearing across the rear of the Grand Fleet in order to do so. But this absolutely vital piece of intelligence was ignored by Jellicoe. Why? The C.-in-C. had good reason for doing so. By this time any signal from the Admiralty was suspect in his mind. Not only had he earlier been told that Scheer was still in harbour when he had been at sea for eight or nine hours. More recently, in a signal transmitted from London at 9.58 p.m., and read by Jellicoe at 10.45 p.m., he had been given the position of the rear ship of the German battle fleet many miles from where he knew it to be, based on his own cruiser sightings. 'Which should I trust?' Jellicoe asked later. 'Reports from my own ships which had actually seen the enemy, or a report from the Admiralty?'[32]

By the time he heard from the Admiralty again on the not unimportant subject of the enemy's position and course, it was too late. At 3.30 a.m., with misty daylight flooding across the North Sea, Jellicoe was informed that the High Seas Fleet, an hour earlier, had

been thirty miles north-*east* of the *Iron Duke* on a south-*east* by south
course, 16 knots, and just one hour's steaming from Horns Reef at this
speed.

So, the elusive German battle fleet, which had been glimpsed only
twice for a few minutes the previous day, and then only three or four
battleships at a time, had slipped through Jellicoe's grasp; had
outwitted and outmanoeuvred him by steering behind him. 'This
signal made it evident that by no possibility could I catch the enemy
before he reached port, even if I disregarded the danger of following
him through the minefields . . . '33

Jellicoe failed to pass on to Beatty this crushing news, and
consequently the battle-cruiser commander proposed at 4.04 a.m.
that he should make a sweep to the south-west to locate the enemy
whose proximity was suggested by a scouting Zeppelin. Shortly before
5 a.m. Beatty learned the worst. Chalmers was in the chart-house
when his Admiral entered. 'Tired and depressed, he sat down on the
settee and settling himself in a corner he closed his eyes. Unable to
hide his disappointment at the result of the battle, he repeated in a
weary voice, "There is something wrong with our ships", then
opening his eyes and looking at the writer, he added, "And something
wrong with our system." '34

What, if anything, was 'wrong with our ships' will be considered
later. As to the system, the failure here was evident to many
commanders and their officers, most clearly perhaps to Commodore
Tyrwhitt of the Harwich Force with its fast modern cruisers and
destroyers. Its role in a fleet action had been clearly defined in an
Admiralty letter of 14 November 1914. It would join Jellicoe if a fleet
action was imminent. Naturally enough, Jellicoe and Tyrwhitt had
based their tactics on this assumption ever since. Accordingly, at 6.20
p.m. on 30 May Tyrwhitt was ordered to be ready to sail at daylight.
When he was not ordered to sea, Tyrwhitt sent an urgent telegram to
the Admiralty. He was told to remain at one hour's notice. All that
morning, Tyrwhitt was straining at the leash. In the afternoon he
could bear it no longer. Intercepted W/T signals told him that a fleet
action was taking place. At 5.12 p.m. he proceeded to sea and
informed the Admiralty, only to be ordered immediately back to
harbour.

Tyrwhitt's temper scarcely improved when he was at length
allowed to join Jellicoe at 2.52 a.m. on 1 June when it was all over bar
the tidying up. His five light cruisers, two flotilla leaders, and sixteen
destroyers, all superbly trained for day and night action, were reduced
to escorting damaged men o'war back to their bases.

This last-minute reversal of long-established policy by OD was explained afterwards, in answer to complaints from Jellicoe and Tyrwhitt, by the sudden fear that Scheer's old pre-dreadnoughts, supported by light forces, might make a raid on the Channel and the Channel ports, even cutting off communications with France by sinking themselves as blockships at the entrance to Calais, Dover and other ports. The Admiralty did not learn, according to Oliver, that the pre-dreadnoughts were accompanying Scheer until 'very late on the night after the battle'. But it was for this very contingency that the 3rd Cruiser Squadron and 3rd Battle Squadron of pre-dreadnoughts were brought down from Rosyth on 29 April. If, according to Jellicoe, it was a 'sufficiently strong covering force to encounter enemy battle cruisers', it was certainly capable on its own of dealing with Admiral Mauve's 'five-minute' ships. 'I'll never forgive that old figurehead Oliver, who was at the bottom of it all',[35] Tyrwhitt complained, with some reason, to Keyes.

At noon on 1 June, a funeral service was held in the *Lion*. The Chaplain was among those killed, and it was left to Chatfield to officiate. Beatty stood behind him on the poop 'while ninety-nine bodies of the flagship's company were committed to the deep, in the traditional manner of seamen'.[36]

The same ceremony was followed on board other ships of the Grand Fleet with fatalities as they swept north-west through waters thick with wreckage and, here and there, the bodies of German sailors. The mood was solemn among some of the men, elated among others. Like the passing of any experience long anticipated, feared or hoped for, the battle left in its wake for all to savour the satisfaction of achievement. The mystery had faded with the last sound of gunfire, and for those who had felt it, fear had been overcome. There was not a man, from stoker to admiral, who did not feel matured by the ordeal. Now they could say, 'I was at the Battle', and no one could take that away from them.

And the last, rare slice of luck was, after all, for the British. Due to a German signalling failure, the U-boats from which so much had been expected, did not learn that they were to remain on patrol off the British coast for a further twenty-four hours to attack the Grand Fleet as it returned. Chance sightings led to the firing of a few torpedoes, but none found a target, and every ship was anchored safely in its base by 2 June. Forty-eight hours after the *Indomitable* fired her last salvo of 12-inch shells, Jellicoe reported to the Admiralty that the Grand Fleet was ready for sea.

The passage home of the High Seas Fleet south down the Danish coast in the channel swept for this purpose had its alarms and excursions. Admiral Behncke's flagship *König*, badly holed forward, had taken in so much water that she had to wait three hours for the tide before she could cross the Amrum Bank. The *Seydlitz* was in an even worse condition, and lagged far behind looking more like some giant half-submerged submarine than a battle-cruiser. She did eventually manage to crawl back to the Jade, but it took her thirty-six hours, and then she had to beach herself at the entrance. At 5.30 a.m. there was a colossal explosion in the battleship *Ostfriesland*, which convinced the fleet that the area was swarming with British submarines. There was some firing at these phantom submarines, and the sense of alarm was heightened by the weary condition of officers and men after their long ordeal. The *Ostfriesland* managed to keep her place in the line.

In fact there were British submarines in the vicinity but all three of them had orders to remain submerged and resting on the seabed in order to conserve their batteries until 2 June and neither saw nor heard the entire High Seas Fleet passing above them. The fast British minelayer *Abdiel*, commanded by the intrepid Commander Berwick Curtis, had penetrated this enemy territory ahead of the German Fleet and laid eighty mines so cleverly that it was scarcely possible for the German Fleet to pass through them unscathed. With the good fortune that had blessed Scheer since he had left harbour, his ships escaped them all, and it was a mine that the *Abdiel* had laid almost a month earlier in these supposedly clear waters which caught the German battleship. That field caught no other German man o'war, however, and by 6.30 a.m. the bulk of the High Seas Fleet was anchored safely in the Jade.

15

JUTLAND: A RETROSPECTION

*The need for GFBOs, but their needlessly detailed, restrictive and defensive nature –
Jellicoe's unwillingness to consider alterations to them – Contrasting qualities of British
and German men o'war – The 'flash' clue to battle-cruiser losses and the attribution of
blame – British shell and the reasons for its poor quality – Gunnery records examined –
British weakness in reporting and signalling, and its cause – Admiralty failure to inform
Jellicoe of intercepted German signals – The absence of the* Campania *possibly a grave
loss to the Grand Fleet – Post-engagement speculations and the acrimonious aftermath to
the battle – The performance of individual commanders*

ANY consideration of the Battle of Jutland from the British view must
begin with the Grand Fleet Battle Orders around which Jellicoe's
tactical policy was built. They were, for better or for worse, every
officer's guide, a decision manual as sacred in the Grand Fleet as a
written constitution to a statesman, or the laws of cricket to players in
a test match. It was inevitable that with the *matériel* advances since
Trafalgar greater and more formal guidance should be available to
officers. It was all very well in the Napoleonic wars to state that you
could do no better than lay close alongside your enemy. This was
adequate for 1805 when the ships and weapons had changed little for
centuries. As Chatfield put it:

What would happen [in Nelson's time] when two ships met and engaged
was, as far as material was concerned, known within definite limits from
handed-down experience and from a hundred sea-fights. [Nelson] knew
exactly the risks he ran and accurately allowed for them. He had clear
knowledge, from long-considered fighting experiences, how long his ships
could endure the temporary gunnery disadvantage necessary in order to gain
the dominant tactical position he aimed at for a great victory . . . We had to
buy that experience, for our weapons were untried. The risks could not be
accurately measured without that experience . . . Dreadnoughts had never
engaged; modern massed destroyer attack had never taken place.[1]

At Trafalgar Nelson's approach was at 1–3 knots and some five
hours passed between sighting at dawn and opening fire. At the
conclusion of four and a half hours of cannon fire, at ranges down to
ten yards, not a ship had been sunk. It was ships boarded and
captured that counted. At Jutland Beatty's speed frequently exceeded
26 knots, eighteen minutes passed between his sighting of Hipper and
the opening of fire. In less than an hour a third of his battle-cruisers

had been blown up. The cannon and carronade with their effective range of about 1,000 yards had become the dreadnought's gun and the destroyer's torpedo with a range of around 20,000 yards. Mines added to the hazards a C.-in-C. had to face. The lowliest powder monkey had a good idea what he was in for at the Battle of the Nile. No one really knew what a modern battle would be like. Even the lessons of Tsu-Shima were now out of date. With such complex, expensive, vulnerable, and *untested* men o'war, no wonder their movements and conduct had to be placed under some sort of control. But how much?

By definition rules restrict, and they restrict initiative as much as they define conduct and lead to centralization and leader-dependence. This is what Jellicoe wanted and what he achieved by the GFBOs, which poured from the flagship in a steady stream, so that in the first year of his command he had issued 200 close-printed pages covering every contingency the Fleet was likely to encounter, and covering it moreover in sometimes completely inflexible detail. For example:

Method of Attack No. 1
The Vice-Admiral leading the 'D' line is not to circle the enemy's rear unless ordered to do so (Signal '94'), nor alter course inwards more than two points beyond the direction of deployment.

The GFBOs reveal in almost every line the subordination of the offensive spirit to the defensive spirit, and by consequence to the likely non-decisiveness of any engagement. Although it was the big gun that dominated naval thinking in the construction of the Grand Fleet's dreadnoughts, it was the underwater weapons and the threat that they posed that dominated much of the GFBOs, and the tactics employed when these dreadnoughts first went into action. The precautionary turn-away accepted as sacred doctrine in the face of a torpedo attack was also a gesture of genuflection to alternative underwater weapons. What could be more restricting of initiative and movement and more likely to lead to disengagement and an indecisive conclusion than Paragraph 14?

Caution as to enemy's mines in a fleet action
When engaging the enemy's battle fleet it must be borne in mind that all German destroyers carry mines, and that it is therefore highly dangerous to cross a locality that has been occupied by these vessels.

This is indeed a far cry from 'something must be left to chance' in Nelson's Trafalgar Memorandum.

A further factor which tended towards caution was surprise. So swift had been *matériel* development (the torpedo increasing its range twentyfold in a decade for example) that the possibility that the enemy had made surprise advances in weaponry had to be taken into consideration. Jellicoe was absolutely convinced that German sub-marines would work with the Fleet – 'certain to get among the battleships' – when they were still quite incapable of the high speeds, submerged or surfaced, of a modern engagement. German destroyers did not in fact carry mines at Jutland. Not long before the battle, Jellicoe got wind of the Germans supposedly refitting their battleships with 17-inch guns, and the Admiralty had the greatest difficulty in disabusing him of this belief. Beyond the construction of such giant weapons, it would have taken prodigious measures to carry out the modifications to the turrets, barbettes, hoists, loading chambers, magazines, etc. etc. All would have had to be changed, quite apart from the strengthening of the ships' hulls to take account of the new recoil stresses. But Jellicoe reckoned that he had to be prepared for any surprise.

Surprise in *matériel* contrasted with predictability in tactical thought, the one element (besides the spirit of the men) which remained unchanged since Nelson's day. The single line of battle was sacred, because it was safe and proven and no one could think of anything better. This is not *quite* true as a few Young Turks like Richmond and Dewar favoured a manoeuvre battle. Sturdee might not have possessed a very incisive brain but he was a good tactician and favoured divisional tactics as opposed to monolithic fleet tactics. He was the only squadron commander at Jutland who favoured a deployment to starboard towards Scheer and was shocked when Jellicoe deployed to port.

Although the GFBOs presupposed a slugging match in a single line of battle, the detached activities of the Battle Cruiser Fleet and the existence of the 'free wing' 5th Battle Squadron pointed towards greater flexibility than the written word suggested; and so it turned out.

Nevertheless the GFBOs provided a stifling influence on independent thinking and action, which can be seen from the outset to the conclusion of the battle. They also included a paragraph which might have been written prophetically for Jutland, and confirms how rigidly Jellicoe stuck to his own self-imposed rules:

If the Action has been indecisive
It may be necessary, however, to force or accept action so late in the day that a decisive stage will not be reached before darkness necessitates breaking off the main engagement, and retiring the Fleet clear of the enemy so as to move to a flank unobserved before turning to renew the attack at daylight . . .

While the GFBOs laid down a complex defensive policy against the underwater threat, they also defined precisely the conduct of gunnery. The 13.5-inch gun was to open fire at 15,000 yards (increased to 18,000 after Dogger Bank), the 12-inch gun at 13,000 yards. 'At extreme range fire should be by deliberate salvoes until the enemy is hit or straddled.' Even after Dogger Bank had showed up the folly of slow opening fire, the GFBOs continued to instruct firing every fifty seconds in order to allow the fall of salvoes to be spotted: 'A ship's outfit of ammunition will not last long if fire is continuous, and it must therefore be used with discretion.' 15,000 yards was also beyond the estimated maximum range of German torpedoes and had the advantage of scoring hits with plunging fire on a steep trajectory against the relatively thinly armoured enemy decks in preference to the 12-inch-thick armoured sides. Beatty with his much lighter side armour was a strong advocate of long-range firing, but also (after Dogger Bank) favoured a faster opening rate of fire. His ideal was 16,000 yards, well within the maximum range of 18,500 yards for his 12-inch-gunned ships. At this range the shell took just twenty-six seconds to reach its target, and this he found was perfect for controlling double salvoes and attaining a high rate of fire.

The deposed Callaghan had favoured decentralization of command. Jellicoe was shocked to discover that his predecessor's 'Instructions for the Conduct of a Fleet in Action' covered only two or three pages and laid down that 'In carrying out the intentions of the Admiral, Commanders of Squadrons, divisions or sub-divisions should be given a wide discretion as to the conduct of the ships under their immediate control.' Within two weeks Jellicoe began to change all that, and the first GFBOs arrived in his ships on 18 August 1914. King George V did not enjoy an over-abundance of brains, but his sailor's instinct was as sound as anyone's. He was right to fear the worst if Fisher was brought back. And he may have been right to have preferred Callaghan to remain as C.-in-C. If that admiral had been allowed to exceed his retirement age, the King's son and future George VI who served as a midshipman at Jutland might have been present at the twentieth-century's Trafalgar instead of an indecisive engagement. Callaghan was also very fit and never complained about his health and how exhausting it was to command a fleet.

The defensive note in Jellicoe's GFBOs extended to every class of ship. While the torpedo by inference was the most dangerous weapon, the activities of all ships must be subordinated to the primary need of the battle fleet to destroy the enemy's battle fleet with its guns. Battle-cruisers were for destroying battle-cruisers, light scouting

30. HMS *Invincible's* magazines blowing up at Jutland

31. HMS *Lion* (centre) receiving a hit on 'Q' turret

32. SMS *Kaiser* at gunnery practice with her main armament of 12-inch guns

33. HMS *Invincible* broken in half and resting on the sea-bed. Destroyer
HMS *Badger* approaches to pick up the six survivors

34 and 35. SMS *Seydlitz* after Jutland, showing some of her battle damage

36. Sir Eric Geddes, First Lord 1917–18 [*From the painting by James McNalty*]

37. Admiral Sir Rosslyn Wemyss, First Sea Lord 1917–19

38. A new shape in the Grand Fleet: Admiral Hugh Rodman's flagship, USS *New York*, one of five American battleships which served with the Grand Fleet in the closing months of the war

39. Victorious admirals of the Grand Fleet entertain the King and Queen of the Belgians

A GUN'S CREW WITH THEIR GAS MASKS READY WATCH THE ARRIVAL OF THE GERMAN WARSHIPS

On the way to the place of surrender the crews of the British vessels were all at action stations, with gas masks ready for use in case of need. The men watched eagerly for the first sight of the surrendering German fleet. But there was no cheering, no triumphing over the fallen foe, and equally no fraternising with the crews of enemy vessels when later our bluejackets went on board them. For more than four years the navy has kept the seas free for the Allies, and the sailors of the fleet—officers and men—had their reward when they watched the p'ck of the Germany Navy that was to sweep them from the sea go steaming by them to their berths in a British harbour

40. British sailors with gas masks and wearing anti-flash gear watch the surrender of the High Seas Fleet [The Sphere, *7 December 1918*]

41. Admiral Beatty answering the cheers of his officers and men at the
surrender of the High Seas Fleet, 21 November 1918
[*Photograph by Humphrey Joel*]

cruisers their opposite numbers. Above all, destroyer flotillas had as their first duty to help preserve the battle fleet by fighting off German destroyer attacks, with attack against the enemy battle fleet as a secondary role. In short, the object of destroying the enemy's battle fleet 'should not be diverted by the proceedings of other classes of enemy vessels' which must be dealt with by their British equivalents. 'If you have to decide between his battle fleet and destroyers,' British destroyer commanders were instructed, 'the latter are to be given primary attention, so as to stop them before they can fire their torpedoes at our fleet.'

Beatty, however, preached the opposite gospel. 'I believe that if the Enemy Torpedo Craft attack first, ours would never get into a position to enable them to frustrate it. The moral effect of the first attack with these vessels, I think, will be very great.' This principle was aired in a letter to Jellicoe of 12 August 1915 so that the C.-in-C. clearly accepted a different role for Beatty's destroyers. At Jutland both Beatty and Jellicoe adhered to their own battle orders with the result that Beatty's destroyers greatly interfered with Hipper's tactics, and Jellicoe's destroyers were effective in defending his big ships against German destroyer attack.

Apart from their stifling effect, the GFBOs may be criticized on several other levels. First, they presupposed a German willingness to face the Grand Fleet in a full-scale battle of the line. If the enemy turned away you did not chase him, and therefore, especially under typical North Sea weather conditions, the action was likely to be broken off, as it twice was at Jutland. There was nothing in all those 200 pages to provide for dealing with an unwilling enemy. And yet, in spite of Jellicoe's tendency to ascribe greater strength to Scheer than he ever possessed, he knew that the Grand Fleet had an abundant superiority in numbers of dreadnoughts and a vast superiority in total weight of broadside. Jellicoe never asked himself: 'Why *should* Scheer steam in a long outnumbered line and be knocked to pieces?' It was much more likely that his tactics would be governed by the need to isolate inferior detachments of the Grand Fleet and destroy them piecemeal in order (with the help of mines and U-boat torpedoes) to bring about a superiority in numbers to his advantage before venturing into a full-scale battle. Moreover, North Sea weather favoured these tactics, and in the event Scheer came very near to success when he appeared out of the mist to surprise Beatty and Evan-Thomas. Without his Battle Cruiser Fleet Jellicoe would have been crippled – as crippled as Scheer was by the temporary elimination of his own battle-cruisers.

The GFBOs were also over-detailed, and this did raise criticism at the time and later. Nelson's instruction to his captains before Trafalgar was that 'they might adopt whatever [tactics] they thought best, provided it led them quickly and closely alongside the enemy'. As Admiral Dewar was to write,

Only the initiative of Captains and Divisional Commanders was likely to achieve decisive results in a very large area where 154 British flags and pendants were flying. Elaborate instructions for cruising formations, station keeping, deployment, etc., may have been necessary, but they were of subsidiary importance. *The main thing – perhaps the only thing – for the Commander-in-Chief, was to issue a general idea of attack, so that everyone could act with confidence and determination in destroying the enemy's force.*[2]

By contrast, the German Battle Orders were brief and allowed considerable latitude to individual commanders.

The inflexibility of the GFBOs was matched by Jellicoe's own inflexible view of them. By contrast with Nelson's 'Band of brothers', with whom he frequently exchanged ideas over plans and tactics in a comradely manner, Jellicoe did not encourage consultation and did not care for any questioning of what he had laid down. Discussions with his flag-officers did take place when they were requested but not with alterations to the dogma of the GFBOs on the agenda. Sturdee tried on several occasions to persuade Jellicoe to change his mind on, for example, the tactics to be used in closing a retreating enemy. Jellicoe would have none of it, and took him to task for disturbing the status quo and causing questioning among his commanders. 'I am afraid that the controversy that has arisen over this matter is doing harm in the Fleet', he wrote to this much admired senior officer and squadron commander. 'I hope you will take my word for it that it *is* doing harm, and is causing a feeling of unrest and possibly criticism of the manner in which I intend to handle the fleet, which is bound to be injurious.'[3]

There is tragic irony in the fact that Jellicoe commanded a fleet of dreadnoughts whose design and construction signified offensive, risk-taking tactics, when he was concerned primarily with the survival of his ships and the avoidance of risks. The Grand Fleet had been built on the calculated policy of risk: more and bigger guns to destroy the enemy at the cost of protection from the enemy's gunfire. Jellicoe favoured long-range action with plunging fire when the upper deck of his flagship was protected by 1½–1¾ inches of steel armour. But Scheer's flagship, *Friedrich der Grosse* boasted 2–2½ inches and was structurally better equipped to take plunging fire. Especially when considering Jellicoe's great respect for German long-range gunnery, it would have seemed more productive of results to close to a relatively short range, using his superiority of speed to do so, and smother Scheer's battle line with a fusillade of low-trajectory shells, greater in weight and numbers than Scheer could answer with. Jellicoe's tactical policy was better suited to German than British battleships.

Much criticism has been made in the past of British warship design, citing the heavier losses at Jutland and the sturdy manner in which German armoured ships stood up to British gunnery. At the Falkland Islands and the Dogger Bank the *Gneisenau*, *Scharnhorst*, and *Blücher* all took a terrible beating from heavy shellfire before succumbing. With the exception of one flaw which was to prove fatal and was the cause of the loss of all three battle-cruisers and the *Defence*, the design and construction of British men o'war was quite as good as the German, bearing in mind the priorities applied. From the start, as laid down by Tirpitz, the German first priority was to survive in order to fight again; the British, to destroy the enemy. Class for class, German battleships with their broader beam were better able to resist shellfire than their British counterparts. Their wide beam also gave them superior stability and a slower period of roll as gun platforms. Because of more and better internal subdivisions German capital ships were much better able to resist underwater damage. The *Seydlitz* struck a mine before Jutland and was torpedoed at least once during the battle, but was little affected. When the *Ostfriesland* was mined on the way home, she was able to keep her station. When the *Audacious* struck a mine she went down and the *Marlborough* finally had to leave the line when she was torpedoed. All German ships were honeycombed with compartments to reduce the risk of flooding. For their tight internal sub-division and unpierced bulkheads, the Germans had to pay the price of accommodation cramped by British standards. Officers were berthed four or six to a cabin, the men lived claustrophobically on top of one another, something that should not be forgotten when considering the causes of the 1917–18 Fleet mutinies. For the British seaman, his ship was his home, the centre of his way of life for a minimum of seven years and usually much longer. He might be at sea for weeks at a time, and travel to the other side of the world through different climates. German ships, manned by short-term conscripts, did not have to contemplate the tropics, only the North Sea where ventilation invariably meant cold air! A German man o'war was like a tank, *keine Bequemlichkeit, keine platz*! – neither comfortable nor roomy.

An officer recalls exploring the *Friedrich der Grosse*, Scheer's flagship, when she was docked upside down at Rosyth after being salvaged from Scapa Flow: 'What impressed me most', he writes, 'was the honeycomb of small boiler rooms, all in completely separate watertight compartments, whereas our boiler rooms were vast compartments stretching athwart the ship. To pass from one to the other one had to climb up to the main deck! Again, I was impressed by the use made of coal bunkers to add to the protection of the side armour. No wonder they lost some speed. One certainly got the impression she would have been the very devil to sink!'[4]

German battleships were also, class for class, slower than their British equals. A knot does not read as statistically significant; tactically, it is all that is needed to gain an advantageous position in relation to the enemy. The first German dreadnoughts could not make 20 knots. The most modern in Jutland – the *König*s – could be pushed up to 22 knots but were still 2½–3 knots slower than the *Barham*s as well as being relatively undergunned – 12-inch against 15-inch.

The same relative merits and demerits applied to the battle-cruisers at Jutland. The *Derfflinger* was a magnificent ship, strong and fast and adequately gunned. But the *Lion*, *Princess Royal*, and *Tiger* all stood up to enemy shellfire as well as the German ships, and their superior speed (as Hipper ruefully noted) allowed them to get ahead on the run to the north and 'bend' the German battle-cruisers round to the east and prevent them from sighting Jellicoe's battle fleet until it was right on top of them. The *Lützow* took some twenty-four heavy shell hits and had to be abandoned and sunk. She was little more than a twisted wreck with not a gun working and probably 10,000 tons of water in her. The *Lion* – which received only half that number of heavy shells, it is true, but the German shells were much more lethal – could steam at full speed at the end of the battle and only two of her guns were out of action. Tea had been laid in the *Lion*'s wardroom just before action. 'Some fourteen hours later,' Chalmers noted, 'the furniture was found to be still intact. The cups, saucers and plates of cake were all in proper array and even the flowers stood proudly in their vases, as if in defiance of the death and devastation that lay on the other side of the bulkhead.'[5]

Another twelve hits *might* have sunk the *Lion*. But it is wrong to draw the conclusion that British battle-cruisers were like tin cans by contrast with the well-nigh impregnable German battle-cruisers. Hipper's battle-cruisers were virtually *hors de combat* after suffering some fifty heavy shell hits in all. Beatty's *Lion*, *Princess Royal*, *Tiger*, and *New Zealand*, which had been in the heat of the engagement like the enemy from the start, had endured some thirty heavy shell hits but still made up a fit, fast fighting force. These figures also suggest that British gunnery was not as weak as some critics have made it out to be; nor is the fact that the *New Zealand*, always in the heat of the fighting, remained unscratched to the end a great credit to German shooting.

But before too many bouquets are presented to Beatty and to British naval architects, the uncomfortable truth must be faced – that the Germans had only one battle-cruiser sunk and the British had three, even if two of the British ships were obsolescent and expendable. Was something indeed wrong with our bloody ships that day? What was the one fatal flaw?

The reason for the loss by explosion of three British battle-cruisers was one of the great tragedies of Jutland. Although Jellicoe and Beatty blamed the battle-cruisers' loss on weak construction and inadequate armour protection, the failure did not lie there. The one flaw was the lack of internal protection which allowed an explosion inside the turret to ignite cordite there which led to instant 'flash' transmission by way of the trail of cordite in the hoists, the hoppers in the handing room, and at the magazine bulkheads to the magazines themselves. It is true that if the turret itself had been impenetrable by heavy shell, this would not have occurred. But the turrets were relatively well protected with 7-inch plate and in the case of the *Queen Mary* 9-inch, only one inch less than her German contemporaries. Both British and German turrets proved penetrable. It is what happened afterwards that decided the fate of the ship. After the *Seydlitz*'s narrow escape from magazine explosion at Dogger Bank, all German dreadnoughts were fitted with protection to prevent a repetition. That hit by the *Lion* sixteen months before Jutland was a most fortunate one for the German Navy.

Flash risk was not some new and unprepared-for factor in a modern naval battle. There were flash doors in the hoists and the working chamber, but these proved inadequate to exclude the enormous and spontaneous heat given off by cordite, and might have been made of cardboard. There is good reason to believe that there had earlier been better protection but that it had at one time been removed. In an urgent telegram from Beatty to Jellicoe immediately after their return to base, he wrote:

Present arrangements of flash doors are ineffective when turret armour is penetrated. Flash from shell may reach cordite in main cages and handing rooms ... Almost certain that magazines of three lost battle cruisers exploded from such a cause. Consider matter of urgent necessity to alter existing communication between magazine and handing rooms by reverting to original system of handing room supply scuttles . . . [6]

The last sentence suggests that flash-proof scuttles originally fitted had at some time been discarded. The reason for this no doubt lay in the Navy's cult for rapid fire and the intense gunnery competition between individual ships and squadrons in peacetime. It is possible to imagine a gunnery officer, always on the look-out for time-saving short cuts, saving several seconds by leaving open these scuttles to allow for a continuous flow of charges to the handing rooms, and thence to the main hoist. Word of this dodge would inevitably spread, in time the flash-proof scuttles would be removed altogether on account of disuse, with the justification that the flash doors in the hoists and working chambers were adequate on their own.

Such an impromptu modification could not have occurred in a German ship. It was against the German character to tamper with official design and procedures, and against the German principle of ship-survival and emphasis on protection to reduce safety precautions. Those three battle-cruisers were, quite simply, a gambling loss, part of the price paid for the element of self-confident aggression in British naval tradition. The firm belief existed that there was something weak and even effete in giving too much attention to caution and protection from the enemy.

It was the gunnery system and the gunnery officers themselves which may have been more responsible for the loss of those three great ships and some 3,000 men than the ships' architects or builders. If those scuttles had been retained, it is very probable that the Grand Fleet would have had no capital ship losses at Jutland. The *Indefatigable* was quite able to stand up to five shell hits. From the foretop of the *Invincible* Dannreuther observed – one imagines with clinical interest – the hits suffered by his ship below. 'Then I saw the roof of this turret ['Q' turret on the starboard side] hit by a heavy shell and blown off like a bit of scrap metal. Almost immediately there was a huge explosion as Q and P magazines blew up, destroying and cutting in half the ship.'[7] He had no doubt that the two other battle-cruisers, and the *Defence*, went up the same way.

The second great tragedy of Jutland had nothing to do either with the design of the ships or the gun crews but relates to the quality of the shell they were given to fire, and these were not even designed and produced by the Navy. The Ordnance Board, controlled by the War Office, was responsible. Fisher had long before wrested control of the Navy's guns from the Army but in 1916 the design and testing of shell was still the Ordnance Board's responsibility, with only nominal naval representation until 1919.

The grim and indisputable fact was that the armour-piercing (AP) shell fired at Jutland should have pierced the armour of the German ships at any angle and exploded inside, and did not do that. On striking at an oblique angle, British heavy shell broke up either on impact or before complete penetration. The intelligent and down-to-earth Dreyer calculated that during one period of the battle alone, between 7 p.m. and 7.30, effective British armour-piercing shell would have sunk three or four battle-cruisers and four or five battleships. It was a heartbreaking experience for gunnery officers, and for that most senior gunnery officer, Jellicoe, to witness the relatively harmless effect of their heavy gunfire in the short time in which they had the High Seas Fleet in their sights. 'We thus lost the advantage we ought to have enjoyed in *offensive* power due to the greater weight of our projectiles,' Jellicoe later wrote, 'while suffering the accepted disadvantage in the protection of our ships due to the heavy weights of our guns and ammunition which reduced the total weight available for armour plating.'[8]

The Admiralty is not immune from blame for this catastrophic state of affairs. When it was belatedly recognized in 1910 that future naval battles were likely to be fought at ranges above 5,000 yards (at which the Navy carried out gunnery practice), greater attention had to be paid to shell impact at a relatively steep angle as a result of the longer range and consequent steeper trajectory. The specification for an AP shell to meet this need was passed by the DNO to the Ordnance Board, and in due course the shell provided was tested, but on normal impact at or near a right angle and *not on oblique impact*. Jellicoe, the Controller at the time, insisted on realistic long-range trials. They were disallowed for reasons of expense. The argument was still raging when he took up a seagoing command and was finally lost after his departure. Heavy shell was tested, but it was of such a haphazard nature, in favour of the manufacturers, that there was small likelihood of the defects revealed in action being discovered in Proof.

This is how Vice-Admiral Sir Francis Pridham, one-time President of the Ordnance Board (1941–5), explained the system of checking:

The shell were manufactured in 'Lots', of four hundred, each Lot being subdivided into Sub-lots of one hundred. When a Lot was brought forward by the shell maker for Proof, two shell were picked out at random from Sub-lot No. 1, to be tested at an armour plate of specified thickness, at a specified striking velocity and at a specified angle of impact. If the first shell fired succeeded in penetrating the plate whole, the full Lot of 400 shell passed into service. If this first shell failed the second from the same Sub-lot was fired. If this was successful the full Lot of now 398 were accepted. If the second shell also failed, the Sub-lot was sentenced 'Reproof' and the shell maker was given the option of withdrawing the whole lot from Proof, or allowing the remaining 300 to proceed to Proof. Needless to say they generally chose the latter. Proof then commenced with the next Sub-lot.

Now suppose that there was in fact as many as 50% dud shell in a Sub-lot, then the chance would be three to one against two successive failures! Mathematical deduction shows that there is an even chance that a Lot of Shell which has been accepted as a result of the above system of Proof, may include from 71% to 84% duds.

The Ordnance Board's Professor of Statistics, having been given the results of Proof firings of the heavy shell then in the Fleet, calculated that from 30% to 70% were probably dud shell, but that the data from these Proof firings was insufficient to enable him to give a nearer approximation.

The irony and the tragedy for the Navy is that although they suffered political cheeseparing like everyone else, for the fraction of the cost of a new dreadnought, comprehensive trials could have been carried out that would have revealed this weakness long before the war. But like secure bases for the Fleet, effective AP shell was sacrificed on the altar of dreadnought numbers. Jellicoe's insistence upon opening fire at long range for fear of the efficiency of German torpedoes unfortunately only served to show up the deficiencies of British shell. When fired at ranges under 10,000 yards hits by British AP shell had a devastating effect.

German shell was by no means wholly reliable either. The proportion of duds was much higher than expected by the British. After action against Hipper during the Lowestoft Raid five weeks before Jutland, Tyrwhitt wrote to his friend Walter Cowan, 'The more I see of their shell, the less I think of their efficiency . . . so I don't think you need worry much about the brutes, if only you can set about them.'[9]

There is good reason to believe that British armour was superior to German armour, although statistical evidence is insufficient to form a reliable judgement owing to the short duration of time in which the two main fleets were in action. German armour of 10 and 11 inches thickness was pierced by British heavy shells, but only once was British armour above 9 inches penetrated by German shell.

German instruments for night fighting were vastly superior to British, and all German lenses, and the range-finders themselves, proved superior. The British were at a severe disadvantage with their coincident range-finders in poor visibility, which applied almost throughout the engagement. This is the first reason why the Germans were quicker onto the target, and gave the impression (especially to those at the receiving end) that their gunnery was superior. It was indeed impressive, but when, for instance, the battle-cruisers' duel warmed up, so did British gunnery. The reason for this was that with the British 'bracket system' for finding the target by spotting a short or over before firing the next salvo until a straddle was achieved led to slow firing at the outset. The Germans used the 'ladder system' in which salvoes were fired in rapid succession at ranges increasing by several hundred metres and nearly always found the target more rapidly, although they could lose it again just as quickly in face of enemy evasive action. Also, under intense fire and adverse conditions the Germans tended to lose their concentration relatively earlier and more seriously than British gunners. For example, between 7.10 p.m. and 7.30, records show only two hits on the British Fleet and thirty-five on the German capital ships.

Ship for ship, and class for class, there was little to choose between the men o'war engaged at Jutland, although the priorities applied by British and German architects revealed themselves to the advantage of one side or another: British superiority in speed in the battle-cruiser engagement was highly advantageous, and the overall greater weight of shell had a damaging moral and material effect on the Germans. Even the fastest German dreadnoughts could not have intervened in the 'run to the south' as the 5th Battle Squadron succeeded in doing. On the other hand, German ship resistance to shellfire probably saved the *Seydlitz*, *Derfflinger*, *König*, *Grosser Kurfurst*, and *Markgraf* from going to the bottom, and the failure to sink German ships had a demoralizing effect on the British gunners, even though a number of them thought at the time that they had done better than the results later showed.

The British had a high respect for the *Derfflinger*, the newest German battle-cruiser, and had expected her sister ship *Hindenburg* to be present. It was as well that she had not yet completed her trials. If the *Derfflinger* was the best battle-cruiser present at Jutland, credit for being the best battleships must go to the *Barham*, *Valiant*, *Warspite*, and *Malaya*. Their guns were much feared by the Germans and their speed proved of decisive importance in the 'run to the north' as well as earlier, and their robust construction and armour protection (to German standards) stood up to ferocious and accurate enemy fire. After suffering mechanical failure in her steering mechanism, the *Warspite* received at least thirteen heavy shell hits. But she had only a few casualties and remained in fighting order although Evan-Thomas ordered her home because of her now restricted speed and unreliable steering.

Of the pre-dreadnought ships present, the Germans lost one of six (*Pommern*), the British three of eight (*Defence, Warrior, Black Prince*). None should have been present: they all belonged to an earlier era of naval warfare.

All the German ships present were coal-burners, and many had reciprocating engines. All the British dreadnoughts were turbine-engined and the most recent were oil-fuelled. The standard of efficiency and reliability in both German and British fleets reflected highly on the marine engine of its time and the engineer branches.

The weakness of British reporting was a great handicap to Jellicoe, whose own record was not faultless: for example the *Iron Duke*'s failure to inform Beatty that Scheer had reached Horns Reef. Time and again the inability of British commanders, whose job it was, to transmit information was shown up. There were notable exceptions, and the work of Goodenough and Alexander-Sinclair was a fine example of courage as well as intelligent scouting. One reason why Jellicoe was both disappointed and angry at the poor service he received ('Why doesn't anyone tell me anything?') was that too much was expected from the signals branch. Equipped as the fleet was with short-range and long-range W/T (in the bigger ships), semaphore, searchlights, as well as the traditional signal flags, it was thought that messages must get through, however adverse the conditions. This proved not to be the case, and was another example of placing too much reliance on the *matériel* and too little on the human element. Aerial antennae were carried away, wireless sets damaged by shock and vibration or shellfire, transmissions jammed by the Germans. Searchlights, too, were shot out and even the most powerful were sometimes unable to penetrate the dense smoke and haze. Signal halyards were shot away, flags were impossible to read at long range and difficult to see at short range in the uncertain visibility. The lot of the signalman was not an easy one, and though there were some duffers – especially Beatty's Seymour – most were bright and efficient. Their disappointing performance overall was the consequence of expecting too much and inability to anticipate how difficult it would be on the day.

The failure of ship commanders, whose first function was not scouting, to report sightings to the flagship was caused by the rigidity of the system, the discouragement of initiative, the belief that 'father knows best', and Jellicoe's failure personally to impress the importance of reporting on his subordinates. Although the GFBOs stated that 'reports of sighting the enemy should reach the Admiral without delay', Jellicoe also emphasized that 'W/T should be reserved for messages of the first importance'. Was the distant sighting of a dim, unfamiliar silhouette 'of the first importance'? Captains tended to be on the safe side and judge not; although on more than one occasion that night the shape was that of a crippled German battle-cruiser ripe for the picking.

The 'father knows best' attitude was typified by the flag-captain of the *Barham*, Arthur Craig, who wrote, in defence of his reticence, 'It is certainly doubtful whether the various observations of enemy ships made by ships of our battle fleet ought to have been reported to the C.-in-C. I was on the bridge all night with my Admiral [Evan-Thomas], and we came to the conclusion that the situation was known to the C.-in-C. . . . A stream of wireless reports from ships in company with the C.-in-C. seemed superfluous and uncalled for.'[10] 'Never imagine that your C.-in-C. sees what you see', Jellicoe lectured, but that was in 1934, eighteen years too late.

Of Jellicoe, one of his biographers has written that 'it is impossible that he did not realize the extent to which the whole long chain of command with its memoranda, orders and instructions, might build a wall of reticence which only the exceptionally strong, independent character would break through'.[11]

Beatty recognized how damaging to the Fleet the over-elaborate system had proved to be, and was determined on reform. In his post-Jutland *Battle Cruiser Orders* he stated that it had been proved 'again and again that nothing is more fatal than "waiting for orders". The Senior Officers may be closely engaged, their signal apparatus may be destroyed, or for many other reasons they may be unable to issue orders by signal. It therefore becomes the duty of subordinate leaders to anticipate the executive orders and act in the spirit of the Commander-in-Chief's requirements.'

German signalling worked well, and it was particularly strong on recognition signals. The British system was 'practically nil', Jellicoe admitted later. The Germans picked up our night code recognition signal, passed it through the Fleet, and as a result on several occasions extracted themselves from tight corners by using it.

The worst signalling failures were perpetrated by the Admiralty, and Jellicoe was right to distrust what he was told and vent his spleen about what he was not told during the night. After the Admiralty passed to Jellicoe the 10.41 p.m. signal, which the C.-in-C. had discounted, between 11.15 p.m. 31 May and 1.25 a.m. 1 June a number of German signals, all of paramount importance to Jellicoe, were intercepted by Room 40, decoded and passed to OD. The first, when Jellicoe was steering south confident in the knowledge that Scheer was also on a southerly heading and to his west, was a report from Scheer that he was steering SE by S. Then the commander of the 1st Torpedo Division was heard to order all the flotillas to assemble at Horns Reef at 4 a.m., or steer a course round the Skaw into the Baltic.

At 11.50 p.m. OD were informed that Scheer reported his position at 11 p.m. as 56 15N 5 42E, course SE ¾E, which would have told Jellicoe that both his position and heading meant he was making for Horns Reef. Scheer's 1.20 a.m. position clearly showed that he had crossed over behind the Grand Fleet's course to the north of Jellicoe. This crucial fact was confirmed by a further signal five minutes later.

Not one of these signals was passed to Jellicoe, and he was right to describe these errors as 'absolutely fatal'. How could such criminal negligence have come about? It is not easy to depict clearly and certainly what happened in the Admiralty on this the most important night in its long history. But a picture can be built up from knowledge of the workings of Room 40 and OD and relations and communications between them. This has been valuably supplemented by information obtained from James when he was retired and elderly but possessed of a clear memory and incisive mind: by 1917 he was at work in Room 40 as a thirty-six-year-old commander. Oliver was Chief of Staff, and like Jellicoe he did not sufficiently trust those working under him and ran a one-man band. His DOD Jackson, was an officer not remembered for his sharpness of intellect. Then there were several duty captains, officers who were either unfit for sea service or were awaiting a ship; and none of them was encouraged to show what initiative he had.

That night, in accordance with procedure, decoded German signals from Room 40 were sent to Oliver, or in his absence, to his deputy, the DOD, or one of the duty captains. It seems that Oliver, either for all the time or some of the time, was taking a break when these signals came in, and that – perhaps because of his absence too – they did not pass through Thomas Jackson and therefore went direct to Allan Everett, a forty-eight-year-old captain who was naval secretary to the First Sea Lord, and during these crucial hours duty captain. It might be thought that interest alone would bring the professional head of the Royal Navy to the OD in the midst of this most critical battle. But Admiral Henry Jackson (not to be confused with his subordinate) appears to have had such confidence in his Chief of Staff that he made only intermittent visits; Captain Jackson was resting or elsewhere;

and thus Captain Everett carried the final burden of responsibility. He had much else on his mind. OD was buzzing with signals and this officer had little or no experience of German operational signals. Nor is there any reason to believe that he was an exception to the generally distrustful view taken of Room 40 by OD. The signals were put on file, and it is likely there was a failure to draw attention to them when more senior officers had returned to their posts later.

A combination of lethargy (Henry Jackson), failure to depute (Oliver), lack of intelligence (Thomas Jackson) and lack of initiative (Everett), all suffering under the weak and inflexible organization of OD, resulted in the failure to inform Jellicoe of the whereabouts and destination of his enemy before it was too late to catch him.

While Jellicoe was unquestionably the victim of poor intelligence in this (and other) cases, he had only himself to blame for the possible loss of earlier vital intelligence which might equally have swung the tide of battle decisively in his favour.

The reason why Jellicoe sent the *Campania* home was not only his fear that she might be torpedoed or that she would be too late for the action; if he had had greater confidence in her usefulness he would no doubt have risked the U-boats or sent a couple of destroyers to protect her. The *Campania* had been with the Grand Fleet since April 1915. Early trials had not been very successful. The seaplanes' floats broke up in a rolling sea. The experimental wireless had proved unreliable. Then came the first successful take-off from the flight deck with a seaplane fitted with a detachable wheeled trolley. After being threatened with withdrawal, the old ex-liner was now sent to have her flight deck lengthened so that two-seater reconnaissance aircraft could take off into wind and a reconnaissance balloon be flown from her stern. She rejoined the Fleet at Scapa Flow in April 1916, and on 30 May was proving her worth on exercises with her three Short seaplanes, three Sopwith 'Babys' and four Sopwith Schneider seaplanes. With these ten machines and an effective flight deck for rapid take-off, the *Campania* had a first rate capability for launching spotting and reconnaissance machines and fighters to attack roving Zeppelins. But Jellicoe's rating of her usefulness was not high, and this was confirmed by her obscure anchorage and his failure to learn that she was not with the Fleet until 2 a.m., three hours after she should have sailed.

Like any pioneer enterprise, the Royal Navy's Air Service was supported by enormous enthusiasm and determination to succeed. If the *Campania* had a first rate capability for launching spotting and around 6 p.m. when Jellicoe was in such sore need of information on the bearing, course, and distance of the High Seas Fleet it is scarcely conceivable that none of her aircraft could have learned some intelligence of use to the C.-in-C. and transmitted it back to its mother ship. The eager young pilots, it is certain, would have flown fearlessly and Scheer's anti-aircraft protection was negligible. The aircraft had a speed of 50–60 m.p.h and a duration of four hours, longer than that of many seaborne aircraft in the Second World War. The ceiling was low, visibility poor, some of the intelligence might have been inaccurate, but some of it must have given Jellicoe more information than he was receiving from elsewhere, which had been almost nil up to that time.

More than three hours earlier, at 2.40 p.m., Beatty, also in great need of information on the enemy, had ordered the little *Engadine* to send up a seaplane. Without the benefit of a flight deck, it took twenty-eight minutes to move from its hangar, hoist out, start up, and take to the air. Twenty minutes later Flight Lieutenant Frederick Rutland and his observer George Trewin, confirming Admiral Scott's prediction that no fleet would be able to hide itself from the aeroplane's eye, were reporting: 'Three enemy cruisers and five destroyers distance from me 10 miles bearing 90 degrees steering course to the NW.' Two further valuable and specific signals followed, informing the *Engadine* of the turn to the south of Hipper's 2nd Scouting Group. Rutland was still transmitting details of numbers when a fuel pipe broke and he was forced to land on the sea. He carried out repairs on the spot, took off and returned to his mother ship, concluding the first-ever aircraft reconnaissance flight against an enemy fleet in action. Rutland wanted to take off again but was refused permission. 'We could have been of great use if we had gone on again', he wrote later. 'It was the fault of the Navy entirely that we were not employed to better effect.'

It does not diminish the importance of this single flight that Rutland's intelligence did not get through to Beatty due to poor signalling, and that the *Galatea* was, fortunately, able to pass on the burden of the messages a few minutes later. Jellicoe's failure was that, while regarding successful spotting and reconnaissance and especially attacks on Zeppelins as useful, he did not want with him (as Rutland wrote) 'any unit that had not been proved 100% efficient'. It is safe to assume that Jellicoe was thankful to be relieved of the burden of that big almost defenceless 20,000-ton ex-liner with her unreliable machines. These aircraft, however, could have been of inestimable value to him, and if the *Campania* had been sunk the loss would have been negligible. As it happened, the *Engadine* proved her worth in a second capacity, towing the crippled *Warrior* and taking off all the survivors when she sank.

Over the years since the battle was fought, Jellicoe has been the victim of heavy criticism and the subject of the highest praise. His performance has been compared to Beatty's, in his favour and against; and for two decades and even after their deaths, supporters of the two admirals have fought bitter battles of words as relentlessly as in the Fisher–Beresford feud of the years before the Great War at sea. Feuds in the Royal Navy have commonly been more ferocious than in other closed communities, like the Army or Civil Service. Lord Mountbatten used to say that this was because of the physical conditions of life, in a confined shell often for weeks or months at a time, and, since the days of sail, with not enough to do and cheap drink readily available. Naval service at sea is a highly artificial life, rarely dangerous in the twentieth century in peacetime but often tedious and uncomfortable, especially in the smaller men o'war, and lacking the natural presence of women.

Be all that as it may, the Beatty–Jellicoe feud was one of the hardest fought, with the tide running first one way and then the other. On the whole, though, the criticism of Jellicoe has been sharper than that of Beatty, in part because there was nothing heroic about Jellicoe's style and appearance, which Beatty possessed in abundance.

Jellicoe has been taken to task for deploying to port rather than to starboard and towards the enemy; for twice turning away from destroyer attacks during the critical German 'battle about-turns'; for failing to follow Beatty when the battle-cruisers regained contact; for failing to anticipate Scheer's line of escape and renewing the action the next day; and for much else.

The pros and cons of these points have been debated at all levels, from the intellectual down to the emotional, and only a summary and conclusion are called for here. A number of authorities, from Churchill who was not there, to Doveton Sturdee who was, argued that by deploying to port Jellicoe with only a few hours of daylight left to him delayed the moment of contact and thus reduced the chances of a decisive victory. Many more commentators, and not all of them uncritical supporters of the C.-in-C. argue that any other deployment would have resulted in chaos, the German Fleet being so near that its van would have butchered the first Grand Fleet battleships it encountered in the midst of a complex evolution, with many of their guns masked and in no fit state for close action against a powerful enemy. Additionally, Jellicoe knew from reports from his light cruisers, earlier detached on this errand, that the light was more favourable for gunnery with the enemy to the west; and he also recognized that deployment to port placed him between the Germans and their bases.

Jellicoe was absolutely right to deploy as he did, his timing was brilliant, and the result all that he could, quite rightly, hope for. He deprived Scheer of the chance to carry out the manoeuvre he had so often rehearsed, to concentrate on a part of the British line with gun and torpedo, commit the maximum damage swiftly, and retire behind a smoke-screen. Instead, Scheer found himself faced with the entire strength of the Grand Fleet spread out in an arc and concentrating their fire on his van. No wonder Scheer's Chief of Staff was 'emphatic that Jellicoe acted rightly'. He had crossed his enemy's 'T' and placed himself in the ideal tactical situation with the light advantage previously enjoyed by Hipper against Beatty.

In accordance with Jellicoe's own rules, he had no alternative but first to turn away from Scheer's destroyer attack to cover the enemy fleet's first turn-about. He did all that he could within his self-imposed restraints on an immediate pursuit to position himself favourably for a renewal of action, by placing 'himself as soon as possible athwart their line of retreat to the Bight, for along that line, sooner or later, they were almost certain to be discovered'.[12]

After the battle it was possible to recognize that the massed destroyer attack with torpedoes had been a greatly overestimated menace. Ever since the French had built up a powerful torpedo boat force in the 1880s and 1890s, the Royal Navy demonstrated in its tactics and *matériel* great concern for the threat of the mass torpedo attack. The lessons of battle were limited to the Russo-Japanese War, and since then the torpedo had been improved in power, range, and accuracy many times over. The threat of the flotillas was an unknown quantity but every navy reckoned it as high and there was no reason before Jutland to believe anything else. The Germans were just as nervous as the British were and took as many precautions against the flotillas' swarm attack. In the event, after numerous attacks by both sides in daylight and darkness, the destroyer's torpedo proved if not a bent weapon a much less effective one than had been feared, damaging only one British dreadnought and sinking one German pre-dreadnought.

In view of the commonly held view of the torpedo threat, Jellicoe could do nothing else but turn away from that first destroyer attack by Scheer's flotillas, even though it was later seen to be a relatively limited attack, all torpedoes being easily avoided. (The Germans had been less successful than the British in concealing the track of their torpedoes, and towards the end of their run they travelled very slowly anyway).

The turn-away during the second encounter is less easy to justify. Fate, and Admiral Beatty, had been abundantly generous to Jellicoe by presenting him once with the High Seas Fleet on a plate. That it did so a second time was perhaps more than the British C.-in-C. deserved. Certainly for Jellicoe to allow one plate to be snatched away a second time is hard to explain and forgive. The turn-away was carried out in two stages, at 7.22 p.m. and 7.25, each turn of 2 points (45 degrees total), leaving the fleet on a south-easterly heading, and with the chances of a renewal of contact that evening now out of the question.

Jellicoe had just seen how relatively inoffensive the first German flotilla attacks had been. But he stuck by his own rule book. The inflexibility of mind which had led to the formulation of the GFBOs in the first place was now applied to the critical moment of battle, and was found as unyielding as ever. Only Jellicoe's rear was seriously threatened by this second attack so why turn the whole fleet away? This was the moment when to turn from the defensive to the offensive posed none of the risks Jellicoe had always feared. He knew that he held in his hands the fate of Britain and her empire, that so long as the Grand Fleet survived, they would survive. But he failed to grasp the opportunity (which would never come again) to destroy the enemy, with all the untold benefits this could bring to his country's cause.

Sturdee's second in command wrote, 'To meet the situation all that was necessary was to turn away our tail. What [Jellicoe] did was to turn the whole battle fleet away . . . and thereby lose all hope of a decisive action which until then it was in our power to force by turning our van *towards* the enemy.'[13] There was consternation on the *Lion*'s bridge, too, when this turn-away was observed. One of Beatty's Staff said that he was 'horrified'. 'I felt instinctively that here was the sad climax of all our long discussions about defensive tactics.'[14]

This failure to follow up the enemy, whose tactical position was a shambles, and destroy almost certainly Hipper's battle-cruisers, and very likely half a dozen of Scheer's most valuable dreadnoughts, is a serious and valid criticism of Jellicoe's leadership.

Certainly Jellicoe's opportunity to 'cut off whole of enemy's battle fleet' as advocated by Beatty twenty minutes later was greater at this second enemy turn-about than at the time Beatty used this phrase in his signal beginning 'Submit van of battle fleet follow battle cruisers'. There was for a time much spurious criticism of Jellicoe by Beatty supporters who claimed that if only Jellicoe had acceded to Beatty's plea 'to follow' the battle-cruisers, the whole High Seas Fleet could have been sent to the bottom. This much-repeated theme underlines the caricatured image of the two admirals which developed in the emotional aftermath of the engagement, with Beatty seen as the dashing, bold commander intent only on the complete annihilation of the enemy, à la Nelson; and Jellicoe the anxious, fussy commander flinching back from a showdown.

In fact, at 7.30–7.45 p.m. it was Beatty who, in touch with the enemy, wisely called for support, not wishing to risk facing the full strength of the High Seas Fleet alone. And Jellicoe at this time, as he wrote later, 'was steering 4 points more in the direction of the enemy than were the Battle Cruisers'.[15] The 'Follow me and we will sink the whole German Fleet' controversy lasted until the publication of the *Official Despatches* in 1921 settled the matter. Both admirals maintained a discreet silence over the affair, and the only hint of Jellicoe's feelings was contained in an entirely private remark to a friend after the war. 'To tell the truth,' he was reported to have remarked quietly of Beatty's signal, 'I thought it was rather insubordinate.'[16]

Deprived of reports to the contrary from both the Admiralty and his own forces, Jellicoe steamed through the night certain in his knowledge that Scheer was to the west of him. He was right to complain so vehemently at this absence of intelligence to the contrary. But was he right to conclude that all the firing to the north stemmed from attacks by the German screen against Grand Fleet destroyers at the rear? At least he could have asked for reports, but he did not. He had made up his mind, and that was that. It was equally possible that this firing was the German screen clashing with Grand Fleet destroyers preparatory to a German break-through to the east; which is what it was.

It was the British C.-in-C.'s tactical inflexibility as much as the failure of reporting that led to Scheer's safe arrival at Horns Reef at dawn. The German C.-in-C.'s first bold attempt to break through to the east had been mistimed and was foiled by the Grand Fleet. After this warning of Scheer's intention, there was no excuse for Jellicoe not to anticipate a second attempt. It was, after all, as obvious as a householder, deprived of his key to the front door, going round to the back.

Whatever tactical successes or failures Jellicoe experienced at Jutland, given the conditions and time of day, the rigid centralization of his command, the strict limitations of initiative allowed to his subordinates, the unexpected failure of the torpedo, the unwillingness of the enemy to face a full-scale general engagement, and his own belief that the survival of the Grand Fleet battle squadrons was more important than the destruction of the enemy's battle squadrons, a decisive victory was well-nigh impossible to achieve.

If Beatty had had the 5th Battle Squadron with him from the opening rounds, he would probably have sunk two or three of Hipper's battle-cruisers instead of one. If Jellicoe had turned away only the rear of his line at the second turn-about and destroyer attack and pursued Scheer to the west with his other battle squadrons, he could have severely mauled the High Seas Fleet before it got away. If Jellicoe had received – and believed – earlier news of Scheer's night route he might have cut him off before he reached Horns Reef, but any dawn engagement would have been bedevilled by much worse conditions than the previous afternoon. 'Visibility was so poor that we couldn't see beyond a squadron length', reported Scheer's Chief of Staff. 'We could hardly even find the entrance to the Amrum Bank passage.'[17]

Whatever tactical errors were committed on the British side, therefore, the chances of an annihilating victory were negligible, even if British shell had been less fallible and the battle-cruisers less vulnerable to magazine explosion. The first day of June would still have seen Germany in possession of a formidable enough fleet to sustain the future U-boat campaign, keep the Baltic closed and the trade routes open to Scandinavia, and oblige Britain to keep an Army of 100,000 men at home against the invasion risk. All that Germany would have lost by sustaining a partial defeat was the propaganda advantage of claiming a victory and the boost to morale in the Fleet and at home which she gained by sinking more ships than she lost.

A *decisive* defeat by either side would have had catastrophic results for the loser. For Germany the effect of defeat on neutral opinion, especially American opinion, on the Russian campaign, the renewed U-boat war, the Army, the civilian population, and her allies would certainly have been serious, quite apart from the knowledge that Britain's Trafalgar reputation for supremacy at sea would be sustained. For Britain defeat at sea would have meant total defeat within a few months, with the nation exposed to landings, trade and supplies and troops from overseas exposed to an Atlantic blockade, and even communications to France severed. The relatively worse consequences of defeat for Jellicoe than for Scheer would have justified greater boldness than shown by the German C.-in-C. and provided some justification for the greater caution shown by the British C.-in-C. Churchill wrote a good deal of nonsense about Jutland but it is his definition of Jellicoe as being 'the one man who could lose the war in an afternoon' which history will remember.

On 1 June 1916 Britain still controlled the world's trade routes and sustained the blockade of Germany. Her Fleet was ready for action within twenty-four hours, bunkers and magazines full, the spirit of the men unimpaired, except by disappointment that they had been deprived of a great victory. As one midshipman wrote after the battle,

We have met the Germans at sea and only weather conditions of the most unfavourable sort, in Admiral Jellicoe's words 'robbed the fleet of that complete victory which I know was expected by all ranks and which one day will be ours'. The technical experience gained in every department has been immense, but the general effect on the morale of the Fleet cannot be over-estimated. Our one desire is to meet the enemy once more on his own ground and under any conditions, our only stipulation being that the visibility and the disposition of our Battle Fleet will force him for the first and last time to accept a general action which can and will be fought to a finish. The British Navy has entire confidence in the result.[18]

Germany's Fleet was unfit for sea, and would be for many weeks. And when it was it took no further risks of a gunnery duel with the Grand Fleet. The spirit of the men, who were at first elated at the damage they had inflicted and the victory they were accorded by their Emperor, their C.-in-C., the populace, and the newspapers, which hailed 'the victory of Skagerrak', began rapidly to decline when they returned to the barren and austere regime they had endured previously in anticipation of this great victory. Disillusionment in the Navy led eventually to political restlessness which ended in mutiny.

Two commentators, one a British statesman, the other a German naval officer, deserve the last words on the results of Jutland.

Two months later, Balfour claimed: 'Before Jutland, as after it, the German Fleet was imprisoned; the battle was an attempt to break the bars and burst the confining gates; it failed, and with its failure the High Seas Fleet sank back again into impotence.'[19]

Then many years later Korvetten Kapitän Friedrich Forstmeier wrote:

The greatness of personality of a Jellicoe perhaps rests in the very fact that he did not yield to fighting impulse, but evinced a statesmanlike mind . . . To him it was more important to keep his country's fleet intact at all costs for the main strategic task – remote blockade of the German Bight. A total victory over the High Seas Fleet might well have hastened the defeat of Germany . . . but the risk inherent in such an attempt was not justified when the blockade, slowly but with deadly certainty, achieved the same end.[20]

For Beatty the battle was a shattering disappointment, and he always refused to celebrate its anniversary. He felt a great opportunity had been missed and that Jellicoe had let him down by failing to gobble up the fleet he had, in effect, presented to him ready-cooked. Dannreuther recalled a conversation with Beatty at Rosyth after the *Lion*'s return. 'I spent an hour or more alone with him in his cabin on board the *Lion* while he walked up and down talking about the action in a very excited manner and criticizing in strong terms the action of the Commander-in-Chief in not supporting him.'[21] Outside the privacy of his cabin and the letters he wrote to his wife, Beatty was discretion itself and showed an unwavering loyalty to his chief during the months that followed. He regretted as deeply as Jellicoe the internecine strife the engagement aroused.

Beatty's courage and dash were never in doubt. But he was strongly criticized for (1) failing to ensure that the 5th Battle Squadron was in close support on meeting Hipper; (2) for failing to ensure that the 5th Battle Squadron turned before being forced dangerously to confront Scheer; (3) for failing to keep Jellicoe fully informed of the progress of the battle and of Scheer's whereabouts; and (4) for crossing in front of the Grand Fleet during and after deployment thus obscuring the High Seas Fleet from Jellicoe.

Chatfield validly argued that if Hipper had identified the four 15-inch-gunned ships he most feared, in addition to Beatty's battle-cruisers, he would never have opened the action, and would simply have warned Scheer and fallen back on the High Seas Fleet. Beatty kept Evan-Thomas's big battleships in reserve for just the situation that developed. He was very conscious of Jellicoe's strict orders referring to his use of the 5th Battle Squadron. Jellicoe, according to Beatty, 'was obsessed with the ideas that the ships of the 5th Battle Squadron were not as fast as anticipated [and] that the German Battleships were faster than anticipated'. Just as Hood believed that Beatty would misuse the precious 15-inch-gunned new ships, Jellicoe had been most reluctant for Beatty to have them at all when the 3rd Battle Cruiser Squadron went up to Scapa for gunnery practice. Jellicoe 'only consented to agree to my urgent request', continued Beatty, 'on the strict understanding and definite instructions that they were only to be used as a Supporting Force to avoid the possibility of their being engaged by a superior force when their lack of speed would prevent them from making good their retreat. Consequently, they were disposed as they were 5 miles away from the anticipated position of sighting the enemy.'[22]

The fact that they were further delayed in their support of Beatty was due, once again, to faulty signalling. Signalling failure then accounted for (2): (3) is a more difficult charge to answer. Besides the failures of signalling, all the scouting forces, British and German, except Goodenough's 2nd Light Cruiser Squadron and Boedicker's 2nd Scouting Group, tended to forget their primary function when in action. The best training in the world could not have prepared these light-cruiser officers for the distractions of real shellfire and the tumult and terrors of close-fought battle. Time and again, on both sides, the primary function of communicating information on what could be seen was lost in the hurly-burly of fighting the enemy and surviving.

As to the fourth major criticism of Beatty, it is true that by altering course to the east he cut across the battle fleet's intended course, forcing it to reduce speed temporarily and delaying Jellicoe's deployment. It has been suggested that Beatty made this alteration on the assumption that Jellicoe would deploy to starboard – to the west. But Beatty was much too able a tactician, and reader of his C.-in-C.'s mind, to make such a fundamental wrong assumption. It is much more likely that he wished to conceal for as long as possible from Scheer the presence of the British battle fleet, his priority intention throughout 'the run to the north'. He had every reason to suppose that he had succeeded so far, and he would naturally aim to draw Jellicoe's victim as deeply into the trap as possible before it was sprung upon him.

No praise is too high for Beatty for sustaining his aggressive tactics against Hipper in spite of his own serious losses and the damage to his flagship. He was less successful in another important duty, in keeping his C.-in-C. informed of what he saw and what was happening. It is quite extraordinary, for example, that Jellicoe did not learn until the following morning of the loss of the *Indefatigable* and *Queen Mary*, and even more extraordinary that Chatfield, twenty years later, expressed surprise when someone questioned this omission on his Admiral's part. But it is equally extraordinary that Jellicoe, knowing what a hot time Beatty had been having, never enquired about any ships he may have sunk or losses he had sustained. With the superiority the Battle Cruiser Fleet's commander enjoyed, it was possible that he had already sunk the greater part of Hipper's force, but Jellicoe either had no time, or no inclination, to find out.

It is quite clear that Beatty had taken no steps to improve his fleet's deplorable signalling organization. The same carelessness and lack of intelligence displayed on earlier occasions was repeated, and once again signals were not repeated by searchlight, a procedure on which Jellicoe was always most insistent. Beatty must also be held responsible for the numerous failures of his Staff, especially his Chief of Staff, the inadequate Captain Rudolph Bentinck, and, of course, for his retention of Seymour after his clear failure to match up to his job. The signalling staff of the *Princess Royal* and *Tiger* especially appear to have been insufficiently trained.

One further point has to be made before leaving the subject of reporting and signalling generally. Many of the failures, especially during the night action, can be accounted for by exhaustion. Even if most officers and men had enjoyed some sleep on the night of 30–31 May, the late-night departure and the imminence of action had not led to much rest. Then, for all those of the Battle Cruiser Fleet the action had been almost continuous for seven hours even if contact with the enemy had been broken from time to time. The strain of that second night was appalling, and many collapsed with tiredness as they had at the Battle of the Nile in 1798.

Of the Grand Fleet's squadron commanders, Evan-Thomas came in for the most criticism, especially by the pro-Beatty school. His failure to turn to concentrate his strength on Beatty at once can be accounted for by the fact that, due to Beatty's poor signalling organization and especially the failure to confirm by searchlight and W/T, the signal never reached him. It can as well have been caused by Evan-Thomas's knowledge that he had been ordered to station himself as a link between Beatty and Jellicoe and his first responsibility was to maintain that link, only breaking it when ordered to do so. When Beatty's signal to his destroyers to take up screening positions was received in the *Barham*, Captain Craig did suggest that the 5th Battle Squadron should turn to the east on its own initiative, but Evan-Thomas decided to await orders – an early example, even before the battle began, of the negative initiative instilled by the GFBOs.

A further major difficulty lay in the fact that Evan-Thomas was a newcomer to the Battle Cruiser Fleet and his 5th Battle Squadron was only on temporary assignment to Beatty. Highly as Beatty prized these super-fast super-dreadnoughts he had worked very little with them, and Evan-Thomas was unfamiliar with Beatty's tactical style, which was far less rigid than Jellicoe's because of his relatively smaller size, high speed, and different function. When Evan-Thomas received no signal (and when working with Jellicoe he invariably received searchlight confirmation) he presumed that 'the Vice-Admiral wished 5th BS further to northward to prevent enemy escaping in that direction – that was the idea at the moment in my head'. It is difficult not to accept the validity of this defence, and sympathize with the gallant Rear-Admiral when he continued with the question, 'After all, isn't it one of the fundamental principles of naval tactics that an admiral makes sure that his orders are understood by distant parts of his Fleet before rushing into space, covered by a smoke screen?'[23]

The earlier arrival of the 5th Battle Squadron would certainly have given Beatty the chance to cripple Hipper's squadron, and might have saved the *Queen Mary*. For this Beatty must take the lion's share of the blame, and while Evan-Thomas demonstrated a certain lack of imagination, he did not deserve the vilification he suffered from some quarters. There remains to be said that, once in action, both Beatty and Evan-Thomas performed heroic prodigies of leadership, handling their ships in a manner beyond praise. The 5th Battle Squadron's gunnery revealed the advantage of the superior facilities for practice at Scapa Flow compared with Rosyth.

Of the other battleship squadron commanders there is little to say. The seamanship of all of them was first class, as expected, and there was little opportunity to reveal any other qualities, least of all individual initiative, although in the last stages of the daylight action Jerram managed to get well ahead of Jellicoe in pursuit of Beatty. Hood's performance as C.-in-C. 3rd Battle Cruiser Squadron was all that might be expected of this splendid officer. He had a brilliant future at the time of Jutland, and his loss was sorely felt in the Navy. The most tragic squadron was Arbuthnot's. Three of the four old armoured cruisers were sunk, which did not matter, but over 1,800 officers and men died, and no nation and no navy can afford that. It was particularly unfortunate that this squadron, which was so unsuited to face the High Seas Fleet at any range, should be hurled by its bold commander into the barrels of Scheer's and Hipper's guns, at the same time seriously impeding British gunfire.

With few exceptions, the flotillas performed magnificently, with dash and with many examples of sharp-thinking initiative. The night actions they fought, blinded by seachlights and muzzle flash, deafened by small-calibre gunfire at sometimes point-blank range were the most nerve-testing of all. Many heroes were made that night, among them Captain Charles Wintour in the *Tipperary*, and so many of his officers and men of the 4th Destroyer Flotilla. The *Spitfire* got home with only six dead and part of the plating and anchor gear of the German dreadnought she had rammed. Other destroyers went down as a tangled riot of smashed and twisted steel after a single German salvo, and, in all, eight of these little craft failed to come home.

Admiral Scheer was highly praised for his tactical skill and his handling of the High Seas Fleet. This praise is deserved for his conduct of the two turn-abouts and for his training of the Fleet for this manoeuvre. But great commanders are not made by skilful evasions of the enemy, and an intelligent appreciation of the events following his sighting of Beatty at the end of the 'run to the south' would have made these turns-about unnecessary. Scheer could and should have concluded from Beatty's northerly heading that the High Seas Fleet was being led into a trap. If Beatty was flying for his life, why was he not steering north-west for home? Scheer's second tactical error was to presume, without the confirming evidence of his scouting forces, that Jellicoe was far enough south at 7.10 p.m. for the High Seas Fleet to make a dash for Horns Reef behind its rear. Scheer calculated that Jellicoe would be going at full speed, probably close to 20 knots, in pursuit of him to the south when in fact Jellicoe was still attempting to sort out his line following the last German destroyer attack. To attempt this same movement a second time does not suggest original thinking on the German C.-in-C.'s part, and presupposed a great deal of luck, which again came his way. Scheer's boasting and misrepresentation of the battle afterwards is irrelevant and is not contributory to history's judgement on the stature of this Admiral.

Admiral Hipper, on the other hand, after that early lapse of leaving his west flank unprotected, played the part of a maestro – a maestro of some Wagnerian epic. He manoeuvred his ships superbly, kept his nerve under the most daunting and intimidating circumstances, and extricated all his ships from the famous 'death ride' following his C.-in-C.'s second turn-about. He and his captains deserve the highest credit.

And so, who really won the Battle of Jutland, and with what weapons? To deal with the *matériel* first, there can be no doubt that the torpedo was the weapon that dominated the tactics on both sides, and yet fell far below expectations in the damage it caused. The flotilla attacks caused convulsive movements of the fleets but little harm. The submarines, blinded by being submerged (British) or deaf (German), played virtually no part in the proceedings, although juicy targets by the score passed near or over them. German air reconnaissance came too late on the morning of 1 June, and was never allowed to prove its value on the British side. With the exception of the 'flash' catastrophes on the British side, heavy shell proved to be less destructive than expected. No British gunnery officer expected that a German battle-cruiser (*Seydlitz*) would survive twenty-four heavy-shell hits, any more than a German gunnery officer expected a British battleship (*Warspite*) to survive the ferocious battering she received –

and in fact they claimed to have sunk her. In *matériel*, Fisher's theories were proved correct. The battle-cruiser fulfilled its functions satisfactorily, scouting and drawing the enemy battle fleet into a tactically disadvantageous position. Fisher as a proponent of high speed was once again vindicated. It was also Fisher who had advocated only the smallest secondary armament for his dreadnoughts and deplored the introduction of a 6-inch secondary battery. Jellicoe's fear of the overall heavier secondary armament of German dreadnoughts was not realized. The 4-inch gun was quite adequate against German flotillas, and because of the long range of the German 5.9 fitted in all dreadnoughts, gunnery officers were tempted to use them against the enemy battle line, which confused spotting.

In simple numbers, there was no doubt who had come off worse. The British losses were three battle-cruisers, three armoured cruisers, and eight destroyers, against German losses of one battleship, one battle-cruiser, four light cruisers, and five destroyers. Of these the German battleship *Pommern* and the three British armoured cruisers can be discounted as of negligible value. The serious losses were the *Lützow* and the four modern light cruisers for Germany, representing 20 per cent and 36 per cent of these two essential classes of fighting ship; and the *Queen Mary* for Britain, the relatively old and slow *Invincible* and *Indefatigable* together equally perhaps the value of one modern battle-cruiser, but statistically representing 33 per cent of British battle-cruisers participating. The balance, therefore, was marginally in Germany's favour. But damaged ships must also be taken into account, and here the balance turns to Britain's favour. Hipper's battle-cruiser force was *hors de combat* on 1 June and was quite incapable of putting to sea. In spite of frantic efforts in German dockyards, it was six months before the last of those battered battle-cruisers were fit for service. Scheer had only ten undamaged dreadnoughts after the battle while Jellicoe had twenty-four, and all the damaged British ships were repaired within eight weeks.

In the tragic human toll, because four of Jellicoe's ships blew up with only a handful of survivors, the British dead numbered 6,097 against the German loss of 2,551.

Both sides exaggerated enemy losses, but only the Germans loudly proclaimed a victory, and made great propaganda capital out of doing so immediately the fleet put into harbour. The first British official communiqué reporting the heavy losses suffered by the Grand Fleet filled the nation with anxiety and disappointment, and enraged Jellicoe's men, who thought they had done pretty well. Subsequent announcements from the Admiralty cheered everyone up, and while the regret that this had been no Trafalgar lingered, it was recognized that the German Fleet had escaped only by the skin of its teeth.

Germany could play with figures for as long as she wished, but British control of the world's sea lanes was unimpaired, the blockade of the enemy as tight as ever. The High Seas Fleet had come out with the intention of trapping and destroying *part of* the Grand Fleet, had failed to do so, and had retreated hastily back home, leaving the field of battle firmly in British hands. It is strategy that finally wins wars, and strategically there could be no doubt that Jellicoe had been the winner, whatever shortcomings he and his fleet's performance might have revealed. Of course it would have been infinitely more satisfactory if he had been a decisive tactical winner, too, but he judged the risks of attempting to achieve that to be too great. It is quite impossible to declare responsibly whether he was right or wrong not to take those risks. And no one can say he had not made his tactical policy amply clear beforehand. The evidence of that was in the GFBOs, all 200 pages of them.

16

THE DEFEAT OF THE U-BOAT, SURRENDER AND SCUTTLE

Post-Jutland reforms – The 19 August sortie – Jackson replaced by Jellicoe, Balfour by Carson, at the Admiralty – The advent of unrestricted U-boat warfare – The Navy's countermeasures inadequate – Jellicoe's resistance to the introduction of convoy – American entry into the war – Convoy again provides the antidote to the guerre de course – Geddes replaces Carson, and Jellicoe's peremptory sacking – Harmony prevails between the RN and USN – The success of the Geddes–Wemyss administration but failure to exploit air power – The abortive Zeebrugge raid – Surrender of the High Seas Fleet

The Great War was not yet at its halfway stage when the Battle of Jutland was fought, and grievous setbacks lay ahead on land and at sea before the final and rapid German descent towards defeat in the late summer of 1918.

On the same day when Jellicoe declared the Grand Fleet ready for action again, the second Battle of Ypres began on the Western Front, and just a month later (1 July 1916) the gigantic and bloody Somme offensive opened. On 15 June Woodrow Wilson, the man who was to take the USA into the war in April 1917, was re-nominated Democratic presidential candidate.

As a reaffirmation of the first lesson of Jutland, and of the new face of sea warfare, the underwater weapon struck again, on the evening of 5 June, when the armoured cruiser *Hampshire* with Kitchener on board and *en route* to Russia, was sunk by a mine laid by a U-boat off the Orkneys. The Field Marshal, a national hero who had, in the public's view, created the new armies as Fisher had created the Grand Fleet, had lunched with Jellicoe and discussed the Battle of Jutland before embarking in the cruiser, rejecting Jellicoe's suggestion that he should delay his departure.

Amidst the cries of lamentation which sounded out in the country for the loss of Kitchener, and the loss of so many fine ships and brave men at Jutland, sweeping naval reforms were swiftly put in hand. Following Beatty's urgent message to Jellicoe on the subject of his ships' destruction, the 'flash' menace was investigated by a newly formed Protection Committee. Anti-flash gear and devices were introduced throughout the Fleet. Flash-tight scuttles in the bulkheads between magazines and handling rooms were re-introduced. But the Fleet was equally concerned with what they regarded as the inadequacy of the armour, especially on the battle-cruisers, and battle-cruisers under construction were considerably strengthened. Only the Admiralty remained satisfied that British projectiles were beyond criticism. But when Jellicoe became First Sea Lord, oblique tests confirmed Beatty's suspicions about the reasons for the failure of British AP shell. On the other hand, no one could find fault with British director gear and for this reason the fitting of it in cruisers and for secondary armament in capital ships was accelerated.

The failure to transmit vital information to the Fleet by the Admiralty was thoroughly investigated, but it took another fourteen months before Oliver could be convinced that Room 40 must become an integral part of the Intelligence Division, under Hall. Room 40 grew in size and efficiency, supported in its work by yet another piece of good fortune. German intelligence had at last replaced the signal book retrieved from the *Magdeburg* in the first days of the war. But on 24 September 1916 the Zeppelin *L-32*, which had been shot down, conveniently yielded up a copy of the new signal book, which allowed Room 40 to continue its valuable work with hardly a break.

The GFBOs were little altered as a result of Jutland. In spite of the relative ineffectiveness of the torpedo, this weapon still dominated tactics. Mass destroyer attacks, submarines, and mines remained greatly feared, and Jellicoe was still not going to risk pursuit of a fleeing enemy or approaching within torpedo range until 'the enemy is beaten by gunfire'. Greater flexibility in the line was permitted and Jellicoe bowed to criticism of his second turn-away – which many officers thought had led to the failure to force a decision – by permitting squadron commanders greater discretionary powers.

But by August 1916, when the greater part of the High Seas Fleet was ready for sea again, nothing had occurred on either side that made a decisive battle more likely to take place. This was confirmed when, with a somewhat hollow show of bravado, Scheer ventured to demonstrate to the world that 'the enemy must be on the watch for attacks by our Fleet'.[1] On 19 August the High Seas Fleet with eighteen dreadnoughts and its only two serviceable battle-cruisers came out with the intention of effecting the aborted pre-Jutland raid on Sunderland in association with U-boat traps.

Again, Room 40 did not let down Jellicoe who was again at sea to meet Scheer before he had left harbour himself, this time well covered by scouting Zeppelins. The two Fleets were never in serious risk of making contact. Jellicoe flinched away when one of his light cruisers was torpedoed for fear that he might be entering a new minefield, and Scheer made a rapid retreat when one of his Zeppelins misreported the Harwich ships as 'a strong enemy force of about 30 units' including dreadnoughts.

The loss of two British light cruisers to U-boats on this sortie caused even greater reluctance to commit the Fleet to coming south when and if the German Fleet approached the east coast unless 'there is a really good chance of engaging it in daylight'.[2] It appeared more and more unlikely that this would ever again happen, and senior officers began to face up to the reality of victory without battle.

By November 1916 the Admiralty was again in deep trouble. This was brought about by a number of factors, one of them stemming from the failure to destroy the High Seas Fleet six months earlier. But more important was the great increase in merchantmen losses from the newly intensified U-boat campaign, with tonnage sunk doubling to over 120,000 monthly by contrast with 56,000 earlier in the year. Two raids on the Channel by German light craft did not help the standing of the Admiralty either. The Navy itself escaped criticism; it was the men in Whitehall who had again lost the confidence of the nation.

'The Navy has done wonders', ran a leader in *The Times* on 21 November 1916. But confidence did not extend to members of the Board at Whitehall. 'They have been a long time in office, and shore life for eighteen months tends to benumb a sailor's sense of the sea . . . The feeling that they have become "stale" is almost universal.' Jackson made no difficulties about quitting his post. 'I think it is quite time I made way for a more energetic and more experienced Admiral than I can claim to be . . . ',[3] he announced with modesty and truth. Jellicoe was his natural successor, but he made a great show of reluctance to leave, and when at last Balfour persuaded him to come down to London from his northern fastness and he bade farewell to his beloved Grand Fleet, 'there was not one completely dry eye on the quarterdeck' of the *Iron Duke*, according to an eyewitness. Jellicoe not only enjoyed the affection and admiration of his men. He had indeed forged a fine weapon, and even if it was never fully unsheathed its keen edge had been a sufficient deterrent to preserve the nation from catastrophe.

Beatty was a less obvious successor as C.-in-C. There were eight vice-admirals senior to him, among them Sturdee who was greatly put out when he was passed over. The only other serious contender was Jellicoe's Chief of Staff, Vice-Admiral Charles Madden. The rest were inadequate for one reason or another, and short of a surprise appointment from the pool of rear-admirals, there was really no one else but the hero of Jutland and the people's choice, David Beatty.

Balfour was not long in following Jackson out. Fleet Street had correctly surmised that he was also ineffective as the Navy's professional head, and the term of office of the other half of this thoroughly weak partnership expired with that of the man who had appointed him, Herbert Asquith. In fact Lloyd George, the new Prime Minister, had made it clear to his predecessor that Balfour was to be 'eliminated from the Admiralty'. In Balfour's place came Sir Edward Carson, 'uncrowned King of Ulster' and MP for Dublin University. He was a very considerable advocate, had been an able Attorney-General, possessed a mind as keen as Balfour's, supplemented by a kindness and friendliness in stark contrast to his predecessor's remoteness. Balfour had never gone near to the hurly-burly of grease, noise, and movement of a naval base. Carson took the Fleet into his confidence and was soon rewarded with its affection. And, unlike Churchill, he had no intention of becoming 'an amateur in naval strategy or tactics'. His presence boded well for the future.

By the end of 1916 it had become apparent that U-boat warfare against shipping would be the first threat and first preoccupation of the new Board. Germany had intensified her campaign in the autumn of 1916, but on a restricted basis. The failure of the German armies to break through on the Western Front, economic near-bankruptcy at home, and the increasing pressure of the British blockade introduced a note of desperation into Germany's war plans.

'A decision must be reached in the war before the end of 1917,' wrote the German Chief of Naval Staff, von Trotha, on 22 December 1916, 'if we can break England's back the war will at once be decided in our favour. Now England's mainstay is her shipping . . . ' Scheer himelf put it thus: 'Our aim was to break the power of mighty England vested in her sea trade in spite of the protection which her powerful Fleet could afford her . . . if we did not succeed in overcoming England's will to destroy us then the war of exhaustion must end in Germany's certain defeat.'[4]

A renewal of unrestricted U-boat warfare proved complex and difficult to undertake. Von Trotha many years later recalled the political machinations:

Scheer and I both held the view that the first half-hearted attempts at submarine warfare were a profound mistake as they gave notice to the British Admiralty to prepare for future eventualities. We both felt this limited submarine war was a waste of both life and material as it could not be expected to achieve anything in the nature of a blockade of England.

We were however restrained by the Government on the representations of the Army from starting unrestricted submarine war. Nevertheless we pressed for authority to start it.

The characters of the Kaiser and of von Holtzendorf [head of the *Admiralstab*] had a great influence on the question. The Kaiser had vision but lacked nerve. In the building up of the Navy in the years before the war, Tirpitz faced crisis after crisis, and each one took more toll of the Emperor's nerve . . . von Holtzendorf was a good staff officer but not a man to ride the storm . . . We never submitted the plan of an operation to Holtzendorf until it was too late for him to stop it. He was the class of man, rather like Ingenohl and Pohl, who stuck closely to the book.

It was with such men that Scheer and I were dealing and Scheer at last decided to send me straight to the Army Headquarters to urge our point of view. If the Army accepted, the politicians would follow. At last Ludendorff telegraphed for me to meet him at GHQ at Pless to discuss the U-boat campaign. I dined with him and Hindenburg very simply. It was my first meeting with Hindenburg. The Hindenburg–Ludendorff combination was a gift from heaven.

Ludendorff took me into his room and rang up the German Army Headquarters in France. The telephone had a loudspeaker and the Commander at the other end described the situation as very bad. The Somme battle had claimed all our efforts and we had put our last reserves in the line. Ludendorff then said to me that . . . the unrestricted U-boat war advocated by Scheer must be implemented.[5]

It was as a result of this lobbying for support by Scheer's Chief of Staff that on 1 February 1917 Germany reopened unrestricted U-boat warfare in the North Sea, English Channel, the Mediterranean, Western Approaches, and soon the eastern seaboard of the United States. She could muster 154 craft of a radically more effective specification than those of 1914. In fact, there were never more than 70 at sea at any one time because of the need for refitting and repairing, and resting the crews. But that number turned out to be sufficient to bring Britain almost to her knees and the war to an end in Germany's favour. Total losses of British shipping by U-boats alone rose from 35 ships in January 1917 (110,000 tons) to 86 in February, 103 in March, and 155 in April, or over 516,000 tons, in addition to another 30,000 tons from striking mines; while the grand total of shipping losses to Britain and her Allies, and neutral ships carrying Allied supplies, reached the catastrophic figure for April of 869,103 tons.

But even those figures do not tell the full story of the paralysis that was seizing up sea communications. In addition, many more ships were damaged and put out of action, were delayed in sailing due to real or false alarms, or did not sail at all, or were delayed by safety diversions. The real figure that counted, the figure that was beginning to paralyse war production (despite the rationing of raw materials and food for civilians and servicemen alike) and halt the movement of war material, was the fall from 1,149 ships entering British ports in February and March 1916 to under 300 a year later. And the U-boat campaign was only just getting into its stride.

By late 1916 the Admiralty would no doubt have given deeper thought to anti-U-boat defences and counter-attack if Germany's offensive up until that time had been more consistent. But international political considerations and internal dispute led to a frequent changes in policy from completely unrestricted commerce warfare to a very muted and strictly legal offensive which deceived the Admiralty into believing that existing protective methods were adequate.

The only major countermeasures introduced in the first two years of the war were patrols, the arming of merchantmen, and the laying of minefields. Patrols were enormously expensive in terms of manpower and ships required to cover the most vulnerable areas. No fewer than 3,000 vessels, from armed yachts and drifters, to torpedo boats and sloops, were in use at the end of 1916, although only fifteen U-boats were lost *from all causes* including accident during the second half of the year. Arming merchantmen was the most effective deterrent but thousands of guns were required for this to be effective and the demand for artillery for the various theatres of war was unremitting. Mining had no restricting effect on the movements of U-boats. Net barrages in association with mines proved useless in the Channel. The U-boats simply ducked under them.

Devices ranging from the eccentric to the practical and effectively destructive had been tried out from the early days of the war, and were discarded or introduced according to results. A towed sweep carrying explosive charges was used by small ships working together, sometimes at high speed. When the location of the U-boat was known a depth charge containing TNT or Amatol was dropped or discharged carrying a hydrostatic pistol set to explode the charge at predetermined depths.

The most romantic, if hair-raising, method of hunting down U-boats was with 'Q-ships'. These were innocent-looking merchantmen manned by volunteer naval crews with a powerful but carefully concealed armament. In the past, merchantmen had often been painted to look like men o'war with dummy wooden guns. This ruse which saved many a ship from pirates or its country's enemies was effectively reversed in the Q-ship, which rapidly assumed a legendary wolf-in-sheep's-clothing reputation in the service. The formula for success with these vessels was to invite attack by proceeding alone in danger areas. At least until 1917, the U-boat usually surfaced on sighting its intended victim and then, with or without warning, opened fire and sank the ship by gunfire, reserving torpedoes for special occasions and targets, like ocean liners and warships. On sighting a surfaced U-boat, a 'panic party' would noisily take to the Q-ship's boat, perhaps complete with a parrot cage, while the gun crews remained concealed awaiting their opportunity of giving the enemy a short, well-aimed, and fatal volley.

To lie in concealed waiting while the U-boat conducted a cautious examination from a distance, sometimes through its periscope, required nerves of steel, and after the Germans rumbled this ruse, U-boats were known to torpedo the Q-ship and depart with no more ado. However, early Q-ship successes were encouraging. The most famous Q-ship commander was Gordon Campbell, who earned a VC and DSO for his dangerous work. His first victim was *U-68* which first fired a torpedo at the Q-ship. It just missed, and the carefully posed nonchalant crew on deck pretended not to have seen it. The U-boat then surfaced, subjected the vessel to an exhaustive examination after firing a shot across her bows, and the 'panic party' left the 'deserted' ship with a great deal of noise, while another shot was fired.

'He was now about 800 yards off, showing full length, and although the range was a little bit greater than I wished,' Campbell wrote later, 'the time had come to open fire before he might touch off our magazines. I therefore blew my whistle. At this signal the White Ensign flew at the masthead, the wheel-house and side ports came down with a clatter, the hen coop collapsed; and in a matter of seconds three 12-pounder guns, the Maxim, and rifles were firing as hard as they could.'[6] The U-boat submerged, badly damaged, was forced to the surface with depth charges, when the *coup de grâce* was given at point-blank range. The effectiveness of the Q-ships waned as the Germans became more wily.

Death in a crippled U-boat was a particularly distressing business, and if anything was worse than trench warfare it was the cruel war at sea in which thousands of merchant sailors were roasted or choked to death by oil, went down in their ships, or were left to drown or freeze to death in the North Atlantic.

In answering a letter of protest from Fisher at his laying down of the Grand Fleet's command, Jellicoe wrote to him,

It is *because* I agreed with you that the great danger now threatening us is the submarine menace that I have now left the Fleet to come to the Admiralty. I could do nothing with the Fleet to cope with that menace. I may be able to do something at Head Quarters. I may not succeed, but I am here to try. I know of course that all the criticism hitherto aimed at Jackson will now fall on me, but I am prepared to face that in the hope that I may, with the help of those coming with me, be able to cope with the submarines.[7]

Alas, the choice of Jellicoe was not a successful one, and before long the new Prime Minister recognized that he had made a mistake. This able, intelligent, likeable, and loyal sailor was less well equipped to deal with the problem of running the Navy at war from Whitehall, and in the depths of a life-and-death crisis at that, than he was at commanding a great fleet. Jellicoe's two great weaknesses as a C.-in-C. Grand Fleet, his inability to delegate and his inflexibility of mind, were even more apparent and damaging in the First Sea Lord's office. Beatty's first shock at taking over from Jellicoe was the quantity of paperwork his predecessor had been prepared to cope with. He soon had it cut to the bone and handed most of what was left over to his Staff. But anyone with an appetite for paperwork and the minutiae of administration could have his fill in the First Sea Lord's office where bureaucratic excesses had constantly to be held at bay.

There is no surer formula for stress leading to ill-health and a deterioration in performance than conscientiousness combined with a distrust of others to work to one's own high standards, pressure from above and from all sides, and a fundamentally weak constitution. As an admirable, loyal, and thoroughly decent man, Jellicoe's personal tragedy is one of the greatest of the war at sea.

The first step he took after arriving at the Admiralty was to set up an Anti-Submarine Division to co-ordinate existing measures and seek new weapons and policy. This was an excellent idea in principle and, after a chaotic start characteristic of reorganization at the Admiralty, it began to produce new ideas. The first difficulty to overcome was that of recognizing the nature of the threat. In its characteristics and its method of attack the submarine was something entirely novel in commerce warfare, and in the struggle for survival at sea the fact that the U-boat was only a raider in another guise was lost in a smoke-screen of new weaponry.

A glance back in history and a cold, hard look by an intelligent Staff committee, would have led to the simplest solution much earlier than it was reached. Like so many of his contemporaries, Jellicoe was a 'numbers man'. In the Grand Fleet he fretted constantly about numbers – inadequate numbers of destroyers to protect the Fleet against the growing number of enemy submarines, inadequate numbers of dreadnoughts to face the supposedly huge increase in numbers of German dreadnoughts. In this new war against the U-boats he applied the same policy, the gospel of numbers. One officer described it as 'the thousands scheme' – thousands of nets, mines, depth charges, guns, patrol craft, thousands of every new development worthy of joining the vast arsenal of anti-U-boat weaponry. There was, Jellicoe frequently proclaimed, no single way of defeating the U-boat. Victory could only come by suffocation, the smothering of the underwater threat by weight of numbers.

The convoy was as old as war at sea. The convoying of merchantmen protected by men o'war had been repeatedly resorted to from the thirteenth century to, most recently, the Napoleonic wars when, from 1798, it ceased to be a convenience for merchants and their merchantmen and became obligatory. Its efficacy was beyond doubt. Yet by 1914, when commerce was even more essential to the survival of the nation than it had been in 1814, the convoy was discredited in naval policy despite Churchill's recent introduction of a Naval Staff.

The problem of protection of trade was under constant review. The first reason why the convoy principle had been discarded was the same reason which had led to the emphasis on offensive gunpower and speed rather than defensive armour and strength of construction in the Navy's men o'war. In the end it came down to a state of mind in which the Nelsonian principle of attack (albeit distorted) was applied to the training of officers and men and the design and construction of the men o'war. In short, defence was an unacceptable principle, offense correct – right-minded, valorous, glorious, and correct. To protect merchantmen, to scurry about them like a sheepdog, was *defensive*. To send out hundreds of men o'war to hunt down and destroy commerce raiders was *offensive*. That such a policy was flying in the face of reason was considered only by a small minority of 'thinkers' at the Admiralty.

When losses began to rise alarmingly and several voices were raised in favour of introducing the traditional convoy system, the opposition arguments were:

1. Convoys would require vast numbers of escort vessels better employed in search-and-kill patrol operations.

2. Convoys with the delays entailed in collecting the vessels in port, in organizing merchantmen skippers and crews untrained for station-keeping, in the imposition of slow speeds on faster vessels, the

alternating congestion and slackness in loading and discharging cargoes, would lead to a greater loss of trade than the U-boats could ever accomplish.

3. The greater the number of ships forming a convoy, the more vulnerable it must be to U-boat attack.

The administration of a convoy system was indeed mountainously complex and difficult. Trade had multiplied many times and destinations were more numerous since the French wars, but convoys had in fact already been instituted for the Channel coal trade with France, without which French industry would have ground to a halt. Convoys had also been resorted to for the Dardanelles operations and for the great troop movements from the far corners of the Empire in the opening weeks of war. When the success of these was cited, convoy opponents declared that there was a great difference between troop-ships manned by the cream of the merchant service and the vast quantity of ships on the Atlantic or Cape run and in the Mediterranean of diverse size, speed, and quality of manning.

As figures for U-boat construction and the sinking of merchantmen both rose out of all proportion to U-boat losses, and political and Press agitation became more clamorous, the Admiralty were forced to examine the problem and present counter-arguments to justify their stand. No voice condemning the convoy was more authoritative than Jellicoe's, and it was his insistence more than anyone else's in refusing to introduce the system that led to his eventual downfall. Jellicoe, whose own Grand Fleet Battle Squadrons had formed the biggest and safest (nil losses) convoy of all time since October 1914, remained inflexible in his opposition, as did Duff and Oliver and numerous less influential senior officers.

Richmond, now serving at sea with the Grand Fleet, observed Jellicoe's inaction at the Admiralty with despair. 'Having missed two chances of destroying the German Fleet,' he wrote in his diary, 'he is now busy ruining the country by not taking steps to defeat the submarines.' Beatty was equally exasperated, and in a talk in the flagship with Richmond said that Jellicoe's ignorance of war was astonishing. 'Every proposal of Beatty's for convoy has been opposed', wrote Richmond. 'It was "impossible". Everything was impossible. "It is like running your head against a brick wall – no, a wall of granite – to try & get any ideas through", said B.'[8]

The official and obdurate Admiralty opposition to the principle of convoy was cracked at last by three events. The Scandinavian trade had been operating for some time at the unacceptable loss rate of

25 per cent. Beatty set up a committee to consider this crisis, and its first urgent recommendation was in favour of the convoy principle as a trial. It was difficult for the Admiralty to brush this aside, and on 20 April 1917 the OD, and the next day Jellicoe, agreed. The loss rate instantly fell to 0.24 per cent, or 120 times.

On 6 April America entered the war, and although the immediate impact was slight, the expected addition of numerous destroyers and other escort vessels for the Atlantic trade demolished all arguments about the lack of escorting numbers. The April loss figures provided the fatal blow against the convoy opponents. But the ship took a long time to sink, and Jellicoe was still expressing the gravest doubts about the practicality of the convoy system even on a limited scale as late as 23 April, at a War Cabinet meeting.

In the end, Lloyd George, increasingly disenchanted with his new First Sea Lord and his refusal even to listen to arguments, and fed with facts provided by dissidents within the Admiralty, decided to intervene. At another War Cabinet meeting two days later (25 April) Lloyd George announced that he would make a personal visit to the Admiralty on the 30th in order to investigate 'all the means at present in use in regard to anti-submarine warfare'. Carson and Jellicoe and OD recognized the element of threat in this unprecedented decision, and, while the motives behind the actions of the days preceding Lloyd George's visit, and the actual sequence of events, were to be disputed later, the fact remains that Jellicoe received from Duff, on 26 April, a memorandum on the subject of convoy. It suggested that there was now 'sufficient reason for believing that we can accept the many disadvantages of large convoys with the certainty of a great reduction in our present losses'.[9]

On the following day both Oliver and Jellicoe agreed that some sort of convoy scheme should be worked out 'to judge how far it will be practical'. And on the very day of the Lloyd George visit, Jellicoe informed the newly appointed American commander, Rear-Admiral William Sims, that 'there was every intention of giving [convoy] a thorough and fair trial'.[10]

Lloyd George made himself exceedingly unpopular later by insisting that it was only the threat of his visit that 'galvanised the Admiralty' into re-examining their strategy in the anti-U-boat campaign and discovering 'that protection for a convoy system was within the compass of their resources. Accordingly, 'continued the ex-Prime Minister in his *Memoirs*, 'when I arrived at the Admiralty I found the Board in a chastened mood.' It was, claimed Lloyd George, his 'peremptory action on the question of convoys'[11] which forced the

Admiralty to introduce the system, and so save the country from certain strangulation. For this, Carson called him a 'little popinjay' who had told 'the biggest lie ever told'.

It was the eighteenth-century military theorist Clausewitz who said, 'Everything is very simple in War, but the simplest thing is difficult.' It had certainly been a difficult task to persuade the Navy's high command to revert to a commerce protection policy which had proved itself time and again in the past and was the most effective and economical method of securing the nation's trade. No single figure, and certainly not Lloyd George, can reasonably claim sole credit for the belated introduction of convoys. However, their inception could very well have been fatally delayed but for the heroic work of the Young Turks in the Navy – officers like the indefatigable if petulant Captain Richmond and Commander Reginald Henderson in the Admiralty. They risked their careers by advancing the convoy cause and preparing memoranda demolishing the anti-convoy case, then feeding information to the War Cabinet through the back door.

The introduction of convoys was by no means an overnight business, and the machine ground into action with the speed of a long-disused motor handled by mechanics who are not all well trained or enthusiastic. The United States Navy did not help matters by expressing its doubts. 'The Navy Department', reported the British Naval Attaché in Washington, 'does not consider it advisable to attempt . . . convoy . . . In large groups of ships under convoy, fog, gales, inexperience of personnel, and general tension on merchant vessels make the hazards of the attempt great and the probability of a scattering of the convoy strong.'[12]

The Americans can hardly be blamed for basing their policy on the powerful and much-reiterated arguments of the British Admiralty, but the Secretary of the Navy was soon listening to the arguments of Sims. 'It would seem suicidal', he wrote, 'if the convoy system as proposed by the British Admiralty is not put into immediate operation and applied to all merchant vessels thus forcing submarines to encounter anti-submarine craft in order to attack shipping.'[13]

Prejudices were slowly ground down, the complexities of mass assembly of heterogeneous merchantmen overcome, new skills acquired by British, Allied, and foreign skippers. From every convoy sailing, new lessons were learned, and confidence increased with the startling decrease in losses. Out of 800 vessels convoyed in July and August 1917, only five were lost. By the end of September, a mere five months after the Admiralty's change of heart, the tide had turned so strongly that there could no longer be any question that the U-boat

had been mastered. With the destruction of ten U-boats in that
month, for the first time sinkings exceeded new construction figures.
Moreover, it was naturally the bold and most successful U-boat
commanders who took the greatest risks and became the first
casualties in convoy escort counter-attacks, so that by early 1918 the
most daring commanders had almost all gone. Scheer cited 'the loss of
seasoned commanders' as a primary cause for the steady decline in
the success of the U-boat campaign.

For all U-boat commanders the introduction of convoy led to a
sudden dearth of targets. As Admiral Karl Doenitz wrote in his
Memoirs, 'The oceans at once became bare and empty; for long periods
at a time the U-boats, operating individually, would see nothing at
all.'[14] A convoy of twenty ships is only marginally more likely to be
sighted by a single U-boat than a single ship. The majority of convoys
were never sighted at all. When they were, the attack was made much
more hazardous by the presence of escorts with increasingly effective
countermeasures, and it was a rare occurrence for a U-boat, after
sighting and stalking a convoy and manoeuvring to within a range of a
target, to get in a second shot.

During 1917 and early 1918, with the introduction of airships,
long-range flying boats, seaplanes, and towed kite balloons, more and
more convoys enjoyed the additional protection of an air umbrella.
The deterrent effect surprised the most enthusiastically air-minded
naval officers. In 1918 there were only six attacks against air-
protected convoys, with a total score of just three ships.

Replacement of lost shipping was accelerated many times over by
the arrival in the maritime world of a figure who instilled new life into
the British shipbuilding industry. This remarkable man was Sir Eric
Geddes, an authority on running railways and much else, who had
been brought in to the Admiralty as a civilian controller. Lloyd
George was a great admirer of Geddes, with good reason, and when
Carson's star began to wane with general disillusion in the naval
administration's conduct of the war at sea, he made him First Lord on
20 July 1917. It was the first time the Navy had had a straightforward
businessman as its chief. Evan-Thomas described him as 'a bullet-
headed sort of a cove who anyway looks you straight in the face which
is more than those confounded Politicians will do. So perhaps he will
suit us quite well.'[15] He did, and presided over the affairs of the
service with an intelligence and brisk efficiency which showed up all
too clearly the shortcomings of his predecessors – the overbearingness
and egotism of Churchill, the languidness of Balfour, the stubborn-
ness of Carson.

Carson's tenure of office was one of the shortest on record. But he went without rancour and always said that his eight months in the Admiralty had been exceedingly happy. Jellicoe's departure was a very different affair, stained by scandal and darkened by anger. The year 1917 was the most anxious and dismal of the war. The Western Front offered little but blood, tears, and disappointment. The war seemed interminable, with no end in sight. At home there were deprivations brought on by losses at sea and the cutting of inessential imports. As always, the public looked to the Navy for cheer and for glorious victories. But the senior service remained as silent as ever. The war against the U-boat was gradually being won. But it was an unsensational campaign and the shipping loss figures were still much higher than they had been before unrestricted U-boat warfare was introduced. As for the continuing blockade of Germany, as a negative campaign it attracted even less publicity. It had taken the nation a hundred years to appreciate, through the writings of Mahan, the war-winning achievement of the British blockade of France in the Napoleonic Wars by those 'far distant storm-beaten ships upon which the Grand Army never looked'. But that lesson had been forgotten in the anxieties and aroused passions of war, and once again, towards the end of 1917, the man in the street, the voter, demanded action and sought a sacrificial victim. Among the numerous and often shrill voices of criticism was that of the naval correspondent of the *Daily Mail*: 'No one can feel the smallest confidence in the present Admiralty. If it does not fall soon, it will bring down our country with it.'

From national hero, Jellicoe's stock had fallen so low that, like Battenberg before him, his work began to reflect his depression and disillusion. Nor was his departure any more graceful than that of the Prince.

Jellicoe's pessimism and complaints of bad health were increasingly irritating to everyone, especially to Geddes, who dismissed him with the peremptoriness of a managing director sacking an inadequate executive, on Christmas Eve at that. The King was 'greatly surprised', Churchill 'greatly regretted the decision'. Asquith reassured Jellicoe that 'when history comes to be written, you will have no reason to fear its verdict'. The *Daily Telegraph*'s naval man, Archibald Hurd, commented that 'Jellicoe was dismissed with a discourtesy without parallel in the dealings of Ministers with distinguished sailors and soldiers.' But the Press did not come out well with most of Jellicoe's Navy admirers. 'And so another great man goes down under the sea of Mud of the Gutter Press',[16] wrote one lieutenant-commander.

Richmond, with no time for sentiment, merely noted that 'one obstacle to a successful war is now out of the way'.[17]

Although it is true that adverse comment of Jellicoe in the Press played its part in his removal, there can be no doubt that he was no longer up to a job for which he was not best suited in the first place. At the same time, Asquith was right in his verdict. The plain, unassuming figure did great things for the Navy and the nation; and, just as Fisher had successfully striven to drag the service into the twentieth century amidst cannonades of oppostion and bad feeling, so his friend Jellicoe consolidated his achievements and, above all, regained for the service he loved the harmony and unity Jacky Fisher's bloody revolution had destroyed.

On 1 January 1918 Jellicoe faced a year in which his chief activity would be the writing of his memoirs and the story of the Grand Fleet. The Navy faced a year, under an astute, efficient, and admired administration, which would see the realization of all the achievements for which Jellicoe had laid the foundations, created the indestructible framework, and striven so hard to complete.

After the disappointment of Jutland in 1916 and the acrimony and desperation of 1917, the war at sea took on a more hopeful and certainly happier condition in 1918. The first reason for this was that at last there was relative harmony in Whitehall and a strong, united, and efficient administration established in the Admiralty; while in the Fleet the hard-won lessons of almost three and a half years had brought about dramatic reforms in every department, and there was real confidence in the new Board.

The new First Sea Lord, who was to see the Navy through until victory was won, was Vice-Admiral Sir Rosslyn ('Rosy') Erskine Wemyss, an able and likeable officer who had been Deputy First Sea Lord since 7 August 1917, and had for long been the favourite to replace Jellicoe among the Young Turks at the Admiralty. He did so on 27 December.

The second reason for optimism was the arrival of the US Navy in substantial strength. The reinforcement of the Grand Fleet by, eventually, five dreadnoughts was as welcome in itself although there was a tendency in the Fleet at first to say, 'We can beat 'em on our own.' The light forces which began to arrive in great numbers towards the end of 1917, with the promise of many more from the unsurpassed shipbuilding resources of America, were even more valuable and took much of the burden of providing patrols and convoy escorts off the Royal Navy.

Best of all, and perhaps surprisingly considering the differences in background and temperament and the potential for dispute between the war-weary proud veterans of the British Fleet and the much younger and equally proud American service, the USN and the RN got on famously. There was good will on both sides, the British welcoming and anxious to teach, the Americans fresh and warm-hearted and anxious to learn.

Much of the success lay in the choice of commanders. Sims was an officer of great experience and depth of character, one of the most remarkable figures produced by the USN. His frank and open dealings with Jellicoe and Beatty, Carson, and then Geddes, led to mutual confidence and the Admiral's freedom to visit all departments at the Admiralty and see anyone he wanted to see, from Lloyd George down. Wemyss found Sims's loyalty and co-operation 'extraordinary'. His tribute continued, 'I very much doubt whether any other United States Naval Officer would have achieved the same result as he has . . . The manner in which the United States Naval Forces co-operate with ours, the way in which their Officers consider themselves part of our forces, are facts which I believe to be mainly due to him.'[18]

The commander of the American battle fleet was Rear-Admiral Hugh Rodman. He was almost as big a success at Scapa Flow and Rosyth as Sims in London. 'Our friendship ripened into a fellowship and comradeship', he wrote, 'which in turn, became a brotherhood. I realized that the British Fleet had had three years of actual warfare and knew the game from the ground floor up; and while we might know it theoretically, there would be a great deal to learn practically.'[19]

The most active seagoing co-operation was established in the Western Approaches where the difficult and curmudgeonly Admiral Sir Lewis 'Old Frozen Face' Bayly commanded the mixed Anglo-American force of light craft, mainly destroyers and U-boat-chasers, responsible for the safety of the vital sea traffic in the western Atlantic. Allaying all fears of difficulties in relations, Bayly warmed to the American sailor, his style and cheerful cockiness, who responded by calling him 'Uncle Lewis'. 'Relations between the young Americans and the experienced Admiral became so close that they would sometimes go to him with their personal problems', wrote Sims. 'He became not only their commander, but their confidant and adviser.'[20]

The successes scored by Bayly's mixed command in the U-boat campaign were of vital importance in the closing stages of the war. The introduction of convoy had resulted in all the benefits its proponents had predicted. But this sea war of attrition continued and the U-boat remained a menace to the end. The world total of merchant shipping losses (the vast majority from U-boat attack) had fallen from an April 1917 peak of about 881,000 tons to under 300,000 in November. But this scale of loss was still very serious, and in the early months of 1918 the figures began to rise again.

Convoy had made the defenders' task simpler, as had been expected, by drawing the U-boats to them instead of patrol ships having to search the vast expanses of the ocean for their prey. A further method of countering the menace was to destroy the U-boats in their bases, where they spent at least as much of their time as they did at sea. This had been considered from the earliest days of the war, but the difficulties were immense against well-defended harbours behind minefields.

As long before as 21 November 1916 the War Committee discussed a possible plan to neutralize Ostend and Zeebrugge, the Flanders bases for the major force of U-boats as well as the German light forces which remained a constant threat to the Channel communications. Over the following weeks it was decided that the main British effort on land in 1917 would be made in Flanders with the aim of destroying this wasps' nest. At the same time, the Navy was requested to consider plans for the destruction of these bases by bombardment from the sea. Jellicoe gave a firm 'thumbs down' to this idea. It was 'an operation which I am sure that no responsible naval officer would recommend, and it is, indeed, hardly practicable',[21] he wrote in a memorandum.

At the same time Jellicoe was claiming 'a naval bombardment alone will never turn the Hun out of Zeebrugge and Ostend' he was emphasizing the absolute importance of capturing and occupying these two bases, or the U-boat would never be crushed. From the depths of his pessimism, Jellicoe further declared (20 June 1917) that because of the shortage of shipping 'it would be impossible to continue the war into 1918'. This 'startling and reckless declaration', as Lloyd George called it, did not add to Jellicoe's already declining stature among the politicians, and he knew it: 'I have got myself much disliked by the Prime Minister and others . . . '

In June and July 1917 a combined operation with the Navy landing a division, complete with tanks and artillery, was proposed. This was conditional on a sufficient advance on land in a new offensive by Haig. But Haig never got near his target, and the joint operation was called off on 23 September.

In a paper written by Beatty and forwarded to Jellicoe on 26

August 1917, an idea was revised which had earlier, and independently, been promoted by both Bayly and Tyrwhitt. This was for a Navy
blocking operation. There was no chance whatever of destroying the
flotillas of U-boats and destroyers once they were inside their bases
because they could simply fade away into the maze-like canals and
channels inland. Bruges itself, eight miles from Zeebrugge with
which it was still linked by a ship canal, made a marvellous, virtually
invulnerable, hide-out. There was, however, this alternative blocking-
in means of dealing with the intractable problem.

'The port of Zeebrugge', wrote Beatty, ' is so narrow that blocking
it is practicable. A blockship built of concrete, fitted with a crinoline
with mine-mooring cutters to take it through the minefields, and
directed by wireless from aircraft, would have many chances in her
favour of reaching the entrance to the locks.'[22]

The means and details of 'putting a cork' into these vital bases were
modified over the following weeks, and it finally fell to Roger Keyes,
now a vice-admiral and commanding the Dover Patrol, to put forward
his plan to a new Admiralty administration. He received the green
light in the last days of February 1918. The 'cork' was to be made up
of three old cruisers loaded with cement which were to sink
themselves against the main lock entrance and the mouth of the canal.
In a subsidiary operation two old submarines loaded with high
explosive were to blow themselves up under a railway viaduct.

As a preliminary and diversion to this main part of the daring
operation, the old cruiser *Vindictive*, supported by two shallow draught
ferry steamers, was to approach under a cover of a smoke screen and
lay herself alongside the mile-long mole which covered the entrance to
the Bruges canal. She would then put ashore a landing party of
bluejackets and marines who were to storm the guns before the arrival
of the blockships and then blow up as many installations as possible
before withdrawal.

On the night before St. George's Day, 23 April 1918, and in bright
moonlight, this gallant little armada approached its objective. But the
patron saint's good fortune did not sail with it. The wind turned at the
vital moment, blowing aside the smokescreen so that the *Vindictive*
made its attack in the open and blasted by enemy gunfire. Clouds and
drizzle hid the moon. All this led to the cruiser positioning herself
incorrectly so that her guns could give no support to the landing
party, whose leaders had already been killed.

Under withering fire, the blockships were unable to sink themselves
in their allotted positions. One of the submarines failed to arrive in
time, though the second completed her mission and blew a 100-foot

gap in the viaduct. The *Vindictive* withdrew, towed by one of the little steamers.

There were over 500 casualties, and a similar operation on Ostend failed as badly. The overall result provided only a mild inconvenience to the Germans. For a few days the larger U-boats and destroyers were obliged to use Ostend instead, but a new channel was soon dug, and within a few weeks it was as if no raid had taken place.

On the other hand, the Zeebrugge raid was a resounding morale-raiser at home, in the Fleet, and in the trenches. Paradoxically, the preliminary reports on Jutland issued by the Admiralty implied limited defeat while the Germans, without any justification, proclaimed a great victory. Zeebrugge in its relatively much smaller way, was an expensive British rebuff and defeat, and was instantly hailed as a great victory, with St. George slaying the dragon in accordance with tradition. It was put about that the nest of the hated U-boats had been destroyed. Keyes, the hero of the hour, was made a baron.

Zeebrugge was a courageous and thrilling exploit deserving its place in history, not for its tangible results, which the Admiralty really believed for a time were considerable, but for its inspiration. And example and inspiration were sorely needed in April 1918. The people of Britain had never lost their faith and confidence in the Royal Navy, only repeatedly in its administration. Zeebrugge confirmed this faith in the most glorious manner, and gave to the Board of Admiralty the reputation for high quality which it deserved in spite of the Zeebrugge failure.

German minefields and the threat of the U-boat prohibited any consideration of a return to the close blockade abandoned in 1912. But it was a reflection of Beatty's more daring approach to the command of the Grand Fleet that he abandoned Scapa Flow for the base he knew best and had favoured for the Grand Fleet in order to take it closer to the High Seas Fleet.

Beatty always felt that the Battle Fleet at Scapa Flow was too far away from the enemy, [wrote Chalmers,] and . . . he took the whole Fleet to the Forth. Many people doubted the wisdom of this, as the waters above the bridge are congested and the tide runs fast. Strong nerves were needed to turn thirty battleships 'at rest' through 180 degrees on an ebb tide after the anchors had been weighed. Under Beatty's leadership it soon became a matter of routine, and at no time did weather conditions prevent him from taking this huge armada of 150 ships to sea at any state of tide by day or by night . . . the superb seamanship of the Captains and Navigators overcame all hazards.[23]

In 1918 the Grand Fleet was a magnificent fighting force which had come to terms with the realities of twentieth-century sea warfare. It had secure bases, boasted excellent gunnery, possessed efficient shell in its well-protected magazines, improved its signalling. No contingency was uncatered for, the U-boat was respected but no longer feared, all that had been unknown in 1914 was now known.

The vast superiority in numbers and improved *matériel* generally (even the mines worked now) had been multiplied by American reinforcement, so that an unlikely German decision to face a full-scale battle would be an act of suicide.

In only one important branch had the old tradition of conservatism prevailed. Jellicoe's failure to recognize the value of an aircraft-carrier with his Fleet at Jutland was compounded by his failure, and the failure of the administration that succeeded his at the Admiralty, to develop the air arm with the resolution and speed it warranted, in spite of the earlier successful pioneering work in the Dardanelles. It was left to a small band of dedicated enthusiasts, like Rutland, Williamson home from the Dardanelles, Commodore Murray Sueter, Squadron Commander E. H. Dunning, Flight Commander C. H. K. Edmonds, and others to fight the battle for the aircraft-carrier and the production of machines like the Sopwith 'Baby' seaplane and highly effective Sopwith 'Cuckoo' torpedo plane.

On 20 December 1916 Sueter put forward proposals for a mass torpedo plane attack on the German Fleet at Wilhelmshaven and the Austrian Fleet in the Adriatic. These were at first received sympathetically at the Admiralty, but with the loss of Sueter's driving force when he was sent to Italy the momentum was lost, and Beatty (always an air enthusiast) never had a chance to prove the devastating power of the airborne torpedo before the Armistice.

The aircraft-carrier was regarded with the same suspicion as the submarine little more than a decade earlier, and development was slow. After the battle-cruiser losses at Jutland, the Fleet did not welcome the completion of Fisher's 'large light cruisers' he had ordered back in 1914. The ultimate Fisher battle-cruiser was the *Furious*, armed with two 18-inch guns, protected by 3-inch (maximum) side armour, and capable of 32 knots. Before she was completed, her forward turret was removed and a flat deck, like the *Campania*'s, built forward of the bridge for aircraft to fly off. Unfortunately, Dunning attempted to land on her and, after succeeding once, was drowned in a subsequent attempt when a tyre burst. The uncompleted battleship *Eagle* was also put in hand for conversion to a carrier role along with the ex-liner *Argus*. But none of this work was pursued with any great vigour, and the world's first designed and laid-down carrier, *Hermes*, which was started in July 1917 was not in commission until 1923. The RNAS became known more for its land-based operations in Flanders than for its operations in the North Sea. This lack of enthusiasm by the Admiralty was a very important factor in the decision to form the RAF in 1918 and, later, the loss to the RAF of the Navy's control of its aircraft between the two world wars.

In spite of tepid official encouragement and the limited resources available, by the end of 1917 Beatty had wrested control of the air over the North Sea from the Germans. One of the objections put forward against the early carriers was that they were too slow to keep up with the Fleet. In January 1917 Beatty set up the Grand Fleet Aircraft Committee to work on this problem before really fast carriers could be made available. One of the successful solutions was to construct platforms over the conning tower and forward gun of light cruisers. These were a mere 20 feet long, but this was quite enough to get a Sopwith 'Pup' fighter airborne with the ship steaming into wind. When the first of these platforms was used operationally in August 1917, Flight Sub-Lieutenant B. A. Smart made history by taking off when a Zeppelin was sighted and shooting the huge craft down in flames, subsequently ditching his 'Pup' in the sea.

An alternative to the ship's platform was a lighter fitted with a 30-foot flight deck and towed at high speed by a destroyer. On 31 July 1918, Flight Lieutenant S. D. Culley took off in a Sopwith 'Camel' and shot down the Zeppelin *L-53*. By this time most battle-cruisers and light cruisers had been fitted with fixed or turntable platforms so that quite a swarm of reconnaissance as well as fighter aircraft could be launched. Now the sky as well as the sea was dominated by the British Fleet, in spite of the opposition of numerous gunnery officers and encrusted old salts, the senior admirals with 'solid ivory from the jaws up, except for a little hole from ear to ear to let useful knowledge go in and out'.

Beatty's most important contribution to the successful pursuit of the Great War at sea was his sustaining of the optimism and spirit of the Grand Fleet from June 1916 until the end, during which time his own popularity among the officers and men never wavered. 'The outstanding characteristic of British Sea Power', wrote one American officer, 'was its extraordinarily high morale in the face of great handicaps.'[24] Beatty himself never gave up hope that a second opportunity of meeting the enemy in strength might occur. Like many of his captains and squadron commanders, Beatty found the awful winter weather and boredom of life at Scapa Flow and Rosyth a great burden. There was additionally the sense of helplessness when the Army continued to fight and suffer so heavily. 'It frets me terribly that with all this terrible fighting going on that we cannot help',[25] Beatty once wrote in anguish to his wife.

On 21 March 1918 the German Army attacked the British front on the Somme in great strength. A dense fog, far thicker than the North Sea mist which had assisted the German Fleet at Jutland, concealed the German attack until it was too late. The Germans advanced deep into British- and French-held positions, deeper than at any time since 1914. In the throes of this crisis, Marshal Ferdinand Foch took overall command. The Allied armies were forced at last into a war of movement, and the farther they fell back the more disadvantaged were the Germans. Moreover, like the British battle-cruisers at Jutland – 'the many-headed hydra' – there seemed to be no end to the Allied reserves. By the end of April the German attack had run out of steam. Supplies could not be sustained; nor could the spirit of the men. Germany knew she was beaten in spite of victory against Russia earlier in the year. Food was becoming desperately short and certain factions were fermenting revolution.

Unrest in the High Seas Fleet was sharpened by well-founded rumours that they were to participate in some sort of 'death ride'. What had the C.-in-C. in store for them at the end of October, when all seemed lost on land and an armistice could not be long delayed? 'It is impossible for the Fleet to remain inactive in any final battle that may sooner or later precede an Armistice', Scheer declared. 'The Fleet must be committed. Even if it is not to be expected that this would decisively influence the course of events, it is still, from the moral point of view, a question of the honour and existence of the Navy to have done its utmost in the last battle.'[26]

When the Fleet was ordered to assemble in Schillig Roads outside Wilhelmshaven on 29 October 1918, mutiny broke out in varying degrees, from insubordination and refusal to report for duty to threats of violence. Cheers for peace were heard throughout the Fleet, and even cheers for the American President, Woodrow Wilson. By 4 November, the red flag of revolution was flying at all the German naval ports.

After some inter-service and inter-Allied altercation, the naval terms for an armistice were agreed. 'The war of exhaustion', as Scheer described it, was heading for 'Germany's certain defeat.' To be surrendered for internment in neutral ports – or failing them, Allied ports – were 160 submarines, 10 battleships, 6 battle-cruisers and a proportionate number of cruisers and destroyers.

So neglected were the ships of the High Seas Fleet, that it was difficult to get even this reduced force to sea. But at last they did, and Beatty, denied a second Trafalgar, reached the summit of his life and his achievement when he sailed to meet them and take the surrender on 21 November 1918, just ten days after the armies had ceased fighting, with 370 ships and 90,000 officers and men under his command.

Like 31 May 1916, the date on which the Fleets had last met, the weather was sunny but misty. The filthy, neglected condition of the German ships, the scruffy, ill-disciplined state of the German crews on deck, told their own story of what had happened during the previous thirty months to one of the toughest, most professional and skilful fighting forces in the world. Here, forty miles east of May Island off the entrance to the Firth of Forth, was the tangible proof of British naval omnipotence, and the meaninglessness of Jutland's pluses and minuses in ship losses.

By 11 a.m. the two Fleets were safely inside the Firth of Forth, where Beatty made a general signal: 'The German flag will be hauled down at sunset today, Thursday, and will not be hoisted again without permission.' The German ensigns were duly hauled down as all hands in the flagship *Queen Elizabeth* were piped aft. On the sounding of the bugle 'making sunset', Beatty was given a great round of cheers by the ship's company and the men of the entire Grand Fleet as well as the American 6th Battle Squadron and the representative French ships.

Beatty answered the cheers with his famous hat held aloft, smiling at the unprecedented scene. 'I always told you they would have to come out', he told his men.

Any last pride left to the German Fleet was sunk just seven months later in the biggest act of self-immolation in naval history. On 21 June 1919, in a well-kept conspiracy, the High Seas Fleet scuttled itself in Scapa Flow. The spectacle could also be interpreted as a symbolic act of genuflection at the scene of Britain's power-base during those years of blockade which had brought about the enemy's downfall.

The victory of 21 November 1918 was a bloodless and silent one. But it was none the less the greatest naval victory in history, brought about by the sustainment of spirit and distantly and continuously applied superiority in a battle lasting 1571 days and nights. From time to time during this long-drawn-out conflict the two protagonists had brushed up against one another, exchanged fire, suffered and caused losses. Sometimes the engagements had occurred for all to see, as at the Falklands, at other times in the dim visibility of sunset as at Coronel and Jutland, and more often blindly and beneath the ocean. But whether the Grand Fleet was lying at its anchorage at Scapa Flow or engaging enemy destroyers in a tumult of fire and North Sea darkness early on 1 June 1916, the application of superiority remained unchanged. The date 21 November 1918 was important only because it was the day Germany finally resigned herself to the state of affairs which had applied since 11 p.m. on 4 August 1914.

It is no reflection on the prodigious and continuing effort and glorious courage of the armies in France and the numerous other theatres of war, or of the airmen who gave them such valiant assistance, to say that the Royal Navy provided the greatest contribution to victory by its perpetual and mainly unseen and soundless pressure. It was the blockade that finally drove the Central Powers to accept defeat. At first mild in its application, the blockade's noose gradually tightened until, with the American entry, all restraint was cast aside. Increasingly deprived of the means to wage war, or even to feed her population, the violent response was insurrection; apathy and demoralization the mute consequence of dashed hopes and thin potato soup.

'No historian', wrote a great military historian of the Great War, 'would underrate the direct effect of the semi-starvation of the German people in causing the final collapse of the "home front". But leaving aside the question of how far the revolution caused the military defeat, instead of viceversa, the intangible all-pervading factor of the blockade intrudes into every consideration of the military situation.' The blockade, concludes Basil Liddell Hart, was 'clearly the decisive agency in the struggle.'[27]

The effort of sustaining that blockade and the Fleet that made it possible was prodigious, demanding an incalculable toll on human ingenuity, courage, patience, spirit, and belief in the cause, and on the material and economic resources of the nation and its empire. The price paid could be seen by 1921 in tangible terms in the enforced reduction of the size of the Royal Navy to that of its ex-ally the United States, whose own naval competition with the Japanese Empire was already set on its compass course to Pearl Harbor.

NOTE ON SOURCES

THE most important source of unpublished papers on the naval war at sea 1914–18, and on the years leading up to the Great War, is the Public Record Office at Kew, London, where the Admiralty Record Office MSS are essential for any serious student of this period. Also held at the PRO are The Foreign Office MSS, the Additional (Add.) MSS, and British Documents. Other important sources are the British Library in London (e.g. Jellicoe MSS: MSS 48989–49057); Naval Library, Ministry of Defence, London (e.g. Jackson MSS); National Maritime Museum Library, Greenwich (e.g. Richmond MSS); and Churchill College, Cambridge (e.g. Drax MSS).

The most comprehensive published guide to manuscript sources is in Arthur J. Marder's *From the Dreadnought to Scapa Flow* v. 346–61. However, this was published in 1970 and some of the addresses are out of date. For example, the highly important Beatty MSS may now be consulted at the National Maritime Museum, Greenwich. This same volume also contains an invaluable list of published works with comments, sometimes of a cryptic nature.

NOTES

CHAPTER 1 (pp. 1–11)

1. Cadet Stephen King-Hall to his parents, 3 February 1906; *My Naval Life* (1952)
2. Including *The Influence of Sea Power upon History 1660–1783* (1890) and *The Influence of Sea Power upon the French Revolution and Empire 1790–1812* (1892)
3. *Observer*, 18 July 1909
4. Commander G. Lowis, *Fabulous Admirals* (1957) p. 35
5. *Pall Mall Gazette*, October 1904

CHAPTER 2 (pp. 12–21)

1. Charles Middleton, first Lord Barham (1726–1813), Controller of the Navy 1776–1806
2. Quoted by F. Lascelles to E. Grey, Foreign Secretary, 16 August 1906; British Documents, viii. 192
3. *Manchester Guardian*, 29 December 1907
4. *The Times*, 6 March 1908
5. Captain Philip Dumas RN to F. Lascelles, 12 January 1908; British Documents, vi. 124–5
6. Cabinet paper, 'Naval Estimates 1914–15', 10 January 1914; Asquith MSS
7. Sir Francis Knollys to Lord Esher, 10 February 1909; Esher MSS
8. Winston S. Churchill, *The World Crisis, 1914–19*, 5 vols. (1923–9), i. 37.
9. *Daily Express*, 20 March 1909
10. Rear-Admiral Sir Robert Arbuthnot
11. Churchill, *World Crisis*, i. 74–5
12. Admiral Lord Fisher to Lord Esher, 2 February 1910; Kilverstone MSS

CHAPTER 3 (pp. 22–36)

1. 3 March 1910; Lennoxlove Papers
2. Churchill, *World Crisis*, i. 70
3. *Standard*, 5 July 1911
4. Churchill, *World Crisis*, i. 81–2
5. J. S. Sandars to A. J. Balfour, 14 November 1911; Balfour Papers
6. Arthur J. Marder, *From the Dreadnought to Scapa Flow*, 5 vols. (1961–70), i. 253
7. 21 December 1912
8. Admiral G. von Müller to Admiral F. von Tirpitz, 4 June 1914; German Ministry of Marine MSS
9. Lennoxlove Papers
10. Fisher to Churchill, 16 January 1912; Arthur J. Marder, *Fear God and Dread Nought: the Correspondence of Admiral of the Fleet Lord Fisher of Kilverstone*, 3 vols. (1952–9), ii. 426

11. Churchill, *World Crisis*, i. 123
12. Churchill to Fisher, 11 June 1912; Admiralty MSS
13. Add. MSS 49694, 6 January 1912 and 9 January 1912
14. 5 June 1914
15. Randolph Churchill/Martin Gilbert, *Winston S. Churchill*, ?7 vols., with *Companion* vols. of Papers (1966–   ), ii. 688. Hereafter referred to as Churchill/Gilbert
16. Lennoxlove Papers
17. *Army and Navy Gazette*, 17 May 1913
18. Admiral Sir William James to A. J. Marder, undated but probably 1967; Marder Papers
19. James to Marder, 23 February 1967; Marder Papers
20. James to Marder, 3 February (?) 1967; Marder Papers
21. Churchill/Gilbert, *Companion* ii to *Churchill* ii, p. 1304
22. ibid., p. 1312

CHAPTER 4 (pp. 37–52)

1. Churchill, *World Crisis*, i. 37
2. Foreign Office MSS 800/87
3. Tirpitz to Bethmann Hollweg, n.d. (?5 October 1911); German Ministry of Marine MSS
4. Memo on 'Suddenness in Naval Operations', 1 March 1905; Balfour MSS
5. 118th meeting of Committee of Imperial Defence (CID); Asquith MSS
6. Captain Hugh Watson, RN, to Sir Edward Grey, 30 June 1913; Marder Papers
7. Foreign Office MSS 800/87
8. Rear-Admiral Sir Edward Troubridge, 20 June 1912; British Documents, ix (Pt. i). 413–16
9. Foreign Office MSS 800/87
10. 23 August 1912; quoted in Churchill, *World Crisis*, i. 112
11. 29 January 1914; Asquith MSS
12. Rear-Admiral William S. Chalmers, *The Life & Letters of David, Earl Beatty* (1951), p. 99
13. Captain Hugh Watson, RN, to Sir Edward Goschen, 13 October 1913; British Documents, x (Pt. 2). 716

CHAPTER 5 (pp. 53–68)

1. Churchill, *World Crisis*, i. 190
2. Richard Hough, *Mountbatten; Hero of our Time* (1980), p. 27
3. Richard Hough, *Louis & Victoria: the First Mountbattens* (1973), p. 280
4. Churchill, *World Crisis*, i. 212
5. G. Callender, *The Naval Side of British History* (1924)
6. CID Report 54–A (PRO)
7. Beatty MSS
8. Churchill/Gilbert, *Churchill*, iii. 15
9. John Winton, *Jellicoe* (1981), p. 144

10. Sir Julian S. Corbett/Sir Henry Newbolt, *History of the Great War. Naval Operations*, 5 vols. (1920–31), i. 177

11. 18 August 1914; Jellicoe MSS

12. Chalmers, *Beatty*, p. 161

13. ibid., p. 158

14. Churchill/Gilbert, *Companion* iii to *Churchill* ii, p. 222

15. 24 October 1914; Richmond Papers

16. W. S. Chalmers, *Full Cycle: the Biography of Admiral Sir Bertram Home Ramsay* (1959), pp. 20–1

17. R. Blake, *The Unknown Prime Minister: the Life and Times of Andrew Bonar Law* (1955), p. 232

18. Asquith MSS

19. 'Errors, Blunders, & 'orrible examples'; Richmond MSS

20. Beatty MSS

21. H.G. Thursfield, *The Naval Staff of the Admiralty* (1929), Naval Staff Monograph, p. 29

CHAPTER 6 (pp. 69–86)

1. Richard Hough, *First Sea Lord: an authorized life of Lord Fisher* (1969), p. 316

2. Fisher to Commander T. E. Crease, 18 August 1914; Marder, *Fear God*, iii. 52–3

3. Lieutenant-Commander P. K. Kemp to the author, 25 February 1982

4. Churchill, *World Crisis*, i. 240

5. Captain John Creswell, RN, to Marder, 17 July 1971; Marder Papers

CHAPTER 7 (pp. 87–98)

1. Churchill, *World Crisis*, i. 414

2. Vice-Admiral Harold Hickling, *Sailor at Sea* (1965), p. 50

3. Quoted in Richard Hough, *The Pursuit of Admiral von Spee* (1969), p. 115

4. Hickling, *Sailor at Sea*, p. 50

5. Quoted in Hough, *Pursuit of von Spee*, p. 116

6. ibid.

7. Admiral Sydney Start to Marder, 10 November 1966; Marder Papers

8. Captain Geoffrey Bennett, *Coronel and the Falklands* (1962), p. 20

9. Captain C. R. O. Burge, DSO, RN, to Marder, 21 October 1966; Marder Papers

10. Churchill, *World Crisis*, i. 424

11. Start to Marder, 10 November 1966; Marder Papers

12. Churchill, *World Crisis*, i. 419

CHAPTER 8 (pp. 99–120)

1. Beatty to Lady Beatty, 19 October 1914; Chalmers, *Beatty*, p. 178

2. Churchill/Gilbert, *Companion* iii to *Churchill* ii, p. 188

3. Beatty to Lady Beatty, 18 October 1914; Beatty MSS

4. 24 October 1914

5. Churchill/Gilbert, *Companion* iii to *Churchill* ii, p. 230
6. Churchill to Balfour, 17 September 1915; Balfour Papers
7. Chalmers, *Beatty*, pp. 160–1
8. Admiral Sir Roger Keyes, *The Naval Memoirs of Admiral of the Fleet Sir Roger Keyes*, 2 vols. (1934–5), i. 130
9. Churchill, *World Crisis*, i. 427
10. Sturdee to Sir Henry Newbolt, March 1924; Sturdee MSS
11. Hough, *Fisher*, p. 327
12. Kilverstone MSS
13. Jellicoe to Fisher, 11 November 1914; Marder, *Fear God*, ii. 70
14. Hickling, *Sailor at Sea*, p. 66
15. Bennett, *Coronel*, p. 126
16. Quoted in Hough, *Pursuit of von Spee*, p. 135
17. Captain R. F. Phillimore (commander of the *Inflexible*, which rescued survivors from the *Gneisenau*), letter of 11 December 1914; Phillimore Papers, Imperial War Museum (IWM) 75/48/2
18. Hickling, *Sailor at Sea*, p. 74
19. Sturdee MSS
20. Churchill, *World Crisis*, i. 436
21. Rear-Admiral R. K. Dickson, letter of 11 December 1914; Marder Papers
22. Captain Hans Pochhammer, *Before Jutland: Admiral von Spee's Last Voyage* (1931)
23. Hickling, *Sailor at Sea*, pp. 81–2
24. ibid.; quoted in Hough, *Pursuit of von Spee*, p. 158
25. ibid., p. 80
26. Conversation with the author, May 1968
27. Quoted in Hough, *Pursuit of von Spee*, p. 158
28. Commander L. Peppé, conversation with the author, September 1982
29. Rear-Admiral R. K. Dickson, letter of 11 December 1914; Marder Papers
30. Chalmers MSS
31. Crichton F. Laborde, Captain's Clerk HMS *Inflexible*, to his father, Commander H. W. Laborde, 13 December 1914; IWM Ref/77
32. Kilverstone MSS
33. Sturdee MSS
34. Kilverstone MSS
35. Sturdee MSS

CHAPTER 9 (pp. 121–143)

1. Filson Young, *With the Battle Cruisers* (1921), p. 49
2. James to Marder, 18 March 1968; Marder Papers
3. Churchill, *World Crisis*, i. 467–8
4. Beatty to Jellicoe, 19 December 1914; Admiralty MSS
5. Young, *With the Battle Cruisers*, p. 111
6. Marder, *Dreadnought to Scapa Flow*, ii. 140n. (2nd corrected printing)
7. Creswell to Marder, 20 March 1966; Marder Papers

8. 21 January 1915; Beatty MSS

9. Add. MSS 49006, ff. 72–3

10. Captain M. von Levetzow to Admiral von Holtzendorff, 15 January 1915; Levetzow Papers, German Ministry of Marine MSS

11. 20 December 1914

12. Churchill, *World Crisis*, ii. 129

13. Young, *With the Battle Cruisers*, pp. 175–6

14. Addendum to Diary, 24 January 1915 entry; Drax MSS

15. ibid.

16. ibid.

17. ibid., p. 183

18. Downing to Marder, 6 July 1966; Marder Papers

19. Addendum to Diary, 24 January 1915 entry; Drax MSS

20. Beatty to Keyes; quoted in Captain Stephen Roskill, *Admiral of the Fleet Earl Beatty* (1980), p. 114

21. Creswell to Marder, 13 March 1964; Marder Papers

22. Jellicoe to the Secretary of the Admiralty; Add. MSS 49012, ff. 23–5

23. Beatty to Keyes, 10 February 1915; Keyes, *Naval Memoirs*, i. 163

24. Fisher to Jellicoe, 8 February 1915; Jellicoe MSS

25. Fisher to Beatty, 31 January 1915; Marder, *Fear God*, iii. 150–1

26. Captain H. Watson, RN, to Jellicoe, 28 February 1915; Beatty MSS

27. Jellicoe, 'A Reply to Criticism'; Jellicoe MSS

28. Downing to Marder, 6 July 1966; Marder Papers

CHAPTER 10 (pp. 144–168)

1. Beatty to Lady Beatty, 4 December 1914; Beatty MSS

2. Marder, *Fear God*, iii. 99–100

3. ibid., p. 91

4. ibid., p. 138

5. Captain T. Crease to Admiral Sir R. Hall, 7 November 1914; Crease MSS

6. D. Brownrigg, *Indiscretions of the Naval Censor* (1920), p. 12

7. Diary, 12 August 1914; Richmond MSS

8. Admiral Sir Reginald Bacon, *The Life of Lord Fisher of Kilverstone*, 2 vols. (1929), ii. 188

9. Marder, *Dreadnought to Scapa Flow*, ii. 177

10. ibid., p. 86

11. Memorandum, 20 December 1906; Lennoxlove MSS

12. Vice-Admiral K. G. B. Dewar, *The Navy from Within* (1939), p. 190

13. Marder, *Fear God*, iii. 117–18

14. Marder, *Dreadnought to Scapa Flow*, ii. 205

15. ibid.

16. M. Hankey, *The Supreme Command, 1914–1918* (1961), i. 265–6

17. Jellicoe's marginalia to his copy of Churchill, *World Crisis*, ii; Jellicoe MSS

18. Marder, *Fear God*, iii. 133

19. David Lloyd George, *War Memoirs of David Lloyd George*, 6 vols. (1933–6), i. 395

20. Arthur J. Marder (ed.), *Portrait of an Admiral: the Life and Papers of Sir Herbert Richmond* (1952), p. 140; Diary entry, 9 February 1915

21. 10 November 1915; Balfour MSS

22. Balfour to Churchill, 8 April 1915; Add. MSS 49694

23. Corbett, *History*, ii. 145

24. The unpublished memoirs of Group Captain H. Williamson; Marder Papers

25. ibid.

26. Captain H. C. B. Pipon to Marder, 18 October 1965; Marder Papers

27. Foreign Office MSS 800/88

28. Churchill, *World Crisis*, ii. 256

29. Pipon to Marder; Marder Papers

30. Keyes, *Naval Memoirs*, i. 209–10

31. ibid., p. 26

32. Captain A. C. Dewar, quoted in Marder, *Dreadnought to Scapa Flow*, ii. 243

33. Group Captain Williamson memoirs; Marder Papers

34. Marder, *Dreadnought to Scapa Flow*, ii. 232

35. ibid.

36. Dardanelles Commission report

37. Add. MSS 49703; Balfour MSS

38. Dardanelles Commission report

39. Churchill, *World Crisis*, ii. 234

40. Marder, *Fear God*, iii. 179

41. Churchill, *World Crisis*, ii. 358

42. Lennoxlove MSS

43. ibid.

44. ibid.

45. Marder, *Fear God*, iii. 247

46. Lennoxlove MSS

47. ibid.

48. Cynthia Asquith, *Diaries 1915–18* (1968), p. 31

CHAPTER 11 (pp. 169–189)

1. Diary, 11 February 1915; Duff MSS

2. Admiral Sir Percy Scott, *Fifty Years in the Royal Navy* (1919), pp. 289–90

3. Jellicoe Papers

4. H. Bauer, *Führer der U-boote* (1956), pp. 17–18

5. P. K. Lundeteg, 'German Naval Critique of the German U-boat Campaign', *Military Affairs*, Fall 1963

6. *Die deutschen U-boote in ihrer Kriegführung 1914–18*; quoted in R. H. Gibson and Maurice Prendergast, *The German Submarine War, 1914–18* (1931), p. 25

7. Admiral Lord Fisher, *Records* (1919), pp. 177–8

8. Hough, *Fisher*, p. 169

9. Churchill/Gilbert, *Companion* iii to *Churchill* ii, pp. 1960–1

10. Churchill, *World Crisis*, ii. 280

11. Corbett, *History*, ii. 393

12. Churchill, *World Crisis*, ii. 292

13. A. Spindler, *Der Krieg zur See 1914–18. Der Handelskrieg mit U-boote* (1932–41), iii. 72

14. Lieutenant-Commander P. K. Kemp to the author, 30 November 1981

15. Corbett, *History*, i. 238

16. Captain Richard Phillimore to Keyes, 21 January 1916; Paul G. Halpern (ed.), *The Keyes Papers*, 3 vols. (1972–81), i. 333

17. Lieutenant-Commander K. Edwards, *We Dive at Dawn* (1939), p. 117

18. Lieutenant William G. Carr, *By Guess and by God: the Story of the British Submarines in the War* (1930), p. 21

19. ibid., p. 30

20. *Keyes Papers*, i. 139

21. Sir Walter Raleigh/H. A. Jones, *The War in the Air*, 6 vols. (1922–8), ii. 11

22. Captain Stephen Roskill (ed.), *Documents Relating to the Naval Air Service*, vol. i, 1908–18 (1969), i. 310

23. Raleigh and Jones, *The War in the Air*, i. 487

CHAPTER 12 (pp. 190–210)

1. 'Earl Balfour as First Lord of the Admiralty', Graham Greene MSS

2. *Dictionary of National Biography*

3. Diary of Admiral Sir Frederick Hamilton, Second Sea Lord, 20 May 1915; Hamilton MSS

4. Hankey, *The Supreme Command*, ii. 335

5. Selborne to Balfour, 19 May 1915; Balfour MSS

6. N. Macleod to Marder, 22 January 1966; Marder Papers

7. Jellicoe to Beatty, 7 August 1915; Beatty MSS

8. Jellicoe to Beatty, 23 March 1915; Add. MSS 49008, ff. 27–8

9. Churchill, *World Crisis*, i. 401–2

10. Lloyd George, *War Memoirs*, ii. 107

11. Jellicoe to Admiral Sir Edward Bradford, 15 September 1915; Bradford MSS

12. Jellicoe to Jackson, 9 August 1915; A. Temple Patterson (ed.), *The Jellicoe Papers*, 2 vols. (1966–8), i. 167

13. ibid., 7 August 1915, i. 177

14. Jellicoe to Hamilton, 12 September 1915; Hamilton MSS

15. *Jellicoe Papers*, i. 221

16. ibid., p. 231

17. Corbett, *History*, iii. 276

18. Jellicoe MSS

19. Jellicoe to Beatty, 11 April 1916; Jellicoe MSS

20. ibid.

21. Corbett, *History*, iii. 321

22. ibid., p. 320

23. G. von Hase, *Kiel and Jutland* (1921), pp. 86–7

24. Admiral Sir Reginald Bacon, *The Life of John Rushworth, Earl Jellicoe* (1936), p. 163

25. F. C. Sillas, 'Note of conversation with Vice-Admiral von Trotha of the German Navy', 1939; Marder Papers. Von Trotha visited England in May 1939

26. E. Raeder, *My Life* (1960), p. 40

27. Unfinished MS of book on Jutland by W. S. Chalmers; Chalmers MSS. Quoted in Roskill, *Beatty*, p. 148

CHAPTER 13 (pp. 211–234)

1. *Jutland Official Despatches* (1921), p. 130

2. ibid., p. 198

3. ibid., p. 143

4. von Hase, *Kiel and Jutland*, p. 147

5. ibid.

6. Chalmers, *Beatty*, p. 229

7. Admiral of the Fleet Lord Chatfield, *The Navy and Defence* (1942), p. 149

8. Chalmers, *Beatty*, p. 231

9. ibid.

10. ibid., p. 233

11. von Hase, *Kiel and Jutland*, p. 148

12. ibid., p. 161

13. Marder, *Dreadnought to Scapa Flow*, iii. 67

14. *The Times*, 9 June 1916

15. Corbett, *History*, iii. 339

16. ibid., p. 337

17. Goodenough, BBC talk in 1938. Quoted in Marder, *Dreadnought to Scapa Flow*, iii. 70n.

18. Quoted in letter from Captain C. V. Marsden to Marder, 26 March 1976; Marder Papers. Marsden was a sub-lieutenant in the *Southampton*

19. Lieutenant Stephen King-Hall of the *Southampton* in an unpublished account in the possession of Admiral Sir Harold Burrough. Quoted in Marder, *Dreadnought to Scapa Flow*, iii. 71

20. Quoted in Marder, *Dreadnought to Scapa Flow*, iii. 72n.

21. Lieutenant William Tennant, quoting from his diary entry for 31 May 1916. This account was published in Lieutenant-Commander H. W. Fawcett, and Lieutenant G. W. E. Hooper (eds.), *The Fighting at Jutland* (1921). Tennant became an admiral and survived the loss of his ship, *Repulse*, 10 December 1941

22. *Jutland Official Despatches*, p. 199

23. ibid., p. 200

24. *The Times*, 5 June 1916

25. von Hase, *Kiel and Jutland*, p. 24

CHAPTER 14 (pp. 235–266)

1. Marder, *Fear God*, iii. 274

2. Admiral of the Fleet Earl Jellicoe, *The Grand Fleet, 1914–16: its Creation, Development and Work* (1919), p. 274

3. Dreyer, *The Sea Heritage*, p. 145

4. ibid.

5. Corbett, *History*, iii. 354

6. Admiral Magnus von Levetzow to Rudolf Hess, 10 August 1936; Levetzow Papers, German Ministry of Marine MSS

7. Chatfield, *The Navy and Defence*, p. 146

8. Quoted in Marder, *Dreadnought to Scapa Flow*, iii. 113

9. Chalmers, *Beatty*, p. 251

10. Corbett, *History*, iii. 366

11. Admiral Drax; quoted in Marder, *Dreadnought to Scapa Flow*, iii. 115

12. Conversation with the author, May 1968

13. Admiral Reinhard Scheer, *Germany's High Seas Fleet in the World War* (1920), pp. 151–2

14. Commander Lionel Peppé, a lieutenant in the *Superb*. Conversation with the author, May 1982

15. *Jutland Official Despatches*, p. 18

16. ibid., p. 36

17. ibid., p. 53

18. ibid., p. 61

19. ibid., p.65

20. Corbett, *History*, iii. 371

21. Scheer, *Germany's High Seas Fleet*, p. 152

22. Corbett, *History*, iii. 372

23. Bacon, *Jellicoe*, p. 277

24. Corbett, *History*, iii. 378

25. Chatfield, *The Navy and Defence*, p. 147

26. Quoted in S. W. Roskill, *HMS Warspite* (1957, paperback edn 1974), p. 126

27. Corbett, *History*, iii. 393

28. Vice-Admiral Adolf van Trotha to Tirpitz, 18 July 1916; Tirpitz MSS

29. Jellicoe to Jackson, 4 June 1916; Jackson MSS

30. ibid.

31. Corbett, *History*, iii. 384–5

32. Jellicoe, 'The Admiralty Narrative of the Battle of Jutland'; Jellicoe MSS

33. ibid.

34. Chalmers, *Beatty*, p. 262

35. Keyes MSS

36. Chalmers, *Beatty*, p. 262

CHAPTER 15 (pp. 267–297)

1. Chatfield, *The Navy and Defence*, p. 149

2. Dewar, *The Navy from Within*, p. 30

3. Jellicoe to Sturdee, 17 November 1915; Sturdee MSS

4. Commander Anthony Pellew to the author, 15 July 1982

5. Chalmers, *Beatty*, p. 262

6. Beatty to Jellicoe, 3 June 1916; Jellicoe MSS 265

7. Conversation with the author, June 1968

8. Jellicoe's autobiographical notes quoted in Bacon, *Jellicoe*, p. 163

9. Tyrwhitt to Captain W. Cowan, RN, 5 May 1916; Cowan MSS

10. Vice-Admiral Craig Waller (he changed his name), *R.U.S.I. Journal*, November 1935

11. Captain Edward Altham, *Jellicoe* (1938), p. 116

12. Corbett, *History*, iii. 372

13. Diary of Rear-Admiral Alexander Duff, 22 June 1916; Duff MSS

14. Admiral Drax's letter to Marder, 28 April 1960; Marder Papers

15. Jellicoe's unpublished notes 'The Grand Fleet at Jutland'; Jellicoe MSS

16. Jellicoe in conversation with Captain O. Frewen, RN, 29 November 1919; Frewen MSS

17. Vice-Admiral Adolf von Trotha to Tirpitz, 18 August 1916; Tirpitz MSS

18. 'Account of the Battle of Jutland' by Midshipman R. K. Dickson, HMS *Benbow*, 18 June 1916. National Library of Scotland; Dickson MSS

19. Press Statement, 4 August 1916

20. *Marine Rundschau*, June 1966

21. Admiral Drax to Marder, 5 November 1962; Marder Papers

22. Beatty's marginalia on his copy of L. Gibson and Vice-Admiral J. E. T. Harper, *The Riddle of Jutland* (1934); Chalmers MSS

23. Evan-Thomas's letter to *The Times*, 16 February 1927

CHAPTER 16 (pp. 298–321)

1. Scheer, *Germany's High Seas Fleet*, pp. 185–6

2. Beatty to Jellicoe, 6 September 1916; Jellicoe MSS

3. Marder, *Dreadnought to Scapa Flow*, iii. 336

4. Scheer, *Germany's High Seas Fleet*, p. 49

5. Note of a conversation with Admiral von Trotha by Mr. F. C. Sillas in the course of the Admiral's visit to England, May 1939; letter to Marder, 4th October 1966. Marder Papers

6. Vice-Admiral Gordon Campbell, *My Mystery Ships* (1928), p. 105

7. Jellicoe to Fisher, 1 December 1916; Lennoxlove Papers

8. Richmond diary, 15 May 1917; Richmond MSS

9. Quoted in Marder, *Dreadnought to Scapa Flow*, iv. 159

10. ibid., p. 160

11. Lloyd George, *War Memoirs*, iii. 1162–3

12. Quoted in Marder, *Dreadnought to Scapa Flow*, iv. 187

13. ibid., p. 258

14. Admiral Karl Doenitz, *Memoirs: Ten Years and Twenty Days* (1959), p. 89

15. Marder, *Dreadnought to Scapa Flow*, iv. 214

16. Lieutenant-Commander L. Frewen, diary, 27 December 1917; Frewen MSS

17. Richmond diary, 28 November 1917; Richmond MSS

18. Wemyss to Beatty, 23 August 1918; Beatty MSS

19. Admiral Hugh Rodman, *Yarns of a Kentucky Admiral* (1928), p. 266

20. Rear-Admiral William S. Sims, *The Victory at Sea* (1920), p. 65

21. Jellicoe's memorandum, 'Attacking Ostend and Zeebrugge', 18 June 1917; Jellicoe MSS

22. Beatty's paper, 'Mining Policy'; Jellicoe MSS

23. Chalmers's unpublished MS 'Running Free'; Chalmers MSS

24. E. E. Wilson, 'Grand Fleet Morale'; *Shipmate*, January 1964 (Organ of the US Naval Academy Alumni Association)

25. Beatty MSS

26. Captain Otto Groos/Admiral Walther Gladisch, *Der Krieg in der Nordsee*, 7 vols. (1920-65), vii. 341

27. B. H. Liddell Hart, *History of the First World War* (1970 edn), p. 588

SUGGESTIONS FOR FURTHER READING

GENERAL

Barnett, Corelli, *The Swordbearers: Studies in Supreme Command* (1963). Worthwhile for the Jellicoe chapter. Critical of the social element's influence on the Royal Navy's performance.

Bennett, Captain Geoffrey, *Naval Battles of the First World War* (1968). Excellent balanced accounts and judgements.

Bingham, Commander Barry, *Falklands, Jutland and the Bight* (1919). A participating officer's view of these actions.

Chatfield, Admiral of the Fleet Lord, *The Navy and Defence* (1942). Narrative and observations by Beatty's flag-captain.

Churchill, Winston S., *The World Crisis, 1914–19*, 5 vols. (1923–9). Compulsive and magnificent reading, but the rich prose does not entirely conceal prejudice and distortion in the naval passages.

Corbett, Sir Julian S./Newbolt, Sir Henry, *History of the Great War. Naval Operations*, 5 vols. (1920–31). The official semi-popular history, Corbett being responsible for the first 3 vols. Readable and reliable.

Dewar, Vice-Admiral K.G.B., *The Navy from Within* (1939). Prejudiced but highly informative.

Dreyer, Admiral Sir Frederic, *The Sea Heritage: a Study of Maritime Warfare* (1955). Untidy and unbalanced but interesting, especially on Jutland.

Grenfell, Commander Russell, *The Art of the Admiral* (1937). Very good on strategy. As so often with clever naval officers, crossness and perversity are never distant.

Groos, Captain Otto/Gladisch, Admiral Walther, *Der Krieg in der Nordsee*, 7 vols. (1920–65). Groos responsible for the first 5 vols. The official German history. Stately and irreplaceable.

Jellicoe, Admiral of the Fleet Earl, *The Grand Fleet, 1914–16: its Creation, Development and Work* (1919). Dull but an essential source.

Liddell-Hart, Sir Basil, *The Great War* (1967 revised edn). The soundest single-volume history, with the Royal Navy's role seen in balanced perspective.

Marder, Arthur J., *From the Dreadnought to Scapa Flow*, 5 vols. (1961–70). The culminating work for which this historian will be remembered. Essential reading which is unlikely to be superseded. The last two vols. highly detailed.

BIOGRAPHICAL

Asquith

Oxford and Asquith, Earl of, *Memories and Reflections, 1852–1927*, 2 vols. (1928). See especially vol. ii.

Jenkins, Roy, *Asquith* (1964). Highly readable, somewhat uncritical.

Battenberg

Hough, Richard, *Louis & Victoria: the First Mountbattens* (1973). American edition, *The Mountbattens* (1974). The official family history.

Kerr, Admiral Mark, *Prince Louis of Battenberg, Admiral of the Fleet* (1934). An interim and uncritical study.

BEATTY

Chalmers, Rear-Admiral William S., *The Life & Letters of David, Earl Beatty* (1951). Written with access to the family papers, and very well done. Prejudice not too evident considering the author was on Beatty's Staff from 1915–19.

Roskill, Captain Stephen, *Admiral of the Fleet Earl Beatty* (1980). A more recent authorized biography by the distinguished official naval historian of the Second World War.

CHURCHILL

Churchill, Randolph/Gilbert, Martin, *Winston S. Churchill,* ?7 vols., with *Companion* vols. of Papers (1966–   ). Randolph Churchill wrote the first two vols. The official biography, readable, scholarly, definitive. See especially vols. ii, iii, and iv.

Roskill, Captain Stephen, *Churchill and the Admirals* (1977). The only worthwhile study of this fascinating subject.

FISHER

Bacon, Admiral Sir Reginald, *The Life of Lord Fisher of Kilverstone*, 2 vols. (1929). The first authorized biography by one of 'Jacky's' closest satellites. Predictable prejudice.

Hough, Richard, *First Sea Lord: an authorized life of Lord Fisher* (1969). American title, *Admiral of the Fleet*. With more emphasis on the man than below.

Mackay, Ruddock F., *Fisher of Kilverstone* (1971). The most recent biography with special emphasis on Fisher's earlier work.

Marder, Arthur J., *Fear God and Dread Nought: the Correspondence of Admiral of the Fleet Lord Fisher of Kilverstone*, 3 vols. (1952–9). With the editor's sagacious interpolated biographical essays, these volumes provide the finest portrait of the idiosyncratic, brilliant, and not wholly lovable admiral, though the third vol. can be skimmed.

JAMES

James, Admiral Sir William, *The Sky was Always Blue* (1951). Vivid and enthusiastically recounted memoirs of 'years that were never dull, always happy and sometimes exciting'.

JELLICOE

Altham, Captain Edward, *Jellicoe* (1938). Sound.

Bacon, Admiral Sir Reginald, *The Life of John Rushworth, Earl Jellicoe* (1936). Authorized and too uncritical but essential reading.

Patterson, A. Temple (ed.), *The Jellicoe Papers*, 2 vols. (1966–8). Brilliantly edited for the Navy Records Society.

Winton, John, *Jellicoe* (1981). A critical, balanced study of this fascinating admiral.

KEYES

Aspinall-Oglander, Brigadier-General C. F., *Roger Keyes* (1951). Authorized and uncritical.

Halpern, Paul G. (ed.), *The Keyes Papers*, 3 vols. (1972–81). See especially vol. i, which superbly evokes the man, his relationships, and his work.

Keyes, Admiral Sir Roger, *The Naval Memoirs of Admiral of the Fleet Sir Roger Keyes*, 2 vols. (1934–5). Opinionated and belligerent but not without interest.

LLOYD-GEORGE

Lloyd George, David, *War Memoirs of David Lloyd George*, 6 vols. (1933–6). See especially vols. iii and iv.

RICHMOND

Marder, Arthur J. (ed.), *Portrait of an Admiral: the Life and Papers of Sir Herbert Richmond* (1952). Reveals the brilliance as well as the contentiousness of this officer.

SCHEER

Scheer, Admiral Reinhard, *Germany's High Seas Fleet in the World War* (1920). Egocentric, idiosyncratic, unreliable, and execrably translated, but should be read.

SIMS

Morison, Captain E. E., *Admiral Sims and the Modern American Navy* (1942). Admirable, authorized.

Sims, Rear-Admiral William S., *The Victory at Sea* (1920). Irreplaceable for its account of the American contribution and the introduction of convoy.

TIRPITZ

Tirpitz, Grand-Admiral Alfred von, *My Memoirs*, 2 vols. (1919). Self-righteous and self-satisfied but an essential contribution.

WESTER WEMYSS

Wester Wemyss, Lady, *The Life and Letters of Lord Wester Wemyss* (1935). The essence of the officer is not lost in this amateurishly compiled collection.

ENGAGEMENTS

CORONEL, AND THE FALKLANDS

Bennett, Captain Geoffrey, *Coronel and the Falklands* (1962). Excellent and with new material.

Hickling, Vice-Admiral Harold, *Sailor at Sea* (1965). A moving and revealing account by an officer of the *Glasgow*.

Hirst, Paymaster Commander Lloyd, *Coronel and After* (1934). The story told by another of the *Glasgow*'s officers.

Hough, Richard, *The Pursuit of Admiral von Spee* (1969). American title, *The Long Pursuit*. The two engagements seen more from the German view.

Pochhammer, Captain Hans, *Before Jutland: Admiral von Spee's Last Voyage* (1931). A moving narrative by the senior survivor of the *Gneisenau*.

DARDANELLES

Aspinall-Oglander, Brigadier-General C. F., *History of the Great War. Military Operations. Gallipoli*, 2 vols. (1929–32). The official account.

Brodie, C. G., *Forlorn Hope 1915: the Submarine Passage of the Dardanelles* (1956). Heroic.

Chatterton, E. Keble, *Dardanelles Dilemma* (1935). Sound, dramatic.

James, Robert Rhodes, *Gallipoli* (1965). The best popular account.

Samson, Air Commodore Charles R., *Fights and Flights* (1930). Good on the air side.

DOGGER BANK

Young, Filson, *With the Battle Cruisers* (1921). Includes a graphic account as seen from the *Lion*'s foretop.

JUTLAND

Bacon, Admiral Sir Reginald, *The Jutland Scandal* (1925). Heavily pro-Jellicoe but must be read. The title indicates its contentiousness.

Bennett, Captain Geoffrey, *The Battle of Jutland* (1964). As balanced as Bacon's is prejudiced.

Fawcett, Lieutenant-Commander H. W., and Hooper, Lieutenant G. W. E. (eds.), *The Fighting at Jutland* (1921). Personal narratives, some very vivid.

Frost, Commander Holloway H., *The Battle of Jutland* (1936). Critical and comprehensive, but now superseded by that of his fellow-countryman, Marder, in vol. iii of *From the Dreadnought to Scapa Flow*, q.v.

Legg, Stuart, *Jutland* (1966). Personal accounts well strung together.

Pastfield, the Reverend J. L., *New Light on Jutland* (1933). Interesting on the technical aspects.

NB Accounts of the battle, often of a personal nature, appear in numerous volumes of naval memoirs, e.g. Chalmers's *Beatty*, q.v.

ZEEBRUGGE

Carpenter, Captain A. F. B., *The Blocking of Zeebrugge* (1922). The best account by a participating officer, the *Vindictive*'s captain.

Pitt, Barrie, *Zeebrugge* (1958). An enthusiastic more recent retelling.

MISCELLANEOUS

AVIATION

Macintyre, Captain Donald, *Wings of Neptune: the Story of Naval Aviation* (1963).

Popham, Hugh, *Into Wind: a History of British Naval Flying* (1969). Both books cover the field ably and accurately.

Raleigh, Sir Walter, Jones, H. A., *The War in the Air*, 6 vols. (1922–8). Raleigh responsible for vol. i only. This official history covers all aspects of its subject and is especially good on the early days of naval aviation.

Roskill, Captain Stephen (ed.), *Documents Relating to the Naval Air Service*, vol. i, 1908–18 (1969). This Navy Records Society volume, the first of a proposed two, does not lack for detail or comprehensiveness.

NAVAL INTELLIGENCE DEPARTMENT AND 'ROOM 40'

Ewing, Alfred W., *The Man of Room 40: the Life of Sir Alfred Ewing* (1939). A filial tribute.

James, Admiral Sir William, *The Eyes of the Navy: a Biographical Study of Admiral Sir Reginald Hall* (1955). American edition, *The Code Breakers of Room 40* (1956). Lively, authorized.

SCAPA FLOW SCUTTLING

Reuter, Vice-Admiral Ludwig von, *Scapa Flow: the Account of the Greatest Scuttling of all Time* (1940). By the commander who carried it out.

van der Vat, Dan, *The Grand Scuttle: the Sinking of the German Fleet at Scapa Flow in 1919* (1982). A comprehensive and entertaining account.

SHIPS

Hough, Richard, *Dreadnought: a History of the Modern Battleship* (1964). The emphasis on illustrations, diagrams, and statistics.

Marsh, Edgar J., *British Destroyers* (1966). Plans, statistics, photographs, authoritative text. Can never be superseded.

Parkes, Oscar, *British Battleships* (1957). The massive and definitive study of Royal Navy capital ships since the end of sail.

NB Issues of *Jane's Fighting Ships* up to 1919 also relate, as does Breyer, Siegfried, *Schlachtschiffe und Schlachtkreuzer* (1970).

SUBMARINES AND U-BOATS

Bauer, Admiral Hermann, *Reichsleitung und U-Bootseinatz, 1914–18* (1956). A notable German submariner's invaluable history.

Carr, Lieutenant William G., *By Guess and By God: the Story of the British Submarines in the War* (1930). An entertaining, lightweight book on the great exploits.

Chatterton, E. Keble, *Fighting the U-boats* (1942). A comprehensive history of one great U-boat campaign published in the throes of a second.

Edwards, Lieutenant-Commander K., *We Dive at Dawn* (1939). A concise and useful history of the submarine and its exploits during the Great War.

Gibson, R. H., and Prendergast, Maurice, *The German Submarine War, 1914–18* (1931). Comprehensive and invaluable.

Jameson, Rear-Admiral Sir William, *The Most Formidable Thing* (1965). Another submariner's excellent account. Reliable and entertaining.

INDEX

OXFORD

MORE OXFORD PAPERBACKS

Details of a selection of other Oxford Paperbacks follow. A complete list of Oxford Paperbacks, including The World's Classics, Twentieth-Century Classics, OPUS, Past Masters, Oxford Authors, Oxford Shakespeare, and Oxford Paperback Reference, is available in the UK from the General Publicity Department, Oxford University Press (RS), Walton Street, Oxford, OX2 6DP.

In the USA, complete lists are available from the Paperbacks Marketing Manager, Oxford University Press, 200 Madison Avenue, New York, NY 10016.

Oxford Paperbacks are available from all good bookshops. In case of difficulty, customers in the UK can order direct from Oxford University Press Bookshop, 116 High Street, Oxford, Freepost, OX1 4BR, enclosing full payment. Please add 10 per cent of the published price for postage and packing.

GERMANY 1866–1945

Gordon A. Craig

This is the history of the rise and fall of united Germany, which lasted only 75 years from its establishment by Bismarck in 1870. It is a history of greed, fear, cruelty, and the corruption of power on the one hand; of courage, struggle for liberty, and resistance to tyranny on the other; and Gordon Craig, Professor of History at Stanford University, tells it brilliantly.

Professor Craig's study has become standard reading for students of modern German history.

'the best account so far available of Germany from Bismarck to Hitler' *Times Literary Supplement*

THE FIRST WORLD WAR

Keith Robbins

This book gives a clear chronological account of the campaigns on the Western and Eastern Fronts, and then moves on to investigate areas that many studies ignore—war poets, the diplomacy of war aims and peace moves, logistics, and the 'experience of war'.

It was soon seen that 'war has nothing to do with chivalry any more', but it was harder to say what the First World War was fought for, or what the combatants gained. Professor Robbins approaches this problem from two angles: he analyses the complex political and diplomatic background to the alliances between the Great Powers; he also explores the mood of Europe between 1914 and 1918 by examining the experience of war from the different standpoints of the nations and individuals caught up in it.

'a most interesting, indeed compelling, analysis' Bruno Derrick, *Tablet*

An OPUS book

THE STRUGGLE FOR MASTERY IN EUROPE
1848–1918

A. J. P. Taylor

This book describes the relations of the great European powers when Europe was still the centre of the world. Though primarily diplomatic history, it seeks to bring out the political ideas and economic forces which shaped day-to-day diplomacy. The author has gone through the many volumes of diplomatic documents which have been published in the five great European languages, and the story is based on these original records. With its vivid language and forceful characterization, the book is a work of literature as well as a contribution to scientific history.

'one of the glories of twentieth-century history writing'
Observer

THE AGE OF ILLUSION
Ronald Blythe

'*The Age of Illusion* accomplishes more than any orthodox history . . . a moving and stimulating study.' *Sunday Times*

In this brilliant reconstruction of Britain between the wars Ronald Blythe highlights a number of key episodes and personalities which characterize those two extraordinary decades. The period abounds in astonishing figures: the Home Secretary, Joynson-Hicks, cleaning up London's morals while defending General Dyer for the massacre of 379 Indians at Amritsar; Mrs Meyrick, the night-club queen, being regularly raided at the '43'; John Reith putting the BBC on its feet and the public in its place; headline stealers such as Amy Johnson, T. E. Lawrence and the body-line bowling controversy. And behind this garish façade we are shown the new writers emerging from their embarrassingly middle-class backgrounds, and the birth of Britain's first radical intelligentsia.

Ronald Blythe writes with perception, humour and conviction and provides a vivid and compelling portrait of Britain over twenty turbulent years.

SPEAK FOR YOURSELF

A Mass-Observation Anthology, 1937–1949

Edited by Angus Calder and Dorothy Sheridan

It would be hard to find more realistic glimpses of British life in the 1930s and 1940s than are provided in this selection from the remarkable Mass-Observation Archive at Brighton. One of the main projects Tom Harrisson established was the investigation into 'Worktown'—in fact, Bolton—and this material is represented here with special attention to pubs and drinking. 'The Blitz and its Aftermath' gives first-hand reports of air-raids, tube-dwellers, and pin-up girls; 'Women 1937–45' covers subjects as diverse as cotton-winding and the intimacies of marriage; and 'Aspects of Politics 1940–49' includes everything from the Eddisbury by-election to an interview with the King of Poland.

Incidents from everyday life suddenly come into focus, incidents too inconspicuous to have reached the newspapers, far more vivid than memory could supply them—some hilarious, some poignant—all fascinating because they aim to be 'objective' truth.

THINKING ABOUT PEACE AND WAR

Martin Ceadel

In the nuclear age the ethics of war, and the policies of pacifism, have become matters of increasingly urgent concern. Martin Ceadel analyses the various arguments and describes, rather than prescribes, the standpoints of the twentieth century's most crucial debate.

The author is Tutor in Politics and a Fellow of New College, Oxford.

'a masterly analysis' Reconciliation Quarterly

'The book sets out to remedy what the author rightly describes as "an astonishing deficiency in popular or international-relations theory". It does this in a lively and perceptive manner . . . an admirable book.' Adam Roberts, New Society

An OPUS book

THE RUSSIAN REVOLUTION 1917–1932

Sheila Fitzpatrick

This book is concerned with the Russian Revolution in its widest sense—not only with the events of 1917 and what preceded them, but with the nature of the social transformation brought about by the Bolsheviks after they took power.

Professor Fitzpatrick's account, widely praised on first publication for its clarity and for its historical objectivity, confronts the key questions: what did the dictatorship of the proletariat really mean in practice? And was Lenin's revolution, in the hands of Stalin, accomplished—or betrayed?

'a crisply written, lucid, descriptive analysis from an independent point of view' *British Book News*

'a lucid and indeed instantly classic explanation of the revolutionary spirit in its pre-1917 and Lenin-then-Stalin dominated stages' *Tribune*

An OPUS book

WAR AND THE LIBERAL CONSCIENCE

The George Trevelyan Lectures in the University of Cambridge, 1977

Michael Howard

Is war not rooted in the vested interests of the ruling classes? (But have not democracies proved as bellicose as other states?) Should not political disputes be settled by civilized negotiations? (But what if the adversary is not, by your standards, 'civilized'?) Ought states to steer clear of other states' internal conflict? (Or should they help liberate oppressed peoples?) Which is better, appeasement or a war to end war? Such questions reflect the confusion that still besets liberal-minded people in the face of war, despite centuries of trying to discover its causes and secure its abolition.

Michael Howard traces the pattern in attitudes from Erasmus to the Americans after Vietnam, and concludes that peacemaking 'is a task which has to be tackled afresh every day of our lives.'

'So well written that it could be read as a novel—except few novels are so interesting. To take one strand of history and unravel it in this way is not only a service to historians but to the ordinary bus-riding liberal anxious to clarify his own thought.' Jo Grimond, *Books and Bookmen*

WAR IN EUROPEAN HISTORY

Michael Howard

This book offers a fascinating study of warfare as it has developed in Western Europe; from the warring knights of the Dark Ages to the nuclear weapons of the present day. It illustrates how war has changed society and how society in turn has shaped the pattern of warfare.

'Wars have often determined the character of society. Society in exchange has determined the character of wars. This is the theme of Michael Howard's stimulating book. It is written with all his usual skill and in its small compass is perhaps the most original book he has written. Though he surveys a thousand years of history, he does so without sinking in a slough of facts and draws a broad outline of developments which will delight the general reader.' A. J. P. Taylor, *Observer*

'It is, at one and the same time, the plain man's guide to the subject, an essential introduction for serious students, and in its later stages a thought-provoking contribution.' Michael Mallet, *Sunday Times*

An OPUS book

THE OXFORD ILLUSTRATED HISTORY OF BRITAIN

Edited by Kenneth O. Morgan

'The best buy of the year in historical publishing. It belongs in every school satchel, on every student's desk, in every library's catalogue . . . on everyone's coffee table . . . wherever readers have a real curiosity to discover, in words and pictures, the current stage of historical inquiry in the field of British history, from the Romans to Thatcher.'
Peter Clarke in *History Today*

'Without doubt, this will serve as the standard one volume history of Britain for the rest of the century.' *Sunday Times*

WAR AND THE LIBERAL CONSCIENCE
The George Trevelyan Lectures in the University of Cambridge, 1977

Michael Howard

Is war not rooted in the vested interests of the ruling classes? (But have not democracies proved as bellicose as other states?) Should not political disputes be settled by civilized negotiations? (But what if the adversary is not, by your standards, 'civilized'?) Ought states to steer clear of other states' internal conflict? (Or should they help liberate oppressed peoples?) Which is better, appeasement or a war to end war? Such questions reflect the confusion that still besets liberal-minded people in the face of war, despite centuries of trying to discover its causes and secure its abolition.

Michael Howard traces the pattern in attitudes from Erasmus to the Americans after Vietnam, and concludes that peacemaking 'is a task which has to be tackled afresh every day of our lives.'

'So well written that it could be read as a novel—except few novels are so interesting. To take one strand of history and unravel it in this way is not only a service to historians but to the ordinary bus-riding liberal anxious to clarify his own thought.' Jo Grimond, *Books and Bookmen*

THE 'HITLER MYTH'
Image and Reality in the Third Reich

Ian Kershaw

A remarkable new study of the myth that sustained one of the most notorious dictators.

'A book which should be read by everyone interested in the history of 20th-century Europe . . . perhaps the most revealing study available of popular opinion in Nazi Germany.' Richard Bessel, *Times Higher Education Supplement*

TOWN, CITY & NATION

England 1850–1914

P. J. Waller

By the outbreak of the First World War England had become the world's first mass urban society. In just over sixty years, the proportion of urban dwellers had risen from fifty to eighty per cent, and during this period many of the most crucial developments in English urban society had taken place.

This book provides a uniquely comprehensive analysis of those developments—conurbations, suburbs, satellite towns, garden cities, and seaside resorts—which so fascinated the rest of the world. Nevertheless, while proper recognition is given to the importance of London, the provincial cities, and manufacturing centres, the author emphasizes the continuing influence of the small country town and 'rural' England on political, economic, and cultural growth. In many respects, P. J. Waller's book is a general social history of late nineteenth- and early twentieth-century England, seen from an urban perspective. Vividly written, it will appeal both to the student and to the general reader who is keen to understand the exuberant and melancholy features of modern English towns and cities.

An OPUS book

LIFE IN THE THIRD REICH

Edited by Richard Bessel

This volume offers a series of short articles, originally published in *History Today,* which present some new approaches to the study of Nazi Germany. Some of the subjects may be familiar, but their treatment is not.

HEART OF EUROPE
A Short History of Poland
Norman Davies

In this book Norman Davies provides a key to understanding the social and political inheritance of modern Poland. By delving through the historical strata of Poland's past he demonstrates that the present conflict is but the latest round in a series of Russo-Polish struggles stretching back for nearly three centuries.

'Another masterpiece; *Heart of Europe* has sweep, a rare analytical depth and a courageous display of the author's personal convictions. The book begins and ends with Solidarity; the unique labour movement thus serves as a frame for the nation's history.' *New York Times*

'should never be out of reach of anyone . . . who wishes to keep track of the infinitely complex interplay of forces in Poland today and tomorrow' *Catholic Herald*

'A deep, heartfelt analysis which sets Poland's poignant, but currently stalemate, situation in its historical context.' Linda O'Callaghan, *Sunday Telegraph*

HITLER AND THE FINAL SOLUTION
Gerald Fleming
Introduced by Saul Friedländer

'should finally lay to rest David Irving's provocative theory that Hitler neither ordered nor wished the destruction of the Jewish people' Gordon A. Craig, *New York Review of Books*

'puts the record straight and adds many interesting new details to a terrible but still compelling story' Hugh Trevor-Roper

THE OXFORD HISTORY OF BRITAIN

Edited by Kenneth O. Morgan

The Oxford History of Britain tells the story of Britain and her peoples over two thousand years, from the coming of the Roman legions to the present day.

The dramatic narrative of developments throughout the British Isles is taken up in turn by ten leading historians, who offer the fruits of the best modern scholarship in an authoritative and accessible form. The relationship between the political, economic, social, and cultural transformations in British history is explored revealing a vivid and sometimes surprising picture of a continuous turmoil of change in every period. But there also emerges a pattern of continuity in British cultural and social ideals, and a special awareness of nationality and patriotism which has been such a distinctive feature of British society.

'Without doubt, this will serve as the standard one-volume history of Britain for the rest of the century.' *Sunday Times*

CONTEMPORARY INTERNATIONAL THEORY AND THE BEHAVIOUR OF STATES

Joseph Frankel

This book provides a brief survey of the major theoretical approaches to international relations: systems analysis, integration theory, the action of states, and states in interaction. In a concluding chapter some of these approaches are applied in a case study of the relations between Britain and the European Economic Community.

LABOUR IN POWER 1945–1951

Kenneth O. Morgan

Kenneth O. Morgan's book is a uniquely detailed and comprehensive account of the Attlee government. It is the first study to be based on the vast range of unpublished material from the period, and draws on numerous personal papers as well as public records.

'a remarkable achievement of political history' A. J. P. Taylor, *London Review of Books*

'history at its very best' *New Society*

'A considerable achievement . . . it will be required reading for students of modern history for at least a generation to come.' *The Economist*

'a marvellous account of how this most gifted, intelligent and idealistic Cabinet applied its collective mind to the great questions of the age' Michael Foot, *Observer*

REBIRTH OF A NATION

Wales 1880–1980

Kenneth O. Morgan

This comprehensive survey of Wales during the past century was described by the *Times Literary Supplement* as 'a crowning achievement', while the *Guardian* said that it would 'serve as a fulcrum of historical debate for a generation'.

MAIN CURRENTS OF MARXISM

Volume 1: The Founders

Leszek Kolakowski

In this first volume, Leszek Kolakowski examines the origins of Marxism, tracing its descent from the neo-Platonists through Hegel and the Enlightenment. He analyses the development of Marx's thought and shows its divergence from other forms of socialism.

'The most commanding, the most decisive, the most properly passionate and yet also . . . the most accessible account of Marxism that we now have. It is a work of surpassing lucidity and power, of the sharpest and most sensitive judgement, of a far finer quality than almost all of that with which it deals. It is, in short, a masterpiece.' *Times Higher Education Supplement*

BRITAIN AND THE JEWS OF EUROPE
1939–1945

Bernard Wasserstein

'Bernard Wasserstein's outstanding book . . . tells his terrible story with such exemplary calm and scholarly restraint that the reader is left fuming with impotent chagrin and grief . . . For all its attention to balance, and its scrupulous fairness, his book leaves a stain of moral ignomity on the history of the British official class that no future account of the war will ever efface.' Simon Schama, *New Society*

This book examines the British policy towards the Jewish problem during the Second World War. Based on archival sources, it explores the reasons for the near-total ban on Jewish refugee immigration to Britain, the restrictive immigration policy in Palestine, the failure to aid Jewish resistance in Europe, and the rejection of the scheme for the Allied bombing of Auschwitz. What emerges is a lamentable story of bureaucratic complacency, inhumanity, and blindness to the Jewish catastrophe in Europe.